IN THE FOOTSTEP OF THE BUDDHA

for Sanghashura,
with much mettā.

Atthavajit

A Sri Lankan stupa

With retreatants at Nilambe Laymen's Meditation Centre

IN THE FOOTSTEP OF THE BUDDHA

By Ashvajit

OLA LEAVES

May 2014

SECOND EDITION - August 2014

Published by Ola Leaves
Adhisthana
Coddington Court
Coddington
Ledbury
Herefordshire HR8 1JL

© Ashvajit 2014

British Library Cataloguing in Publication Data:
A catalogue record for this book is available from the
British Library

ISBN 978-1-292-78247-9

Ordering :

Special discounts are available for individuals and bookshops.
For details, contact the publisher at the abovementioned address
or at ashvajit.dh@gmail.com

Dedication

To my Sri Lankan and Indian friends, to all my Buddhist brothers and sisters, to the members of the Adhisthana Community, who have seen less of me while I have been preparing this book than would otherwise have been the case, and to those friends and relations who know little or nothing of what I was doing in the East between 1985 and 1990.

With gratitude to my Preceptor and Kalyana Mitra, Urgyen Sangharakshita, without whom nothing recounted in these pages would have happened, and to all those who have helped me on my journey in ways small and large and who continue to do so.

That Enlightened One whose sphere is endless, whose victory is irreversible, and after whose victory no defilements remain to be conquered, by what track will you lead him astray, the Trackless One?

Dhammapada, v.179, Section XIV: The Enlightened One
(tr. Sangharakshita)

CONTENTS

List of Illustrations

A note concerning my use of diacriticals

I have sometimes employed diacriticals, the little dashes, dots and tildes (~) above or below a letter in a word of Pali or Sanskrit origin transliterated into Roman characters. Whilst usually employing them in the first occurrence of a word in my text and generally omitting them later, I may occasionally have been inconsistent in my usage. Scholars may recognise specific instances as 'correct' or else be pretty sure that they are peculiar to myself.

Foreword

It was a warm summer's day in 1956 and I was fifteen. Seated on a terrace overlooking the school cricket pitch, occasionally glancing up at the slow-moving match, I was dipping into a book. It was a book on comparative religion, and I was trying to make sense of the author's rather rambling and disconnected account of Buddhism. I put the book down, and gazing into the middle distance, saw appearing in my mind's eye a curious and arresting figure. A man draped in patched, earth-coloured robes was walking amongst the trees of a forest glade. The vision continued to unfold: approaching a particularly large and shady tree, the russet-robed man seated himself at its foot in a regal, cross-legged position, back upright, hands folded in his lap. His face was calmly composed, and a beautiful, soft golden aura began to emanate from his head and body. At this point the smack of leather on willow on the cricket pitch roused me from my waking dream, but not before I had thought to myself 'I want to do that!' Suddenly, I very much wanted, not to score a six, but to meditate, as perhaps I had done ages ago, and to cultivate a golden aura once again.

Reflecting now on this experience, or this irruption into my consciousness of something strange and new, I find it even more unusual and surprising than when it occurred. The book I was reading - and I have since checked my recollection of its contents against a recently-acquired copy - had painted no word-picture of a man in reddish-brown robes, and I had at that time seen no illustration remotely comparable to what I saw at that moment in my mind's eye; indeed, there was no such picture, so far as I know, in existence in those days, in the UK in 1956. From whence had it come? Its appearance both in hindsight and in the light of my experience since, leads me to conclude that mind, contrary to what many, perhaps most scientists until recently believed, is much more than an epiphenomenon, a mere frothy by-product of matter. Mind, though usually presenting itself in terms of images rooted in experiences supposedly imprinted during this lifetime, is not limited by them; it is transcendent. Of course, one could simply dismiss 'visions' as 'just one's imagination', but that would be to underestimate or to limit the faculty that goes by that name. Imagination, though immeasurable, can be electrifying and profoundly influence our lives.

Ashvajit, Adhisthana, 1 August 2014

Preface

Some twenty-five years after my vision of the Buddha with the golden aura, and following the advice of my Buddhist preceptor Sangharakshita, the story of my meeting with whom I will have to recount in another book, I found myself resident between 1985 and 1990 in Sri Lanka. The Buddha is supposed by many Sinhalese to have left his footprint on Adam's Peak as he alighted on that highest point on the Island; one can ascend the peak even today, if one is prepared to undertake the arduous climb, and see it for oneself. However, study of the historical records and a little common sense suggest that the Buddha never ventured far from Central India in his physical body. Thus, that footprint on the Peak, whatever it may be, is not the footprint of Shakyamuni, the historical Sage of the Shakyas. Rather, it embodies a spiritual truth, and perhaps more than one truth. The idea of the Buddha miraculously flying to Sri Lanka and alighting on the highest point of the Island is suggestive of the *yogic* experience of meditation, in the course of which the subtle influence of the transcendental consciousness is said to enter in at the highest point - the top of one's head. From there, in the course of sustained practice it gradually descends, transforming, transfiguring and transmuting the whole ego-based consciousness into what becomes, eventually, the Buddha-consciousness: the mind awakened to the realisation of the true nature of ordinary human consciousness, to transcendental awareness and to Enlightenment itself: the goal of all spiritual striving. One might also, of course, take the singleness of the footstep on Adam's Peak to mean that the Buddha used Serendib (as the Island used to be called) as a stepping stone to a further destination. No doubt being a stepping stone for Buddhahood is as praiseworthy — and just as much in keeping with the Dharma – as being a temporary abode for it.

During the four years whilst I was resident in Sri Lanka I became familiar with modern Theravada Buddhism and its monastic exclusivism - the idea widely held not only by the *bhikkhus*[2] but also by many, perhaps most of the so-called laity, that it is only the shaven-headed robe-wearers who are the 'real' Buddhists. Furthermore, I soon found that it was commonly believed that of all the forms of Buddhism, only Theravada is the 'real' one – which Sri Lankans often referred to as 'the pure dhamma' or even as 'the pure, pristine dhamma'. This belief was often accompanied by an almost complete lack of knowledge of the Mahāyāna, Vajrayāna, and Zen varieties of Buddhism. A curious counterpart of the exclusive monasticism of this modern Theravada, I also discovered, was the phenomenon of exclusive 'laicism': the belief on the part of some Sri Lankans at least that Buddhism should be pursued without the co-operation of the orange-robed *bhikkhus,* all of whom were assumed by people of this persuasion to be degenerate. Soon after my arrival I began to form certain impressions of my own concerning the phenomenon of Sri Lankan Buddhism. It moved me sometimes to joy and sometimes to tears.

As for the political scene, I kept as far as possible from it, though violence and the threat of violence sometimes came so close that I had to be prepared for the worst. There was of course a two-way traffic of ideas as well as a sparking-off of experiences between me and the Sri Lankans. No doubt my own Buddhist talks and meditation instruction had an effect upon them, and indeed, most seemed very much to appreciate what I imparted. A few reactionary individuals, however, came to regard me, one single powerless Westerner, as a threat to their 'Pristine Buddhism', and eventually succeeded in preventing me from having my residence visa extended. I had not expected such antagonism from people whom I had supposed were my spiritual brothers. However, apart from this uncharacteristically Buddhist behaviour, I was treated with much kindness and generosity by the Sri Lankans, and was able to communicate the art of meditation to many hundreds of men and women, young and old, and therefore, presumably, to help them to some extent to go for refuge to the three great universal ideals of Buddhism more deeply and more effectively than they had hitherto done.

The charges levelled against me at the Ministry of the Buddha Sāsana[3] by a few anonymous persons were, amongst other things, eating after midday in public - moreover eating sausages - ridiculing the *bhikkhus*, and being 'a Mahayanist' - a follower of what was commonly thought by Sri Lankans to be a later, 'degenerate' form of Buddhism. I was also suspected of being a CIA agent, and was, I was told later, 'shadowed' on my trips into Colombo for a fortnight before my eventual departure. I did indeed eat in public and a little after after midday on a few occasions. Sometimes I had a busy schedule, was far from friends and without a begging bowl. Feeling hungry and wishing to keep my energy up in order to communicate the Dhamma later in the day, I would resort on such occasions to a meal in a restaurant. In any case, I was an *anagārika*[4] - a sort of freelance monk – and the *anagārika* does <u>not</u> undertake the precept to avoid so-called untimely meals[5] by refraining from beginning his meal after noon. So there was in truth, for me, never any question of breaking the eating-before-twelve precept. In any case, a precept is a training principle, not a rule in the ordinary sense. As for the second charge, that of eating sausages, presumably if I had been seen eating a good respectable type of meat of the sort often demanded of their devotees by the *bhikkhus*, like beef or chicken, it would have been less of a sin. In point of fact, being a vegetarian, I did not eat meat at all, regarding it (when one actually has the practical alternative of vegetarian food) as a species of cruelty. I did not touch a morsel of meat or fish during my whole stay in Sri Lanka, contrary to the practice of many *bhikkhus*, some of whom even went so far as to provide their supporters with menus (I was shown one) demanding not only meat but specific types of meat.

I was never given a chance to formally answer my accusers, whose names and accusations were in any case not disclosed to me, and at the end of my fourth year I received a letter from the police saying that, since my residence visa had expired, I was to leave the country not later than a fortnight hence, or 'measures would be taken' against me. I appealed to the President but this was of no avail - I received merely a formal acknowledgement of my communication from one of his secretaries. Given just two weeks notice, I had to abandon, after four years of dedicated work, the hundreds of friends whom I had made and who were beginning to look to me for some sort of spiritual guidance. I left also a Meditation Centre on which I and my friends had lavished much care, effort, work and money, a library, and a considerable sum of money. Furthermore, unfortunately, there was at that time no one ready to take up the work I had begun.

During my first year in Sri Lanka I gave upwards of one public talk a week, sometimes in a school or college, but more usually at a *pirivena* or temple. The temple might be a wealthy city temple, or it might be an *āraṇya* or forest hermitage with the bhikkhus subsisting on no more than the daily requisites specified by the *vinaya*, the monastic 'rules and regulations'. This *vinaya*, that consisted of precepts, training principles, pithy pieces of advice or, in a few cases, binding exhortations given by the Buddha to his full-time disciples, had in some – perhaps many - cases to be updated during his lifetime, and were usually, I found, praised uncritically by both bhikkhus and laymen - especially by laymen - and observed by the bhikkhus chiefly in public. I knew my Buddhism well enough to know that the Theravada bhikkhus had through the ages proved themselves unable or unwilling to follow the advice that the Buddha had given to his companion Ananda. Shortly before his passing-away he called Ananda who, having a highly retentive memory was invaluable to later generations of disciples, and told him that all the minor precepts could be changed. The Buddha being the Buddha knew very well that conditions would change, and that those changing conditions might well necessitate different means of discouraging unskilful and encouraging skilful behaviour, especially in cultures different from his own. I therefore regarded the lip-service given to the ancient *vinaya* - revered simply because it was ancient - as being at the least myopic and at worst, psychologically damaging - especially for those who promised to keep its precepts and then chose to ignore them. As for the major precepts, that was quite a different matter, one covered amply by Sangharakshita in his *Ten Pillars of Buddhism*[6], in which he explores the canonical bases for this *mula pratimoksha*, or set of basic training principles

There was thus, I found, widespread confusion concerning the Dhamma itself, about what was truly helpful for one's spiritual development. There was, so far as I could ascertain, little or no effective practice of meditation. There was also something that had a more direct and personal impact - doubt and hesitation as to whether I was a bona fide *bhikkhu* or a layman, the only two categories of Buddhist individual recognised by officialdom. Despite all this, I found that usually I was given a very warm welcome by the *bhikkhus*. Whether I had been invited to visit or simply turned up unexpectedly at a forest hermitage or at a city temple, I would usually be greeted at the very least with politeness, and often with real friendliness and enthusiasm, by the Nayaka Thero or 'Chief Priest'. I would then be taken into the Chief Priest's residential quarters and in due course, usually after being offered a cup of sweet black tea, be introduced to a group of the faithful assembled in the Temple if it happened to be a Poya or full-moon day. At least ninety-five percent of such an assembly would be women and children. All would be dressed in the traditional white dress, sari, or sarong, symbolizing purity and renunciation, at least during the period of attendance within the sacred precincts, and many of them would be, judging by the lean and careworn looks on the older faces at least, from the less well-to-do sections of society. Occasionally there would be a few women of quite extraordinary beauty and modesty, like dark tropical flowers arrayed in white, who seemed to have come not so much from a wealthy part of society but from some heavenly region. Occasionally also - though to my disappointment even less often - there would be a few young men, their dark skins and glossy black hair radiant with health, in appearance not unlike the Bodhisattvas depicted in Buddhist art and sculpture, and described in glowing terms in so many places in the classics of Buddhist literature.

The pattern which then unfolded soon became familiar to me, and almost a matter of routine. I would be asked to give a dhamma talk to the assembly or give them meditation instruction, or both, with my Sri Lankan friend Siri Goonasekara, as he then was, ably translating. The bhikkhus and novice bhikkhus, dressed in their resplendent orange robes, would then stand around for a few minutes not sure, apparently, whether to pay attention to me or not. Usually they would soon wander off, whilst the remainder of the audience would listen with undivided attention until the end of the introduction and actual meditation session perhaps an hour and a half later. It was not however that the bhikkhus had heard what I had to say before, or had already familiarized themselves with the meditation techniques I imparted; almost always they had not, as I discovered from my many private conversations with them. I began therefore to suspect that their indifference might even be a symptom of a lack of real interest in the *dhamma*[7]. There was also their self-confessed unwillingness, I discovered, to be seen on an equal footing with the 'lay' audience by sitting with them. Of these two unfortunate attitudes, the most unfortunate it seemed to me, was the first; since the *dhamma* is the Way to Enlightenment, lack of interest in it would be tantamount to ignoring the very Path to which one is supposed, as a Buddhist, to be committed. Regular practice of meditation was a vital feature of the Buddha's life, and has always been regarded by the great Buddhist teachers of the past as one of the most important activities (or from an uninformed perspective, non-activities) of those bent upon Enlightenment. Even the Buddha, after he had gained the supreme spiritual experience of Enlightenment under the Bodhi Tree, even after he had experienced the co-emergence of Bliss, Wisdom and Compassion in their perfection in his own human body and Enlightened mind, meditated regularly, one might even say habitually. Thus not to meditate formally, that is to say by seating oneself mindfully, composing one's limbs, closing or half-closing one's eyes, turning one's mind away from objects of mundane perception and towards the Transcendental, would mean not to appreciate, not to wish to savour, at least occasionally, and for the sake of all sentient beings, the bliss of uttermost freedom. It would be a perverse attitude, perhaps amounting to the false view of the Path as one of mere asceticism in the narrow sense of self-punishment. Knowing this, the bhikkhus' apparent indifference to meditation therefore appeared to me tantamount to indifference to the principial *dharma* itself. Whilst in a Temple addressing 'lay-people', I thus became, unwittingly, a double source of embarrassment to the bhikkhus. They would become on the one hand ashamed and perhaps even envious of the apparent ease with which I held the attention of my audience by means of what from the point of view of my own Order was unexceptional knowledge and practice of the dharma, and on the other hand contemptuous of the fact that I placed myself on such familiar terms with ordinary people, not holding myself aloof as most of them did. The bhikkhus were used to insisting, I soon discovered, on a particular way to be treated - in particular that they be accorded a seat covered with a white cloth and higher than anyone else's. There was even a special language, or mode of address, to be used when speaking to bhikkhus, as well as a 'proper' way of presenting gifts to them. The lay people however were anything but embarrassed by me, as all too often I had seen them become in the presence of an incompetent dhamma preacher. They would listen carefully to my instruction and often become fully absorbed in the subsequent meditation practice. On the few occasions that bhikkhus did attend my introductions to meditation sessions, they would invariably sit on benches or comfortable high chairs, whilst the rest of the assembly, including old women bent with age and toil, would sit on thin rush matting laid over a cold concrete floor. I would be told, however, if I suggested an alternative arrangement: "It is not our custom to do so", and that was the end of the matter, as if things could not or should not be done in any other way than that in which they had been done for as long as anybody could remember. I was invariably expected to assert my superiority by accepting a high position, rather than demonstrate friendliness and practical common sense by adopting seating arrangements suited to people's physical condition and seating myself in a position which encouraged communication.

Sometimes I was happy to adjust to local custom, as for instance when I participated in the ceremonial worship of the Buddha image. Such worship has sometimes been censured, but so far as I was able to ascertain, no Sri Lankan ever thought that he or she was worshipping the actual stone or wooden image itself; the image was simply a convenient means of bringing to mind the qualities of Enlightenment and the recollection of the Buddha Shakyamuni. The ceremony involved melodious chanting by everyone, and many extraordinarily beautiful and fragrant flower-offerings would be passed by the devotees to the line of monks in which on occasion I stood, and would then be reverentially placed before the Buddha-image. Then again, hundreds of lovely little flickering cocoanut-oil lamps were lit and offered in a similar way. To other occasions I was far less happy to adjust - for instance the ritual offering of the mid-day meal. This was usually taken by the bhikkhus on comfortable seats, either in their own Temples or else in the houses of their lay-supporters, whilst the householders sat on the floor or stood around uneasily. The fare usually included meat and fish, which I always declined to accept. And after the meal, gifts, sometimes very expensive ones, given the poverty of the household, would be handed around to each bhikkhu from the seniormost, the stubble of his shaven head touched with silver, to the youngest stripling at the other end of the line, with down just appearing on his chin. Then would come the worst part as far as I was concerned: one of the senior bhikkhus would start to give the *bana*[8] or preaching. Though I understood very little of what was said, because it was in Sinhalese, I very soon got to know the usual pattern, and was also sensitive to the emotional tone of the preacher and his utterances, and to the response of the audience. The bhikkhu would first praise the head of the household which had offered the food, and then recite the names, the status and qualifications of each of the other bhikkhus present. This could take quite a long time if the chapter of bhikkhus invited to the meal was large. Then would follow the recitation of a verse from the Pali and a commentary upon that. It was a bit like a non-conformist Christian sermon. And I could tell from the manner of the delivery and the attitudes of the listeners that the content was usually uninspiring. More often than not, the *bana* was all too clearly devoid of spiritually positive content - probably the mere recitation of platitudes, half-truths, or even, perhaps, things which were not the *dhamma* at all. Thus I often had the experience of participating, at first, in a highly positive atmosphere, full of faith and devotion on the part of the donors, until the *bana* was given. At this point the feeling of faith, of pleasure and happiness at the presence of the bhikkhus and the expectation of something good happening, would evaporate, giving way to boredom or even downright embarrassment. At first I would check my intuition of what was happening with Siri, asking him for a translation and for an explanation of what was going on, but I found I was always correct in my surmise, and came to realize that this dramatic change in atmosphere was regarded as normal. It was, as it were, a penalty the donors had to accept if they wanted to 'earn merit'. They were required to arrange for the performance of this ceremony perhaps once a year, at considerable expense, and in return they would thereby gain social orthodoxy, perhaps material reward, and most importantly, rebirth in a heavenly realm, which is of course really a more subtle version of material reward. In this way they would be performing the role allotted to them by those concerned to preserve the special status of the priest as 'practising and meritorious Buddhist' whilst they accepted the implicit role of 'honorary, or non-practising' Buddhist. In reality, however there is no such thing as a non-practising Buddhist, since what makes someone a Buddhist is the actuality of their Going for Refuge to the Three Jewels - i.e. their practising of ethics and meditation and the development of Wisdom to the fullest extent they are able with the guidance of those more spiritually developed than themselves.

During my second year on the Island, when the Indian Peace-keeping force arrived and the whole atmosphere began to feel poisoned, I avoided attending ceremonial meals so far as possible, and gave less and less talks in Temples, feeling that it was more important to concentrate on the teaching of meditation and developing deeper friendships with a few people, in the hope that they would begin to take to the practice of meditation. This strategy began to pay off to some extent, and a few people did indeed begin to take up fairly regular meditation practice, in contrast to the usual layman or woman who would only meditate, if at all, on Poya or Full Moon days. Not only that, a few individuals asked to become a *mitra*[9] - a formally acknowledged associate - of the Movement then known in the UK as the Friends of the Western Buddhist Order, but which eventually would be given a different name. In due course, those people whom I felt were both sincere and ready, became mitras by means of a simple but effective ceremony conducted in a similar way throughout the Movement worldwide.

During my third year in Sri Lanka, the troubles with which the Island had been plagued almost since Independence began to escalate with a vengeance. Tourists, some of whom I was able to initiate into meditation, dwindled in numbers to almost zero; murders by bomb, gun and torture throughout the country reached horrific proportions, and the tension, especially while travelling, was palpable. I had witnessed personally by this time bhikkhus preaching racial hatred, asking for money for machine guns and telling the armed forces to go North and kill the Tamil[10] extremists in order to protect Sinhalese Buddhism. I had also heard from reliable witnesses of bhikkhus inciting mobs to destroy public property. Not that I had much sympathy for the violent Tamil insurgents either. I eventually came to feel that Sri Lanka and perhaps South East Asia generally was a rather bloodthirsty place and that, contrary to my expectations, those who were really interested in spiritual development there were few and far between.

However, not all bhikkhus by any means were like the villains I have described. Many were sincere, friendly, very helpful to me personally, and deeply disturbed by what was going on in the country. Nevertheless, I heard of not one bhikkhu out of the twenty thousand or so in Sri Lanka who was willing, during my time there, to initiate a campaign of reform, to continually bring to the attention of the public the atrocities being carried out in an ostensibly Buddhist country, and to say that what was happening was a disgrace to Buddhism and to the people of Sri Lanka. The fact was that some of those bhikkhus were grossly violating both the letter and the spirit of the *vinaya*, and all this without receiving censure or expulsion from the sangha. Yes, there were mealy-mouthed newspaper articles by some senior bhikkhus, but that was all. There was no sustained effort to bring about radical change. This was probably because, had any bhikkhu tried to do so, he would have been in imminent danger of his life at the hands of extremist nationalists. In the circumstances, it was therefore not surprising that there was so little open criticism of officialdom, so little attempt to get to the root of the malaise gripping the country. Civil war was brewing and there was an atmosphere of hostility, fear and endemic mutual distrust.

So what, it may be asked, had 'gone wrong' in Sri Lanka? This was a question I was asked many, many times by the Sri Lankans themselves, both lay and monastic. What had gone wrong with modern Theravada Buddhism? After all, with twenty thousand bhikkhus practising *sila*[11], *samadhi*[12], and *pañña*[13] - Morality, Meditation and Wisdom - the universally acknowledged path of spiritual development which it is the implicit duty of every Buddhist spiritual aspirant to tread - one might have expected Sri Lanka, a small island with a population of about fifteen million people, to be a paradise on earth. Tragically, however, the duties of the bhikkhus were 'more evident in the breach than in the observance'; and if this was largely true - and everything I heard and saw tended to confirm this - the majority of bhikkhus were renunciants in name only. Certainly, of those whom I met individually and personally in Sri Lanka, few appeared to be bhikkhus in the sense of having that depth of practice that would lead to spiritual insight and from there to Enlightenment. Rather, the bhikkhus I observed, especially in the better-endowed city temples, were like well-fed, urbane college professors, amiably engaging in word-play before their post-prandial snoozes. They did not even approach the picture of the spiritually-inspired individual earnestly striving for Enlightenment that is painted in the Buddhist scriptures.

A complaint that I heard many times while speaking to individual bhikkhus was that there was no real Sangha – no spiritual fellowship or spiritual community amongst them. Certainly, I saw no evidence of spiritual community strong enough to transcend boundaries of formal membership and to unite all Sri Lankan Buddhists in one body able to act unitedly and effectively. Part of the problem was that the Theravada Bhikkhu Sangha of Sri Lanka was no longer in command of itself. Its affairs came under the jurisdiction of a secular body, the Ministry of the Buddha Sasana. This Ministry is still today under the watchful eye of the Executive President - a lay person - who has draconian powers. By the Ministry of the Buddha Sasana I was regarded with extreme suspicion from the first. My yearly visits to its officers in pursuit of the requisite letter of recommendation were an exercise in forbearance.   The trouble stemmed in part from my appearance. In order to be taken seriously by the Buddhist community in Sri Lanka, one's head had to be shaved. This in any case I had already had done in India as part of my formal undertaking of the precept enjoining celibacy and chastity. Moreover, as was traditional, I was wearing the plain, unstitched orange robes of an *anagārika*, which any observant person could see were not the expensively cut-and-stitched-in-imitation-of-patchwork robes of the modern Theravada bhikkhu. Nevertheless, I was nearly always taken for a bhikkhu, and therefore liable to be accused by reactionaries of masquerading as one. Even when I had the chance to explain that I was not, I was often treated with the extreme deference usually accorded a bhikkhu. At first my ego was stroked by what appeared to be the devoted attention of so many people. However I became less and less happy about this as an unwelcome truth began to dawn on me concerning the bhikkhus on the Island. It seemed to me that many of them were simply playing a power game, lording it over their 'lay' brethren, when they had not an ounce of spiritual practice under their belts. So by my robe-wearing, it occurred to me, I was implicitly demonstrating my solidarity with the bhikkhu sangha, the behaviour of the majority of whom I felt left very much to be desired. On the other hand my own practice of demonstrating solidarity with the devotees and disciples by sitting on the same level with them and so forth, was evidently not approved of by at least some of the bhikkhus. When I was asked to leave the Island, one of the accusations made against me was that I was ridiculing the bhikkhus, although I had never publicly or privately ridiculed their essential role, and in point of fact always cultivated an attitude of respect towards everyone, robed or not.

I came to the conclusion, not entirely unexpected, and not unforeseen by Sangharakshita, that Sri Lankan Buddhism had by and large degenerated into what he has called 'religio-nationalism'[14] - a religion related to its own eminently worthy version of the Pali *Tipitaka*[15], one of the chief canonical collections of Buddhist texts, not by that penetrating 'doubt' or intelligent questing which may lead to insight and 'worth more than all the creeds', but in fundamentalist fashion to the letter of the texts, and often in complete disregard of the spirit. This is what Sangharakshita had to say in 1957 concerning the Theravada Buddhism of the type I encountered all too often in Sri Lanka:

Theravada Buddhism however resembles the tombs of the Egyptian Kings; while preserving the outward forms, it has not succeeded in preserving that life itself. Not only do they believe, in the face of even canonical evidence to the contrary, that every word of the Tipitaka *was uttered just as it stands today, by the Buddha himself, but they vehemently insist that their form of Buddhism alone is orthodox, and that all other schools - which nowadays they never study - are corruptions and degradations of the original teaching. Only an influx of Mahāyāna Buddhism as a living spiritual force will save the Theravada countries from parrot learning, blind faith and rigid formalism, and enable its peoples to appreciate the true value even of their own tradition.*

A Survey of Buddhism, Sangharakshita, Ch.1, Section 19, Bangalore, 1957

By this Sangharakshita did not mean to say that Theravada Buddhism was without great and enduring value, neither did he mean that Theravada and Mahāyāna are opposing schools, but that a return to real sutra-style Buddhism, a Buddhism based on intelligent and faithful study of a wide range of doctrinal and inspirational texts and their commentaries, elucidating and inculcating the spirit of radical practice is what is needed in Sri Lanka. A re-invigoration of the whole spirit of Buddhism will involve re-imagining the Buddha, will involve the creative, imaginative and compassionate flight of the spirit taking wing as a result of wholehearted practice based on profound spiritual teachings. This is what the Mahāyāna is really all about. Today in Sri Lanka, so-called Buddhists worship side by side the Buddha and the Hindu god Vishnu, the National gods Skandha and Kataragama, and regard the god of Christianity as the protector of the Dharma. Those truly inheriting and transmitting the Buddha's great tradition of Vision and Insight, those truly practising 'pristine Buddhism', would be incapable of coming to such conclusions or of engaging in worship of such doctrinally-opposed systems. Thus far has the great and noble tradition which we call Buddhism fallen in the land where 'the entire Buddhist Canon' was first committed to writing. Properly speaking, of course, Buddhism - the Dharma - the principial path to Enlightenment in its pristine truth, its pristine purity - cannot fall. Only those who claim the name of the Buddha without striving to realise it can fall. Sri Lankan officialdom moreover has long added to the confusion by placing its secular stamp on a religion which has simply ceased to be Buddhism. Disestablishment in the sense of the removal of external, governmental jurisdiction over Buddhist affairs is therefore necessary before there can be a widespread revival of the True Doctrine, the Lotus of the Good Law, in Sri Lanka.

Despite my early and reluctant recognition that the modern forms of Sinhala Buddhism I encountered were all too often corrupt, I did not doubt the genuineness of the old Sinhalese *saddha* (faith in the Buddha and in the Triple Gem). I was often deeply moved by the devotion of many of the lay Buddhists, and of a quite a few bhikkhus too. I was also continually inspired by the recollection of the great personality of Anagārika Dharmapala, the 'Lion of Lanka', who brought about more than any other figure a revival of Buddhism in Sri Lanka a hundred years ago and paved the way for a Buddhist revival in India and throughout the world.

Thus was I resident for four years in Sri Lanka. During this time there was an armed uprising against the Government of the Island and the arrival of the Indian peace-keeping force. I wrote a series of letters recounting my novel and often strange experiences during those four years to my friends in the West. This book consists of a collection of forty of these letters, some long, some short, thirty-two of which I wrote whilst in Sri Lanka itself, seven in India and one in England during the period 1986-90. I often wrote them hurriedly, whilst on the hoof, not always pausing to choose the most felicitous word or expression, so I have lightly edited the collection for publication. I have provided an index, and bearing in mind a readership possibly unfamiliar with Buddhist terminology or with certain Buddhist terms as they are used by members of the Order and Community of which I am a member, I have added footnotes where appropriate. These are located at the end of each chapter. The letters were originally published in *Shabda*, the monthly in-house journal of what used to be the Western Buddhist Order and is now known as the Triratna Buddhist Order. I now offer these Letters to a wider audience: to those within the Triratna Buddhist Order, greatly expanded from what it was when I wrote them; to those few Order members who may have read but forgotten them; to the worldwide Community associated with the Triratna Buddhist Order; and to those who, perhaps having as yet no more than a passing acquaintance with contemporary Buddhism, might be interested not only in my sojourn in Sri Lanka and travels in India, but also in spiritual matters that tasked the heart and mind of at least one Buddhist in the twentieth century.

NOTES

1 Bodhisattva: literally, a *bodhi*-being (*bodhi* = the state of being spiritually awake); a person who, having awoken from all illusions and delusions concerning human existence and seeing the ultimate nature of things, strives to attain human perfection or Buddhahood for the sake of all sentient beings.

2 A *bhikkhu* (fem: *bhikkhuni*) is one who begs for alms. In Theravada Buddhism, he (or she) is enjoined to celibacy and observes the *pātimokkha* or code of conduct consisting of 227 rules for *bhikkhus*, 311 for *bhikkhunis*. The use of the English words 'monk' or 'nun' as translations of these Pāli originals is really quite

inappropriate and may lead to false assumptions on the part of those unfamiliar with Buddhist tradition.

3 *sāsana* : meaning dispensation, or teaching-and-example. It indicates the whole legacy of the Buddha's spiritual teachings, life and personal example. The website of the Ministry of the Buddha Sasana, has in its main menu a tab wholly devoted to Complaints (with a sub-menu).

4 *anagārika* : the lifestyle which I undertook in 1983, one year after basing myself in India, and continued to observe in Sri Lanka. An *anagarika* does not formally commit himself (or herself) to the strictly cenobitical monastic restraints (such as finishing one's begging round for food before midday, and not handling money) of a caenobium or monastery. Instead he or she simply observes (in addition to the Ten Principles of skilful behaviour pertaining to body, speech and mind) the training principle of *brahmachariya*, i.e. the precept of celibacy and chastity, thus ensuring that one remains free from family and sexual ties to work with the maximum freedom for Enlightenment and the spiritual welfare of others. One of the finest exemplars of the lifestyle of the anagarika in recent times was Anagarika Dharmapala (see *Anagarika Dharmapala, A Biographical Sketch, and Other Maha Bodhi Writings* by Sangharakshita. Ibis Publications, 2013).

5 untimely meals: the precept forbidding the taking of untimely meals was promulgated by the Buddha in response to a local scandal. One evening a *bhikkhu* had been going on his begging round and, standing in the shadows, had severely frightened a pregnant woman. Shortly afterwards she miscarried, and the bhikkhu concerned was regarded as the cause of this misfortune. In response to this the Buddha had been obliged (amongst other things) to institute the rule of not begging after noon. The bhikkhu Sangha has not felt itself able to modify this minor rule even after two thousand years of changing circumstances and even though they had the Buddha's express permission to do so. For a thorough examination of the question of the difference between major and minor rules, see *The Ten Pillars of Buddhism*, (note 6 below).

6 *The Ten Pillars of Buddhism*. Sangharakshita, Windhorse Publications, Cambridge, 2010.

7 *dhamma* (*dharma* in Sanskrit) is an ancient Indian word rich in meaning and used variously in Buddhism to indicate the Buddha's own Teaching, the Way to Enlightenment, a principle, a quality, a thing, a law, or a mental state.

8 *bana*: the 'sermon', homily or exhortation usually delivered by a *bhikkhu* after the midday meal has been ceremonially offered by the *dayakas* (lit: 'helpers' - of the Chapter) and eaten.

9 *mitra*: when a Friend attending spiritual activities of the Triratna Buddhist Order feels happy making three 'declarations', he or she may be accepted as a mitra. These are: 1) I feel that I am a Buddhist. 2) I am trying to practise the five ethical Precepts. 3) I want to deepen my practice within the context of Triratna. The only stipulation is that they have been attending a Triratna Centre for approximately six months.

10   Tamil: one who identifies him- or herself primarily in terms of their ancestral links with Tamil Nadu, one of the Southern States of India. Descendants of the people who invaded Sri Lanka from Southern India in ancient times and ruled the northern part of the country. Traditionally Hindu, but nowadays also Christian, they are of Dravidian rather than Aryan stock, and tend to be literate and well-educated.

11 *sila*: morality. Two broad kinds of morality are distinguished in Buddhism: conventional morality and 'natural' morality. The first denotes those aspects of group or social behaviours which are matters simply of custom and tradition. If one does not observe the dictates of conventional morality, one is liable to encounter the disapproval or censure of those group members who insist that certain forms of

behaviour are 'acceptable' and others not. 'Natural' morality however is concerned with what eventuates from the wellsprings of one's motivation; from deliberate, willed action and its direct, natural reaction upon the mind and being of the doer of the act. The reaction is more or less weighty according to the quality of the intention that informs the act. This is the principle of *kamma* (Skt. *karma*) and its results. One's *kamma* or *karma* is thus whatever deliberate intention, skilful or otherwise, that precedes or underlies any personal act of body, speech or mind. The Buddhist ethic is therefore, through and through, one of intention: the goodness or rightness or skilfulness of an act is seen to be commensurate with the intention that underlies it and of which the act is a more or less adequate outward expression. Any *karma* - any willed action of body speech or mind - is productive of results which will ripen sooner or later to produce a *vipaka*, i.e. a result appropriate to and commensurate with the original volition; will ripen whenever conditions arise which can serve as the basis for the fruition of that act..

12   *samadhi*: an almost untranslatable term meaning both healthy one-pointedness of mind and a state of higher consciousness involving the harmonious integration of various highly positive psychic factors, together with the presence of *upeksha* - a state of profound inner tranquillity and imperturbability.

13   *paññā* [Skt: *prajna*] : a purely spiritual faculty for discerning spiritual truths. Developed by the progressive unfolding of three aspects: (i) the wisdom that comes from attending mindfully; reading and absorbing the words and the meaning of the spiritual teachings that are being communicated [Pali: *sutta-maya paññā*, Skt: *sruta-maya prajna*] (ii) the wisdom that comes from calling to mind, reflecting upon and understanding spiritual teachings [Pali: *citta-maya paññā*, Skt: *cinta-maya prajna*] (iii) the wisdom that comes from profound meditation during which a spiritual truth is seen, understood and recognised directly in personal experience. [Pali: *bhavana-maya paññā*, Skt: *bhavana-maya prajna*]. As one of the five spiritual faculties, it is to be balanced with *saddha* (Skt. *sraddha*) or faith, to avoid its articulation becoming cliché or a mere dry, formulaic repetition.

14   *Religio-Nationalism in Sri Lanka*: see *Alternative Traditions*, pp.69-91 Sangharakshita, Windhorse, 1986

15   *Tipitika* : this collection of ancient textual material widely regarded as canonical is divided into three parts: *sutra*, *vinaya* and *abhidharma*, or: miscellaneous discourses of the Buddha and his Enlightened disciples; teachings having to do with monastic discipline; and teachings concerning the nature of all dharmas in the sense of mind and mental events.

* * * * *

Introduction

I HAD ARRIVED in hot, steamy and once-beautiful Bombay (now, of course, 'Mumbai') in 1982. I was dressed in ordinary clothes, being a Dharmachari[16] or 'Follower of the Buddha's Teaching', who eschews the projection-attracting tendencies of priestly garb. Basing myself in Pune, Maharashtra, I had continued with the Buddhist studies that I had pursued since my discovery in my late twenties of books on the Dharma, and had persevered with the regular practice of meditation, especially the sadhana or spiritual discipline into which I had been initiated in 1972 by Sangharakshita. I soon found that meditating in the tropical heat of India was a much more natural and congenial thing to do than in the cooler climate of my native land, and after a few weeks of practice found myself slipping quite regularly into the *dhyanas*, the states of superconsciousness described by the Buddha in the early Buddhist texts.

However, I had not come to India simply to meditate, wonderful though it was to find my efforts in that direction beginning to meet with success after ten years of practice. As arranged before my departure from the UK, I started working with Trailokya Bauddha Mahasangha Sahayaka Gana ("The Association of Helpers of the Great Sangha of the Buddha of the Three Worlds"), the new Buddhist organisation set up by Dhammachari Anagārika Lokamitra (as he then was) in 1977 under the guidance of Sangharakshita, the founder of the Western Buddhist Order[17]. Inspired by Lokamitra's example as a Buddhist teacher, and attributing a not insignificant part of that to his being an anagārika and to the pathways that that opened for him, I myself began to consider becoming an anagārika. I wrote to Sangharakshita, and he advised me to find out what the Indian Order members thought of my proposal. All of them encouraged me to go ahead. So, one year after my arrival in India, both to facilitate my teaching of Buddhism in towns and villages, and also in pursuance of a long-cherished spiritual ambition, I had my head shaved and donned the orange robes - the 'robes' which were of course originally, in the days of the Buddha, made of discarded rags stitched together and dyed with *garua mati*, a reddish brown earth-dye. They were symbolic of renunciation, not only of the romantic ties of family and the hankering after sex, but also renunciation of social status and ultimately of all ego-conceits. Witnessed by Sangharakshita, who was then on a brief visit to India, and by my fellow Indian Dhammacharis, I undertook the brahmachariya precept, the precept enjoining celibacy and chastity. Soon after this I began to give public talks on Buddhism, mainly to the ex-untouchable Buddhists in the towns and villages of West Central India, and this I continued to do for several years.

In July 1985 I became extremely ill with jaundice, which I had caught by drinking polluted water whilst on a Dhamma-teaching tour in the Kokan area south of Bombay during the hot season. I flew back to the UK, where after two months I was well on the road to recovery and returned to India. During my convalescence, I had visited my teacher and preceptor Sangharakshita and had responded enthusiastically to his suggestion that I visit Sri Lanka. Three months after my return to India, therefore, having meanwhile continued to teach the Buddha-dhamma, I made my way to Sri Lanka.

NOTES

16   Dharmachari (masc.) Dharmacharini (fem.) : literal meaning: one who conducts his life according to the principles of the Dharma. In this context: a member of the Triratna Buddhist Order. Traditionally, one who Goes for Refuge to the Enlightened One, to His Doctrine and Discipline, and to the spiritually developed members of the Spiritual Community, i.e. those really practising (and therefore exemplifying in their work and lifestyle) the Teaching of the Buddha. Ref: *Going for Refuge*, Sangharakshita, Windhorse, 1981.

17   WBO: the Western Buddhist Order, known nowadays as the Triratna Buddhist. The nucleus of the spiritual movement founded by Venerable Sangharakshita in 1968 in London, U.K. It was Western in the sense that it arose in response to a Westernised, that is to say a secular, industrialised and English-speaking people. Now, however, it consists of an increasingly large number of Centres worldwide, each of which bears the name Triratna Buddhist Order (or the equivalent in the local language), each is registered as a Charitable Organisation or its equivalent. Each Centre is directed by a Council of Members of the Triratna Buddhist Order and has as Aim and Object the propagation of the Buddhist faith in accordance with the Dharma, the principial teaching of the Buddha as communicated by the canonical texts of Buddhism and in accordance with the spiritual vision of Sangharakshita. Order members affirm this not due to any narrow view or sectarian bias, but out of a firm faith in Sangharakshita's vision of the Dhamma, having thoroughly examined it in the depths of their own life-experience, compared it with the canonical texts and with the testimony of the wise. See: *New Currents in Western Buddhism,* Sangharakshita, Windhorse, 1990.

* * * * *

1   Attaining 'ethical purity'

The three o'clock flight from Trivandrum, coasting under a cloudless azure sky only a few hundred feet above the choppy sea, had just crossed the Palk Straits from Southern India. Overflying a palm-fringed littoral, it traverses a large lagoon on the rippling surface of which are borne side by side two lone boats with square, wind-filled sails, and dips its nose for the landing at Colombo International Airport. Drawing up alongside a sleek jumbo-sized jet on which is emblazoned in large Cyrillic characters the legend 'Aeroflot', the passengers issue forth into the immigration section of the airport building.

I JOINED THE SUBMISSIVELY-WAITING QUEUE of pink-skinned, coffee-complexioned and mahogany-coloured people attired in a great variety of national costume, and in due course had my passport stamped with a visa expiring after one month; on 9th January 1986, to be precise. While I was waiting for the conveyor belt to deliver my carry-all, I had the opportunity to observe two large groups which I took to be of Russians; at least, they were of pale, Slavonic features, and spoke something which sounded to my ears very much like Russian. The first group consisted of schoolboys in their late teens, headed by two very severe-looking men, presumably their teachers, one of whom, with pinched nose and dark-shadowed eyes, tall and grey-suited, looked consumptive. The other was short and stocky, wore a stylish sports jacket, and from his podgy, tightly clenched fist jutted a cigarette. These two men appeared to detest their charges, who, perhaps victims of a repressive discipline, looked at their masters from time to time with a mixture of fear and loathing. I wondered what on earth they would get up to on this fabled island paradise, but they were soon ushered out of my sight and my attention turned to the other group of adults. This second group consisted of some handsome-looking men and women, perhaps from Uzbekistan, I thought, since their faces bore Mongol characteristics. In addition to half-a-dozen healthy-looking men, there were a couple of ancient peasants wearing Muslim skull-caps, and a few women whom I took to be unmarried, dressed in l950's European style, looking slightly dowdy and a bit miserable. Some of the men looked at me with curiosity; perhaps I was the first orange-robed man they had ever seen. I smiled at them, they smiled back, and the mood of the whole group seemed to lighten a bit. I wondered what they would do with their taste of freedom.

My carry-all having at last arrived on the conveyor belt, I picked it up and walked through the 'nothing-to-declare' exit into the airport entrance hall. Having changed some of my five-dollar notes into the much more colourful-looking and much higher-denomination Sri Lankan currency, I exited through one of the outer doors of the air-conditioned building into the open air. My nose immediately prickled and within a few seconds my skin began to feel damp. I wondered momentarily whether I would be able to acclimatize to this hot-house atmosphere from which there would be no exit, and made a mental note to slow down. Enquiring of a bystander at the airport bus stop how long it would take to reach Galle, the town in the South where my friend Siri Goonasekara was living, I was told I would arrive in the capital city too late to board the southbound train from Colombo. I might, however, catch a bus, I was told. Thinking I would arrive at Siri's too late for his convenience, I decided to take a lodging that night in Colombo, and to proceed southward next morning.

As we drove towards the city, with the softly luminous evening light casting a warm glow on the ubiquitous tall palm trees, I noticed crowds of people walking on the pavements. The women, to my surprise, wore mostly western dress, of a very colourful variety, even more colourful than the occasional westernised Indian women I had become used to seeing, and also, counter intuitively in view of the apparently greater freedom of dress, the sexes were more segregated - women more often than not being in the company of women, and men with men.

Having found a cheap boarding house run by a Christian Sinhalese, slept well and risen early, I was on a mini-bus to Galle soon after nine next morning. I soon noticed many others of a similar kind plying the roads at high speed. As we passed through Colombo, I noted the cosmopolitan character of the architecture, ranging in style from classical Greek to visceral Hindu, from Art Nouveau to modern European, and also in evidence was a peculiarly Lankan style I had not seen before, with roofs wide-spreading for protection from rain and sun, and elaborately carved timber fretwork at the eaves. Soon we were speeding along the coastal road, with exhilarating glimpses of a turquoise sea pounding the dazzling white sands, and where the grey rocky outcrops of palm-fringed shore met with the huge breakers, great spouts of foam were tossed sparkling into the air. An open window at my elbow alleviated the tropical heat. A cheerful south-sea-island lilt emanated from the buses' loudspeaker, setting off little tingles and sprays of emotion, and I felt in very elevated mood.

Arriving some three hours later at the bus station in Galle and emerging from the hot mini-bus into the now dazzling sunshine and almost overpowering noonday heat, I stood for a moment surveying the scene. The paved surfaces of the bus-station were pot-holed like a moonscape, over which decrepit single-decker red State Transport Buses or STBs lurched from time to time to disgorge their overheated occupants into the welcome shade of the passenger stands. The sun was scorching; I had never felt so hot. Would I be able, I wondered, to do anything at all on this tropical island but put my feet up? However, for the moment my only concern was to meet Siri Goonasekara, at whose invitation I was here in this small and so far undistinguished-looking town. I examined the address he had given me and guessed that he might not be far away. Having enquired, and been pleased to receive reassuring replies in good English from an elderly Sinhalese gentleman that the place I sought was not far, I set off on foot from the bus station. But I soon realized the truth of the saying that only mad dogs and

Englishmen walk in the noonday sun. Soaked with perspiration after only a few minutes, I decided to take a rickshaw. I was set down, after a short ride, in the place I wanted - the Magalle Road - but the houses did not appear to be numbered, and when I enquired of passers-by, some of whom spoke at least some English, I received no helpful directives. I decided to try asking at the houses themselves. It so happened that the first one at which I presented myself - a rather smart, modern, two-storey building with a broad overhanging roof - was the one I sought. I was greeted by a young woman dressed in a denim skirt and white T-shirt who was sitting at the top of the back stairs leading to the first-floor verandah. I asked if she knew Siri Goonasekara, and she informed me that she was his wife, and that she had been expecting me. Apparently Siri was at the Hotel, and Nita - for that was her name - proceeded to tell me how to get there. Polite and helpful, she agreed to let me leave my heavy carry-all at the house to be picked up later. But the one thing I wanted most of all - a glass of water - she did not offer, which I thought was rather curious. In India, to the heat of which I had been accustomed for the last four years, one was invariably offered water on arriving at someone's home. Grateful however that at least Nita was willing to look after my luggage, I thanked her and made off armed with her instructions, deciding to ignore my thirst until I met Siri.

I had not walked more than a few yards from the gate when a man on a bicycle drew up beside me, and in halting English asked me where I was going. I discovered from him that the village of Unawatuna, where Siri's hotel was situated, was "a long way away". "Is it near enough to walk?", I asked. Replying in the negative, he looked me up and down and invited me to take a lift on his bicycle. The heat was intense, and I was keen to get to 'Samma Ajiva', Siri's hotel in Unawatuna, with the minimum of delay. So I nodded my head in assent and hopped as gracefully as I could onto the crossbar of the man's bicycle.

We had not gone more than a few yards when there was a sudden commotion. A man on a motorcycle had drawn up beside us and ordered the man giving me a lift to stop. The motorcyclist seemed to be in a state of apoplexy. As I got off the cross-bar, he addressed me in broken English, letting me know that a bhikkhu should not allow himself to be treated like a sack of potatoes. My protest that I was not a bhikkhu brought a look of puzzlement to his dark face, and he became quiet for a moment. But before we could exchange any more words, a little crowd of passers-by had materialized as if from nowhere and started remonstrating with the cyclist. Evidently they thought it extremely remiss of him to have offered me a lift. The emotional temperature began to rise alarmingly, out of all proportion, I thought, to the apparent misdemeanour, if indeed there was one, and I hastily took my leave. Looking over my shoulder after I had covered a fair distance, I saw the little crowd still arguing with the cyclist at the roadside.

The sky was the most brilliant and beautiful blue I had ever seen, and the flowering trees that peeped above the walls surrounding the houses either side of the road down which I walked shimmered in the intense heat. Their intoxicating perfume was noticeable even above the pungent and prickly smell of the fumes from the traffic. But I soon began to realize that even without the burden of luggage, walking in the middle of the day was not something one did for pleasure in Sri Lanka. The sun beat down mercilessly on my unprotected head, and my robes, now soaked with perspiration, began sticking to me. I decided to take a bus, not wishing to present myself on Siri's doorstep in a state of collapse. Some sun-drenched minutes later I reached a bus stop, and after what seemed an interminable wait, an old red bus, seemingly packed full with people, approached. To my surprise, it stopped at my bidding, and the press of bodies at the door miraculously drew back to let me in. As I penetrated into the sweltering interior, an old woman rose and offered me her place. Suspecting that I was in better shape than her despite the heat, I declined the offer, but several other passengers chimed in: "No, you must take it: the seat is for Priests." Fearing another scene, I accepted as gracefully as I could and sat down. The rickety bus drew off with a terrific roar and rattle, and a blissfully cool breeze began to play over my face as I watched the palm trees and little houses pass swiftly by.

We were soon traversing a particularly narrow village street lined with numerous fish-sellers. This, I was soon to discover, was one of the less pleasant aspects of Sri Lankan village life. The stench of freshly cut fish, the swarms of flies, and the sight of the pitiful remnants with blood and guts strewn in the gutter was ugly indeed. I was evidently wrong in expecting that compassion would be more evident in a 'Buddhist country' than in a non-Buddhist one. But this was only the beginning of my disillusionment concerning the 'Buddhist' nature of Sri Lanka.

Some ten minutes after passing through the village with the narrow main street and the fish-sellers, we pulled up, apparently in the middle of nowhere. The bus had stopped on a long straight stretch of road lined with tall palms, with just a few small houses visible amongst the trees, and a village store nearby. "This is Unawatuna", the driver announced. I dismounted, feeling the curious stares of the passengers at my back. The bus sped away with a loud rattle, leaving behind it a trail of smoky exhaust. I looked around, savouring the sudden silence and the feeling of expansiveness. Then I noticed a sign pointing across the road to 'Samma Ajiva' Whole Food Restaurant', and with mounting excitement, crossed the now-deserted highway.

I found myself in a delightful country lane lined with trees and bushes flowering with brilliant crimson hibiscus, and after a five minute walk came to a sharp bend to the left, on the outer, right-hand corner of which stood a building bearing the sign 'South Ceylon Hotel' and beneath it the words 'Samma Ajiva'. It was a two-storey structure of brick and timber, over which spread a low pitched, tiled roof with a wide overhang supported on sturdy timber pillars. The roof overhung a balcony shaded by a great mass of passion fruit plants on the front and on the two long sides, and on the first floor at the front I could see the restaurant, advertised by gaily painted signs. The signs announced 'Rooms available', and various kinds of exotic-sounding dishes like guacamole and gado-gado.

I climbed the wooden stairway to the first-floor balcony, and immediately spotted Siri, bare-chested and wearing a white sarong around his waist. Not looking carefully at me at first, he said, "Ah, hello, welcome

Bhante"[18], and then he saw who it was and his face lit up with delight: "Oh, hello Ashvajit! How nice to see you!" It was a happy beginning. I was soon made blissfully comfortable, with the offer of a drink, a bath, and a meal, all of which I accepted in due order. I was shown the room that had been assigned to me, which I was to share with a pleasant, dark-skinned curly-haired young man called Ranjit. Ranjit did not appear to take much notice of me, but I told myself that it was certainly early days yet. I felt very much at home. In fact, I felt absolutely delighted to have arrived in what seemed to be such a bright, healthy, comfortable and interesting place.

I soon settled into a routine at 'Samma Ajiva'. I would rise with the loud and exotic dawn chorus, study, then after a cool shower, lead a meditation session in the small shrine room. This was attended by some of the hotel staff and guests, and would begin as soon as Siri had arrived from his home in his battered old Morris 8, which was usually about 7:00am. Siri would translate for me into Sinhalese, for the benefit of those who did not understand English. Then after meditation, at 8:30, there would be breakfast consisting of rice, palm treacle, and papaya or pineapple, together with a small and very sweet banana from one of the plantain trees in the banana grove at the back of the Hotel. On the remaining three sides of the hotel tall and stately coconut palms thrust high into the blue sky their huge and delicate windmill-like array of spiky leaves. After breakfast I would spend some time talking to the guests, especially the newly arrived ones, and after that I would go for my morning walk. All this, including the sport of monkeys and in the evening the flights of the fruit bats, could be surveyed from the first floor balcony surrounding the hotel. It really was a delightful spot.

Five minutes from the hotel was the beach. It was a semi-circular bay about three-quarters of a mile from the tip of one 'horn' to the other, and with pale golden sand of a marvellous softness, onto which the breakers from the Indian Ocean would thud and hiss. The beach was shaded on the land side by an almost continuous growth of palm trees, into which intruded, here and there, small hotels. The air, due to the abundance of trees, and the absence of polluting agents, was wonderfully refreshing to breathe, and it was at first difficult for me to imagine how anyone could be unhappy here. I soon discovered that some people did try very hard, however, and with a combination of wives, mistresses, fish and meat, toddy, cannabis and heroin, contrived to make their own lives and that of others less than perfectly pleasant. Sinhala Buddhism, I soon discovered, did not seem able to provide a real alternative to the reckless, drug-laden hedonism that I began to see in evidence everywhere. Perhaps it did not want to provide an alternative, or else chose to ignore the decadence which Western tourism had brought and which its own youth had begun to emulate with enthusiasm. Perhaps it saw but did not know the answer. Sri Lankan Buddhism itself, though colourful and even attractive, I saw with ever-increasing clarity and certainty as a museum piece; and further evidence of this was provided by the many young people who began to come to me at 'Samma Ajiva' seeking answers to questions about Buddhism that the Sri Lankan bhikkhus had not been able to answer.

The beach at Unawatuna was sheltered from the full fury of the Indian Ocean by two arms of land and sundry rocky islets that lay out in the bay some distance from the shore, so that the main force of the waves was spent on them. The blue waters of the bay were thus subject only to relatively small waves and were ideal for swimming. By the time I usually arrived at the beach, there would be several dozens, perhaps even several hundreds of holidaymakers sunning themselves; many of the women would be topless, and this had the effect of making me more circumspect in my visits. I found that if I took more than a passing glance at the women, my mind all too easily became preoccupied with them, and observance of the Brahmachariya precept, the precept of chastity, would become difficult; indeed, I reflected, even by allowing my gaze to return just once to a woman, I had already broken the precept. I had in effect allowed my mind to fall from the level of insight into the true nature of phenomena back into a more worldly, a more crudely conditioned mode of perception. I found however that if I allowed myself simply to see what sometimes came unbidden into my field of vision, and did not allow my eyes to return, it was possible to regard these human blossoms with the same state of mind with which I contemplated the exotic, colourful and sweet-smelling flowers that grew in such abundance everywhere, and my mind was not entranced. After a visit to the beach and a swim, for which I wore an old lower robe, I would return to 'Samma Ajiva' and lunch. And after lunch, the temperature was so hot that really the only thing one could do was rest. At five in the afternoon another meditation class was oriented towards those visitors who had become bored with the beach, and this was followed by supper. Soon after the rapid and dramatic tropical sunset, Siri would drive off in his rickety old Morris 8, and I would be left to read or meditate alone, unless, as sometimes happened, we had arranged to visit a friend or relative of Siri's or one of the many Temples in the area.

During my first three weeks in Unawatuna, numerous visitors came and went from the hotel; bronzed fair-haired Germans, many from West Berlin, paler and spottier Englishmen, lanky Australians, lounging Italians, slender Frenchmen, tall and well-muscled Americans, a few sallow-skinned, lotus-eyed Japanese, and Sri Lankans with their black hair, dark and healthy-looking skin, and features rounded by the kindness of the climate and land. What with my daily meditation classes and Siri's championing of Sangharakshita and the FWBO[19] there was thus a definite spiritual direction, or spiritual ambience to be found at 'Samma Ajiva'. Siri kept at the back of the restaurant, for use by the visitors, a small collection of tape-recordings of Sangharakshita's talks on the Dharma, and a variety of Buddhist and some not-so-Buddhist books in English, German and Sinhalese. Modern Sinhalese stands in a similar relationship to the language of the Pali, the ancient Buddhist texts of Sri Lanka, as modern Italian does to Latin.

Not long after my arrival in Unawatuna I was taken by Siri in his ancient Ford Popular to visit a temple near the village of Walpola, birthplace of the famous 'political bhikkhu' Walpola Rahula, to whom he was distantly related. As we drew up at the entrance to the Temple precinct, we found eight or nine bhikkhus standing around as if forming a reception committee. However, none of them was actually expecting us or appeared to be doing very much, and so our arrival caused quite a stir. They gathered in a semi-circle eyeing us suspiciously, and I asked who was the seniormost. The bhikkhus looked pointedly beyond my shoulder, and turning round, I could see, sitting idly on a low chair at the end of a spacious corridor, an old man, somnolent and large-eyed. I went up to him and offered him a spray of frangipani or temple flowers that had been given me during my journey, and stirring slightly from his daydream to accept the proffered sprig, he asked if I wanted a cup of tea, to which I assented. The old man hauled himself up and ambled off, leaving me to the tender mercies of the junior bhikkhus. They noticed and proceeded to grill me concerning the apparently seamless robe I was wearing and the precepts I followed, and though of course I gave all the answers promptly, confidently and even inspiringly, the bhikkhus remained somewhat stony. It was only when we came to the question of tea that something happened to raise me in their estimation; asked whether I took milk, I replied: "If milk is offered I accept it, if not, I am happy without." At this, they all smiled and warmed perceptibly to me, offered me a seat and asked me how I became a Buddhist. Siri told me later that there are in Sri Lanka several *nikayas*[20] or monastic institutions, two of which differ concerning what is considered permissible to drink. One of them considers the taking of milk with tea in the afternoon as an infringement of the no-eating-after-twelve rule, while the other nikaya considers it permissible. My reply to their question, apparently, was reckoned to please members of both nikayas.

Within the course of the first month after my arrival, I had personally met, with varying degrees of intimacy, nearly thirty bhikkhus, but my chief Sri Lankan friend remained Siri Goonasekara; indeed our friendship was deepening day by day. Siri, a short and healthy, pleasant-faced young Sri Lankan inclined to portliness, had made contact with the Friends of the Western Buddhist Order in New Zealand in 1978. He had listened to Sangharakshita's audiotaped lectures on Buddhism and was so impressed that a year later he visited London to find out more. He had had an interview with Sangharakshita, and met Subhuti and several other Senior Order Members, including myself. I would occasionally refer to Siri as my *dayaka*[21] - a term commonly used by the Sinhalese, and which means literally, 'one who is kind', but he was much more even than that to me. Without him it is unlikely I would have gone to Sri Lanka, or if I had done, it would surely have been much more difficult and less pleasant to do what I was in fact able to accomplish during the first eighteen months of my stay. Siri's hotel-cum-vegetarian-restaurant was an ideal place for making new recruits to the practice of meditation, as not only was there a cosmopolitan clientèle, but also Siri was well-connected locally. We often seemed to catch the fancy of friends and acquaintances of his, young outwardly or inwardly, who for some reason or another, when meeting us were seized with the desire to learn to meditate, or at least to come and eat at the restaurant and hear something about Buddhism as taught by a Westerner. It was not long before I began to feel that I could be of use as a meditation teacher in Sri Lanka, and what is more, that I wanted to stay there indefinitely.

When, therefore, my first application for a one-year residence visa in Sri Lanka ended in failure, my consternation was very great. What happened was that I had befriended two young visitors to Siri's Hotel, an Australian named Sean and his cockney girlfriend, and they had tagged along with me one day into Colombo and come as far as the Office of the Commissioner for Buddhist Cultural Affairs where I had to apply for my residence visa. It was a very hot day, and as there was no shade in sight anywhere, I suggested that my two friends wait downstairs, on a shady veranda well-provided with seats, while I went upstairs and made my visa application. However, whilst I was making my enquiries and filling in forms upstairs, my young friends had succumbed to the mid-day heat, and lying there in a semi-stupor, were spotted and suspected of being drug addicts. A small crowd of irate orange-robed officials roused them into sudden wakefulness, standing over them and demanding who they were. Sean was asked the preposterous question: "Why are you not wearing robes?" Sean replied, reasonably enough according to his own lights: "Because I'm not a Buddhist". The two were then asked what they were doing there, and replied that they were waiting for their friend Ashvajit, who was upstairs. The rumour of all this arrived at the ears of no less a person than the Commissioner himself just as his pen was poised to sign my papers, and of course, he baulked. The feelings which assailed me are perhaps not hard to imagine. However, I was not to be put off so easily, and within two days I had set about enlisting the help of the Government Agent for Galle District, who was almost as weighty as a Judge in Britain, the Superintendent of the Galle District Police whom I befriended, and the High Priest of Galle, Venerable Akurattia Nandasara Nayaka Maha Thero (B.A.), who happened to be a friend of Siri's family. My fresh application for a Residence Visa, with all that weight behind it, met with success.

The Chief High Priest of Galle was a key to my obtaining a Residence visa, and for that reason, though not for that reason alone, I agreed to accompany him to a *pirit* ceremony (a 'ceremony of protection') in a village some forty miles inland from the village of Unawatuna. Arriving at the Venerable Nandasara's temple not far from the centre of Galle at sundown, I was invited to take a back seat in his modern car. Two other young bhikkhus squeezed in next to me, and off we went. Despite the gathering darkness, I was able to appreciate something of the countryside, with its rice fields, rubber trees, tea plantations, banana trees, coconut palms and a large variety of beautiful flowers whose names I do not know. The *pirit* ceremony was at a place called Galle Vidya Shanti Pirivena, Weihena, which we reached after traversing what seemed in the darkness to be an alarming series of hairpin bends that took us well above the surrounding plain. Emerging from the car, I was advised by Venerable Nandasara to go and make offerings to the Buddha, and wondering how this was to be done, I wandered in the direction that I now saw many dozens of bhikkhus slowly walking. They were walking towards what appeared to be the centrepiece of the *pirivena* or monastic college; it was a newly erected temple in which were housed two seated Buddha images each more than twice the height of a man. One of them had evidently just been completed and was gleaming with fresh paint. It was a sort of amalgam of the popular Indian Buddha-image with its very sweet, rounded features, and the Tibetan or Nepalese, which is more angular and austere. This very beautiful image had been sculpted, I was told, by a sixteen-year old boy. I looked around at the growing numbers of people, both golden-robed and white-robed who were thronging the Temple, and feeling suddenly in need of fresh air, I sought the exit and the cooler air outside.

I noticed that not far from the great wide-open Temple doors stood an ancient white-painted *stupa*, a burial receptacle embodying symbolism of cosmic significance, about forty feet high and of classic bell-shaped proportions. Further away stood a long low building accommodating, I was told by a helpful bystander, about twenty bhikkhus; and at right angles to that, there were two large lecture halls. Between the elements of this tastefully arranged complex, gay with coloured lights, fragrant with incense, and adorned with masses of beautiful flowers I now strolled, but despite the presence of thirty or more bhikkhus of impressive and pleasing appearance, it seemed I was attracting rather a lot of attention. Doing my best to blend unobtrusively with my surroundings, I found myself unwittingly being drawn and urged into what seemed to be some sort of ceremony. Low chanting was beginning to issue from the throats of the gathering crowd, and I sensed that something momentous was about to begin, from which it might be difficult to extricate myself. Not knowing what it was all about, I felt for a moment reluctant to proceed. However, as the chanting swelled and grew in clarity, it suddenly became comfortingly familiar to my ears: it was a long-drawn-out recitation of the *ti-ratna vandana* - the verse-salutation to the Three Jewels - which is chanted by the faithful throughout Buddhist lands. Whatever was about to happen, I reflected, we were all Going for Refuge to the Three Jewels, so what did I have to worry about? The bhikkhus amongst whom I now found myself walking and completely surrounded, entered the Temple and took up a position in front of the new Buddha image, and ranging themselves in a line, proceeded to accept flower offerings from the assembly who had followed them in. I did likewise, and accepting a fragrant and colourful little basket of flowers from a dark-skinned, white sari-clad female devotee, went and ritually offered it beneath the benign gaze of the golden Buddha. It was a beautiful and moving ceremony. The chanting from the now perhaps two thousand strong gathering was becoming hypnotic, in a completely positive sense, the participants seeming to be in an almost *dhyanic*[22] state.

Hundreds of baskets of flowers were tendered to the bhikkhus and myself and ritually offered, and eventually the chanting of the *ti-ratna vandana* came to an end. The bhikkhus then all at once turned away from the flower-bedecked altar and began to exit through the Temple doors and to walk towards the stupa. I had no choice but to follow. We all went and seated ourselves on the sandy ground close to the stupa. While we were doing this, the assembly began chanting, and this time I recognized the verses of the Buddha Puja[23], the ceremonial worship of the Buddha, swelling again to an hypnotic rhythm and intensity into which it seemed perfectly natural to join, hands pressed together in the *anjali* or gesture of respect or worship. I felt as if I were a little rivulet joining a great stream or river of worship. After many repetitions of the well-known verses during which time seemed to stand still, the bhikkhus began to seat themselves in pairs facing each other cross-legged on the carefully-swept sand around the stupa, and I had no choice but to do the same, finding myself seated opposite a very thin bhikkhu with a care-worn face. Luckily, he spoke a little English, and was able to explain that we were to engage in the ceremony of Confession, and that the seniormost would begin. He then asked me 'how many rainy seasons?' meaning how many rainy season retreats had I observed. I replied that I had received ordination in 1972 and done a substantial retreat every year since that time. 'Ah', he said, 'Then I am a little senior to you, so I will begin'. He then began to recite, quite mechanically, the Pali verses of confession known as the *cetiyadi vandana* and the *khama yacana*, the translation of which goes something like this:

'I salute every stupa wherever it may be, the bodily relics [of the Buddha], the Maha Bodhi[-tree, symbolising the perfection of Wisdom], and all the images of the Buddha; I salute and revere the words of the Teacher, and His last exhortation to strive [with mindfulness]. All the shrines, too, I salute, (together with) my preceptors and teachers. By virtue of this salutation, may my mind be liberated from evil.'

'If by way of body, speech or mind I have acted unmindfully, forgive me oh Teacher, oh greatly wise one, Tathagata'

Stopping and looking at me with wide-open eyes, the thin bhikkhu pressed his palms in the gesture of salutation and bowed. Then it was my turn. Not having the verses by heart, and in any case not regarding them as constituting an authentic personal confession, beautiful though they were, I looked at the man in front of me and confessed in slow, clear English, to pride, greediness, and laziness, and then asked the Buddha's forgiveness. The thin bhikkhu smiled and bowed once again, pressing his palms together. At this point, all the bhikkhus began to rise and to walk away from the vicinity of the stupa. I did the same. At that moment, some very deep chanting indeed began to sound forth from a point somewhere beyond my sight. It sounded, in its initial stages at least, as if it was another slow and particularly lugubrious rendering of the *ti-ratna vandana*, and after sauntering as unconcernedly as I could to the side of the new Temple, I saw that *pirit* (i.e. *paritta* - 'verses of protection') was being chanted by a number of Theras or senior bhikkhus who had seated themselves in a small covered dais open on all sides and were gently fanning themselves with their heart-shaped palm leaf fans. Despite my initial impulse to laugh, or at least to smile, the effect of their chanting was to lull one into a very pleasant state even more deeply relaxed than that induced by the previous communal chanting. The *pirit* chanting went on and on and on; I sauntered several times around the temple complex, and was beginning to feel more and more sleepy. But despite my sleepiness I could not help noticing that some of the younger bhikkhus (or perhaps they were *samaneras*, novice bhikkhus) were also sauntering, or rather, strutting around, like spoiled, pampered and clever schoolboys, several of them in the first flush of manhood, and reflecting the positive emotions of the faithful lay-onlookers like jewelled ornaments or young peacocks.

Spotting an empty and comfortable-looking seat near a group of senior Theras who were chatting urbanely amongst themselves, I sat down and began to listen to them. They went on chatting, apparently taking no notice of me, occasionally laughing politely at each other rather in the manner of highly-polished college professors at high table, which is probably what many of them were. They were all dressed in resplendent robes, had freshly shaven, gleaming pates, and appeared to be in sleek good health, no doubt the result of enjoying the privileges that conventional morality brings. Then to my surprise - because I thought I had sat down unobserved - a portly and senior-looking Thera sitting nearby turned and spoke to me over his shoulder. He said: "Are you the bhikkhu who was seen being given a lift on a bicycle in Galle recently?" At this I felt intensely embarrassed, and suddenly fearful of being censured and perhaps even refused a visa for this petty offence, I replied obliquely: "I'm not a bhikkhu", I said, "I'm an *anagarika*." The Thera, after a peremptory "Ah", turned his attention back to his opposite number, and I was left feeling uneasy. Some minutes later, however, the Thera got up from his seat and coming over to me, asked me in kindly fashion whether I would like somewhere to sleep. Receiving my assent, he directed me to his own room, which was equipped with two beds, and having made sure I was comfortable, left me to rest. I awoke some time later to find the Thera on his bed, resting on one elbow and looking at me. I again felt uneasy, and knowing exactly why, I decided to 'open up'. I said: "I was the person who accepted a lift on a bicycle ride in Galle: I didn't know it was an offense." "Yes", the Thera replied with a little smile: "we mustn't do that sort of thing." And with that, he turned to the wall and took no further notice of me.

At this point I noticed that the *pirit* chanting was coming to an end, and quickly getting up and adjusting my robe, I made for the door and went to look for Ven. Nandasara's car. To my relief I located it just as the driver and the bhikkhus with whom I had come were about to depart. Within minutes we were on the road to the coast, and Ven. Nandasara announced to me portentously that I was now '*silavant*' - ethically pure, 'possessed of *sila*' (morality, in this case skilful morality) - as a result of participating in the ceremony. Of course, I did not regard the matter of moral purification as quite so simple. However, I settled back into the depths of the back seat of the car and tried to sleep. We got back to Ven. Nandasara's temple at three thirty in the morning, and he invited me to take the other bed in his room. I awoke at six, to find the Chief High Priest of Galle still sleeping blissfully, and after taking a cold bath and catching an early bus, I managed to reach the South Ceylon Hotel in time for the morning meditation at 7am.

NOTES

18 Bhante: the term of friendly respect traditionally used to address a senior bhikkhu, especially one's Preceptor, or someone whom one regards as one's spiritual superior. Used by members of the Triratna Buddhist Order and Community when referring informally to Sangharakshita.

19 FWBO: Friends of the Western Buddhist Order (now known as the Triratna Buddhist Community). This was the name of the spiritual movement founded by

Venerable Sangharakshita in 1968 in London, U.K. It was Western in the sense that it had arisen in response to a Westernized, that is to say a secular, industrialized and mostly English-speaking society. It was already made up of an increasing number of Centres worldwide, each of which bore the name FWBO (or the equivalent in the local language), each was (and still is) registered as a charitable organization or its equivalent, was directed by a Council of Members of the Western Buddhist Order (WBO - see note 17, Introduction) and had as Aim and Object the propagation of the Buddhist faith in accordance with the Dharma, the principial teaching of the Buddha, particularly in accordance with Sangharakshita's exposition; not that they did so out of any sectarian bias, but out of a firm faith in Sangharakshita's vision of the Truth having thoroughly examined it in their own hearts and minds and compared it with the testimony of the wise. See: *New Currents in Western Buddhism*, Sangharakshita, Windhorse, 1990.

20   *nikaya*: a division of the Theravada sangha on the basis of Ordination lineage. Such distinctions usually also involve minor differences of dress and custom. *De facto* recognition of one nikaya by another is commonplace, but there is no *de jure* recognition of one *nikaya* by another.

21   *dayaka*: lit. a 'carer' - the term used to describe a layman who reveres and supports a bhikkhu or a Temple.

22   *dhyanic*: pertaining to *dhyana* [Pali: *jhana*] : the state of being 'fixed' or firmly established in a superconscious state. The state experienced, for instance, by the yogin who successfully takes up the practice of the contemplation of the breathing process, or Mindfulness of Breathing, [Pali: *anapanasati*] particularly as described in the Sattipatthana Sutta of the Pali, and taught and practised in public classes by members of the Triratna Buddhist Order. The Buddha continued to perform this practice after his initial Enlightenment experience, during the three-month Rainy Season Retreat, and considered it a practice for heroes. It is a subtle, profound and spiritually efficacious exercise leading to the firm establishment of mindfulness and the ability to enter *dhyana* at will.

23   *Buddha-puja*: literal meaning: Buddha-worship. Ceremonial veneration of the Buddha Image or Shrine as a symbol of Enlightenment. Such veneration includes ritual obeisance, offerings of flowers, lights and incense, and the recitation of devotional verses, usually of great beauty and spiritual significance.

* * * * *

2   To Stay or Not to Stay?

In the course of the first few weeks after my arrival in Sri Lanka I begin to feel optimistic, not to say euphoric, concerning the prospects for spreading the real spirit of the Buddha's teachings on this island. I experience not for the first time, because I had begun to do so in India, but this time more as a pioneer, as it were, the potency of the actual Path to Enlightenment as communicated by Sangharakshita. As my own confidence in it deepens, I enjoy passing my knowledge and experience of the Dharma on to others in this ethnically Buddhist island.

My early mood of optimism is gradually being tempered by a growing awareness that I am spiritually quite alone in Sri Lanka, and that I need to withdraw from time to time deeply into myself to re-contact my sources of inspiration. I make a special point of doing this once a month when members of the Order are meeting world-wide in Chapters to meditate, engaged in 'Spiritual Workshops' and just enjoying one another's company. Doing this, I am surprised - and delighted - to discover that I do indeed feel in contact with the Order on a subliminal or perhaps telepathic level, and that such withdrawal from my everyday affairs has an immensely invigorating and inspiring effect upon me. I feel as if I am in actual contact with other Order members on a transcendental plane of spiritual awareness. This monthly communing with the silent 'presence' of other Order members is a very real experience for me, and very supportive of my continued work.

Not only do I feel the necessity of a regular personal retreat; I am beginning to explore the possibility of holding group meditation retreats in conjunction with an American bhikkhu who seems sympathetic to our Movement. He subsists in a little wooden hut up on the rocky western, wooded promontory of Unawatuna bay. I have by this time of course obtained a Residence Visa. My future in Sri Lanka looks assured by now, so I am setting about finding the most suitable places and opportunities to spread the Dharma to the Sri Lankans as well as to deepen my own spiritual practice. I want to deepen my spiritual practice on two main fronts: more intensive and prolonged meditation practice in accordance with Sangharakshita's system of meditation, and deepening friendships. One of my new friends is an American Bhikkhu who calls himself Yogavachara Rahula. Soon after my arrival in Unawatuna I had been taken by Siri to Rahula's 'Seaside Kuti' on the promontory overlooking the sea and about twenty minutes walk along the beach from the South Ceylon Hotel, and introduced to him. He had told me that he was teaching at the Nilambe Meditation Centre what he called Vipassana meditation. Having subsequently sat in on a meditation class which I had suggested Siri allow him to give at the South

Ceylon Hotel, I saw that he taught in a very dry, laconic fashion which I feared could not but turn quite a few people off. I also saw that his teaching of 'vipassana' was not really vipassana, that is to say, not taught from the point of view, as it were, of insight. Not that one can teach vipassana directly, in any case, though one can of course teach insight-type practices - those which are best undertaken after a suitable preliminary course of meditation has been assiduously and successfully practised. Rahula's 'vipassana' was simply a particular application of the very important practice we know as Mindfulness, but taught in such a way as to render the development of an integrated awareness more difficult than it actually is. The many people I have met both in India and here who have attended so-called vipassana courses have apparently been told that meditation can be categorised into two great types known as *samatha* and *vipassana*, or Tranquillity and Insight. They have also been told that 'vipassana' or spiritual insight is the ultimate goal of spiritual practise. This emphasis, however, subtly encourages completely 'green' beginners to feel that they are not doing things properly unless they are practising this 'higher' type of meditation. Their choice, however, is I suspect, exercised in ignorance of two circumstances: that real spiritual insight is the natural outcome or flowering of the two great Tranquillity practices, mindfulness and the meditation of loving kindness, and secondly gives rise to Compassion - to the profound, heartfelt aspiration to gain full and perfect Enlightenment for the sake not only of oneself but for all sentient beings. Thus, Insight manifests in a compassionate regard for other human beings and in a responsiveness to their needs based not on personal opinion but on Wisdom. So many of the 'vipassana' enthusiasts I have met appear to be ignorant of the fact that without the necessary basis of concentration and positive emotion generated by the *samatha* or Tranquillity types of meditation, the practice of vipassana or 'Insight meditation' is not only ineffective, but can be positively dangerous. I have on many occasions listened to first-hand reports of beginners to meditation attending a ten-day 'Vipassana' course and being instructed to sit for up to eleven hours per day - without moving. So-called 'Insight meditation' practices of this sort, undertaken without a full preparatory course of instruction, without properly qualified guidance and a supportive context of positive, inspiring communication whilst undertaking such practices, can lead to the development of alienated states of consciousness from which, I have seen, it is very difficult to extricate people. The practitioner may even start thinking - of course erroneously - that he is enlightened, and has nothing further to learn. One has had one's 'Enlightenment experience', and that is the end of the matter! People may well have an 'experience' of sorts after completing such a 'Vipassana' course, but it would not be an experience of Enlightenment, it would be an experience of the sort of relief one might get after stopping beating one's head against a brick wall. I was rather pleased therefore to find that at least one of the people to whom I had taught meditation at the South Ceylon Hotel - a German – and who had subsequently joined Rahula's course, was using it as an opportunity to get on with the Mindfulness of Breathing, a basic samatha-type practise, and with the *mettā bhāvana*, the cultivation of loving-kindness.

Despite my reservations concerning Rahula's teaching of meditation, I felt he was at heart a good man. Besides, I did not know whether he himself advocated such extreme methods of practice. So I sought to deepen my friendship with him, and was pleased when he invited me to visit him at the end of a ten-day retreat he would soon be leading for men and women in an up-country meditation Centre called Nilambe, the 'Sadaham Mithuru Samithiya' or 'SMS Laymen's Meditation Centre.' I discovered to my relief that Rahula's teaching at Nilambe did not involve an eleven-hours-a-day regime, but he himself, he proudly told me, had completed such a course, and spoke in a way that suggested to me that he thought he was enlightened. My wish to stay on good terms with him means that I am not going to challenge him prematurely on what I consider to be alienating methods of meditation teaching. I feel that I need a stronger basis of friendship with him before it will be possible for me to do that without provoking a reaction.

The journey to meet Rahula was delightful. Taking a train which ascended at first slowly from the green paddy fields around Colombo then up the precipitous, densely wooded hillsides to Kandy, and from Kandy taking a bus even higher up into the mountains, I reached the village of Nilambe. From there I walked for an hour up a winding dirt track to a small group of buildings constituting the 'Laymen's Meditation Centre' to which I had been invited. Rahula was not present on my arrival; the young Sri Lankan who greeted me told me that he was staying in a tiny meditation hut even higher up the mountain. I was then shown to quite a spacious room at the end of one of the two rows of buildings situated some distance from the main shrine room and kitchen. Left alone, I found myself gazing spellbound at the prospect of the distant hills and mountain ranges. The gently sloping hills, backed by steeper and higher ranges disappearing blue-green into the distance, were planted here and there with tea bush, and elsewhere covered with a wonderful variety of beautiful trees such as the eucalyptus, rubber, palm, and banana, and on the highest slopes, the fir. As I continued to contemplate the scene, the silence seemed to deepen; I began to hear the cool breeze rustling the leaves of the trees, and the calls of numerous birds - some low, monotonous and repetitive, and others high and musical.

Beautiful though the Nilambe Meditation Centre was, I had not come just for the view and not even simply to deepen my friendship with Rahula; I had come to consider and to decide whether it was practical to conduct a ten-day meditation course there myself sometime in the future. The premises were well-equipped for twenty or thirty people, and it appeared to me eminently possible to have a good retreat there. I reflected that I will have to commit myself quite soon, and to decide, for instance, whether the retreat will be single-sex or mixed.

My feelings have thus begun to clarify: I realise I am no longer in any doubt that I want to settle in Sri Lanka. Having obtained a one-year residence visa, with the enthusiastic help of Venerable Nandasara Thero, the 'Chief High Priest' of Galle District, I will surely have no difficulty in renewing that visa every year for as long as I wish. What is more, I will be able to come and go from Sri Lanka as necessary, with a little co-operation from the Indian immigration authorities. I will be able to pay occasional visits to my friends in India when time, money, my friend Lokamitra and my need for peer companionship conspire to draw me there.

I have been wondering from time to time what I will do in Sri Lanka, with all my limitations; whether and for how long I will be able to stay and serve the Dharma here. The food is good and the climate, at least in the hill country, suits me. The people do not seem too difficult, and what little money I have goes further here than anywhere else I have been. I have made a start with teaching a little meditation - to the staff of Siri's hotel, to some of the local bhikkhus, and to an association of old age pensioners at the Temple of Baddegama near Unawatuna which houses a very beautiful, twenty-foot high Buddha-image with a smile of unusual subtlety and refinement. I have also addressed a large group of people assembled at a country house belonging to Mr Albert Edirisinghe, the President of the World Fellowship of Buddhists, and obtained an invitation to stay at his town house in Colombo. Having taken Sangharakshita's advice and taken up residence in Sri Lanka, I have discovered that I feel disinclined to go anywhere else.

Feeling that I am likely to be on the island for quite some time, my mind has begun to turn to building a library of Buddhist literature. Dharma books other than those relating to the Theravada are scarce in Sri Lanka; I will need also to amass a collection of periodicals published by the FWBO such as *mitrata*[24] and *Golden Drum*[25]. I have written to my fellow members of the Order in Britain asking for all those who could, to send copies to me. I have also begged for copies of Sangharakshita's seminars and taped lectures. My friend Siri has a small collection of tapes at the 'Samma Ajiva' guest house, but most of them are already damaged by the heat and moisture, and are difficult to hear properly. I have begun composing a letter appealing for help to get our new Buddhist movement established in Sri Lanka on a proper footing.

I have received a letter from Lokamitra a few days ago announcing the names of newly-ordained Order Members in India, and I want to emulate his success in spreading the Dharma in such an effective way. But in the midst of all this activity, all this planning, I am beginning to experience my aloneness.

NOTES

24 *Mitrata* : a three-monthly periodical issued mainly for the benefit of the mitras of the FWBO/TBMSG.
25 *Golden Drum*: (later to become *Dharma Life*) then the three-monthly English-language journal of the Western Buddhist Order.

* * * * *

3   Why do Bodhisattvas not declare themselves?

As week succeeds week and month succeeds month, as my sense of aloneness deepens, I begin to wonder whether I should become a bhikkhu, thereby availing myself of the warmth and implicit approval of the bhikkhu sangha and the Sri Lankan laymen. However, I quickly reject that thought, reflecting that I rejoice in my membership of the Western Buddhist Order, and even more importantly, if possible, even than that, that I am a disciple of Sangharakshita. I rejoice in the perspective and clarity that he has given me on the Buddhist path. That perspective is an immensely valuable one, a unique one; it enables me to see with increasing clarity just what is going on in Sri Lanka, to see just how religio-nationalism[26] vitiates almost everything that goes by the name of Buddhism on the Island. I am also gaining confidence in my ability to spread the Dharma single-handedly as it were, and to all kinds of people, from school children to the aged, from villagers to holiday makers.

ABOUT THREE MONTHS AFTER MY ARRIVAL in Sri Lanka, I have suffered my first illness, albeit a minor one. It was no more than a very bad cold and a splitting headache, but in the tropics, things with which one can relatively easily cope in temperate latitudes can be considerably more difficult when the prevailing temperature is thirty degrees in the shade and the humidity ninety percent. Also, my legs, particularly the hip joints and ankles, began to trouble me and occasionally became extremely painful. I did not know what was the cause, unless it was that I had been sitting more in the half- and full-lotus posture than in the past, and not doing any exercises to loosen up the joints. However, the pain gradually eased off over a period of a month or so, and I was able to regard the experience as not having been wholly without its merits. The experience has helped me to develop a more compassionate attitude towards my own body. On the negative side, exacerbated by the illness and pain, my patience with those at the Hotel amongst whom I live and teach has worn a bit thin. I have been considerably more direct with them than I had been in the past, giving expression to my feelings, which were sometimes less than charitable. This might not be a bad thing in some ways, but I cannot excuse myself any expression of harshness, much less of anger. I am living in an area where not long after my arrival a throat was cut in an argument over a few fish - the village people are extremely volatile. In an effort to curb my own impatience, I reflected that one might not know how one stood with Sri Lankans until they were wreaking their revenge. Fear and anger, confusion and panic and the resulting reactions are sometimes, I feel, not far away. I tell myself that I should watch my step. At nights I can sometimes hear the tom-toms ominously beating, and one morning I discovered a large scorpion near my meditation cushion while sweeping the room before sitting. I gingerly removed it with the help of a pot and a plate, reflecting that it was as it were 'my own'. And the same day I narrowly missed treading on quite a big snake - a beautifully coloured, four foot long fellow with glittering green eyes. I am beginning to feel that creatures of the depths, some of them not altogether wholesome, are trying to gain entry at the door of my mind.

In an effort to extend my Dharma teaching activities beyond the confines of the little fishing village of Unawatuna, I have arranged, amongst other things, to lead a 'Meditation and Dhamma Course' at the Young Men's Buddhist Association of Galle[27], the nearest town of any significance. The YMBA has its headquarters in Galle Fort, the picturesque old town built by the Portuguese and later heavily fortified by the Dutch. The Association owes its origins to the inspiration of the great Anagarika Dharmapala nearly a hundred years ago, and numbers amongst its presidents F. L. Woodward. Woodward, a large and ancient photo of whose handsome features hang on the wall of the entrance hall together with other past Presidents of the YMBA, was one of the famous translators of the Pali into English; he had also, by all accounts, been a much-loved headmaster of one of the most prestigious boys' colleges in Galle. Now however, the chief interest of the young and not-so-young men of YMBA Galle is such that, I once only half-jokingly remarked, the 'B' of YMBA stood not for Buddhist but for billiards. I was however assured by the Secretary that a Course of the kind I was proposing would be met with enthusiasm, and such indeed turned out to be the case. The main hall was full on the first night of the course, and remained so for each of the following five weeks. Siri was as usual the vigorous translator of my introductions to Meditation and my talks on Buddhism into Sinhalese, and as we stood in the cool and dimly-lit main hall of the YMBA, I found our words being listened to with close attention by the sixty or so people who attended the course each week. The audience consisted mostly of middle-aged ladies, but there were also a few enthusiastic men. The ladies invariably wore white saris, which, contrasting sharply with their healthy dark skin, gave a wonderful impression of elegance, coolness and purity. In preparing my talks for the Course I went over some of the truly excellent expositions of the Dharma produced by Sangharakshita, and felt really happy and inspired passing on the essence of that material to my YMBA audience. It was quite evident that they enjoyed and appreciated it too, as their bright and attentive faces indicated, and as their effusive personal thanks afterwards often testified. Even more than giving the talks, I enjoyed instructing my audience in meditation. This, I felt, especially in the context of the dharma talks, would have a great potential for good in the future. I spoke to my audience about the Buddha, the Dhamma, the Sangha and Morality, leaving *samadhi* and *prajna* - Concentration and Wisdom, respectively - for some further sessions.

Another occasion for Dharma-teaching occurred when I visited the Girls High School in Galle Fort, near the YMBA. The diminutive headmistress of that august establishment was herself a devout Buddhist, and soon after Siri had introduced her to me, she became very keen for me to speak to her girls. Thus it was that I found myself early one morning addressing a group of five hundred fifth and sixth form girls, ranging from fifteen to eighteen years of age, all deeply attentive. When after my introduction we sat practising the mindfulness of breathing, they really did seem to be getting quite absorbed.

During the same week, I also addressed a similar sized, mixed and more varied congregation at the largest Buddhist Temple in Galle. This was at the invitation of the chief bhikkhu there, Venerable Dayasara. He wanted, I suspected, to provide his full-moon day proceedings with a touch of the 'exotic', a white, orange-robed Buddhist, and I suppose my presence did supply it, though displays of exoticism were not my intention. I wished only to communicate the Dharma. In this sort of way I have begun extending and deepening my friendships in the locality, feeling that there is much to be done in reviving enthusiasm for spiritual practice in Sri Lanka.

My early experience of the Island is provoking reflection on my existential predicament as the sole active member in Sri Lanka of the Western Buddhist Order / Trailokya Bauddha Mahasangha. I am based on an island which some are saying is on the verge of civil war, though there have been until recently no more than a few hints here and there in the newspapers about the ethnic violence in the North. My own 'political stance' has been very provisional and reticent, but it has begun to be more definite. Though I have tried hard not to come to any premature conclusions, it is difficult to avoid the view that the burgeoning ethnic violence is due in considerable measure to the activity of the Tamil 'freedom fighters.' Whatever may have been the justification for their grievances, they seemed to have vitiated their cause by their ruthless violence and the killing of defenceless Sinhalese, including women, children, and young monks. The matter has of course been rendered complex by more than two thousand years of history. That history involved entanglement with and occasional subjugation by the rulers of what is present day Tamil Nadu, just over the Palk Straits in India, and also by the contemporary ambitions of the Indian Presidency for world statesmanship. There have also been calls in many Sri Lankan newspapers for 'religious revival', though it is far from clear what is meant by that. I shudder to think of the consequences of a unification of Sinhalese Buddhist Fundamentalism with the reactionary forces of a Sinhalese State. The Prime Minister has been continually egging on the bhikkhus to "solve the problem" and to "find a political solution." He had, however, little or nothing of practical value to say himself except the mouthing of religious platitudes. It has been difficult to discern a gleam of common sense anywhere in the media. It seems to me that if only the politicians cleansed themselves of religious posturing and the bhikkhus refrained from any involvement in practical day-to-day politics and simply communicated the Buddha-dharma, there would be some real progress.

My own growing involvement with the Sri Lankan Buddhist scene has also made me reflect on just what the Western Buddhist Order / Trailokya Bauddha Mahasangha has to offer Sri Lanka in its current predicament, and how it could be spread about. Siri Goonasekara, my *dayaka*, or helper, as such a person is known locally, is not yet a mitra of our Movement, though he has made a request to me to be admitted as such. That request I have passed on to the Order Office in the UK. Siri, already beginning to nurture ambitions, thinks it will be best for us to move to Colombo or Kandy, partly to distance himself from his family and also to extend our contacts. If, how, and when all this is to be done is not clear, and I have stuck tenaciously to Sangharakshita's advice in his letters to me to proceed with caution. Just what outward form our new Movement's kind of Buddhism might take in this 'pure Theravada Buddhist' country is at present a matter of speculation.

The bhikkhus in Sri Lanka are called 'priests' in the English Press, or *hamudru* in Sinhalese; I am addressed in Sinhalese as 'swami mahanse' which means something like 'Venerable Sir'. Monks and lay-people alike are almost without exception friendly and warm to me, some of them markedly so, and I have on several occasions been invited to take up residence in delightful temples, and been offered many gifts, including a begging bowl and bhikkhu robes. It has also been suggested to me several times that I should take *upasampada* or bhikkhu ordination - though presumably I would first of all have had to become a *samanera* or novice monk. It would probably be a very easy and pleasant life-style for me, just studying, reflecting, and meditating, but it really is not an option as far as I am concerned. It would not be a real, or even an effective act of Going for Refuge; it would undermine my commitment to Sangharakshita, and also my membership of the unique, neither-lay-nor-monastic Order which has given me and others so much spiritual sustenance and which provides me with my initial and ongoing inspiration for the spiritual life. The enquiries that I have so far made indicate that most of the *hamudru* do little spiritual practice, and that, well-meaning though many of them are, they usually fall far short, in terms of purity, energy and altruism, of the sublime spiritual ideal they claim to follow. I spoke recently to a small number of *hamudru* meditating in the 'Vipassana' tradition harking back to the Burmese meditation teacher U Ba Khin, but found them, though mentally active, rather dry and uninspiring. And I have seen little evidence of that 'existential communication' characteristic of sincere practitioners of the Dharma in the temples I have visited so far. I feel that I am serving the Dharma in the best possible way by continuing as an Anagarika of the Western Buddhist Order. In fact, I thank my lucky stars that this continues to be the case.

I therefore continue to reside in the South Ceylon Hotel, Unawatuna, near a beach which is an archetype of beautiful beaches. On the land side of the long crescent-shaped beach, the wall of palm fronds stirs atop slender trunks in the gentlest of breezes, and beneath them on the soft golden sand sit young men and women of many nationalities soaking up the sun. The sands slope down to the dazzling blue sea in which swim turtles and little tropical fish of many colours. The air is fresh and unpolluted, and my food consists of nourishing red rice, fresh vegetables and delicious fruit. The main difficulty I have to put up with is the hubbub of voices in the hotel dining room late into the night; the walls and floor of the building are thin, so the sound easily penetrates to my small room on the ground floor. This has seemed at first a small price to pay for the opportunity of sharing what I know of meditation with so many others, and of learning things about the spiritual life and understanding things which Sangharakshita taught which I had not really understood before. The gravitational pull of greed and self-indulgence is very clearly in evidence in the village and hotel, however, and I have constantly to be on my guard to avoid over-indulgence in food and sleep.

Despite the distractions of the hotel, I have led my first meditation retreat there. It lasted two full days, and was attended by two people, a handsome young Norwegian and an elderly North American. They reminded me very much of the young hero and the wise old man. The American was persistent with a question I found difficult to answer to his satisfaction: "Why do Bodhisattvas not declare themselves?" My first suggestion to him was that such a claim might be arrogant, and if made would be considered 'spiritual bad manners'. I also pointed out that such a claim, if uncritically accepted, might encourage dependence and gullibility in the disciple. This however did not satisfy him, so I finally resorted to saying that in my opinion my own Buddhist teacher Sangharakshita and Dr. Ambedkar, the great leader of the mass conversion of ex-Untouchables to Buddhism were Bodhisattvas. This response appeared to mollify my American friend, and also gave me the opportunity to eulogize Sangharakshita. It was the happiest hour of the retreat.

NOTES

26 See *Alternative Traditions* (Sangharakshita, 1980) pub: Windhorse.

27 Galle is the town near the southern tip of Sri Lanka where Colonel Olcott and Madame Blavatsky first 'took pansil', that is to say, ritually recited, after a *bhikkhu*, the Three Refuges and Five Precepts - thus constituting themselves formally, in traditional Buddhist eyes, proper Buddhists, in this case Upāsaka (masc.) and Upāsikā (fem.). They were the first Europeans to do so on Sri Lankan soil, thus becoming in the eyes of the Sinhalese at least, the first European converts to their 'national religion', the Buddha-dhamma. See *Anagarika Dharmapala, A Biographical Sketch, and other* Maha Bodhi *Writings*, p.19, Sangharakshita, Ibis Publications 2013.

* * * * *

Ashvajit with Jinasena (left) and Siri (right) in Unawatuna

4   The Buddha's Tooth, and the Botanical Gardens, Kandy

Within six months of my arrival in Sri Lanka, I begin to relax my rather tightly-disciplined and quite demanding schedule of activities, and to allow the more artistic, or at least, more imaginative side of my personality movement and expression. I give myself permission to do unprogrammed things, and begin by reflecting on spontaneity, on the seating arrangements in buses, on nudity, and to enjoy a trip with a friend to the extraordinary and wonderful botanical gardens at Kandy. I begin to experience an unaccustomed sense of urgency - perhaps due to the fact that I am approaching my fiftieth year, perhaps due to the highly unsettled political atmosphere that is beginning to develop on the Island.

> *"When I have fears that I may cease to be,*
> *Before my pen has glean'd my teeming brain"....*

I SAT DOWN EARLIER IN THE MONTH than usual to write my accustomed Letter to Shabda. The thought of dying had been occupying my mind for some months: perhaps I was undergoing a sort of spiritual death for which I felt not very adequately prepared. The dread of dying without having added anything worthwhile to the sum not only of humanity but also of human culture has pursued me on and off for many years, and although I have made sporadic attempts to assuage it, it has been intruding with ever greater insistence. This feeling has been further exacerbated by seeing some of my contemporaries beginning to excel themselves in the literary world. So I have begun, with redoubled zest, to add to my growing pile of 'Travel Letters'. These letters do not constitute a systematic approach to the Buddhist Vision, but I hope that spontaneous and anecdotal accounts of my experiences in Sri Lanka will appeal more directly to certain types of reader than the canonical works, essential though they are for the serious student. They will also be of interest, perhaps, to my friends, and I am therefore prepared to spend quite a bit of time composing them. I have taken seriously Sangharakshita's comment concerning Gray's Elegy, that there are no "mute inglorious Miltons" and wish fervently to add something, however small, to the rich literary tapestry created by the ancient Buddhist masters.

According to Webster's *New Collegiate Dictionary* (the largest I have been able to find on sale in Sri Lanka), spontaneity is a 'voluntary or undetermined action or movement.' And spontaneous, I read there, means, or is derived from, the Latin word *sponte*, - of one's free will, voluntarily. Six principal meanings are distinguished: (1) proceeding from natural feeling or native tendency without external constraint. (2) arising from a momentary impulse. (3) controlled and directed internally, or self-acting, as in "spontaneous movement characteristic of living things." (4) produced without being planted or without human labour. Indigenous. (5) developing without apparent external influence, force, cause, or treatment, e.g. "spontaneous recovery from a severe illness." (6) not apparently contrived or manipulated. Natural. Further synonyms given are: impulsive, instinctive; and we are told that a common denotation of the word is "acting or activated without deliberation." Its antonym is "studied", apparently. These definitions were not, perhaps, as comprehensive as they could be, but what I wanted to point out was that experience shows us that there is no conflict between study and spontaneity - between, that is, study in the spiritual tradition - dharma study with others - and spontaneity. Study helps us to be spontaneous, to articulate at least what we know, and to admit what we do not know, rather than to hesitate for an unduly long time for reflection. My own provisional definition of spontaneity runs along these lines: activity unobstructed and unrepressed, springing from a joyous response to the boundless potentiality of life. It had been suggested to me by a fellow Order Member not long before I wrote this letter that Order meetings were "not spontaneous", and so I thought that some words concerning the meaning of spontaneity might be of some help.

The letter I am writing for Shabda this time concerns itself with a visit from a Friend called David Harre, hailing from Brighton. On his arrival at 'Samma Ajiva', and I recognized him immediately. We had shared, for a few days, a caravan in the Padmaloka vegetable garden whilst he was attending the men's retreat immediately preceding the Order Convention last year. David did not know I was here, and did not recognize me immediately, although it was plain that he thought he had seen me before somewhere. I quickly let him out of his suspense, upon which he confessed that I looked twenty years younger than the grey-faced man he had seen recovering from jaundice back in England. He further confessed, after a few minutes of delighted and animated talk, that I was not at all like the people he usually imagined in robes. It seemed, he said, that I was really healthy and happy and full of the joys of life, and that it was really great to find me here. Well, after all that, I began to feel quite enthusiastic about him, and when, a short while later, he suggested that we spend a few days in Kandy together, moreover at his expense, I was happy to accept, after making sure that my diary pointed to no duties or undertakings during the period in question.

We set off early one morning, just as the palm-tree tops were becoming darkly visible and the birds were beginning their dawn chorus, and having reached the main road about five minutes' walk away, were soon successful in flagging down a 'private bus' - one of the buses of Japanese manufacture which ply a busy trade along the coast road. 'Priests', as the bhikkhus are called, are not allowed by local custom to stand on buses, and to all but the most critical I appeared to be a 'priest'. This circumstance taught me a number of lessons. As the private bus approaches, the first question that arises in the driver's mind will be: "how many more can I cram in?" On the State buses, everything is cut and dried - certain seats up near the driver (and therefore, incidentally, the very noisiest) are labelled 'Reserved for Clergy'.

But on the private buses this is not so. If the private bus, or mini-bus, is pretty full, it will therefore simply drive on. But if there are only a few people standing in the bus, it may stop and the driver will then eye you somewhat suspiciously, as will all the other occupants of the bus who are in a position to be able to see you. If you make the slightest suggestion of expecting to be let in, the bus will drive off, but if you just stand quite still, one of the people in the seats next to the driver may get up and stand to the rear of the bus. Alternatively, you may be asked by the conductor to enter by the rear door. Any display of eagerness for a seat, especially a front one, may provoke a reaction and cause the bus to drive off. This habit pattern seems to have evolved as a sort of anti-authoritarian reaction in semi-conscious opposition to the absolutist "reserved for clergy" system, which I have seen provoke considerable resentment, as for instance when a young bhikkhu I saw recently imperiously waving his finger at a middle-aged man who was slow to give up his seat.

At the start of my journey with David to Kandy, I was offered a front seat in the minibus and David went "backside". We arrived in Galle (pronounced something like 'Gaul') with plenty of time for breakfast before having to board the train, and made for one of the restaurants. Galle is a rather scruffy little town with few buildings of merit in it. Its chief claim to fame, apart from the Dutch Fort, is that it is the place where Madame Blavatsky and Colonel Olcott first "took pansil" - formally recited the Three Refuges and Five Precepts of Buddhism, thus formally constituting themselves Buddhists and technically the first white Christian converts to the faith on Ceylonese soil. A statue of the enterprising little American Colonel who amongst other things devised the Buddhist flag, stands in the centre of the town, surrounded by fly-blown sacks of rice and mangy dogs. Such buildings as there are look mostly very much in need of repair, or at the very least in need of a coat of paint. Into one such poorly lit, scruffy establishment we penetrated, and sat waiting for our breakfast of 'string hoppers', a sort of bird's nest of thin spaghetti or vermicelli, served with dhal and curries. After we had fumbled around for a few minutes in the semi-darkness, a fluorescent tube was switched on by one of the waiters, providing a semblance of illumination, and we were able not only to taste but also to see what we were eating. David professed himself unused to eating such spicy food so early in the morning, and said that he felt as if his stomach had been assaulted. Having become accustomed to 'meals of fire' in India, and especially as I was feeling quite hungry, I found the breakfast at least palatable, and was glad to get a fair sized meal under my belt before twelve. Beyond the confines of the South Ceylon Hotel, I have found it difficult to get anyone, without embarrassment, to serve me after midday, hungry or not, in this stronghold of religious formalism where bhikkhus are supposed to begin eating their one-meal-a-day before twelve. Having drunk our tea and paid our bill, we were ready to go.

We sauntered out. The already brilliant sunshine was as yet no more than very pleasantly warm, and leaving the vicinity of the bus station we made our way along a road dominated by a larger-than-life statue of Anagarika Dharmapala gazing reflectively into the distance, and entered the railway station. Sri Lankan railways provide three classes of travel, none of them very good by Western standards, and David purchased second class tickets, perhaps thinking that first class would be too extravagant and third class a bit uncomfortable. I bought myself a copy of The Daily News, and we walked onto the platform. David asked a Ceylonese gentleman where the second class carriages would stop, and was told 'Here.' I put my carry-all on the ground and stood quietly waiting, but about fifteen seconds later the Ceylonese gentleman changed his mind and decided that the second class carriage would be stopping further down the platform, so we followed him. Some minutes later, a small number of ancient-looking carriages, drawn by what seemed to be an enormously oversized diesel engine manufactured, according to a plate fixed to its side, in Japan, drew ponderously up. We got in, making ourselves comfortable in preparation for the two-and-a-half hour journey into Colombo. I read my newspaper from beginning to end during the first half-hour of the journey. The newspaper contained nothing in the least surprizing or even interesting. Ceylonese newspapers seem to lack even the amusement value of their Indian equivalents' quaint language. They are couched in a sort of denatured, inter-continental English, with a fair peppering of grammatical, typographical and stylistic errors. However, one is spared the grisly details, which often appear in Indian newspapers and magazines, complete with photographs, of caste or other violence, and is told only of a small number of 'terrorists', and an equally small number of policemen or soldiers killed in the North or East. I wondered which was more trustworthy, or less untrustworthy – the Sri Lankan or the International press. Were the realities of the situation being magnified and distorted by the media and by other power groups? The 'ethnic problem', tragic and deplorable in itself, has I suspect become a 'media problem' also, involving international, religious, political and business interests, misinformation and perhaps also, plain deceit.

Soon we were well on our way to Colombo. With tropical rain forest to our right and golden sand and sea to our left, the journey was a pleasant one. At 9.30am we drew into Fort Station, Colombo, where we decided to refresh ourselves before proceeding. We entered the slightly more salubrious-looking of the two station restaurants and sat down at a corner table. David asked me what I wanted and I said 'lemon juice'. He managed to obtain for me a bottle of sweet gassy liquid that bore only the faintest resemblance to the flavour of that ovoid, pale yellow, citrus fruit which one can obtain freshly pressed in less sophisticated places, but which was, nevertheless, refreshing enough. While we sat there enjoying our drink, a young European couple sat down at a table next to ours and directly in my line of sight. They were perhaps in their late twenties - German, or perhaps Austrian - I am unable to distinguish between the two languages, if indeed they are two. Both the man and the woman looked in the bloom of youth, but for some reason or other the man looked uneasy, his gaze darting restlessly here and there. The girl was dressed in a silk skirt and blouse that managed to reveal almost more than it concealed, making it very difficult to avoid that polarization of consciousness about which so many Western women travellers seem to be unaware. Having several times tried to explain to scantily-dressed women visitors to 'Samma

Ajiva' why they got so many peculiar looks from the local men, they would airily profess innocence. Whether these women were simply deceiving themselves or just incredibly naive was impossible to tell.

Living near a 'topless'[28] beach, I have tried as honestly as I can to come to terms with the phenomenon of exposure of the body. The feeling of wind, sun, and rain on the naked body can no doubt be pleasant. On the other hand, it is impossible for anyone who is clearly self-aware and aware of others to be unconscious of the fact that what one wears or does not wear communicates a message to those nearby: leaving aside philosophy, fashion is all the rage nowadays. However, the unguarded mind is liable to be flooded by sexual desire when young attractive bodies are exposed beyond certain limits - limits that are the subject of endless argument and wide cultural differences. Whilst not wanting to inhibit and repress, perhaps it is best to leave such exercises in public self-exposure to the young, whose bodies are still trim, and to the spiritually uncommitted, who will not be surprised or distressed when the their lack of decorum stimulates attention.

After our refreshment, David and I walked into the centre of Colombo, he to confirm an airline booking and I to make an inquiry about importing books. It so happened that our respective destinations were situated exactly opposite each other on the same street, which we reached after passing in front of the Main Post Office where a big reception was being organized for the Chinese President. Having attended to our respective business, we retraced our steps to Fort Station, partaking on the way of neatly de-crusted but tasteless sandwiches in a smart restaurant decorated with pictures from Ceylon's colonial past. On our return to the station, it transpired that the next train to Kandy did not depart for another two and a half hours, so we decided to take a private bus to the 'hill country'. The route, the driver said, would take us through some very beautiful countryside. He was right: the countryside was indeed beautiful. Not long after we had left Colombo, the land began to get more and more hilly, and the tall, rounded forms of the hills became suggestive of Zen paintings, though rendered in vivid greens and blues in the manner of Hokusai rather than the more subdued greys, browns and blacks of the early Zen artists. The bus driver, unfortunately, drove rather aggressively, so it was difficult to relax completely. Once, having overtaken another bus that had seemed reluctant to be overtaken, he braked sharply, causing the bus driver behind to brake sharply to avoid collision. I felt disgusted at his behaviour and raised my voice in protest and warning, saying 'be very careful.' He appeared to ignore me, but there were no further incidents, and we arrived safely in Kandy having traversed some gorgeous mountain scenery, passing through thickly forested areas, and along roads where the hedgerows blushed with an abundance of flowers of intoxicating fragrance and brilliant colour.

Having arrived in the busy little town of Kandy, our first task was to find somewhere to stay. David had some very definite ideas where to look, and we first visited the YMBA (Young Men's Buddhist Association). However, the only room they could offer us was without an outer window and was also a bit expensive, according to David. So we politely declined, and went off in search of the Burmese Rest House, which I had been told provided simple accommodation. Our search took us past a scene of great beauty - a large artificial lake situated on the outskirts of the city. And to complete the idyllic picture, on one side of the lake stood a beautiful temple. While David was simultaneously trying to make inquiries and to throw off the unwelcome attention of a tout, I sat down by the side of the road, within a short distance of the temple, which I knew was the Temple of the Tooth, to savour the scene. It was late afternoon, and low clouds lent a welcome coolness to the scene, a coolness already somewhat accentuated by the elevation of Kandy above sea level. The lake is about a mile long and a quarter of a mile wide. It is surrounded on three sides by steeply-sided hills, covered with a great variety of large and exceptionally beautiful trees. On the fourth side lies the city, (really hardly more than a town) terminating, more or less, with the Temple. Most of the outer part is quite a modern-looking building reminiscent of the art nouveau style, predominantly cream in colour, and with a very pleasing arrangement of columns and windows. It is in fact two buildings, the one seen at first completely surrounding and protecting a smaller and older one, as I was to discover later. For the time being I simply sat there, allowing myself to become absorbed by the outward appearance of this place of pilgrimage. It was very peaceful, and began to evoke in me a feeling that: 'Ah, there's something more here, some imprint of bygone greatness.'

After I had been reflecting in this way for a few minutes, David came over and said that he had found out where the Burmese Rest House was, and we set off. We retraced our steps back along the lakeside, past the Temple on the other side of the road, and towards the town. Finding Trincomalee Street we walked up it for about half a mile, and after overshooting our destination by a few yards, discovered a little notice board indicating that we had arrived at the right place. It might have been the entrance to a rather unprepossessing godown, or a rather down-at-heel publishing house, with large panes of obscured glass framed in black timber flanking a black door. Pressing the bell-push, which was so placed as to be virtually invisible, and almost out of reach, we heard the gentle tinkling of a bell inside. We waited a few moments but no one answered, so we tried again. After a third try and some minutes' wait, we tried the door handle and found that the door opened, so in we went. We were greeted almost immediately by a young man in ordinary European shirt and trousers who ushered us into the presence of a Burmese bhikkhu, as was evident by the far Eastern cast of his features and the black cheroot with characteristic musty smell that he was smoking. He appeared neither young nor old, and sported a pair of legal-looking black spectacles with circular lenses similar to those worn by Dr. Ambedkar in his early years. The bhikkhu told us in quite intelligible English that we could sleep in a dormitory for fifteen Rupees a night (about forty pence English money), and he was sorry he could not offer us a room to ourselves, as they were all occupied. We asked to see the proffered accommodation, and finding it to our satisfaction, we accepted. The dormitory had five beds in it. It was fairly clean and spacious, with a good-sized window, and was indeed occupied, but by only one middle-aged man. Nearby was a quite serviceable toilet and bathroom with running water. What was more, to David's delight, it was down only two flights of stairs from a small but elaborately decorated shrine room, complete with a brass, slightly top-heavy looking Burmese image of the Buddha. The whole place was dusty and neglected, but would, David thought, be good to meditate in. I returned to the dormitory and introduced myself to our roommate, who turned out to be an American named Charlie, hailing from Texas. He looked rather grey and faded, like a number of other things in the room, but this impression was not borne out by my subsequent conversations with Charles, as I called him. Charles's mind, I was to discover, was anything but grey.

Leaving our bags padlocked to our beds - a habit derived from experience of travel in the East - we went back out and down, for the dormitory was situated in a separate two or three storey building situated at the far end of an atrium, but higher up from the building we had entered from the street. The Burmese Rest House, we could now see, was built on the side of a steep hill, and the grass covered, sloping atrium formed the first big 'step', the first little step, as it were, being the entrance hall. In one corner of the atrium was a large mango tree. The whole place, with a coat of paint, the lines of washing removed, and a bit of tidying up, could have been very pleasing indeed in appearance. As it was, there was little either to direct the eye or to inspire visually. In any case, both David and I were by now feeling quite hungry, not having eaten since breakfast, so I suggested that David fetch something for us both, which we could then go and eat in the dormitory. He readily assented and went off, while I remained seated at the lower end of the atrium. Had I accompanied him, people might have thought it rather strange that a 'bhikkhu' was buying food at that time of day, and I did not want to have to go into any long explanations of what was the difference between a bhikkhu and an anagarika. I had often found that despite my best efforts, my listener would come to the conclusion that an anagarika was something a bit inferior to a bhikkhu, which is not what I perceived to be the case at all. After sitting quietly for a few minutes, I was joined by the Burmese bhikkhu. There were at least two young Ceylonese bhikkhus in the place, one of whom lounged lazily in an armchair watching the small colour television that graced the reception room, but neither of them showed the slightest interest in me. The Burmese bhikkhu was however a very different kettle of fish, and though he seemed inseparable from his cheroot, he gave me the impression of being an intelligent and kindly man. He very soon suggested that I go and see the Tooth Relic, or at least, the receptacle in which it resided, for the Tooth itself was displayed only on rare occasions. I responded by saying that I thought the Tooth was not genuine, and asking whether he had any views on the matter. He peered at me intently through his glasses, revealing for a fraction of a second the diamond-sharp lights in his rather small and weak eyes, and lifted up his little finger. 'It is rather large', he said, 'but you see, these people like to think the Buddha was a very big man.' Then he looked at me again, saw that I wasn't buying that one, and tried again. 'All right,' he said, 'supposing it was the actual tooth of the Buddha, you wouldn't worship that, would you?' I smiled, touched by his honesty and practical common sense, and grasping his meaning immediately, decided to visit the Temple of the Tooth after all.

I walked back down Trincomalee Street towards the Lake, then turned left into the very broad, tree-lined avenue which led to the Temple entrance. Passing a row of stalls selling beautiful blue lotuses of exquisite fragrance and other beautiful kinds of flowers, I selected a pannier of little blossoms of a thrilling whiteness, leaving a golden coin in the dana[29] bowl. Thus equipped, I passed through the entrance doorway to the Temple, up a flight of steps and from thence through a floor-to-ceiling steel grille worthy of a prison. Up another flight of steps I went, past a soldier holding an evil-looking gun at the half-ready, and at the top there was a shoe rack where I left my sandals. A short, low tunnel led me through what I took to be the wall of the outer Temple and into the inner precinct, in the middle of which could now be seen a smaller and much older edifice, reminiscent of a Japanese temple, with multiple hammer beams all richly decorated with flower and animal motifs. The entrance to this older temple, up a broad flight of half a dozen steps, was flanked by two stone lions, and the doors that presumably lay beyond were covered by a large square blue cloth bearing a Dharmachakra Wheel in gold. The whole effect was rather pleasing and somehow curiously pagan in appearance. A small number of tourists were standing around with cameras bared, and a few of them were kneeling devoutly with eyes in the direction of the Dharma Chakra and with palms together. I looked around for somewhere suitable to place my little white flowers, and noticed a table on which a number of other flower offerings were already laid. Having placed mine there, I then walked around the space between the outer and inner Temples, savouring the fragrance of sandalwood which emanated, perhaps from the burning incense sticks, but mainly from the extensive use of the dark gold timber itself in the construction of the balustrades and galleries. As I walked around, more and more people began to file in through the tunnel, and I wondered where best to place myself. A feeling of expectancy was beginning to vibrate in the air, but it was not obvious what was going to happen, or whether someone wearing yellow robes would be expected to do anything other than stand around and stare like the others. I was not left wondering for long, for a young man buttonholed me, asking me where I was from, and suggesting that if I asked the permission of the Chief Priest, I could see the relic casket close up. Not waiting for an answer, he motioned me to come with him, and I followed hot on his heels. We went up a couple of flights of stairs, around a corner, and were soon standing in the High Priest's quarters. After a few moments the ochre-robed gentleman himself stepped into view from a side room, and I was introduced by the young man, to whom I had already given my name. The High Priest gave an indistinct answer to my polite inquiry as to whether he spoke English, and sat down on a nearby couch. He was perhaps in his early fifties, smooth-looking and well-fed but lacking any refinement of face. Neither, indeed, did he appear to have any refinement of manners, because he did nothing to ease my discomfiture when I conspicuously failed at first to attract the attention of the young man who would, I had hoped, remain at my side to translate, but who had, embarrassingly, wandered off to join the group of people who stood some distance away in the large hall, and who was now smiling rather inanely at the other bystanders. In fact, I got the fleeting impression that he had done this deliberately, with the intention of intimidating the newcomer. The Chief Priest remained silent, with a faint scowl on his face; perhaps, I thought, he was thinking that I had not bowed low enough, or not offered some expected morsel, be it plum cake or a hundred dollar note. I had become quite accustomed to meeting awkward priests by now, but this one beat them all. However, by speaking loudly across the hall, whilst managing to refrain from actually shouting, I eventually got through to the young man who had escorted me up, called him over, and succeeded in putting to the Chief Priest my request to see the Relic Casket. But again, to my surprise, no clear answer was given, and I began to feel my anger rising. All right, I thought, I can stand around looking as dumb as any of them, which is what I proceeded to do. Perhaps, indeed, that was all one had to do, and no actual communication was expected. However, a few moments later my young escort said: 'All right, you can see the casket, just wait downstairs.'

So downstairs I went, to join the throng which by now almost filled the available space and was pressing around the entrance to the small temple. Within moments of reaching the floor, I was approached by one of a trio of drummers who wore white sarongs, were bare-chested, and sported a broad, bright red sash around their waists. The drummer asked me to sit against a column within a small roped-off rectangle in front of the old temple, and so I did. A few moments later, the bare-chested men hit their drums with a tremendous crash which caused some of those assembled to put their hands to their ears in horror. I continued to sit on the floor, alone in my roped-off rectangle, trying to remain as calm as possible, and preparing myself for - well, I had no idea for what. I had begun to grow accustomed to the shockingly loud drumming which had neither the rhythm of tom-toms nor the stimulating effect that Lamas' puja instruments can have, when another young yellow-robed man standing nearby told me to go with him, so I rose quickly to my feet and followed him through a doorway and up another narrow flight of steps. The steps gave onto a balcony passing along one side of the small temple before entering it. I was ushered past a crowd of worshippers kneeling in front of a centrally-placed archway, and through a very big door where I found myself inside a small ante-room, together with half a dozen bhikkhus. I guessed they were headed in the same direction as I was. One of them, who appeared to know the protocol, indicated that we were to take a golden sash each from a large box and tie it at waist level around our robes, which gave us all a rather sack-like appearance. I had time to notice that the ante-room was hung with rich brocades and fitted with a red pile carpet of prodigious thickness. Or maybe it just seemed that way because I had been quite unused to treading on carpet for some years. Then, a boy of ten or twelve, with curiously bland features, appeared with a tray of small bowls of flowers. I smiled at him and his features recovered their animation. Each of the bhikkhus and myself now being equipped with a small bowl of flowers, a great brocaded gold curtain was swept aside revealing, behind a huge window of plate glass, a beautiful stupa, some four or five feet in height, which appeared to be made of solid gold, and bedecked with ornate necklaces of rubies, emeralds, and sapphires. The goal of our pilgrimage having been reached, we each in turn placed our flower offerings on a broad shelf in front of the stupa and made our obeisance upon the deep pile carpet. Meanwhile, the High Priest had reappeared, now also equipped with a broad gold sash, and looked on at the proceedings with a proprietary air. When all the bhikkhus had finished their obeisance, he inquired as to our countries of origin: Burma, India, Nepal, Thailand, England, came back the replies, which he repeated as if writing up a scoreboard, and at this point an unaccountable mirth possessed us all. It was as if the very idea of the Buddha's Tooth having brought us all together, especially a Buddha's false tooth, was so inconceivable, we just had to transcend it altogether. At this moment the door separating the stupa-reliquary from the sight of the faithful, past whom we had been ushered, was now opened, and a sort of moan or sigh went up, as if what was revealed satisfied some deep yearning. I wondered whether it was the beautiful golden stupa, or the thought of the relic of Shakyamuni in it, or both, that appealed to their hearts, but my reflection was broken off as we were urged back into the ante-room by the Chief Priest, were asked to deposit our sashes, and a enormous silver plate was passed around to receive our offerings. Having placed in it a note of suitable denomination, I turned and went down the stairs, past the thronging crowd, retrieved my plastic sandals, left the building and walked back to Trincomalee Street, feeling unexpectedly elated.

By now it was dark, and David had returned to the Burmese Rest House with some food. In fact, feeling famished, he had already eaten his share. He did not appear to mind at all that I had visited the Temple of the Tooth without him, and I felt that he was gifted with a strong and healthy sense of scepticism. He was certainly not lacking in feelings of devotion, that much I had already discovered, but to the Tooth, apparently, he was indifferent, and there we left the matter. I was hungry, and tucked zestfully into the simple fare he had supplied. After a meditation and Basic Puja in the ornate little shrine room, which we had dusted and set to rights as best we could, we retired to bed, and passed a night punctuated by Charles's uneasy slumbers. I 'woke' feeling exhausted, and spent the next hour suffering from a streaming nose and watering eyes. Something, I thought, had set off an allergic reaction. Perhaps it was the discharge of all the accumulated excitement and tension I had experienced during the last twenty four hours. Or perhaps it was an allergic reaction against something about to happen. David decided to go and meditate in the shrine room while I recovered. Half an hour later, as I was sitting on the periphery of the lower courtyard in the warm morning sunlight trying to let go of the tension, the Burmese bhikkhu emerged from his room and invited me to breakfast. He did not mention David, and I soon discovered he had prepared food for me alone. His dispensation, it seemed, did not extend to my companion, who was still meditating in the shrine room, and as worthy of breakfast as I was, but I decided that it would be ill-mannered to decline the proffered fare and the implicit companionship. I would be able to take tea with David over his breakfast later. The Burmese bhikkhu and I ate our delicious bread and butter in silence, and I enjoyed the cup of tea he lovingly prepared for me. Suitably refreshed, and my allergy having now subsided, I went and sat down once more on the bench where I had been sitting before the invitation to breakfast.

Charles had by now seated himself on one end of the bench, so now was my chance to make his acquaintance. I found him easy to engage in conversation, and soon discovered that he was born within a year of me. I had imagined him to be at least ten years older. Tall, with a slight stoop, he had a mop of greying hair and wore an old blue track suit. His hands looked strong and practical, and the veins stood out prominently. He wore a strongish pair of glasses, but his eyes looked bright and intelligent. He had spent five years, he told me, in Kerala, South India, wearing a big bushy beard and living very simply 'chopping wood.' Whether he meant this literally or metaphorically, I did not discover. But apparently, he had eventually been suspected of spying, and been taken to the local jail where the only people to take an interest in his plight were a group of Marxists who ran the local bookshop. Charles didn't mind that they were Marxists, he said, because 'light came from them', and they had staged a demonstration outside the jail, after which he was released. However, he said, living in that area was now impossible, and he had made his way up to Kathmandu, where he was taken into discipleship by a Tibetan Lama who, it seems, considered that Charles and he had been together in previous lives. I was very doubtful of the wisdom of such a claim, even had the lama been quite sure of his ground. It seemed to me, from what I was quickly discovering of Charles, that despite a formidable rational side, Charles was emotionally very dependent upon the approval of others, in short, emotionally a baby, and therefore needed to cultivate psychological independence. I supposed that Charles's Lama had been utilising skilful means to arouse Charles's faith, and had not been motivated simply by the desire for a compliant disciple. At any rate, Charles had completed a hundred thousand prostrations, and was now plunging into the Abhidharma. His knowledge of textual Buddhism was considerably more than superficial, he was well-versed in Schopenhauer and Hegel, and had researched in behaviouristic psychology at University. In fact he had an interesting story to tell concerning the University. Apparently he had been recruited to carry out an extensive experiment, together with a number of other researchers, to determine the rate of learning by college students, of a string of nonsense syllables. Charles's results had, it seems, turned out to be significantly different from the other researchers; checking and double checking revealed no difference from the others in his technique or his manner of conducting the experiment. The significance of this circumstance, it began to be mooted abroad, was that the experimenter (i.e. in this case Charles) was able to influence external, objective behaviour by private, internal means - a conclusion profoundly disturbing, and indeed totally unacceptable to the Faculty. In fact, Charles was summarily dismissed from his post. Whatever may or may not have been Charles's 'psychic powers', I found communication with him stimulating rather than disturbing, and felt glad to have made his acquaintance. We exchanged addresses, and I told him I would certainly reply if he wrote to me.

David having by now breakfasted by himself, we caught up with each other's news and went off in search of the Buddhist Publication Society headquarters on the shores of the lake above the town. We found the smart modern building quite easily after a very pleasant stroll, and spent the next hour or so browsing - or at least, I did, because David left after about twenty minutes, saying he was going to sit outside. I was glad to see Bhante's Biography of Anagarika Dharmapala[30] in print - a jewel amongst a large collection of booklets, books and pamphlets of rather variable quality. Some of them seemed to me undoubtedly good, others merely informative, whilst some again were even, possibly, misleading. My browsing eventually brought me to the conclusion that though much of the material was excellent, much of it could have been improved on by almost any of our Dhammacharis and Dhammacharinis. The reference library, housed on the same floor, in fact in the same room as the bookshop, was a good one, having a complete set of the PTS edition of the Pali Canon in English, and many other good books on various aspects of the Buddhist world. I was happy to see *Golden Drum* and *Mitrata* there, and both quite well-thumbed. Nevertheless I could not help feeling strangely disappointed at this showcase of Theravada Buddhist literature, and the image of a very large, affable dinosaur came to mind which, having performed something like a hop a skip and a jump, had relapsed back into scoffing its diet of plankton unaware of the larger vistas and greater life in the world beyond its own immediate and myopic gaze.

After enjoying sweet and sour vegetables and vegetable chop suey at the Sri Lankan Cultural Centre, housed in a simply constructed but elegant building beside the lake not far from the BPS, and with a fine view of the surrounding wooded hills, David and I made for the famous Kandy Botanical Gardens. I was looking forward to this visit with eager anticipation, and was pleased to find David appearing to share my enthusiasm. A short bus ride took us to the outskirts of the city, and we strolled over to the large and beautiful wrought-iron entrance gates to the Gardens. Declining the offer of a guide, we had hardly gone a few yards when it became evident that we had entered a plant-lover's paradise. Such was the beauty of the place, in fact, that we were precipitated into a dhyana-like state and remained there almost effortlessly for the next few hours. It is hardly possible even to give an inkling of the magic of Peradeniya Gardens, as they are called. The colours and shapes of trees and flowers enchanted the eye in every direction, and the fragrances that wafted on the gentlest of breezes were of an unutterable sweetness. I had not realized that there was such a variety of palm trees, some with short stout trunks with bulbous bases and topped with coarse, spiky leaves, and others with eighty-foot high trunks or stems that were as straight as an arrow, and which were hardly more than eight inches in diameter. They were topped with leafy sprays of the utmost refinement and delicacy. Bushes with multi-coloured leaves ranging from scarlet to the deepest and most mysterious purples were ranged along the paths, and blossoms of the most exotic kind, like huge orchids, hung from the trees in profusion. And the bamboos! Such bamboos I had never seen or dreamed of. Fully a hundred foot high and grey-green in colour, they shot from the ground in joyful straightness, diverging as they rose and spraying forth a multitude of spiky leaves, bending imperceptibly at first and then with greater abandon as they sought the light. There were gold-green bamboos too, emanating a kind of yellow glow as if they were illuminated from within - huge natural fibres of the utmost refinement and strength, supporting millions and millions of quivering green spikes. And between each 'knuckle' of the stem, as if placed there by an artist's hand, broad and narrow bands of green and yellow in seemingly arbitrary but aesthetically pleasing fashion.

We inspected the beds of medicinal plants, containing aconite, deadly nightshade, and other hardly less formidable drugs, and wondered at nature's profusion and serviceability. We passed down an avenue of fir trees, but such fir trees as are not painted by artists wishing to be believed, unless it was a van Gogh. They twisted and writhed out of the ground as if they could not wait to grow straight, or as if some irresistible force were thrusting them towards an errant sun. And we came across a strange variety of eucalyptus tree that displayed livid streaks of red and green on its trunk as the bark peeled off. We walked under a spreading giant tree, the biggest living thing I had ever seen, covering half a football field of ground with its writhing, far-reaching branches of a pale fleshy colour that resembled human limbs, and holding aloft a canopy of millions of small dark green leaves that gave welcome shade from the sun. And then we were transported by the sight of a huge colony of fruit bats - hundreds of thousands of them, living amongst the branches of a grove of enormous, elm-like trees. The bats chattered wildly and incessantly, with a curious suggestion of glee, hanging upside-down for long periods of time, and every now and again dropping, swooping and gliding with clumsy grace from tree to tree and branch to branch.

Moving on, we discovered a small circular pool covered with thousands of tiny white lotuses, and in the depths of which thronged a shoal of little fish. Invisible at first because of their muted grey and pink colours, as one gazed at the waters' surface they appeared slowly, gawping in the way fish do, and waving their little fins in a sort of fishy semaphore. From the pool we passed to the Orchid House, and gazed in wonder at the appearance of this family of most exotic flowers. Some of them appeared as if in frozen dance, waiting only for the music to start up again to resume their antics. Others were more remarkable for their pure, brilliant colour and luminosity, for all the world like miniature faces gazing steadfastly at the equally curious bipeds passing by. By now I had begun to feel glutted with superlatives, and suggested to a somewhat reluctant David that we make our departure, especially as a bell had sounded which had started other visitors moving towards the exit. We had made a circuit of all but about one-twelfth of the perimeter of the Gardens, and the remainder would have to wait until another visit.

The next day we were to spend visiting the Meditation Centre at Nilambe, high in the hills outside Kandy. The bus took us way out past the beautiful salmon pink neo-classical buildings of the Peradeniya University campus and high into the hills. The bus having taken us as far as it could, we then toiled on foot slowly up the narrow hairpin bends of the mountain path that led eventually to the little collection of buildings constituting the Nilambe Laymen's Meditation Centre perched near the top of quite a high mountain. It was a fitting culmination to our trip. Apart from enjoying a meditative afternoon and evening there, I was able to deal with a matter of some importance. I met Godwin Samararatne, the chief meditation teacher of the Centre, and confirmed that I would indeed be leading the retreat I had undertaken to lead in lieu of Ven. Rahula immediately after Wesak, and confirmed the dates and the arrangements to be made.

Both David and I had a very enjoyable time in Nilambe, and after a cool though comfortable night, returned to Kandy and thence to Colombo feeling that our little spontaneous holiday, trip, survey or exploration, had been very worthwhile. We parted on Colombo Fort station platform on terms of affection. David was to fly to Tiruchchirappalli, known as Trichy for short, in Tamil Nadu, and thence to the Himalayas, and I to take a train and bus to Unawatuna and my Dhamma duties.

The twelve days after my return from Kandy were not idle ones. My six-week course at Galle YMBA concluded with meditation and a talk on prajna, and I was given numerous presents and quite a show of affection, which really touched my heart, since it was difficult to get much idea of how things were going during the course itself. Siri's translation of my talks had improved, and I felt reasonably confident that he was putting across the spirit, if not the letter, of what I was saying. I gave another talk in Galle Fort, this time to an assembly of five hundred schoolgirls, all dressed in immaculate white and perfectly behaved. It was a bit like giving a talk to a single person or a single organism - an organism consisting of five hundred white and golden-brown flowers. The headmistress was a very bright little lady, fluent in English and a Pali scholar, so I had to be careful what I said. I spoke very warmly about Buddhism in England and India, and characterized it as a means of growth for the true individual, which seemed to appeal to them.

Only fifteen minutes after that, I found myself talking to an assembly of three hundred boys in the nearby St. Aloysius' College. They certainly didn't feel or look or behave like a single organism, but my talk seemed to have quite a good effect on them nevertheless. It always took me by surprise what effect a few words from the heart could have on people's faces - how much more alive and in communication they seemed to become. I hope however that my words had more than a passing effect. St. Aloysius' was a prestigious school once run entirely by Jesuits. The big seminary adjoining it had a neglected air, and Father Morali, the Headmaster, his fine aquiline nose reminiscent of a bust of a Roman Emperor, looked rather dejected too. Having been introduced to him by Siri when we passed each other in a Galle street one day, I decided to pay him a visit. We found the tall old man in civvies, whereas he had been wearing a white surplice when we first met. Now attired in a pair of loose-fitting dark trousers and a canary-yellow shirt, he seemed rather puzzled when I explained that I had come just to get to know him a bit more; the idea that someone, especially of another faith, might come to see him simply out of friendship, was evidently strange to him. But eventually he accepted my words in the spirit in which they were meant, and we sat down and had quite a pleasant chat. In fact, I found myself being rather delighted with the old chap, though he was clearly in at least two minds as to how to respond to me. Our conversation remained quite superficial, unfortunately, despite my attempts to go deeper, but after we parted a strange thing happened: my mind was flooded with strong feelings of sadness, and a vision of Father Morali on his knees praying to God, tears streaming down his face, appeared to me. I could not speak to Siri for some minutes, but finally ventured the opinion that Father Morali was guilt-ridden, for reasons at which I could only guess.

The following Sunday, Siri and I visited Galle YMBA in order to arrange a weekend retreat, and it so happened that a karate class was being held there. I reminded Siri that we had planned to speak to the sensei, and no sooner had we exchanged a few words with him than we were invited to give his class a session of meditation instruction on the spot. I did the best I could in the circumstances, and the sensei and boys were so pleased with our few minutes together that I was invited to come again next week. Siri was absolutely delighted to have made contact with something a bit more gutsy than usual, and declared that he very much looked forward to our session with the young men. So did I.

NOTES

28 Nude or topless sunbathing is officially not allowed nowadays.

29 *dana*: Literally: giving, or liberality. The first of the six 'perfections': they are: the perfection of generosity, of morality, of patience, of energy, of means of concentration and the perfection of wisdom. Here however the word is also used to refer to the practice of offering food to the bhikkhus. Such *dana* is usually accompanied by the belief that one gains 'merit' [Sinhalese: *pim*, Pali: *punya*; spiritual positivity] by so doing; in this context, the concern and belief of Buddhist lay-people is not so much to do with spiritual positivity, but with the gaining of rebirth in a heavenly realm by the offering of material goods. This is not considered to be a spiritually worthy goal by those who are altruistically motivated.

30 Recently re-published as: Anagarika Dharmapala – A Biographical Sketch, and other *Maha Bodhi* writings: Sangharakshita, Ibis Publications, 2013.

* * * * *

Statue of Anagarika Dharmapala in the grounds of the
Temple of the Tooth, Kandy

5   Wesak Light, and a Bomb Blast

My Buddhist teaching work increases in scope and intensity, even as there is an increase in the tension and an escalation of the violence in Sri Lanka, both between Tamils in the North and the Sinhalese, and between 'establishment' Sinhalese and 'militant' Sinhalese in the South. An encounter with an elderly bhikkhu produces from him a vehement diatribe against 'disrobing'. I meet Ven. Nyanaponika, an elderly German bhikkhu, who shows himself to be sympathetic towards the FWBO and the Mahāyāna, and I start prison-visiting.

SINCE I LAST WROTE, Bhikkhu Yogavachara Rahula has left for Europe. He has been invited to lead a meditation retreat at his friend Mr. Vig's home in Denmark. From there he is going to Los Angeles, where he intends to settle as resident bhikkhu in a small meditating community devoted to the Theravada. I wished him luck and suggested that he should not be too tightly attached to his bhikkhu life-style. I told him I thought what was important was that he continued to follow the basic precepts. I think he is unlikely to follow my advice, wedded as he is to Theravadin habits, but we shall see. Be that as it may, Bhikkhu Rahula has kindly left his abode, the 'Seaside Kuti' at my disposal. I am now spending some time in it each day, and also sleeping here. It is a little nine-foot by six-foot wooden hut, high on a promontory overlooking the sea. One reaches it by a fifteen minute walk along the beach and up a hill from 'Samma Ajiva'. Here I can escape from the atmosphere of the hotel when it gets too noisy and oppressive, as it usually does at night, when it is often frequented by drugged or drunken worshippers of hedonism. I rise in the mornings at half-past five and meditate, then walk to the hotel for the seven o'clock group meditation. Siri usually comes for this seven-o'clock meditation from his home in Galle, about two miles away. He is now a mitra: we conducted his mitra Ceremony at a retreat in Nilambe Meditation Centre recently, and I felt particularly pleased at this 'first' in Sri Lanka. Siri's presence is a positive inspiration, adding as it does an impression of vitality, energy and mindfulness to the shrine room. When he goes, sometime during the evening, back to his home, his daughter and pregnant wife, I then return to Rahula's kuti. I meditate, perform the Sevenfold Puja, and then go to bed, with the waves resounding on the rocks only twenty yards away.

This morning after breakfast we had the usual weekly hotel staff meeting. It is a difficult process trying to inspire the participants to organize themselves along real 'Right Livelihood' lines, and to help them all, including even Siri, to see their collective work as a path to Enlightenment. Sometimes the going is so heavy that I feel I would rather be on retreat, or leading study, or writing, or listening to some good music. Trying to entice people into Right Livelihood, when they do not seem to want to come into it, is not my idea of the good life. However, it is not as if it takes up very much of my time. And with each tiny improvement, each more open bit of communication, each consensus for a small change, I feel a bit more hopeful about the future. After our Right Livelihood meeting, Ranjit, who was my room-mate on my first arrival at 'Samma Ajiva', and who is one of our more reliable helpers, handed my mail to me. On opening it I found a request to give a talk in Colombo; there were also some minutes of meetings at the Auckland Buddhist Centre, and a large packet containing the long-awaited April issue of the Order Newsletter. I spent an hour or so browsing through the latter, and found myself saying "wonderful, excellent!" from time to time. Eventually I felt moved to make my own contribution, and here I am typing my next Letter from Lanka, after a short interval.

April here has been remarkable for two events. The first was a weekend retreat that we held at Galle Fort Temple, an edifice constructed in the traditional plastered and white-painted masonry, complete with a large reclining Buddha image and a silver-painted, bell-shaped stupa, and situated some fifty yards from the sea-shore. Twenty-eight people attended, though five young men, hardly more than boys, left after the first day. The bhikkhus were eager to see what was going on, but as I had expected, did not participate. However, the Chief Priest, Ven. Dayasara, a young and very positive man, whom I had previously befriended, made it his personal task to see that I was properly fed and watered. His spirit of helpfulness in fact deeply impressed me. He is one of the few senior bhikkhus who I have found who does not appear to expect somebody else to perform the simple tasks. Over the two days, everyone enjoyed themselves, and we departed with requests for more.

The other important recent event was Wesak. Wesak is celebrated in grand style here, with huge, elaborate, brightly illuminated *pandals*[31] erected in prominent positions in all the towns and villages. And all the Buddhists - which means in the South of Sri Lanka, practically everyone - either buys or makes up their own large and beautiful Wesak lantern to hang outside their house. It really is a wonderful sight to see, especially with the full and beautiful Wesak moon hovering above everything in the deep blue tropical sky. The festival spreads over three or four days, and many people spend their time just walking from place to place looking at these extraordinary displays of enthusiastic piety. I was invited to several places this Wesak - to the YMBA Galle, and to a number of Temples to give talks and meditation instruction. I accepted all the invitations, though I had previously thought that I might be able to spend the festival quietly by myself.

Despite the glory of Wesak, however, the Island has fallen since then from the heights almost into the abyss. There has been tension and bloodshed not only between the Sinhalese and the Tamils in the North, but between rival factions of Sinhalese in the South. There have even been stories that port officials on the Indian mainland are allowing boats to be openly loaded with guns. Everyone knows that these boats cross the Palk Straits and deliver their deadly cargo to the Tamil terrorists. Miraculously, riots have not broken out as they did in '83. We ourselves at 'Samma Ajiva' have witnessed some of the violence. For instance, early in May, Siri and I took a train to Colombo. We had planned to start enlarging our circle of friends in the capital. Half way there, a tremor of fearful speculation passed through the carriage. Someone had heard from a railway station bystander that a bomb had gone off in the city. We arrived at Fort Station, Colombo, having seen nothing untoward, and quickly boarded a bus. But after turning a few street corners, the bus was halted by a huge silent crowd gazing wide-eyed at an old colonial building on the other side of the road. The place looked as if a demolition squad had just started work on it. After some minutes, the crowd allowed the bus through, and we proceeded to our destination. We discovered later that we had passed the Central Telegraph Office an hour or so after a terrorist bomb had gone off in it. The blast, we were told, had completely demolished one floor of the building, blown out many windows, killed eighteen people and injured many others. Later in the afternoon, Siri and I visited Albert Edirisinghe, the President of the World Fellowship of Buddhists, Sri Lanka. With tears in his eyes he described to us how he had rushed to the Telegraph Office that morning to enquire after a near relative of his who worked there. The place, he said, was a shambles: prostrate, blood-bespattered bodies lay everywhere, many of them dead, and with their clothes reduced to shreds. Albert's relative was one of the fortunate ones, and had escaped with only minor injuries. "But what can we do?" he asked.

Since then there has been the bombing of the Tri-Star plane at Colombo Airport, and a score of young women and children slaughtered in a village in the North while gathering flowers to offer in the Temple there. Then again, two buses and their seventy or so occupants were shattered by bombs near Trincomalee. What, indeed, can one do or say? Would even oceans of tears help? How long will it be before the India political machine comes to its senses? Surely mainstream Indian politics should vomit up the Tamil rebels. They are a credit to nobody. All this is not to say that the Sinhalese too have not been unskilful and violent. They have perhaps, in some ways, even prepared the stage for violence, as when, for instance, S.W.R.D. Bandaranaike, the fourth of the Sri Lankan Prime Ministers chose, a decade after Independence, to impose a single official language on the whole of the Island, downgrading both Tamil and English. The present situation is complicated by millennia of Tamil-Sinhala rivalry as well as by more recent mismanagement of the multi-ethnic Island. One also can by no means discount the legacy of centuries of successive occupation by the Portuguese, Dutch and British. All this has done nothing to promote the cause of Buddhism or lay the basis for peace.

Be all that as it may, Siri and I have been getting on with teaching meditation and spreading the Dharma. Those few days after the bomb blast in Colombo early in May, we spoke at several places. Most notably I visited Royal College, where five hundred young men in impeccable whites listened to my talk in English. No translation into Sinhalese was necessary. The organiser was warmly appreciative, and at the end of my talk I received a blue bedspread from the young President of the students' Buddhist

Association. We also arranged to give talks at Dehiwala YMBA, the second largest in Colombo. The largest YMBA, I have discovered, is in Borella district, and is impressive for its size and office equipment. It is staffed by elderly men, however, and things did not move fast enough for anything definite to be arranged on my first visit. The President of the women's wing of the Dehiwala YMBA also met us, and impressed me by her warm enthusiasm and devotion. It was her invitation to give a talk that I received in my mail this morning.

We went this morning to meet at his home in Colombo an old man who is, we were told, the last surviving disciple of Anagarika Dharmapala, called Sugatadasa. He offered us a seat and a cup of tea, then began erupting with fire and brimstone, inveighing against every conceivable iniquity. So much so that it became at times a bit difficult to perceive his basic friendliness. He became so violently emotional at one point that I thought he was going to have a heart attack. Some days later, however, Siri and I received an invitation to speak at the Buddhist Society of which he is Secretary. I therefore concluded that he must have been sufficiently self-possessed to form a favourable impression of us. In addition to all this, Siri and the non-working co-owner of 'Samma Ajiva' hotel, Bandula Silva, ferried me to various publishing houses. We even visited the Sri Lanka broadcasting station, trying to find further means of spreading the Dharma. In at least one of these places we were successful; I received an invitation to be interviewed on the radio. So I am beginning to get a little bit 'known' in the South of Sri Lanka. I do wonder, however, how much good it is doing. My health remains good, but whether all this travelling is the best way to expend my energy, I have my doubts. It is important to be inspiring if one appears in public. This is not so easy, however, if one does it often. It requires a constant effort to avoid platitudes and deepen one's insight.

I have by now spoken and given meditation instruction in quite a few Temples on poya (i.e. full-moon) days. As a result of these visits, I have begun to form a general impression of what goes on in them. The assemblies of the faithful usually consist mostly of women, old men and children, all dressed in the traditional white. Many of them, I find on my arrival, are sitting slumped in awkward postures on the floor with no cushions to make themselves comfortable. They sit with their legs turned back and to one side. Some of these unfortunate individuals seem to be either intensely bored or in a sort of catatonic state. So far as I can tell, their condition is the result of the misguided ministrations of the bhikkhus, or sometimes of a lay teacher. They are often expected, I am told, to sit and listen to a 'forest bhikkhu' for instruction. I have, in fact, attended a couple of such sessions myself. Almost invariably, it seems, the content of these talks follows the same course. 'Suffering, the repulsiveness of the body, death, and 'vipassana'. Vipassana, or Insight, is however presented as the mere recognition of impermanence, with no distinction being made between its identification as a bit of received knowledge, and the actual penetration of the true nature of existence.

For experienced and regular meditators with a firm basis of *metta*[32], all this might be of some use, if not actually invigorating. But for these poorly-prepared listeners to the *hamudru*, the outcome is disastrous. If they are healthy and a bit self confident, they quickly become bored, thinking perhaps that they have now developed insight. They then soon begin to think that there is nothing more to learn, and Buddhism becomes for them merely a means of 'earning merit' by feeding the monks, an activity from which all good is thought to proceed. Those listening repeatedly to this kind of message became shocked, it seemed to me, into what appeared to be a sort of emotional rigidity or stoic impassivity. All this is regarded as the Dhamma, the path to Enlightenment, because it bears, as it were, the label 'Buddhist.' I cannot help feeling it is better that the young stay away from all this. For that matter, what even do the old and careworn gain?

The bhikkhus, however, are by no means always the fat and unctuous creatures that are sometimes portrayed in caricature. I have met quite a few like that, but very often they are mild and gentle-looking young men with shy smiles and diffident manners. Sometimes they are naive and callow youths who have been dragooned into the Sangha when very young. The bhikkhu Sangha or spiritual community consisting of bhikkhus is, incidentally, generally referred to incorrectly both by journalists and the bhikkhus themselves as the Maha Sangha, or Great Sangha. The Mahasangha is in point of fact the sangha or spiritual community of all those who Go for Refuge to whatever extent, whether superficially or with complete faith integrated with understanding, to the Three Jewels of Buddhism - a large Sangha indeed. But these young Sinhalese youths, often having donned the robes lacking a true vocation, or by the wish for an easy life, or pressed into the Sangha by destitute or ambitious parents, soon wake up to the fact that they have assumed positions of social prestige and power. The more thoughtful of them try to apply the Buddha's teaching in their dialogues with their devotees, but they are inadequately trained for the task. The result is as I have described, with most people thinking, if they think at all, that this is what Buddhism must be. Other Sri Lankans, the more Westernized ones, apologetically regard Buddhism as a charming but virtually useless ancient custom which is best left to the elderly and very young. It is not, they think, something to be taken at all seriously by modern men and women.

So long as it remains in such a sorry state, Buddhism (or this pseudo-Buddhism, or religio-nationalism, as Sangharakshita has characterized it) cannot be much of a lamp on the path to Enlightenment. It is merely a tawdry flag for power politics and nationalist and racialist ambitions. I see much that is genuinely good, and even deeply moving in Sri Lankan Buddhism. There is much also that is simply no longer appropriate in today's world, and much that might be genuinely helpful which is hopelessly misapplied. One hardly knows where to begin with the much-needed process of regeneration, reformation and renaissance.

There is another facet of the big old, badly-cut Jewel of Lankan Buddhism that is lacklustre. This is what Sangharakshita characterizes as Theravada literalism. The first time I encountered it with a vengeance was at the Vajirārāmaya Temple in Colombo. Siri had described the Vajirārāmaya Temple to me in terms suggesting it was the St. Peter's of Theravada Buddhism, so I would not ordinarily have thought of going there. However, Ven. Nandasara, the Chief Priest of Galle district, who had helped me get my

Visa, one day suggested that I visit a certain bhikkhu resident at the Vajiraramaya Temple. This bhikkhu, according to Ven. Nandasara, was well known for his wisdom. It was difficult, therefore, to avoid following up the suggestion. Besides, I thought, I might learn something. So as soon as it was convenient, I ventured into the Vajiraramaya with Siri one evening. The bhikkhu I had been advised to meet was not there, but Siri and I were immediately directed to another senior bhikkhu. The senior, and as was now evident - elderly - monk was pacing up and down a verandah in the sweetly perfumed semi-darkness of the residential quarters. We approached him very discreetly and gave a bow of middling depth. I said that we had in fact come to see a bhikkhu whom we had been told was at present away. The old bhikkhu then told us that the man we had come to see was away in Europe. After that he fixed his large, strongly bespectacled eyes on me, and asked about my robes. I explained that they were Anagarika robes. He asked me what *silas* (ethical principles) I observed, and I explained that I observed the *dasa-sila* (the ten precepts) including the *abrahmacharia* precept (the chastity precept, or undertaking to refrain from unchastity). He asked about my teacher and I said he was the Venerable Sangharakshita, the seriormost English bhikkhu. So then he said: "Oh, I know him, he's disrobed hasn't he?" I replied: "No, he hasn't disrobed, he wears ordinary clothes as an *upaya kausalaya* (skilful means)." At this, the old man became highly indignant, and began to remind me of nothing so much as Sir Anthony Absolute in Sheridan's play The Rivals: "A monk" he said, "who disrobes" - and here there was a distinct tremor in his voice - "is no better than a robber. It is disgraceful ...." At this point Siri appeared about to explode with indignation, so trying to avert a disaster, I chipped in and said: "Well, whatever Sangharakshita is, he's doing excellent Dharma work in the West. "That may be", the old monk said, determined to make his point: "even laymen can do good work. But he is not a bhikkhu if he has once taken off his robes. He is not a member of the bhikkhu Sangha." I tried briefly to point out the limitations of his standpoint, but it was useless. For the old gentleman, a bhikkhu was defined by the wearing of a particular uniform, and that was that. Siri and I retired as calmly as we could from the Venerable presence, slightly regretting that we had not left the Vajiraramaya Temple the moment we discovered that the person renowned for his wisdom wasn't there. But after all, we had become somewhat the wiser regarding future questions of this sort. Since it was doubtful whether even Sangharakshita still regarded himself as a bhikkhu in the strict technical sense of the term, there seemed little point in us trying to maintain that he was such, technically or non-technically.

My second encounter with Theravada literalism was in the person of the Venerable Nyanaponika Thera. He was so far as I knew, the last remaining disciple of Ven. Nyanatiloka, a German bhikkhu known amongst other things for his authorship of *A Pali English Dictionary*, and *A Guide to the Abhidhamma*. I was looking forward to meeting with Ven. Nyanaponika, since, as well as being a very old bhikkhu - eighty-five years old, in fact - I knew him as author of *The Heart of Buddhist Meditation*, a Dharma book for which I had considerable respect. I decided one day to go and meet him in his forest hermitage in the depths of the jungle known as Uduwattakele that lay beyond the Temple of the Tooth in Kandy, and on no account to enter into any polemics.

Having walked two miles through the forest outside Kandy to his Hermitage, I prostrated myself before Ven. Nyanaponika. He was, after all, the seniormost German bhikkhu, and I had derived inspiration from his book *The Heart of Buddhist Meditation*. Having prostrated myself, I made myself receptive. Venerable Nyanaponika was about the same height as me, but much stouter, and his skin was loose rather like an old elephant's, and discoloured with the signs of old age. His dark brown upper robe draped negligently about him, he directed me with large gestures, resembling those of a sort of ancient hierophant, in the direction of an inner room. To this inner room I repaired while he spoke to his aide and heir-apparent (i.e. to the Editorship of the Buddhist Publication Society, Kandy), namely Bodhi, an American bhikkhu. Some minutes later Ven. Nyanaponika joined me in this small inner room, a gloomy place almost unrelieved in its spartan ugliness. The only attractive object in it to catch the eye was a piece of yellow cloth embroidered with a Dharma Chakra (or perhaps I should say, Dhamma-cakka). I introduced myself as briefly as possible, and Ven. Nyanaponika began, somewhat hesitantly, to speak.

I thought that Ven. Nyanaponika's face showed signs of repressed anger. While speaking he picked, apparently absent-mindedly, at the hairs and skin of his right forearm. However his voice was friendly enough, and his words often interspersed with a characteristic, half-voiced 'nein?', were illuminated from time to time with an old man's slightly child-like grin. He talked at some length on various topics, sometimes lapsing into a long silence. Occasionally I felt it necessary to take steps to resume our verbal communication. Sometimes, he seemed to be day-dreaming. We spent an hour or so together, and towards the end of it he had begun visibly to perk up. I felt sorry that we had to part so soon, and so, it seemed, did he. I was however obliged to leave immediately with a friend who had come to collect me and could not wait.

The next day I resolved to see Ven. Nyanaponika again, this time armed with a tape-recorder. In this way I might have a chance of deciphering his quiet and slightly indistinct speech at my leisure. I walked once more the two miles or so through the beautiful forest, gloriously green and mysteriously silent except for bird calls, hoping that Ven. Nyanaponika would agree to be tape-recorded. Reaching the hermitage, and prostrating myself once more, I was invited to sit down. This time, to my relief, it was in an airy reception room, with Bhikkhu Bodhi also present. I asked them both if they would mind my talking to them and recording our conversation. Remembering that Ven. Nyanaponika had told me that he read the FWBO journal, I said that Nagabodhi, the Editor of *Golden Drum*, might be interested in publishing what he had to say. I had already gathered that Ven. Nyanaponika was very well disposed towards the FWBO. He had told me that he appreciated very much what the FWBO was doing in the West. Furthermore, he had asked me to convey his *metta*[32] to Bhante, and in fact he quickly put my mind at rest on this occasion by assenting to the recorder, and we were able to proceed. We spoke for an hour and ten minutes, touching upon Lama Govinda, Sri Lankan Buddhism, World Buddhism, and the Mahāyāna and Vajrayāna forms of Buddhism. From Bhikkhu Bodhi's occasional interjections, I formed the impression that the Master was rather more flexible and open-minded than the very much younger disciple. Eventually, Ven. Nyanaponika interrupted our talk to enquire about the time. On discovering that it was 11.10am, he rose immediately, almost as if he had been stung. He said brusquely: "We must have our Dana" (i.e. ceremonial mid-day meal) and walked off. Bhikkhu Bodhi followed close on his heels, leaving me suddenly alone. Two minutes later Ven. Nyanaponika returned and asked me if I would like a cup of coffee, to which I assented. He then showed me a little meditation room off the reception room, and departed, saying he would be back later. This surprised me. I had walked two miles into the forest to see them. I would have to walk two miles back and would then be faced with the problem of eating after mid-day. Wouldn't I need a bit of refuelling? There wasn't even a biscuit with the coffee. I reflected on the matter briefly, and decided that my stomach would probably benefit from the rest.

I proceeded to write down an interesting-looking article passed to me by Ven. Nyanaponika on Buddhism and Christianity, of which he had only one copy. Half an hour later he returned and we concluded our interview. Before parting, he asked me if I wanted anything. I asked him if he had a copy of the *Visuddhimagga*[33] to spare. He said he did, and drawing a battered volume from a nearby shelf, he wrote inside the front cover and passed it to me. Whether the old bhikkhu had wanted to teach me a lesson concerning food, I suppose I shall never know. Perhaps he and Bhikkhu Bodhi, in their concern not to miss their one and only meal of the day, had simply been unmindful of their visitor. My last meeting with Ven. Nyanaponika took place following a mixed Beginners retreat at Nilambe. I was disappointed to find that he and Bhikkhu Bodhi did not consider my transcription of our talk worth publishing. After a short conversation, I took a photograph of them both outside their hermitage, expressed my thanks and rather sadly said farewell, knowing that it was almost certainly the last time I would see Ven. Nyanaponika.

The retreat at the Nilambe Laymen's Meditation Centre probably merits a report to itself, but suffice it to say here that there were twenty or so participants shining with vitality at the end. Siri had his mitra ceremony on that retreat, so I was particularly pleased. The consensus was "May there be many more."

Yesterday I addressed twenty inmates in a prison in Koggala, a nearby village, and taught them the *metta bhāvana*. I have committed myself to giving ten public talks shortly in Bandarawela, Colombo, and Galle. I also have a book in course of preparation, so I'm sorry I cannot write more to you this month.

NOTES

31 *pandal*: a temporary stage, sometimes simple, sometimes elaborate, roofed and richly decorated, providing a platform for speakers or performers, religious,

political, dramatic or artistic. They are usually provided with artificial lighting and loud-speakers. Such stages are a common sight both in village and in urban India, and they often attract spontaneous crowds of many hundreds, sometimes many thousands of people.

32 *metta*: strong emotional positivity, which can be cultivated by spiritual practice; a completely positive, wholesome emotion more potent than love or hate. It produces a response of warm friendliness when meeting someone neither elated not depressed, sympathetic joy [Pali: *mudita*] when meeting someone who is evidently happy, com-passion [Pali: *karuna*] when encountering someone who is suffering, and equanimity [Pali: *upekka*], even-mindedness towards a person or persons whose state of mind is not clear, or in fluctuating states, whether positive or negative.

33 *Visuddhimagga* : a non-canonical Pāli text by the renowned commentator Achārya Buddhaghosha. A manual of instruction setting out in great detail an approach to self-purification based upon the principles set out in the third part of the Tipiṭaka, the Abhidhamma.

* * * * *

Ashvajit teaching in a Temple near Matara, with Siri (now Saddhavira) translating

6   Hill country - and a bhikkhu warlord

*My dharma-touring continues in Colombo and elsewhere in the region.
I proceed to Bandarawela district in the hill country, and during quite a
successful tour of the area, I see on TV a prominent bhikkhu giving young
conscripts permission to kill 'for the sake of the dharma'. I learned later that
the terrorist party the JVP had secret hide-outs in the Bandarawela area, and
wondered whether the temple where I felt unaccountably ill was somehow
connected with their outlawed activities. Back at Unawatuna, I conduct a
retreat with the sound of the waves pounding the golden-sanded sea-shore
accompanying our meditations, and Siri and I continue with our visits to
nearby Temples. I journey to Ratnapura and at a Temple there I listen
unwillingly to an incitement to racial hatred by a visiting, supposedly
'learned' bhikkhu, and learn that the bhikkhus of that Temple are raising
money for machine guns. Whilst preparing to go on solitary retreat, I learn of
the purchase by the FWBO of land in Spain, for a Retreat Centre to be called
'Guhyaloka'[34] - the secret realm.*

MY PRESENT LETTER RELATES A JOURNEY into the hill country.
I had set off by bus with Siri Goonasekara who is now a mitra, to
Bandarawela. At first we passed through beautiful countryside green with
paddy-fields and graced by waving palms. Later on we began to climb
steeply, paddy fields rose terrace upon terrace up the steep hillsides, and the
climate grew colder. Then hill gave way to mountain and the paddy fields
disappeared, giving way to plantations of closely-planted small bushes, and
the blue sky to swirling mists. I wrapped my upper robe around me in what
the Sinhalese call 'anagarika' fashion, covering my usually bare right shoulder
in an effort to keep warm. Bandarawela turned out to be a small town of
about 5,000 people, I was told, with no buildings of architectural distinction,
in the 'up-country' or hill province of Uva, famous for its tea. We had
arranged to give, amongst other things, three public talks in the Town Hall. I
had commissioned the hand-painting of twenty large posters, and had sent
them to three friends of Siri's to whom I had been introduced on our previous
visit to have them pasted up in Bandarawela. I had also sent these three
friends several hundred hand bills for distribution. On our arrival after the
eight-hour bus journey from Unawatuna, we were assured that five of the
posters had been pasted up, but in all my subsequent to-ings and fro-ings I
saw only one. The handbills had not been distributed. Not only that, the Chief
High Priest of the area had unfortunately died the day before our arrival, and
his funeral, we were told, would be attended by practically the whole town.
Not only that. The full moon of Poson, which coincided with our visit, was
the occasion, I was only now told, when the arrival of Arahant Mahinda in

Sri Lanka was celebrated and commemorated in grand style. Three continuous days of chanting and ritual offerings had been arranged at the town's main Temple, and not to be seen at that would be a social blunder, to say the least. It seemed I had been decisively upstaged. At any rate, I thought to myself, the other engagements we had, at schools and temples, would not be affected.

I spoke at two mixed schools and two girls' schools. At one of the latter our visit was announced as 'observing *sil*[35] - the Sri Lankan equivalent of a sort of day retreat, and usually held at the Temple on Poya (full moon) Day. We arrived while the assembly of teenage girls were chanting, and it was quite pleasant just listening to the melodious sound. When they had finished, Siri and I were ushered into the long narrow hall and seated on a small dais in the centre of one long side - a difficult position from which to speak. The girls, maybe four hundred of them, all in impeccable white, had faces expanded and bright with bliss, and I felt inspired enough to give a good spontaneous talk. The girls smiled and nodded and laughed almost as one person, and from the perfect synchronization of faces and expressions and movements of most of them, I received the impression once again, as I had in Galle fort school, that I was speaking as it were to a single organism; many bodies, but only one mind, or even, a single, multiple body and one mind. It was rather extraordinary and curious, and I began to wonder whether an audience of equally blissful, mature individuals would be essentially the same[36].

One of the mixed schools was unusually responsive to the talk we gave, which was substantially similar, with only minor variations, at each place we visited. The boys roared with laughter at some of the things I said, but it was not clear what they were laughing at. What I said was simply matter-of-fact. Afterwards I was surrounded by a press of teen age boys wanting me to answer their questions. It was all rather inspiring, as much because of my audience as because of anything I consciously did or said. After this we visited a small temple some miles outside the town where a group of dull and totally unresponsive bhikkhus sat around. I felt completely blocked and quite ill. There was practically nothing I could do there. What I felt like doing was admonishing them, but not being used to doing such a thing, and not seeing immediately how best to go about it, I suppressed the urge. Fortunately we were able to move on fairly quickly, and visit another temple at which a warm reception had been given us on a previous occasion - at least, the High Priest had been notably friendly. This time however, he was cooler - almost aloof. We gave a talk to the Poya day gathering and instructed them in meditation, and they expressed themselves well-pleased with our visit. At yet another temple, closely associated with Sarvodaya, the inter-religious movement started by Dr. Ariyaratne, a large group of people were awaiting us already seated for meditation, and were very appreciative of the lesson. They asked us to visit again. It is a bit frustrating to know that it will probably be quite a long time before it is possible to do any follow-up work in so many of the places we visit, and that, even if anyone was ready to 'leave home' - unlikely though it might be, there is very little we can offer them here in Sri Lanka at present.

Then on the three evenings, my almost un-advertized talks in the town hall were to take place. I was not very happy - not that I am unhappy with a small audience, but in a 1000-seat hall, with only a few people seated here and there tended to create a rather dismal impression. In retrospect, I realized I should have arranged with the Temple bhikkhus to hold my talk there - they would in all probability have been willing, but I had accepted alternative advice, and now it was too late to do anything about it. On reflection, I also realized that my most influential adviser was Siri, who was understandably in a state of reaction against the bhikkhus. About fifteen people attended each of my talks. They sat in the front two rows of seats in one corner of the big hall, and we managed to contrive quite a cosy atmosphere. I sat back in an easy chair, and speaking spontaneously, found myself waxing quite eloquent. The situation was not so bad after all. One member of the audience was a Christian, and although I was quite blasphemous, he persisted in faithfully coming along for each talk. Evidently the Dhamma was able to provide something that God could not. During our three-and-a-half days in Bandarawela, Siri and I also took the opportunity of visiting the director of Education, a big bull of a man bubbling with hyperactivity and forced friendliness. It was very uncomfortable being with him, and I tried, not without success, to put him at his ease. He invited us to the open day of what he called a 'New Sinhala Style' school, and we agreed to come. I found myself sharing a platform with a junior Minister and one of the Directors of Nilambe Meditation Centre where I had conducted a ten day retreat in May. I was puzzled by the half-strangled voices in which these two men addressed the hundred or so audience of parents. I was still puzzling over it when it was time for me to stand and speak. I had had no time to prepare for this occasion, and gave a short impromptu talk on the importance of a traditional Buddhist education, the good example of parents, and the study of the best examples of one's culture, especially people like Anagarika Dharmapala. I spoke in confident tones, and the parents' appreciation showed on their faces, which I had noticed were mostly averted from the other two whilst they were speaking. The Junior Minister stood up afterwards and said "it is clear that the strength is with you (i.e. referring to me), but how can we start?" It was rather a peculiar comment, and I wondered if he had been watching the American film 'The Empire Strikes Back', in which the expression "may the Force be with you" often occurs. Looking more carefully at the people in the audience, who were noticeably wealthier than usual, I began to get the impression that many of them were rather alienated. Perhaps they were victims of 'insight' methods of meditation, or perhaps their condition was simply the result of being well-to-do here, where wealth sharply differentiates some people from the great majority, who are poor peasants and farmers, though even the poor are comfortable enough in a place so abundant with nature's riches as Sri Lanka.

The town of Bandarawela is an old British hill-station, delightfully situated amongst rounded hills alternating with tea plantations and patches of glorious woodland. It is cool, being 4,000 feet above sea level, brilliantly sunny and with masses of colourful flowers everywhere. A sky-blue, and a pink variety of convolvulus is everywhere to be seen, set off by sprinklings of a brilliant yellow bell-shaped flower, and by white and yellow and scarlet bougainvillea. Vegetables grow in abundance, and a visit to the market reveals basketfuls of beans, cucumbers, carrots and all sorts of other tasty-looking and strange varieties of fruits of the earth. Siri and I often walked from place to place, sometimes up and down several hundred feet, and the excercize, coupled with the beauty of the place and the freshness and lightness of the air had a tonic effect. I could hardly believe that in those three and a half days we had given eleven talks, and two meditation classes. It all seemed so pleasant and easy. Only one thing occurred to mar the pleasantness of our visit. On Poson Poya, having arrived back late in the evening at the house of Siri's brother-in-law, where we were staying, we sat down to a well-prepared supper with a guest. The TV was switched on, but I wasn't paying much attention to it, as I had my back to it and my food in front of me. But my attention began to be caught by the sound of a man's voice which suggested something quite sinister. I turned round and saw on the TV a fat, shaven-headed man dressed in the russet robes of a bhikkhu, fanning himself industriously while seated on a throne-like seat with a representation of the Dharma Chakra suspended above. He was addressing young male and female members of the armed forces, over whom the camera panned over from time to time. The first thought that came to my mind was that it was a joke - an elaborate charade such as might have been staged by a young David Frost, in his more iconoclastic days. But no, it was no charade. Wondering whether my intuition of what the man was saying was correct, I asked Siri to translate, and he replied, in a rather matter-of-fact and resigned voice, "Oh, he's just telling them to go and kill the terrorists to protect Buddhism." Neither Siri nor his brother-in-law nor the male visitor, nor Siri's sister, apparently saw anything bizarre in the scene. To me it looked like a nightmare, and I felt slightly nauseous. Apparently the bhikkhu was a well-known pro-Government propagandist. I immediately felt that something should be done about this.

The next day Siri and I left the pleasant hill-station, catching a bus to Colombo. There I gave talks on four successive evenings to an audience of about forty people at YMBA Dehiwala, the second-largest YMBA in the city. I also gave a meditation class to a group of 40 young men at the D. S. Senanayake School, which was a particularly enjoyable duty. I was invited afterwards to "call anytime." We also had interviews with the Permanent Secretary to the Co-operative Ministry and his counterpart in the Youth Service. Though the former, a Mr. Peiris, was a highly intelligent man, they both seemed devoid of imagination, and the latter was very obviously bored.

Each Tuesday this month I have been visiting Koggala Open Prison, about ten miles south of here, to teach a group of twenty prisoners meditation. They all seem to be making some progress, and I've been trying to plant some golden seeds for their future. The prison grounds are beautifully planted and tended and a fine Buddha-image stands in the grounds too. However and it does not require much of a stretch of the imagination to see what the state of mind of the prisoners is like. The place has the stench of fear.

In the middle of this month we held a weekend retreat in a pleasant, airy house right next to the beach, not far from the hotel here. It was one of the easiest retreats I have led so far. Listening to the sound of the waves, watching the sea, and feeling the cool breezes was delightful, and during one of the meditations a wonderful succession of figures appeared before me: Sarvabuddhadakini, who transformed herself into Amitabha, who changed into Bhante, who transformed himself into Shakyamuni, who vanished into a rainbow halo of blissful coolness.

The full moon of July was of course Dharma Chakra Day, and Siri and I were very much in demand. I cannot possibly give you a complete picture here of everything we did. Whilst most people seem to be responding favourably to our talks and classes, a few react with narrow, arrogant, racialist or fundamentalist attitudes when they find we are not peddling the straight and narrow line of the Hīnayāna. My talk of "hundred per cent Buddhism" seems to be meeting with some success, however.

The local ethnic festival began in Unawatuna on full moon night. It is ostensibly to worship the god of Kataragama (Vishnu/Shiva/Krishna), who is supposed to have stopped at this little fishing village on his journey to the South. People pour in by their thousands, strewing paper and leaving excrement everywhere. Crude music blares all day and night, and a vegetable shrine, placed under the nearby holy tree, is worshipped. Many of the visitors are on their way back North, having ogled at Kataragama's festival of spike-and-hook pierced 'peacock dancers' and fire-walkers.

On the last day of the village festival, one unfortunate man was battered to death by an irate colleague, for reasons which are not clear. Siri and I were away in Colombo at the time. We had been giving a talk at a girls' school, the Devi Balika Vidyalaya, where the headmistress was well pleased with our talk. Incidentally, she is going to do a one-year management course in London soon, so she may turn up at the London Buddhist Centre.

A few days ago I presented a paper on 'Samma Ajiva' to the Galle Co-operative Training Centre, and gave talks in Matara, an hour's drive South from here. The most memorable one was given in a temple where there are four 19-year old Nepali bhikkhus being trained in Theravada style. This seems to me a particularly retrograde and stupid procedure. The young bhikkhus' response to me was very warm, but their teacher, a Sinhala Theravadin, regarded me with deep suspicion and refrained from inviting me again although everybody else appeared delighted with my visit.

An even more recent invitation took me to Ratnapura, famous for its gems, where I gave a four hour talk, in two parts, to the Buddhist Society. Then when I had finished that, they asked, and I gave them, meditation instruction. Everybody walked out in a sort of semi-dhyanic state, though it probably didn't stay very long with most of them. After this, I was given no alternative but to accompany Siri and his uncle by van to a Temple where, I was told, a famous and learned monk was to give an address. I was invited to participate in the preceding Puja, which I was very happy to do; passing on beautifully arranged bowls of flowers to be placed in front of a Buddha image is one of the more pleasant tasks that one is asked occasionally to perform here. One is almost dazzled by the brilliance of colour and intoxicated by the perfume of the blossoms.

After the chanting of the verses of Buddha Puja, Siri and I were escorted to the room of one of the young bhikkhus. Here, a short distance from the hall, not far from the speaker's seat, I would be able to listen to his talk in comfort and have Siri translate for me. The 'learned monk' arrived late and began his talk. Though I was unable to see him, as he was seated on a throne with its back to me, some distance away, and though Siri had not even started to translate, the first sound of his voice was enough. I had not heard anything so harsh and hate ridden since listening, a long time ago, to some recordings of Adolf Hitler. I was astounded that such speech could be tolerated in a Temple, and that all the monks could stand around unconcernedly with their eyes downcast while that horrible sound was echoing around. It seemed to penetrate the very pores of my skin and fill my blood with a heavy poison. I felt shocked, and began to wonder what I could do. At the end of his diatribe, the speaker offered a bride to the local deity, promised a beautiful young woman to the largest donor of funds for armaments, and concluded by chanting some beautiful verses of Pali in a voice hoarse with lust. The whole performance was the most disgusting I have ever heard.

I have since written to President Jayewardene voicing my concern over the two bhikkhus I have mentioned, and asking for answers to some questions. It remains to be seen whether I have cooked my goose in Sri Lanka, or whether the sweet voice of the Dharma will prevail. But I felt I would be failing in my duty if I let these examples of flagrant racialism pass without comment, and that I would not feel free to speak the Dhamma unless I had the courage to speak directly to the President concerning these matters.

Having returned to Unawatuna and the 'Samma Ajiva' guest house, I am now getting ready to leave for a one-month solitary retreat at the Island Hermitage, Dodanduwa, where once, Venerable Nyanatiloka, Nyanamoli and Nyanaponika were based. I intend to start writing my first book there. It is a very peaceful place, and they have a good library, at least in Hīnayāna terms. So I should be able to make good progress. The second issue of *Golden Drum* arrived a few days ago, and I was delighted to read about Guhyaloka. Congratulations to everyone who made possible the purchase of the land, including the anonymous donor. Curiously enough, I got to hear about him here in Unawatuna, of all places, a few months ago. The grapevine seems to extend everywhere! Our short sharp lessons with the Karate boys continue, and for the near future, we are organising a ten-day men's 'Meditation and Co-operatives' retreat at Nilambe. I hope it will take us one step nearer the realization of a Centre here in Lanka.

NOTES

34 Guhyaloka: *loka* is the Pali and Sanskrit word for place or realm, and *guhya* means 'secret' - not so much in the sense of deliberately concealed (though it might also mean that), but in the sense of accessible, knowable, only through direct personal experience.

35 to 'observe *sil*' : is a Sinhalese expression meaning to observe (i.e. to undertake not to transgress, usually for the duration of a day's sojourn at a Temple or

at the time of religious festivals or on full-moon days) the 'lay' precepts i.e. the five precepts supposed to be undertaken by 'Buddhist laymen' at all times or else the eight precepts of a samanera/samaneri - novice bhikkhu or bhikkhuni. 'Sil' is short for sila (Pāli) and here means simply ethics, morality, a precept or moral guide-line.

36 It was not until many years later, in India, that I had a number of similar experiences whilst speaking to audiences of adults, though in these cases it was both a more intense and more subtle experience akin, perhaps, to what Sangharakshita characterised as an experience of an 'impersonal force':

'My own spiritual experience during this period was most peculiar. I felt that I was not a person but an impersonal force. At one stage I was working quite literally without any thought, just as one is in samādhi. Also, I felt hardly any tiredness – certainly not at all what one would have expected from such a tremendous strain. When I left Nagpur I felt quite refreshed and rested.'

(*Dear Dinoo - Letters to a Friend*, Sangharakshita,
    Ibis Publications, 2011, p54)

* * * * *

7   Solitary retreatants and priapism at Island Hermitage

Here I give an account of my four trying weeks in 'Island Hermitage', during which the chief bhikkhu there tries to humiliate me. His understanding of the essentials of Buddhism is evidently not mine. I am sorely tempted to become a bhikkhu, thus almost forgetting the important insight of Sangharakshita's that today, in an increasingly Westernized society, the robes that were worn in India two thousand five hundred years ago by the full-time practitioners of the Way to Nirvana, are becoming irrelevant. It is one's Going for Refuge, one's practice of the Path that is of primary importance; the clothes one wears should be a help, not a hindrance to that.

FIVE DAYS AGO I RETURNED to 'Samma Ajiva' from Island Hermitage, the forested fifty-acre island retreat situated in a brackish lagoon near the coast about twelve miles north of Unawatuna where I am normally based. Both Siri Goonasekara, our first Sri Lankan mitra, and Bhikkhu (once Dhammachari) Dhammajyoti, had recommended that I went there for my solitary retreat, and having briefly visited the island and seen that there was quite a good library - in fact the best I have seen so far in Sri Lanka, I decided to act upon their suggestion. As subsequent events were to show, however, I did not think the matter through carefully enough, and found myself placed in a vulnerable situation that almost resulted in my losing my perspective on what I am supposed to be doing here and my intimate connection with Bhante and the Order.

I arrived on the island in mid-afternoon on August 6th, having been ferried over from a point near the coast road by a couple of smiling boys who seemed quite eager to lend their services. Their boat was a modern fibre-glass version of the traditional dug-out canoe, fitted however with the usual timber outrigger to give the tall and narrow hull stability. I had received a letter signed by the chief incumbent of the 'Hermitage' - Ven. Piyaratana, a Sri Lankan bhikkhu - saying that a *kuti*[37] was ready for me. A moment or two after setting foot onshore, I spotted Piyaratana emerging, elegant in his chestnut-coloured robes, from amongst the trees, which had appeared as we approached the island to cover it from end to end.

Approaching me along the path, Piyaratana observed in somewhat broken English that I had not come by the usual boat. I replied that I hadn't, and asked if the two boys waiting on the shore wanted any money. He replied that they were *dayakas* and wouldn't want anything. So smiling my thanks to them, I picked up my bag and the two of us set off towards the main building on the island - the *dana-sala*[38], and the adjoining Library. The atmosphere was very still and quiet, although just above the threshold of hearing I noticed the sound of traffic, presumably coming from the coast road about a mile away. Having walked up a long, gently sloping flight of steps shaded by coconut palms and other trees of less obvious classification, we arrived at the entrance to the dana-sala, stopping beside a large bush of bearing a profusion of deep pink tropical flowers. I was about to ask if Piyaratana could take me to the kuti which I had been assigned when he said, quite abruptly, 'I'm going now', and off he went, leaving me to my own devices. I put my bag down, and stood savouring the fragrance and beauty of the flowers, but as if to remind me that even though I might be standing still, time was not, I heard footsteps behind me and turned to see a young Sri Lankan, perhaps twenty-five years of age, in dark brown robes, with an expression of studious indifference on his not unattractive face. I introduced myself, saying I was Anagarika Asvajit, and he replied in a soft, carefully modulated, musical voice, that he was Samanera Sobhana, and that it was he who had written the letter to me signed by Ven. Piyaratana. I thought to myself that I was lucky to find such an intelligent young man, and English-speaking too, here, when my train of thought was interrupted by his asking if I wanted some tea. I replied that I did, and having indicated a comfortable-looking low chair seated exactly centrally against the rear wall of the entrance verandah and looking out over the bush of pink flowers, Sobhana left. I tried seating myself in the chair, but didn't feel perfectly happy since directly in front of it was placed a normal-height dining table which cut directly across my line of vision. I have begun to get used to such incongruities in Sri Lankan religious establishments and to accept them where they cannot be avoided, but the question of whether to remain in the seat which had been offered to me was hovering in my mind when Sobhana returned with a large bowl of weak, sweet black tea. I accepted it gratefully and began to drink with enjoyment. Sobhana said nothing, and after finishing my tea, I began to wonder what was going to happen next. At this moment another young man, dressed in russet-coloured robes, arrived. Slightly cross-eyed, and with a very robust chest and strong shoulders, he nevertheless contrived to look quite friendly, and Sobhana told me that the newcomer would take me to my kuti. Standing and picking up my bag, I followed this man, whose name I subsequently discovered was Punnaji, and he led me through the dana-sala, out of a rear doorway and along a broad path through the forest. We reached a junction where we took a narrow path to the right. I could see the sunlit surface of the lake glinting through the trees as I walked along behind Punnaji, and was beginning to savour the beauty of the setting when we arrived at the kuti. It was a stoutly-constructed bricks and mortar bungalow consisting of a room about eight feet by twelve, and a toilet, both entered by doors off a covered walkway about thirty feet long in front, which was presumably to be used for walking meditation. The room was equipped with a bed and a mattress, a sturdy desk, a handsome upright chair, and a set of shelves. It looked comfortable enough, and was fairly airy and well-lit by three good-sized windows, each covered with mosquito netting. In front of the walkway there was a small courtyard of bare earth, from one side of which descended steps to a well, and the whole place was surrounded and shaded by tall and leafy trees. I thought that I could be quite happy here for a month. Punnaji handed me the keys, told me that breakfast would be at six tomorrow morning, and that I could have a cup of tea at seven in the dana-sala if I wanted. So saying, off he went with a cheerful smile.

I busied myself for the next couple of hours thoroughly cleaning the place, setting up a shrine, and taking out my few belongings - a Puja book, a large pile of blank paper, pens, toiletries and so forth, and a spare pair of plain robes. The shrine I built around a small square table which was standing at the end of the walkway and which I moved into the room. I draped the table with a plain piece of orange cloth, and placed upon it the small ebony Buddha-image I had been given a few days previously after giving a talk at a school. I also set out a Tibetan block-print of *sadakshari*[39] Avalokiteshvara and a photo of Chintamani's Green Tara, both of which had been sent to me together with a collection of other things helpful for my work from a person or persons who preferred to remain anonymous, either at Ink Printers or the Glasgow Buddhist Centre. Whoever it was, I am grateful for their generosity. Finding a large white jug, I filled it with water and a large spray of long-leaved plants and flowers which had been growing in profusion just outside the kuti, and placed it beside the shrine. Filling a cast-away earthenware pot with sandy soil, I placed that on the floor in front of the shrine as an incense receptacle. The room now being suitably transformed, I could relax. At seven p.m. I went to the *dāna sala* for a cup of tea, and returning to my kuti, performed a dedication ceremony for my new shrine, and to remind me, if reminder were needed, of what I was supposed to be doing there. Then after a session of meditation I did the Sevenfold Puja, retiring eventually to bed at 11:00pm.

At 4:30 next morning I was up, and after ablutions did a session of *metta bhāvana*. The time seemed to pass extraordinarily quickly, since the breakfast bell summoned me while I was still meditating. Stepping quickly down the forest path, criss-crossed with gnarled roots and strewn with brown leaves, I felt like an old-time wanderer, though presumably without the likelihood of encountering wild beasts or robbers. On arriving at the dana-sala, I found six robed men, including the three I had already met - one of them European - seated around three sides of the main dining area upon broad benches equipped with fat cushions, and with food-laden tables in front of them. There were several spare seats behind the tables and nowhere else to sit except the bare concrete floor. On the fourth side of the room was a two-foot high Burmese Buddha-image in *bhumi-sparsa*[40] brightly polished, and with fresh flower and food offerings placed in front of it.

Wondering where I had been assigned a place, I looked around for a clue, but nobody seemed willing to help me - no word, no gesture, not even a glance was forthcoming. So I took my seat on the spare bench at the horn of the "U" arrangement opposite Ven. Piyaratana, and therefore technically the lowest place, since bhikkhus are generally seated in order of seniority going clockwise from the seniormost. In my experience of eating with bhikkhus so far, I had sometimes been asked to sit next to the seniormost - the friendliest gesture - sometimes in a position appropriate to my apparent physical age, and sometimes in the juniormost position, at the end of all the little boy monks. To none of these arrangements I had the slightest objection.

Having sat down in the dana-sala however, I could not help but notice a certain subtle tension in the air, and Sobhana, the young Samanera who was seated to my right, seemed particularly nervous, his movements appearing jerky and his whole manner curiously disdainful and withdrawn, as if he was shrinking back from some unpleasant object. Anyway, I finished my breakfast as calmly as I usually do, no word being exchanged by anyone, and Piyaratana, followed by the others, got up to leave, having washed out their big black begging bowls and rinsed and emptied their mouths into the spittoons. I too got up, preparing to return to my kuti, but as I turned to leave, someone called out in a sharp voice, "Come to the library". The voice was so unfamiliar and peremptory in tone that I thought at first it wasn't intended for me, but the same phrase was re-iterated, though more hesitantly this time, and I turned to see that it was Sobhana, and indeed addressing me with a scowl on his face. I followed him and Piyaratana into the library and was asked to sit down. Piyaratana then spoke to me in Sinhalese, (though I knew his English was quite good) with Sobhana translating. Sobhana said "You are an Anagarika?" I said Yes. Then he asked "What precepts?" So I explained as usual, being now quite familiar with this procedure. The question however was a rhetorical one, because Piyaratana then informed me: "Anagarikas don't sit with monks here." Beginning to feel a little indignant, I said "Well, my ordination is at least equal to a Samanera's, but if that is your custom here, then I have no choice but to follow it." Actually, I regarded my ordination as more thorough even than a bhikkhu's since it involved undertaking the mind precepts, but without getting rather confrontational, I felt I could not really argue the point, especially as I wanted to stay for a month at Island Hermitage. So that, more or less, was that. I reflected that I would at least be able to suppress my feelings, which, though not without reason, were tinged with a certain amount of ego-clinging. It would be good practice for me to try to throw it off. I therefore acquiesced to the rule of the house.

At the early lunch time, for me, of 11:00am, I returned to the dana-sala, having made a start on the first draft of a book on the seven *bodhyangas*[41]. This was something I had been wanting to do for some time, and now I wanted to do some creative writing on this retreat, to whatever extent experiment proved did not interfere unduly with my meditation. However, other matters were about to exercise their influence. Arriving at the dana-sala, I found, rather to my consternation, that not only had a seat been prepared for me on the floor, which was ignominious enough, since there were only two bhikkhus even technically my superiors i.e. in terms of ordination years, not only were there still spare seats a-plenty at the tables, but I was seated in a corner near the exit, far away from the main dining area, which would surely create a very odd impression indeed to any observer. I had never sought to draw undue attention to myself, but this was ridiculous! Not only was my relationship with the other bhikkhus set in sharp contrast, but surely the dayakas who brought the food so faithfully would be very puzzled and confused by the arrangement. Anyway, modern Theravada custom had imposed itself, which I could probably have predicted had I given it a moment's thought, but the consequences of all this were not so predictable.

I found that a number of changes started taking place day by day as a result of my being seated where I was. Outwardly, of course, I sat there without demur and just got on with the business of eating - what else? But inwardly there was quite a lot going on. I experienced moments of anger and frustration and suppressed them. Then I began to think it was all rather ridiculous, laughing inwardly, Milarepa-like, as if to say "Ha ha, this is just ego-clinging, how foolish". But after a few days I began to reflect: "What if I were to become a bhikkhu?" And soon a number of 'justifications' for this idea occurred to me. Not only that, the attitude of the other monks towards me began to undergo a change. Piyaratana, in whose direct line of vision I was seated, began to take on a sort of fatherly appearance, and smiled at me occasionally. I felt like scowling back, but my good nature got the better of me. Sobhana on the other hand now became extremely objectionable and overbearing in his manner. On several occasions before I sat down he added insult to injury by pointing out imperiously which seats I was not to sit upon. And the monk next in seniority to Piyaratana, after the meal was over, began to ask me why I didn't become a sramanera or a bhikkhu. I began to feel resentful; this was emotional blackmail, pure and simple.

My health took a nose-dive. In fact, due to this psychological drama and the sudden change of eating habits, together with the heat, moisture and odour-laden micro-climate, I became quite ill. I had long sneezing fits, and started to feel I was roasting in hell. My temperature rose and I had to spend many hours lying prostrate on my bed. I even tried taking dips in the murky waters of the lagoon in an attempt to cool off. By this time I had more or less convinced myself that I ought to be a bhikkhu and that then everything would be all right - which is, I suppose, precisely what they wanted me to think. Rather to my subsequent shame and remorse, I sent a letter off to Sangharakshita asking him what he thought about my becoming a bhikkhu. It really does seem in retrospect as if I became a bit unhinged for a few days, though while in the midst of the experience, it all seemed very reasonable. Here was my thinking:

Firstly, the case for becoming a bhikkhu: (1) I would be more likely to be taken seriously by the bhikkhu sangha, and would therefore be in a good position to exhort them. (2) Tedious explanations concerning my ecclesiastical status would no longer be necessary. (3) The existence of a member of the WBO[42] within the bhikkhu Sangha would serve to improve communication between the two 'bodies'. (4) The discipline and training necessary to become a bhikkhu would be good for me.

No doubt there are many holes in the foregoing four propositions! Then, against becoming a bhikkhu: (1) Being ordained into the Bhikkhu Sangha would be likely to create a strong sense of identity with people who did not, so far as I had been able to determine, share the same mind, the same attitude as I did myself, and who, in some, perhaps quite a few cases, might be confused concerning the Dhamma and perhaps even malevolent, as for instance were those bhikkhus who raised funds for armaments. (2) Undertaking to observe 225 precepts, some of which by my keeping strictly to them would make it more difficult for me to spread the Dhamma, and which for this reason I would have no real intention of keeping, would be psychologically damaging. (3) Food and money involve a number of important (though minor) precepts in a Theravada bhikkhu's life. Not only would the strictly-observed precepts concerning food not be conducive to my health, they might actually make me ill. (4) Not being able to handle money would make me utterly dependent upon 'the laity' and beholden to them. (5) I might as a bhikkhu be tempted to behave in certain ways simply to avoid popular opprobrium. (6) Very little by way of training was offered by the Theravada Sangha, so far as I had been able to discover. A few establishments offered courses in "Vipassana", which in any case was already an aspect of my practice and View. (7) There was no procedure so far as I had been able to ascertain to induct a postulant into a single, harmonious Bhikkhu sangha. There was in fact, it seemed to me, no integrated Bhikkhu sangha at all in Sri Lanka, despite frequent mention by the Media of 'The Mahasangha', when they should have said 'Bhikkhu sangha'. (8) The method of Abhidhamma analysis, beloved of many bhikkhus, whilst useful in principle, is of limited application in practice, and almost useless in a secular, industrialized society and amongst sophisticated, literate and worldly people. Even for the committed, it can be productive of subtle delusions. (9) Going for Refuge to a preceptor whom I might suspect of delusion would be psychologically damaging, and a gross breach of faith in my own Preceptor. (10) An Anagarika is not someone with a 'higher' ordination, there being in truth no higher ordination than that of the Dhammachari. An Anagarika undertakes to observe celibacy and chastity of body, speech and mind as an intensification of his or her personal practice as a committed Buddhist. (11) I already had ten beautiful and complete precepts with an unsurpassed lineage, and a lifestyle which could be varied according to circumstance and spiritual need. I already had the freedom to conduct my own life skilfully, whatever the prevailing conditions.

This is what I concluded after writing to Bhante asking what he thought. On my return to Unawatuna, a letter from Dharmachari Bodhiraja was awaiting me in which he said that Bhante did not think my becoming a bhikkhu was a good idea at all, and that he was a bit surprised I had even considered it. So that made me feel on the one had rather ashamed, and on the other, pleased that I had by now set out my thoughts clearly enough to make up my own mind. The moral that I draw from all this is that it is no small matter to allow oneself to be undermined, thinking it will have no effect. It can have a very detrimental effect on one's thinking and self-view. Thus the first ten days or so at Island Hermitage turned out to be rather hellish, due to the matters outlined above. I was also experiencing remorse over a number of incidents in my past in which I had been less than skilful, and which stoked the fires of hell for me. However, as the days passed, things did begin to get better. My temperature stabilized, I adjusted, more or less, to the heavy morning eating, and my mind began to calm down. Furthermore, I began to communicate with three of the other monks on Island Hermitage, though not always successfully.

My first attempt at something a bit more than superficiality was with Hitesi Samanera, whom I attempted to communicate with first because for many years I had been sending him copies of *Golden Drum* and *Dhammamegha* from the UK. Alas, he might as well have not received them, as far as I could see. He greeted me pleasantly enough, gave me somewhere comfortable to sit, and then asked if I had any questions. I replied that I hadn't come to ask questions, but just to get to know him a bit, especially as he had been receiving Friends' publications. To my disappointment, this was a total non-starter. He displayed not the slightest interest. After a few minutes of silence, I became rather intrigued as to what, if anything, was going on in his mind. I surmized that he would, or perhaps could only communicate strictly on his own terms. So I made myself completely receptive, and waited. Then, sure enough, he began to speak. I discovered that Hitesi was German, but spoke excellent English. Also, he didn't eat with the other monks, but rowed a little boat over to the mainland where he went on *pindapata*[43] each morning. Then, with bowl full, he returns to his kuti, from where he doesn't stir until next time he is hungry. A real hermit! The first thing, however, that he began to tell me was not about himself, but about Island Hermitage. All the other monks were hypocrites, he said, and Buddhism was in any case virtually dead in Sri Lanka. He was a student of the *vinaya*[44] he said, and he knew that nobody followed it. In fact, he was so unrelievedly bitter in his denunciation of Sri Lankan Buddhism that I began to wonder what he was doing here wearing the robes. It seemed to me that all he wanted was to live alone with his books and to become an expert, it might have been in anything, but it happened to be the Buddhist monastic code of conduct, for some reason or other.

He began to pour out such resentment that I felt quite uncomfortable, and decided to leave, and at the earliest pretext I went. However, Hitesi must have realized he had somehow gone too far, because next morning he appeared at my kuti and said that I could come any time to his kuti and "ask any questions." Clearly this was what most people did who visited him, and I was supposed to toe the same line. However, I was not obliged to communicate with him on his terms, and still felt quite a strong impulse to see him again. I decided to ply him with some questions about the Vinaya. I soon discovered that his memory was faulty, his logic shaky and his penetration minimal, though I did not take him to task on anything. My strategy paid off. After a while he asked me for my opinion on a point concerning the *pārājika*[45] of a bhikkhu who had been on the scene when an execution was taking place, and had asked the executioner to sever the prisoner's head with one blow. Slightly horrified at Hitesi's choice of subject, I nevertheless tried to solve his difficulty. It soon became obvious what it was. He was trying to understand the Vinaya in purely legalistic and logical terms, which is quite impossible, or at least not possible in many cases. I read the passage he was worried about back to him out loud, and explained that it could be understood in the light of the apparent non-emergence of compassion, which was why the Buddha had been obliged to make a pronouncement concerning this particular monk. Hitesi was contemptuous. "Compassion", he said, "the Vinaya has got nothing to do with compassion."

But I had given him something to think about. And the next time I saw Hitesi, his attitude towards me had changed. He began to ask me about what I was doing in Sri Lanka, and I told him I was teaching meditation. This started him off on another tirade - this time against egoistic teachers, and how anybody who presumed to teach who wasn't an Arahant would go to hell. But this was all so theoretical, I thought. Soon Hitesi came round to the question of Stream Entry, and his words became very pointed indeed. So I thought to myself, 'Alright, let's suggest I'm a Stream Entrant, and see what comes of it'. So in a very roundabout way I began to do just this. Hitesi tried to come back at me, but I'd been fairly circumspect in what I said, and there wasn't much he could take exception to. His sails began to flap. Once again a rather more positive element began to emerge in our communication, and the beginnings of respect began to arise between us. I had a couple more meetings with him on subsequent days, and each time our communication became more positive. I began to see that Hitesi had a very gentle side, and he began to see that I wasn't an ignoramus. We had begun to 'spark each other off', parting company both feeling grateful for our meeting.

My second attempt at communication was with Sobhana, the young sramanera who was so objectionable about seats, and apparently so anxious to prove his superiority. We met in the library, in the course of my study in connection with my writing. He came and sat directly opposite me, very obviously wanting to speak, so I put down the passage on *viriya*[46] that I was studying both in Bachelor's and Matics' translations of the Bodhicharya-avatara. I reasoned that if I opened up to him, he might begin to behave in a more gentlemanly fashion towards me. When he began to ask me about the FWBO, so I told him as much as I felt I could about our *tri-yana*[47] approach, about Bhante, about our lifestyles, our co-operatives etc., and a really pleasant flow of energy got going between us. Then Sobhana asked me if we worked with bhikkhus. I said that we hadn't had many bhikkhus develop an active interest in our Movement so far, but that there had been a few who had involved themselves for shorter or longer periods. After we had been in communication for about two hours, Sobhana's attention started to flag, so I thought it wise to bring our talk to an end. Packing up my books and paper, I said that I was going to my kuti as I wanted to do a bit more meditation.

Next morning, after meditation and breakfast, I visited the library again, and found Sobhana already seated there reading a booklet. I selected the two translations of Shantideva[48] from the shelves, and sat down at a distance from him, to one side. I had just started reading when he started talking, quite rapidly, and I turned to see that he was staring at his book, whilst addressing his remarks to me. He was very agitated, and kept re-iterating that what I had told him yesterday was "terrible, terrible, you are going to bring something new to Sri Lanka, you have just come to criticize the bhikkhus, you are a very bad person, you want to involve me in your Movement." I said quite sharply, hold on, Sobhana, you're just reacting, calm down a bit." And he did. I went to sit in front of him, gently took away his booklet, and tried to get into more normal communication with him. But although I was very gentle, it was no good. He remained in a tight aura of fear and reactivity, so I thought it best to leave him. Saying that I was glad at least that he had let me know his feelings and thoughts, and that I had no intention of trying to 'capture' him, I went back to my studies.

I had one more encounter with Sobhana quite a bit later, when towards the end of my retreat I was waiting outside the dana-sala for lunch, and got into conversation with a man who had come to offer food. He had given me a very frank look as I approached, so after sitting near him I asked if he spoke English, and he said Yes. We then started a conversation, but Sobhana, who was lurking nearby, interrupted and said with a disdainful voice and a horrible little laugh which sent shivers up my spine, "Oh, sir, don't speak to that person over there, come over here." I don't think my anger had ever risen so fast. The man got up, and I followed him over to Sobhana and we just stood looking at each other for a few moments before, luckily, the lunch bell sounded, and we all had to sit down. My heart was beating wildly for the next ten minutes, but eventually I calmed down. I wasn't able to speak to Sobhana again, but I put him in the fourth stage of my *metta* practice.

The third person with whom I had more than passing contact was Samanera Jnanobhasa, who hailed from the North of England, and had spent his last few years in the U.K. in a cottage in Cornwall. He looked a very tough customer indeed, with broad shoulders, heavy labourer's hands and stained teeth, some of which were broken. Flickers of worry, or anger, passed constantly over his face, and he blinked rapidly and sniffed every few moments. My immediate impression was that he was ill, and I felt sorry for him. Our first vocal contact was also in the library - I don't now remember the details, but the upshot of it was that we went for a stroll together after he had been quite helpful in looking up a reference in the Pali. He was studying the Pāli language, and had attained some proficiency in it, incongruous though it seemed with such a rugged exterior. Jnanobhasa invited me to his kuti after our walk, and began to pour his heart out to me. It wasn't at all easy to take in, because Jnanobhasa really was ill: every few minutes he would belch, exhaling a miasma of stinking breath. The upshot of it was that he felt suicidal. His health was really bad, he said, and all he wanted most of the time was oblivion. And oblivion he clearly equated with Nirvana; he made no bones about that. At the same time, he seemed to have a genuine love of the Pali Canon, and buried deep underneath all the negativity, a good heart.

His negativity was directed towards the Theravada Sangha in general, as well as towards his companions on Island Hermitage. His critique was quite systematic. First of all, he said, there are 20,600 monks in Sri Lanka. Of these, only six hundred meditate. And of the six hundred, four hundred are in a state of *pārājika*, a serious breach of monastic discipline requiring confession, repentance and re-instatement in the monastic Order. Of the remaining two hundred, he said, there is not a person who is even a stream entrant. Several, he told me, are supposed to be, but so far as he could determine, there was nothing to any of these claims. Those who were not downright hypocrites were simply ignorant, and the real Buddhism was simply dead. Didn't I know that many of the city monks changed into ordinary clothes at night to visit brothels, night clubs and so on, and that many of them had to be treated for venereal disease? And then of course there were those who were merely politicians in disguise. No, Buddhism in

Sri Lanka was simply dead, and that was that. Ven. Piyaratana was an authoritarian twit and Sobhana was dangerously reactive and hate-ridden, in his opinion. Hitesi never spoke to anyone, and Ven. Jñānajyoti, the second seniormost monk, spent his time fanning himself and reading novels. Ven. Jñānamoli (not the man of the same name who is author of *The Life of the Buddha*), said Jñānobhasa, did try to follow the Vinaya, but he was *dosacharita*[49] and could not get out of it. Only Punnaji was alright, but he wasn't very bright and one could not have much of a conversation with him. So now, Jnanobasha said, he avoided everybody as far as possible and got on with his own studies. There were two things which interested him - 'the *sutta*'[50] (which he always referred to in the singular), and the writings of Ven. Jnanavira, a bhikkhu who had been based at Island Hermitage some years ago, and who had eventually committed suicide. From the writings of the latter, Jnanobhasa had come to the conclusion that he might have been a stream entrant. It seemed to me that Jnanobhasa was dangerously close to following the example of his literary hero. I had already discovered some of Ven. Jnanavira's writings there in the library, neatly typed, and I had spent a little time studying them. He seemed to me to have been an intelligent man, but I would want to have known a lot more about him before coming to any conclusions concerning his spiritual attainments. For instance, in one place, Jnanavira had made a curious confession: that he 'suffered from priapism'. The poor fellow evidently considered that he was falling into a state of sin every day simply because was, perhaps only temporarily, suffering from a well-known medical condition. Knowing Buddhism to be eminently sensible about the biological nature of human beings, and knowing that what the Vinaya prohibited was simply actions in pursuit of sensual gratification rather than spontaneous erections, I came to the conclusion that Ven. Jnanavira had been subject to confusion concerning what is considered immoral or unskilful in Buddhism, and was conflating with the Dharma certain Christian ideas about sin. If this had been the case, he would not therefore have been a stream entrant. But the question foremost in my mind was what to do about Jnanobhasa. He seemed to be nursing a psychosis. I decided just to spend some time with him, and to try to draw him away from his interest in or rather, obsession with 'oblivion.'

For the next week or so, I managed to remain in communication with Jnanobasha. We talked about our lives, and he began to mellow. His physical symptoms began to disappear, his twitches lessened in intensity, and he began to remark what a pleasant place the island was. I now began to talk very cautiously about the Friends, about Mahāyāna and so on, and though he professed not to be in the slightest interested, I think something sank in. I also talked quite a bit about the *dhyanas*[51], since he was actually practising meditation, and encouraged him to take careful note of the descriptions of them in 'the sutta' - i.e. the Pali. In this way I hoped that he might begin to discover the occurrence of the dhyanas in his own experience, and to develop them. I suspected that there was a lot of resistance in Jnanobhasha to what I was saying due to pride, but I think that in spite of that, it had its effect. At this point I began to feel that it would be wise to withdraw and leave him to his own reflections, and this is what I did. I hope he is on the road to recovery, and I shall try to visit him occasionally.

I discovered a little more, in the course of my visits to Jnanobhasha and Hitesi, and later on to Jñānajyoti, about the island on which Hermitage was situated. It consists of two pieces of land joined by a narrow strip just wide enough for a pathway, and one can walk from one end to the other quite comfortably in about half an hour. Coconut palms and a great variety of other trees, deciduous and palmiferous grow in profusion everywhere, and there are clumps of bamboo to delight the eye in places - though these seem to have been rather carelessly cropped for their useful hollow stems, which is a pity. Then there are bushes of hibiscus, with their large, deep pink blossoms with prominent stigma terminating in five little pink pads to catch the pollen; there are also bushes of little white flowers in profusion. Dozens of blossoms of an extraordinarily sweet fragrance fall from each bush every day, and I would gather some every morning for my shrine. In many places grew a tall bush which bore gorgeous deep-red chrysanthemum-like blossoms which would last for just one day, and there were smaller bushes producing, variously, little white, yellow and violet bell-shaped blossoms, rather like a large snap-dragon. In an area where a lot of these flowers grew, one of the larger buildings was situated. This was a shrine room in which there was a human skeleton used for the *asubha bhavana*[52] contemplation. I went inside quite often, because the atmosphere was particularly peaceful, and meditated. I would always feel invigorated afterwards.

Mention of the *asubha bhavana* reminds me of the Hermitage Library. It bears the clear imprint of Ven. Nyanatiloka, the German bhikkhu who was instrumental in founding the 'Hermitage' about seventy-five years ago. A strikingly handsome man, his photo stands above the architrave to the entrance door of the Library, and over to one side there is another framed photo of Venerable Nyanamoli, the British bhikkhu, whose *Life of the Buddha* according to the Pali Canon, compiled and translated from the Pali, is well known and recommended by Sangharakshita.

Venerable Nyanaponika, whom I had met not so long ago in Forest Hermitage near Kandy, was of course also here at one time, being Ven. Nyanatiloka's disciple. There have been other European and Sri Lankan bhikkhus here, but none have left their mark so clearly as these. There is a good collection of Pali-English dictionaries and concordances, complete sets of the Tipitaka in Old Sinhala script (i.e. the script with which the Teaching was set down in the original Ola Leaves or Palm-leaf manuscripts), and a very limited collection of Roman-script volumes and English translations. Then there was also quite an extensive section of books in English purveying South-East Asian Buddhism, often prefaced by a picture of an astonishingly sour-looking bhikkhu or "priest", which would put anyone off the study of Buddhism unless they were very determined and perceptive. There is a Mahāyāna section too, many of the books being ones recently published by practitioners in the Tibetan tradition, and there is a section on Zen. I did not however discover a copy of *The White Lotus Sutra*, sad to say, or of the *Avatamsaka*, or *The Sutra of Golden Light*, or *The Life and Liberation of Padmasambhava*, or *The Hundred Thousand Songs of Milarepa* in its complete edition - there is however, a small, rather 'sanitised' collection of Milarepa's 'Songs' in the Buddhist Publication Society series. Many other omissions might be mentioned, but I have probably made my point. Ven. Nyanatiloka was evidently interested in Art, at least religious art, because there is a delightful collection of old books on Buddhist images and Zen art, many of them bearing his signature on the fly-leaf. I also spotted a book by Lama Govinda on Art, which contained some of his own illustrations, and signed by him as a gift to his Preceptor Ven. Nyanatiloka. Then there are extensive sections on Yoga, Hinduism, 'alternative' religions, and many books in German on various aspects of Buddhism. It was altogether a very interesting library, almost as much for its omissions as for what it contained.

There were two more objects, or sets of objects, in the library which perhaps should not pass without comment. One was a *bhava-chakra*[53] painted, judging by the style of the painting and the script, by a Thai bhikkhu, or perhaps a student of Thai Buddhism. Apart from being crudely rendered, it was simply incorrect. Instead of the twelve *nidanas* or links of the doctrine of Conditioned Co-production with which Western Buddhists are familiar, there were twelve non-canonical categories each portraying unrelieved human suffering, and not even significantly connected. I pointed this out to Piyaratana one day, and although he was evidently familiar with the canonical nidanas - he enumerated them, presumably to impress me with his knowledge - he said "It was given by a dayaka, so what can I do?" However, it seemed me that he was unwilling to uphold the Dhamma in the sense of propagating Right View and discouraging Wrong View. The other objects of note were two small photographic albums placed on the South East Asian section shelves and labelled '*asubha bhavana*'. Expecting to see pictures of dead and decaying bodies, I sat down calmly and opened one of the albums, thinking of making my own contemplation of these less pleasant aspects of normal human existence more thoroughgoing. The contents were however horrifying. They were pictures of bodies or parts of bodies, sure enough, and they were obviously dead, but they were photographs in vivid colour of smashed, tortured and horribly mutilated bodies. This was a portrayal of violence of the most brutal and inhuman kind, not the *asubha* meditation at all. Contemplation of simple human impermanence in its unadorned form is considered unsuitable for beginners in meditation and is supposed to be taken up only when metta is firmly established. Images of extreme violence and brutality, on the other hand, are much more difficult to contemplate, tending to arouse as they do in the ordinary healthy human personality, feelings of fear, horror and pity, which are the powerful near enemies of imperturbability, wisdom and compassion. I put the pictures away quickly, wondering what sort of effect those photos had had on Jnanobasha's mind. It was enough to unhinge anyone without a very deep grounding in and practice of meditation, particularly of the fourth dhyana, which leads to unshakeable equanimity.

Why was it necessary to display as it were in public those photos of the remains of those unfortunate victims of criminal violence? Their lives and misfortunes had nothing to do with me or my quest for tranquillity of mind and Insight, or, presumably, with the lives of anyone else on the island.

Would anyone have been the less wise for not seeing them? I happened to notice also, in a recent edition of *The Middle Way*[54], an article by Venerable Sumano from Amaravati, concerning a visit to Thailand, in which he mentions having seen some large photographs of dead bodies, displayed in a Temple in which the Chief Priest is being kept alive by medical science, in a semi-vegetative state, by his well-meaning followers. I began to wonder whether they were the same kind of pseudo-*asubha bhavana* photos that I had found in the Island Hermitage library, and to wonder about the state of the whole dizzying edifice of modern Theravada Buddhism. It seemed to me more and more that it was based on a pessimistic, horrifying view of life and its possibilities, and to have become as life-destroying as Christianity had become for Nietzsche. And to think that I had been contemplating bhikkhu ordination! It even occurred to me to wonder whether the horror photos I had just seen were used to suggest what happened to 'enemies of the Dhamma'. I had already seen painted pictures in several important Sinhalese Temples which showed the gory fate of those who disobeyed the supposed injunctions of the Dhamma. I could no longer say with confidence that it was impossible that an attitude condoning extreme punishment and retribution could be taken by Theravadin monks. So by half way through my 'solitary retreat', I felt that I had, at least in imagination, and, it must be confessed, perhaps an excess of it, descended into the very depths of hell.

The only way out was up. I did very little more writing from this point on, quite a lot more meditation, and some hatha yoga. Bit by bit, things began to clear, both metaphorically and literally. I began to feel healthy and happy and the weather became bright and clear, and strangely still and cool, whereas before it had been cloudy and muggy, fitfully breezy and stiflingly hot. It was as if the Holy Ghost had descended upon everything, and I felt that my visit to Island Hermitage had been worthwhile after all. The island seemed truly paradisiacal for a few days: plants and flowers all seemed to be even more beautiful and more fully in blossom than usual, little blue humming birds appeared, sipping nectar from the brightly blushing hibiscus, the usually murky water around the island became clear, the cats curled up with one another in blissful contentment, and even the ants seemed to be aware of something beyond their usual hum-drum existence. I began to read *The Zen Master Hakuin*, and to feel deeply inspired by him. I felt that the world had been subtly perfumed by the Enlightened mind. .

Returning to 'Samma Ajiva' was a very pleasant experience. Everyone greeted me very warmly, and everything was bathed in a soft golden glow. I felt as if I had landed in a *mandarava*[55]. Next morning, there were ten people sitting with me in our meditation room. A bit of spiritual community at last! I felt immediately as if a space had opened up inside and around me, and that I could 'let go' into it to produce a deeper sense of ease and relaxation. Also, I realize more clearly than ever before that faith is no abstract thing - faith must flesh out into a person's experience as bliss and emptiness.

By faith the flood is crossed
By diligence the sea
By vigour ill is passed
By wisdom cleansed is he.

For some reason or other I found these words from Buddhaghosha's *Milindapanha* very pleasing.

NOTES

37   *kuti*: a small house, often no more than a hut, intended for solitary occupation by someone engaged in spiritual discipline: a hermitage.

38   *dana-sala*: *Dana* means simply: giving, and *sala*, room. The *dana-sala* however is the room or reserved space in the Temple where the bhikkhus eat the ceremonially-offered food and accept the gift of certain requisites from their lay supporters.

39   *sadakshari*: an esoteric form of Avalokiteshvara, the 'archetypal' Bodhisattva of Compassion in male form.

40   *bhumi-sparsa* : lit: 'earth-touching': the gesture that tradition holds the Buddha to have made when challenged by Mara concerning his right to occupy the Vajrāsana, the 'seat of Enlightenment.' The Buddha gently taps the earth with his finger-tip, thus 'calling the earth to witness' - to bear witness to the fact of his austerities throughout countless lives.

41   *bodhyangas* [Pali: *bojjangas*] : Lit: 'limbs of Enlightenment' - steps or stages in the gaining of Enlightenment, or perfected aspects of Enlightenment already established. They are: *sati* or mindfulness, *dhamma-vichaya* or the discrimination of skilful (as contrasted with unskilful) mental states, *viriya* or energy in pursuit of the skilful, *priti* or bodily bliss, *pasaddhi* or calming-down of the psycho-physical energies, *sukkha* or purely mental happiness, *samadhi*, an almost untranslatable term meaning both healthy one-pointedness of mind and a state of higher consciousness involving the harmonious integration of various highly positive psychic factors, and *upeksha* - a state of profound inner tranquillity and imperturbability which is the mundane reflection of the attainment of spiritual axiality.

42   WBO : The Western Buddhist Order. The purely spiritual body founded by Sangharakshita in 1968. Now known as the Triratna Buddhist Order. Its Members are fully-ordained Buddhists known as Dharmacharis (masc.) and Dharmacharinis (fem.). Each has undergone a more or less lengthy process of initiation lasting (usually) between three and ten years after the request for ordination has been made. That period culminates with Private and Public Ordination into the Sangha, the community of spiritually committed individuals. Ordination is not the conferring of a certificate of spiritual attainment; it is a public commitment of body, speech and mind to the service of the Three Jewels.

43   *pindapata* : begging-round. The bhikkhu takes his begging-bowl and walks, no later than noon, with gaze downcast from door to door until he has sufficient for his needs, then goes to a quiet place and eats the contents.

44   *vinaya* : code of monastic discipline; the second collection of the 'Three Baskets' (see note 13) of the Pali: *sutta*, *vinaya* and *abhidhamma*. The *vinaya*, as well as informing us of the strictures which the Buddha was obliged to impose upon his disciples, and to change and modify as occasion demanded, gives us a fascinating picture of the conditions in contemporary society.

45   *parajika* : a 'grave offence' involving dismissal from the Bhikkhu Sangha. There are four such offences, committing which a bhikkhu is said to have gone

completely against the purpose of becoming a bhikkhu. In the parlance of Vinaya, the *parajika apatti* falls upon him; he automatically loses the status of a bhikkhu; he is no longer recognized as a member of the community of bhikkhus and is not permitted to become a bhikkhu again. He has either to go back to the household life as a layman or revert back to the status of a samanera, a novice.

46 *viriya* : energy in pursuit of the Good; the third of the seven *bojjhangas* [Pali] *bodhyangas* [Skt.] (see note 41).

47 *tri-yāna* : an approach to the understanding of Buddhism which regards all traditions tracing their lineage and methods back to the human historical Buddha as more or less comprehensive manifestations of His Teaching, and which regards the three great literary traditions of the Hīnayāna, Mahāyāna and Vajrayāna as successively higher teachings or revelations of the Buddha's original realization.

48 (Acharya - 'teacher') Shantideva : known chiefly as the author of the famous prose-poem the *Bodhicharyavatara,* Shantideva studied at the great Buddhist University of Nalanda, and proved his mastery of the Doctrine when one day he was asked to lecture to a big assembly and astounded everyone with his erudition, poetry, wisdom, and yogic powers. Tradition holds that during his delivery of the last section of his discourse, he rose into the air, from where he delivered the remaining stanzas before vanishing.

49 *dosacharita*: having a mind inclined to anger.

50 *sutta* : lit., a 'thread' - a thread of discourse, especially as recorded in the Pali, and usually beginning with the words *evam me sutam*: thus have I heard. Popularly thought to mean the *ipsissima verba* of the Buddha, though this cannot be proved, and in some cases is obviously not so. See: *The Eternal Legacy*, section 1, Sangharakshita, Tharpa, 1985. The "I" of "Thus have I heard" is traditionally held to be Ananda, the Buddha's cousin and spiritual companion for twenty-five years, and who was endowed with a superb memory. The recollection of his Master's words were very useful to the Order after the passing away of the Buddha.

51 *dhyana, dhyanas:* the superconscious mental states, four 'lower' and four 'higher'. Important for the development of positive emotion and equanimity and leading to knowledge and vision of the way things, in truth, really are.

52 *asubha bhavana*: *subha* means beautiful, *bhavana*, meditation; the negation of the first term joined with the second therefore means the contemplation, investigation, unfolding or penetration of the nature of the unlovely, the ugly, the distasteful. The ancient bhikkhus would undertake the contemplation of the ten stages of decomposition of a corpse as an antidote to intense craving. One reflects upon the less pleasing, the less beautiful aspects of reality, in order to counteract one's own deep-seated tendency towards clinging to objects of sensuous desire. This type of meditation is to be undertaken only when one is in a positive state of mind, a state of mind in which there is a healthy appreciation of one's own positive qualities, i.e. when self-metta is present. Performed at such times this set of contemplations has a positive, liberating and exhilarating effect on the mind.

53 *bhava-chakra*: lit. 'the Wheel of Becoming' - a picture consisting of four concentric circles depicting, in the centre, a snake, a cock and a pig, symbolising the three basic negative emotions of greed, hatred and delusion found in one's unregenerate nature. In the right-hand, black half of the second circle, human beings are shown linked together, descending, miserable expressions on their faces, into hell, whilst in the left-hand, white section of the circle they rise with happy faces to

heaven. This circle, divided into a black segment and a white segment symbolises conventional, worldly morality. The third circle depicts the six realms of sentient existence: the gods or god-like realm; the titans or asuras fighting for a wish-fulfilling tree, the animals, the hell-beings, the hungry ghosts, and ordinary human beings. A fourth, outermost circle depicts a chain of twelve pictures illustrating certain crucial turning-points which condition worldly existence, existence governed by greed, hatred and the confused state of deludedness in which they move.

54 *The Middle Way*: The Journal of the Buddhist Society, London.

55 *mandarava*: a heavenly flower: an enormous, diaphanous flower several yards in circumference, often of golden colour.

* * * * *

8   The Shoe Factory bhikkhu and the Hundred Rupee Note

A bhikkhu whose chief patrons are the managers and employees of a shoe factory invites me to address his congregation and I discover that he considers an anagarika to be the same thing as a bhikkhu. Anagarika Dharmapala Day is celebrated on a full moon day, and I visit a number of places giving Dharma talks. Beginning a retreat at Nilambe, in the hills above Kandy, I am confronted with the intransigence of several of the would-be participants, and of Henry van Zeist, the cross-dressing ex-Catholic priest resident there. I reflect upon Rajneesh (later known as Osho) and Krishnamurti, and find them wanting in comparison with Dr. Ambedkar. A young retreatant tries to tell me how to conduct the retreat. We return later to Nilambe once more, and discover that due to the endemic violence, all the tourists have vanished. I criticize the doctrine of "It's all one" which I hear attributed to Ven. Sumedho of Amaravati in the UK, and which I encounter also at a talk which I give at Ruhunu University.

SINCE LEAVING ISLAND HERMITAGE, a month has gone by, and the peacefulness of an Order weekend once more pervades the atmosphere even here. The sky is a brilliant, luminous blue backdrop to the palm trees. A great unseen convocation of birds is twittering away happily, and in the distance, there is the sound of waves on the pale golden sand. The last thirty days have been less eventful than usual. The first thing that my diary records is a talk at the local teachers' training college. I had arranged to speak on 'Buddhism in the West', and was well into the preparation of this when four young men turned up. They told me that road works were going on outside their college. For this reason, they said, they wanted me to postpone my talk. I sensed an element of reactivity in their manner, and did not feel entirely satisfied with this explanation. I knew that the heat rendered long sustained periods of roadwork in Lanka difficult. So it was likely that things would be quiet in a few hours' time. However, I felt there was no point in arguing. I asked them for another date, and they suggested that I visit them in two or three weeks' time to make a fresh appointment.

The next event of which I have a record was a talk I gave on 14th September at YMBA Galle, when I spoke about Anagarika Dharmapala. The arrangements had been made by Mr. Vijayasinghe, an old gentleman who is honorary secretary of the YMBA. He had suffered a semi-paralysing stroke shortly before I arrived in Sri Lanka. For some reason or other, he took a liking to me, and told me quite a lot about himself. He told me, for instance, that he does not wish to be reborn. Whether he wants to go to heaven, or gain Full and Perfect Enlightenment, he did not make clear, but I suspect he fancies the former. Mr. Vijayasinghe's publicity had however succeeded in attracting about twenty-five elderly citizens. But as soon as I began to speak, it was plain to me that the audience was unable to take in very much of what I was saying. It was as if I was addressing wooden statues, or as if I had more energy and inspiration than they could possibly absorb. I have felt deeply inspired by Anagarika Dharmapala ever since I read *Flame in Darkness* - Sangharakshita's biography of him. But now, for the first time, I felt frustrated at being apparently unable to communicate that inspiration and enthusiasm. I did not feel that communication was possible on this occasion. My audience was simply not open to me.

A day later, I had several opportunities of delivering substantially the same talk. This time it was given to much larger audiences, at temples celebrating Poya or full moon day. Siri and I arrived in style at the first one, having been collected in a brand new shiny Japanese car. It belonged, presumably, to the owner of the local shoe factory who was the chief supporter of the Temple. The High Priest was a chubby and amiable-looking man of about forty-five. His brilliant orange robes draped over a startlingly hairy shoulder, he greeted us and offered me a seat covered with a white cloth. Such a seat is customarily offered only to bhikkhus. Now Siri is very sensitive indeed to any possibility of misunderstanding concerning ecclesiastical status. So concerned was he on this occasion that, as I sat down gratefully in the proffered chair, I overheard him explaining to the High Priest that I was not a bhikkhu, but 'only' an Anagarika. The implication of this, presumably, was that I should not have taken the seat offered. The High Priest however said: "What do you mean? An Anagarika is the same thing as a Bhikkhu." Siri seemed nonplussed by this, and I smiled to myself. It was a very different view from that which I had encountered at Island Hermitage recently. There the Anagarika was very definitely viewed as inferior to the bhikkhus, and was obliged to sit with the 'laymen'. I had thought at first that this treatment would be harmless enough, perhaps even a salutary test of egolessness. But stretched over one whole month, the deliberate and sustained humiliation proved more disturbing than I could easily cope with. The opinion propounded by the Shoe Factory Temple priest was however equally a view, and I refused to allow myself to become elated because of it. I started my talk by explaining, with the help of my seamless robe, the difference between a Bhikkhu and an Anagarika, and stressed that both 'priests' and 'laity' could all equally Go for Refuge. This went down well, and the main body of my talk about Anagarika Dharmapala went down well too, much to my delight. At the end of it, the High Priest offered me a One Hundred Rupee note, and I hesitated a moment before accepting it. Siri seemed suddenly embarrassed, and tried to refuse the offering on my behalf. But the note was pressed firmly into my palm. Attempting to alleviate Siri's distress, I agreed to take half the amount, and everyone was happy. Incidentally, I am opening an account for the support of those wishing to go on retreat with us who are unable to pay their own expenses. This will provide a suitable purse for such donations.

Our second appointment that Poya Day was with a group of young people at a temple in Balapitya. This is the village where Bhikkhu

Dhammajyoti, whom I think of, perhaps rather wistfully, as Dharmachari Bhikkhu Dhammajyoti, has converted an old temple into a hostel for boys. We had been invited by an enthusiastic young man who had been impressed with one of our talks. On our arrival, Siri and I remarked on the liveliness of the participants. It was quite unlike the sleepy semi-stupor that we found all too often. I spoke on 'The Dhamma as Revolution', and felt that everything I said was heard, understood and appreciated. After the talk we gave meditation instruction, and this too, we felt, was appreciated and effective. It was all very gratifying, and Siri too remarked on how inspired he felt. We were invited to return and lead a one-day course, which we happily agreed to do. And as if to seal the success of our meeting, I was presented with a yellow umbrella.

Our next visit was to a group of middle-aged and elderly people in traditional white dress gathered submissively at another Temple. They were determined to practice meditation, so that is what we did, after I had given them a detailed introduction. I did not however ask them to meditate for very long as many of them looked uncomfortable. Most of them were sitting in both legs-at-one-side posture customary for Sri Lankan women. Although easy-looking, this posture twists the spine. But I have found it almost impossible to persuade those accustomed to it to try anything more comfortable and yogically potent. Here also we were asked to come again next month, and it must have been out of compassion that we agreed; it was hard work getting any other response out of this group.

Our last Poya Day assignment was at yet another village Temple. Here our talk had been well publicized and we were welcomed by a good-sized assembly of young, middle aged and even older people. We started by making offerings to the Bodhi Tree. Soon the beautiful and fragrant flowers and the glow of dozens of coconut-oil lamps were accompanied by the low murmur of chanting as we circumambulated the Tree. All this produced a delightful effect. The only other sound to be heard was the croaking of frogs. The effect of the chanting was further enhanced by the full moon sailing above the tall and leafy trees, projecting a great circle of light protecting the whole Temple. After the ritual, everyone sat down and I gave my Anagarika Dharmapala talk, this time in slightly abbreviated form. I put it across with a lot of enthusiasm and emphasis. The audience laughed at first because they are used to slow, solemn, and perhaps rather boring discourses. But after a while they put aside their amusement at the presumably exotic Anagarika, and seemed to enter into the spirit of what I was saying. So much so that I began to feel that Anagarika Dharmapala had re-awakened in the hearts of some of the listeners that evening. One point I made particularly strongly was that it was a mistake to identify Dharmapala with the current nationalist and anti-Tamil groups. Whether I was able to communicate to them the deep spiritual commitment and heroism of Dharmapala I do not know, but at least they seemed able to respond to him as the embodiment of an outstanding folk-hero.

The day after Poya Day a visit had been arranged to Matara, the one-time capital of the ancient Southern (Sinhalese) Kingdom of Rohana. A group of sixteen young men and women involved in the Youth Service had asked me to conduct a day course for them. This we held at a Pirivena or monastic college which, it appeared, had twenty or thirty bhikkhus at least, associated with it. They turned up to gawp at us from time to time.

The course went well; everyone's interest and enthusiasm remaining engaged throughout the day, even through the usually lethargic after-lunch period. We had a question and answer session, by popular request, though there weren't many questions forthcoming. So I started to ask them questions about Hīnayāna and Mahāyāna, but their lack of response to my questions suggested ignorance of these categories. At this point thirty or so bhikkhus gathered around to listen. This rather amused me and put me on my mettle, though again I was surprised by the passivity and ignorance of everyone, and had to do most of the talking myself. After this we had a session of meditation, and the bhikkhus stood about listening to my introduction. Then they began to wander off once they realized that we were going to do some actual meditation practice. Only one young bhikkhu, who, Siri told me, had been appointed an 'observer', participated. On questioning him afterwards, he professed himself interested in 'social work'. I watched him carefully during our conversation, and noticed that his eyes kept wandering over to a couple of the more attractive young women in our group, and I began to suspect that he was not in control of himself. In fact, at one point the young women in question began to comment to each other on his inordinate attention, and I noticed that he became flustered.

When the course came to an end, I was glad to discover that the bhikkhus wanted Siri and I to come and talk with them. Siri however was very obviously eager to be off, so I decided not to try to persuade him to stay longer. The goose that lays golden eggs should not be pressed too much to lay! And since without his skills as a translator I could do very little with the bhikkhus, who spoke little or no English, I decided to leave with him. We set off to catch our bus to Galle, and on the way, Siri with his typical thoughtfulness and kindness, handed out our left-over lunch packets to some undernourished-looking beggars sitting on the pavement.

Towards the end of September, Siri and I, accompanied by a young chap called Seneviratne, decided to visit the Nilambe meditation centre once again. Seneviratne had been working at 'Samma Ajiva' for a few weeks, and had impressed me by his friendly manner and efficiency at work. We had hoped at first to hold a 'meditation and co-operatives' retreat at Nilambe, but had not been able to generate much interest in that amongst our local friends. There is insufficient commitment as yet for anything more demanding than a 'Dharma holiday', it seems, and as such I decided to present it. Unfortunately again, the two or three Sri Lankans at 'Samma Ajiva' with whom I wanted to spend more time could not be spared at what Siri considered inadequate notice. In the circumstances, I hoped that the paucity of Sri Lankans would be offset by quite a few Europeans turning up, as they had on our first retreat at Nilambe. We had put out advertisements in various bookshops, and besides, I thought, there might be a number of people who had just 'drifted in' to Nilambe.

There were in fact seven Europeans there when we arrived, and that evening we had an informal get-together in the 'teachers' room'. This was a comfortable little room for the use of the current meditation leader. It contained a useful library, and was situated next door to the meditation hall. The little room was quickly filled, and I was happy to see so many new faces. However, as soon as I began to speak, I noticed that a number of them looked tense, neither did they relax as I continued to speak. I started to talk a bit about myself and about the Friends, and then invited them to introduce themselves. One by one they began, but there was little enthusiasm and a note of resentment and/or cynicism began to emerge. And when we came to a middle-aged woman who told us that she was of Australian parentage brought up in Spain, the resentment became overt. She launched into a loud-voiced, harsh and defiant tirade, saying that she did not regard me as her guru, and would not co-operate with me. Then she turned to everyone else, an ugly, triumphant grimace on her face, saying "Power!" Whether she was revelling in her own power or resenting my non-existent power was not clear, and I did not consider it wise to ask. I tried pouring oil on troubled waters by pointing out that in the Friends we prefer to speak and act in terms of *kalyāna mitratā*. In the kalyāna mitra relationship, I explained, the two people concerned did not mind who was the 'leader' or the 'dominant' person - it was of no concern to them. Their respective positions might be reversed from time to time, and there was no question of insisting that one person was more developed than the other. The main thing was that they were, first and foremost, friends. This explanation did not however serve to smooth the mood of reactivity that had set in. Four people then declared that they were leaving next morning. At this point I began to suspect that a reaction had been brewing before I had arrived, engineered, possibly by Henri van Zeyst. He was an eccentric transvestite priest who lived in the little house nearby with his pretty young home help and companion Chandra. The atmosphere now prevailing at Nilambe was in sharp contrast to the positivity I had experienced with Sri Lankans in the last few days, and I could not help reflecting that the principal characters in this little drama were all Europeans. I decided there was little I could do objectively, but subjectively, it was an opportunity to practise equanimity and 'leadership from behind.' I could enjoy myself, I reflected, even if nobody else wanted to.

Next day the four rebels departed, which I did not lament, whilst I did regard it as unfortunate that Siri felt it necessary to leave. His relatives had contacted him by means of a phone in a house some way down the hillside, and demanded his return to attend the funeral of an uncle. I pointed out the issues involved; the uncle, after all, was dead, and could not benefit from Siri's presence at the funeral, neither was Siri needed to make funeral arrangements. I reminded him gently that several times before, he had left retreats just after they had started. Perhaps, I said, he might consider whether his presence elsewhere was always as necessary as he assumed it was. But the purpose of committing oneself to a retreat from beginning to end - except in case of dire emergency - seemed to be difficult for him to understand. I added that the merit of remaining on retreat would be considerable. He on the other hand thought it obvious that the requests of relatives for his presence at a funeral would automatically take precedence over attendance at a retreat, and appeared disinclined to take my suggestion seriously. However, I did not press the point, wished him a safe journey, and encouraged him to return to Nilambe as soon as possible.

Thick cloud and torrential rain now began to descend upon the hills, obscuring the magnificent views over the surrounding countryside, and remained for nearly the whole of the next ten days. I found the coolness and misty effects a rather pleasing contrast to the previously hot weather, and adopted an observer-like attitude towards the remaining handful of people. They all seemed to want to continue to 'do their own thing', so there was no question of my taking up my more normal position as retreat leader. Quietly walking up and down in the meditation hall next morning after a 'double sit', I saw Henri van Zeyst approaching me with an air of determination. Henri (or Padma, as he likes to be known), is an 81 year old ex-Jesuit priest and ex-bhikkhu. As well as writing a number of booklets on Buddhism, he has worked as one of the assistant editors on the Buddhist Encyclopaedia (of Ceylon). He is more than six feet tall, has a slight stoop, and is blind in one eye, though you would not know unless he told you. His hair is shoulder length, grey-ginger in colour, and he has a slightly hoarse, piping, womanish voice. The first time I saw him I almost mistook him for a rather ugly old crone, dressed as he was in a full-length dress touching the ground, and with a variety of bangles jingling with the movement of his skinny arms. What alerted me to the possibility that I was looking at a transvestite (or cross-dresser) was that 'she' had a greater stillness and presence than I had seen in an old woman before.

I had discovered, in conversation with Henri on my previous visit, that he was an admirer of Krishnamurti. I also found that he had a very persuasive line of patter which would very soon lull your mind into submission if you were not careful. I had kept my cutting edge in conversation with him, however, taking him up immediately on a number of controversial points he made, of which there were quite a few. It was my refusal to be 'taken over', I suspected, that Henri (or Padma) had reacted to, and, harbouring resentment, had stirred up the other residents of Nilambe against me before my recent arrival. Be that as it may, Henri was now almost upon me, dressed in what might have been a revealing full-length blue dress, if there had been anything to reveal. He evidently meant to impress. Drawing himself up to his full height, he looked at me with his one good eye and said imperiously: "You have let us down. You said you would bring cooks. You said you would be here at 5 o'clock. We did not know what to do. Our cooks are upset, Chandra's menstruation was late, everyone was worried." "Well", I said, "we did say we would cook for ourselves, but I certainly didn't say I would arrive here by five o'clock. Our chief cook has unfortunately had to leave for a funeral, and as for Chandra's menstruation, I don't know what I could conceivably have had to do with that." "You have let us down", Henri repeated, presumably, for emphasis. It was evidently useless to argue, and I contented myself by saying, quite mildly, "I haven't let you down, but I'm sorry Chandra has had trouble with her menstruation." To which Henri replied testily "There is no reason, you have no business to feel sorry for Chandra." He became quiet at this point, and perhaps surprised that I did not say anything else, he flashed a dagger at me with his one eye, and walked, or rather, swept off.

The morning after our arrival, incidentally, proper arrangements had been made for cooking by two of 'our' people, with help from the resident community. Henri appeared either to have ignored this, or to be ignorant of the fact. He again accosted me some minutes later in the kitchen, where we usually took breakfast, and said scathingly: "Where is your cook? You said you would cook for us. Do the cooking yourself. And you're meddling with our programme again." This time I said nothing at all, although I could have. We had already dealt with the question of cooks, and I had previously obtained the consent of the chief teacher and director of the Centre, Godwin Samararatne, to change the programme as I wished. I decided to avoid Henri as far as possible, until he became less reactive, and we did not speak to each other for the remainder of the ten days.

Breakfast arrived without fuss, and as the day went by, everyone's reactivity seemed to lessen. Three or four people began to appear more or less regularly in the meditation hall - regularly, that is, according to the programme I had pinned up, and was myself following, of course. Siri returned, and began to produce some tasty meals. To my surprise, however, even he did not take my programme seriously at first, although he is quite familiar with our procedures on retreat. I was evidently amongst a group of individualists, and it was quite amusing in some ways to watch their behaviour. For instance, I would walk in to start a meditation session with three or four people, make the usual threefold salutation to the altar, and Seneviratne would walk out. Or I might be doing some dharma study with two people in the teachers' room, and a third person would walk in, start a completely independent conversation with my two interlocutors, suddenly stop, looking slightly startled, then go. Almost no thread or continuity of awareness seemed to be established in anyone (apart from myself, of course). I began to regard the other people playfully, though not unkindly, as bits of a jigsaw puzzle, and tried to fit them together. Sometimes I was successful, sometimes not. In any case, I got on with my own meditation practice.

At first there was quite a lot of pain in the bones, especially the joints and thigh-bone of my right leg, which flashed on my inner consciousness as pure white and edged with bright red flames. But after a while it began to 'cool', in fact my whole body began to cool, and felt as if it was pervaded by air and space. I began to feel free, light, comfortable and well-established in mindfulness. My feelings of *metta* grew and seemed to transfer themselves spontaneously to the others. A young Ethiopian named Joseph turned up unexpectedly on the retreat, and after a few moments of shyness, we seemed to be like old friends, and had some really good talks. Having become estranged from the Ethiopian government, Joseph was not keen to return to his motherland. It did not appear that he had been involved in anything terribly unethical, but clearly he was disturbed and fearful at the possible vengeance that he might meet on his return. He seemed to be a good fellow, and though I did not urge him to return to his native land, it would perhaps be a pity from the point of view of the spread of the Dharma if he did not. Joseph seemed to have a quick grasp of essential matters, and a warm heart.

As the retreat proceeded, I seemed to have more and more time on my hands, and began to explore the library. I picked up a book called *The Winds of Sinhala*[56], a historical novel which purveyed a view of Sinhalese nationalism and of the Dharma which the author had tried to present as a sort of distorted, primitive Christianity. I thought that it was extremely unfortunate that what appeared to be a best-seller would be influencing so many people to regard Buddhism in this way. Christianity, with its doctrine of atonement through the sacrifice of the flesh and blood of Christ, was by far the more primitive of the two religio-philosophical systems. Well, it would hardly be possible to regard Christianity as being based upon a philosophy at all, though Bishop Berkeley may be said to have come nearest to providing one.

There were recordings of several popular meditation teachers in the tape library, and I selected one of Rajneesh and one of Krishnamurti to listen to. I was struck by the smallness of Rajneesh's voice this time (I had heard recordings of him before); he sounded very clever, very plausible. But it was as if he was talking to himself. His softly sibilant, trailing consonants reminded me of the character of Gollum, in Tolkien's book *The Lord of the Rings*[57]. Gollum is a strange, disgusting little creature living at the commencement of Tolkien's epic story in a cave, where he lives jealously guarding the ring of power. One could take him as a sort of archetype of the ego, though this was not necessarily Tolkien's intention. Krishnamurti's voice I had not heard before, though I had in my teens read some of his writing with curiosity and mild interest. His voice, however, was not at all what I had expected. It rang with a thirst for power and authority, and, I thought, with more than a hint of pain and bitterness. But these voices paled, I thought, beside that of Dr. Ambedkar, the great Indian Buddhist leader, a recording of whom I had first heard in Sarnath. Dr. Ambedkar was speaking, shortly before his death, to an audience in Kathmandu, on Marxism. And I was immediately attracted and impressed by the measured and mellow quality of his voice, which was without any affectation or pretence. It possessed power of quite a different kind from the other guru-figures to whom I had listened. What Dr. Ambedkar communicated more than anything else in his Kathmandu talk was kindness, which is the real spiritual power, the power of 'heart' and effective reasoning combined.

Seneviratne asked to talk to me as the end of the retreat approached. We arranged a mutually convenient time, and went for a walk along the pleasantly wooded hillside. He seemed to want to impress me, saying that he had sat at the feet of many teachers, and was an admirer of Krishnamurti (who, incidentally, has quite a large following in Sri Lanka). He had studied me very carefully, he said, and wanted to give me some advice. The gist of it was that I should practise simple awareness, and not try to teach anything. However, if I did want to say anything, I should consider it very carefully beforehand. I did not need this gratuitous advice, which in any case I was already following, but listened politely, trying to understand Seneviratne. His dominant emotional state seemed to be one of anxiety, and I recollected that he often belched while meditating. He spoke of friendship, but seemed to be sad and lonely. He went on to say that he respected me, and would like to meet Sangharakshita. But, he said, you should not teach what Sangharakshita teaches, you should teach from your own experience. So far as it went, that was good advice, I thought.

Siri and Seneviratne departed on the afternoon of the penultimate day, taking Joseph and another young man, Kirthisri, with them. I pointed out once again Siri's restlessness and lack of commitment, and suggested that before our next retreat, he makes a firm resolution to attend the whole of it. He left, apparently accepting what I said.

My last afternoon and evening at Nilambe looked like being almost solitary. I would probably not see Henri and Chandra, who kept themselves mostly to themselves in their little bungalow. And Joanna, a young New Zealand woman, would probably keep her distance, if previous experience was anything to go by. At this point I began to feel disinclined to visit Nilambe again, delightful though it could be. It seemed to have become a place where the forces of reactivity were particularly strong. Siri had expressed the opinion that if we had taken a coach load of friends, everything would have gone smoothly. Perhaps he was right, and what is needed is a sort of family tea-party approach at first here. Hardly had Siri gone, however, than three Germans turned up, two women and a man, so I made them some tea, spent a pleasant hour or two getting to know them, and taught them the mindfulness of breathing and the *metta bhavana*. The following morning I left as planned, the only person to have attended the whole of the retreat. By the evening I was back in the Hotel at Unawatuna, feeling pleasantly tired after the six hour bus journey.

Things at the guest house are proceeding in desultory fashion at present. European visitors are few and far between, and the village has almost literally gone to sleep with the disappearance of the tourist trade due to the ethnic violence. Everyone is really feeling the pinch, and were it not for an abundance of cheap vegetables, fish for the catching, and a pleasant and sunny climate with lots of shady trees, things would be quite desperate. As it is, Siri is getting very restless, and has a number of plans up his sleeve for moving. He is not happy unless he is making money. His non-working partners, who put up slightly less than half the capital for the hotel/guest house, have been making demands. But of course, with no tourists, there is no money forthcoming. Siri tells me that he already gives them Bank Rate as return on their capital. This stands at present at 20%, so they have no cause for complaint. Nevertheless, one of the partners visits periodically to ask for more, and sometimes Siri feels like calling for the police. The atmosphere that develops during his visits is quite unpleasant. The co-owners, moreover, are neither willing to buy Siri out, nor to sell their own shares at a reasonable price, so it is stalemate.

Siri has considered putting the hotel under the management of his wife and departing for Japan, where a wealthy friend has invited him to set up and manage a restaurant. He has quite a way with food, and could I think make a success of it. However, Siri's departure would leave me without my right hand, as it were, and him without a companion for dharma practice. I am therefore not keen on the proposal, and prefer to think in terms of us opening a restaurant in Colombo. This might however require quite a bit of money to set up. Anyhow, for the next ten weeks we are conducting meditation courses in three nearby towns, so we have a bit of time to consider or reconsider things.

During the last month I have been catching up on three recently-arrived Shabdas - quite a volume of words to read. I especially enjoyed Suvajra's series of reports, and recalled my own association with Sasanarashmi and Gurudhammo on my pilgrimage to Sarnath in 1983. Being extremely busy in Pune immediately afterwards, I had not written about that experience for Shabda. On my arrival at what was then the Thai Rest House in Sarnath, Ven. Sasanarashmi was acting as host to fifty Buddhists from Meerut. Apparently at a loss as to what to do with them, he had invited me to give them a Dhamma talk that evening. Afterwards he had professed himself much pleased with my talk, and proceeded to tell me his life story - which lasted several hours and appeared to be substantially the same as what he had recounted to Suvajra. As for young Gurudhammo, the Maharashtrian bhikkhu, he had at that time insisted on coming with me, John Bloss and Dharmacharini Anjali, my then companions, all the way to Darjeeling via Bodh Gaya, despite our marked lack of enthusiasm for his company.

I also noted in Shabda, Dharmadhara's report of the events at Amaravati, which reminded me of something Samanera Jnanobhasha said to me at Island Hermitage last month concerning Bhikkhu Sumedho. He said that the head of the Theravada monastic set-up in the U.K. had visited Island Hermitage as part of his 'goodwill visit' to Sri Lanka at the invitation of the President. And during that visit, Jnanobasha told me, he had enquired of Sumedho concerning the relationship of Christianity to Buddhism. He reported Sumedho as saying that "It's all one", at which point, apparently, Jnanobasha had become disgusted and broken off communication with him. I do not know how much weight to give this, but if true, it is rather shocking, and I really wonder what purpose is served by holding 'Joint events' with Amaravati unless such basic points are hammered out.

I am beginning to be more outspoken about Christianity and Hinduism here in my talks, and have already been accused of being 'Un-Buddhistic' - this after a talk to a group of students at Ruhunu University. I think I have detected signs, even during my ten months here, of the 'All's one' doctrine gaining ground - or at least, raising its voice more obstreperously. If the distinctive teaching of Buddhism is not put across, what hope for the survival of the Dharma, what hope for the (True) Individual?

A highlight this month for me was receiving a letter from Bhante. Bhante's letters are just like gold leaf. I wish I was able to impart something of his clarity, warmth and humanity in my communication with others.

NOTES

56 *Winds of Sinhala*: Colin de Silva, Doubleday, 1982
57 *The Lord of the Rings*: J R R Tolkien, George Allen & Unwin, 1955

* * * * *

9   Outreach Courses in Matara and Balapitya

The noises of the world begin to get me down, and I am disappointed by Siri's plans for his departure from Sri Lanka. The enthusiasm of a group of retreatants gives a boost to my enthusiasm for dharma work here. At the end of another successful retreat at a Temple, I begin to feel that I really must have a proper FWBO/TBMSG[58] Centre from which to work.

IT IS THREE-THIRTY LOCAL TIME, when the Order throughout the world is gathering in various places to meditate and report-in. The "thunder of rain on leaves" has temporarily ceased and the great mass of dense green foliage surrounding the South Ceylon guest house looks fresh and glistening. The little Sri Lankan boy adopted by an Australian couple visiting the Hotel has just run off and left me in solitude, and I have an hour or so before I leave for my next assignment. In this case it is a fund-raising visit to a meeting of local pensioners.

This month has been marked chiefly by two events. First, we started three ten-week meditation courses in the towns of Galle, Matara and Imaduwa. And then we set up the association announced on our new letterhead - 'Samma Ajiva Sahayaka Bhavana Samithya'. The name means something like 'The association of meditating helpers of Perfect Livelihood', or, alternatively 'The helpers of the association of meditating perfect livelihood-ers'. It was conceived as a semi-official 'purse' for the receipt of funds for people wishing to go, and able to benefit by going, on retreat. Many of our friends here lead a hand-to-mouth existence and therefore need support if they are to go on retreat even for a few days. In Friends' terms the association is an irregular one. For example, I am named as President, a mitra as Vice-president, and friends who are unfamiliar with our ideals as members. For these reasons I have refrained from inviting Bhante to take his proper place as yet. Some piloting through the uncertain waters of Lankan custom will be needed before I feel confident enough to do that. However, I am confident that it will be possible to steer this 'pilot fish' in the right direction. With a bit of luck, in a year or so the fish may be able to transform itself into something less fishy and more mammalian, more recognizably akin to other FWBO/TBMSG types of organisation.

My 'honeymoon period' with the South Ceylon guest house has ended. I have begun to find it more distracting than enjoyable, and have located alternative accommodation in a quiet room in a nearby house. This does not mean I shall be breaking off communication with its work-force. I am writing this letter in my 'office' in the guest house, and will continue to come here every day. But I will be spending the evenings in my new room which is a bit more commodious and less draughty than Rahula's Seaside Kuti. You may remember that Rahula's kuti was the place I stayed in when things got too boisterous at the guest house.

The last few days have been even more noisy and restless than usual. Guests have begun to return (a very mixed blessing), and I have had three consecutive almost sleepless nights. A local old woman has died, resulting in all-night vigils with voices raised from time to time. On top of this, *pirith*[59] chanting has been broadcast throughout two consecutive nights. My experience of *pirith* chanting has been rather variable, sometimes making me feel blissful for several days afterwards, and sometimes apparently draining my energy. This occasion for *pirith* was the 100th anniversary of the founding of Ananda College, a prestigious Colombo institution. The chanting was played loudly on radios throughout the village, and was monotonous and uninspiring beyond belief. All this has exacerbated an already feverish cold and headache, and produced a state of near-exhaustion. So the honeymoon is over. This evening I am going to move in to this new, quieter room nearby. Well, at least it will be quieter when there is no drilling or dynamite going off in the neighbouring stone quarry. Two old crones and a dog guard the house, which I feel has a slightly mysterious atmosphere, though I cannot say exactly in what it consists.

Siri, my one and only mitra, translator, driver and right-hand man has been another cause of concern to all of us by making definite plans to go to Japan. The texture of my future here will certainly change if he goes. However, it will not, I think, be radically altered. Siri thinks he may be able to earn lots of money, whilst also loosening his dependence on his family. He proposes to set up a restaurant in partnership with a Japanese gentleman who already runs four other restaurants. This plan, which I have done my utmost to discourage, has currently got the staff on tenterhooks. I have been wondering whether it will be a set-back or a catalyst for change.

The meditation courses that I mentioned having started recently differ widely from each other as to numbers. The one at Matara is tended by upwards of three hundred people, mostly, but not entirely, ladies. At the Galle course, there are a mere twelve or thirteen people, whilst at Imaduwa there are about thirty. They are again, however, mostly middle-aged ladies, though enlivened by a few bright sparks both young and not-so-young, male and female. But despite the impressive numbers and few promising individuals, I continue to wonder whether we are deploying our resources to the best advantage. At a big public puja in which I participated at Matara recently, some of the flowers that passed through my hands were offered to an image of Vishnu. I was not amused.

Last Poya day (full moon day) was busy as usual, with four public talks and an after-death ceremony. The assembly in one at least of those temples we visited was sufficiently enthusiastic and on-the-ball to ask us to give a talk and meditation class next Poya Day. The following day we held a one-day course for young members of the Youth Service near Balapitya, Dhammajyoti's village. I found this one of the most rewarding days I have spent so far with any Sri Lankans; I experienced a positivity and intensity of energy much greater than anywhere else we have been, and I hope that we shall be spending more time with such people in future. One of the young men on the course meditates with Dhammajyoti, and wrote to me afterwards expressing the wish that we could arrange something for their benefit.

The next day we gave a one-day course at a temple in Balapitya. The Chief bhikkhu there evidently found the day beneficial, because he not only invited us again to his temple, but also attended at least some of the day's programme. The bhikkhus usually leave me to my own devices, and when that happens, I cannot help thinking that they are not really interested in the Dhamma. Or perhaps they cannot get themselves sufficiently together to listen. It is not that I need their presence. But it seems so uncouth to gawp at me for a few minutes as if I were an exhibit in a zoo, and then slope off the minute some actual Dhamma practise is suggested. So I was quite pleased when the Chief bhikkhu at this Balapitya Temple actually participated in one meditation, and listened to my talk. At the end of the day, however, when there were clamorous demands from the participants for another such course, the Chief bhikkhu remained curiously reticent. I have not heard from him since. I went to visit him recently, but he was out. His young assistant was warmly welcoming, and reported that the lay participants had really enjoyed the retreat. However, no further visits were requested or hinted at, and I did not consider it good manners to press the point. So now, having been in Lanka almost a year, I am beginning to feel that we need a Centre of our own here. There are clearly many lay people who would benefit from regular contact with the teaching we can offer. The bhikkhus, however, or at least, those whom I have met so far, are mostly quite unable to respond adequately. I had previously considered that the idea of 'settling down in a private Nirvana' (or Nibbana) was simply a warning against what might only theoretically happen. But it does seem to be a good way of describing what does actually happen to many of the bhikkhus. They give up on the development of others. Many of them disrobe after a while, presumably having decided that Samsara is more attractive than 'private Nibbana'.

NOTES

58 TBMSG: Trailokya Bauddha Mahasangha Sahayaka Gana. Known at first in the West as the FWBO (see note 17), now designated the Triratna Buddhist Order and Community. Trailokya Bauddha means the Buddha of the Three Worlds, the three worlds being, as Sangharakshita used to say, either the three planes of conditioned existence (the *kāma loka*, *rūpa loka* and *arūpa loka*; the 'worlds' or planes of sensuous desire, pure form and formless or extremely subtle form, respectively) or else the Ancient world, the New world, and the Developing world. Sahayaka means helper, and Gana: association.

59 *pirith*: lit. protection. The ritual chanting of certain verses from the Pali for many hours - often all through the night - usually by a gathering of senior bhikkhus in the Temple premises, is thought to impart much benefit to those who assemble to listen and open themselves to the spiritual influence of the recitation.

* * * * *

10   A Plethora of Bhikkhus

I accompany Dhammajyoti on a journey to Colombo. Having become a bhikkhu, he has placed himself on the periphery of, if not exactly outside, my own Order that transcends the distinction between 'monk and layperson'. As we start out on our journey, it becomes evident that he finds himself unable to re-establish a formal relationship with the WBO/TBM. However, we remain on friendly terms, and go to visit several of his prominent bhikkhu friends. I feel exasperated by the shows of ecclesiastical power that present themselves to me on our perambulations about Colombo with Kah Thong, a mutual friend from Malaysia, and eventually, exhausted, return to the simplicity of my base at Unawatuna. I thank my lucky stars for the Triratna Order and Community. I journey on to lead a meditation course in the Southern town of Matara, and visit the hill station of Nuwera Eliya where I stay with members of the American Peace Corps.

MY LETTERS FROM LANKA have been finding it difficult to keep pace with life; more than a month has gone by without my writing to Shabda. Reviewing the contents of my diary, it is not immediately obvious why life overtook the pen. I was not conspicuously busy, having only three meditation classes a week to conduct, and a small number of talks to give, throughout the month of November. Two events, however, more or less coincided with the time I usually sit down to write. Those, together with a feverish cold, must have prevented me writing my usual Letter.

The first event was a trip to Colombo with Dhammajyoti; the second, closely following, was Siri Goonasekara's departure for Japan. While neither event was particularly demanding physically, both provoked a series of reflections which I wanted to ponder before sitting down to write. I felt too close to my material to trust that I would not be obscuring my account with a veil of subjectivity. So I refrained from setting down my thoughts then and there. Now a month or so has passed, and with it the worst of the turbulence.

Bhikkhu Dhammajyoti, still a putative member of our Order, had invited me to join him on a trip to Colombo Airport to meet Kah Thong, a mutual friend of ours. I had met Kah Thong in New Zealand when I was staying with the Hewitt's Road community in Christchurch, the first FWBO Community in New Zealand. This community came together largely under the inspiration of Lim Poi Cheng, as Dhammajyoti was then known. I had met Lim's friend Kah Thong on several occasions in Christchurch, and been impressed by his friendliness and clarity. I learned that his name meant 'the central pillar of a house'. Kah Thong has since been instrumental in getting some of Sangharakshita's writings translated into Malaysian. He is also in occasional contact with Jayapushpa, our Dharmacharini in Malaysia. Subsequent to Bhante's first visit to New Zealand, Kah Thong was ordained as an Upāsaka in Malaysia and was given a new name, which apparently he no longer uses. He has remained in contact with the FWBO despite his comparative isolation, and two years ago paid us a visit in India. A whirlwind tour was arranged for him by Lokamitra. Some of the Indian Dhammacharis, particularly Bodhidhamma, who translated a talk he gave in Aurangabad, will remember him well.

Kah Thong had arranged to visit Dhammajyoti, not knowing, apparently, that I was in Sri Lanka, and Dhammajyoti, knowing of our friendship, had invited me to accompany him. One Sunday afternoon therefore, Siri and I, after we had finished conducting a one day retreat near the seaside village of Balapitya, made our way to Dhammajyoti's temple which was situated near, well, almost on the sea shore. Siri was accompanying me because he wanted to attend a wedding reception the next day in Colombo. The new groom was his young brother-in-law Keerthi, and the reception was to be held at the Lanka Oberoi, the most prestigious hotel in the city. Dhammajyoti however was in a state of consternation because his van, which he had sent to be serviced, had not been returned. I suggested that we send someone off immediately to fetch it, and having done so, we sat down to wait, with the help of a cup of tea. After tea, Dhammajyoti showed Siri and I around the Shrine room where he and thirty young boys in his care sit to meditate every morning. It was a newly-constructed building, rectangular in shape, with open-grille-work in timber on one side, and a central pillar. This pillar Dhammajyoti had pressed into service as an altar. About two feet off the ground, all around the pillar, was a broad shelf draped with orange cloth; and on three sides of the pillar were placed framed pictures of the Buddha. One of them depicted, in bright chocolate-box colours, a plump and youthful Shakyamuni with a soft, rounded, slightly effeminate face. This however seems to be how many people in India and South-East Asia prefer to see the heroic sage of the Sakya clan. The other two pictures were of a Chinese Shakyamuni; more manly-looking, but with a curiously large head. What, if anything, was on the fourth side, escaped my observation. The thirty boys, Dhammajyoti told us, meditated every morning for forty minutes or so. Part of their practice, he told us, was to gaze at the pictures with concentrated attention while recalling the qualities of the Buddha. Siri told me that he thought the result of this would be that every boy without exception would give up the practice on reaching maturity. Dhammajyoti however, stoutly maintained that such was not the case, and that the training would have a beneficent effect on their youthful minds. I came to the conclusion that the motive for introducing such a practice to the very young should be examined carefully and honestly. It would indeed be a pity if what was considered skilful turned them away from the Dharma in the long run.

Be that as it may, Dhammajyoti was enthusiastic about his shrine room, and most generously offered it to Siri and I for our retreats whenever we wanted. "You don't even need to write," he said, "just turn up with seven or eight people, and everything will be made available for you. Next he showed us an adjoining field which he had obtained with difficulty and for a large sum from the villagers who claimed it was theirs. He was however convinced it had belonged to the Temple at one time. He wished to build a two-storey edifice on it which would provide training facilities at a more advanced level. In this way he hoped to attract international visitors and Dhamma students. Although it seemed in principle an excellent idea, I doubted whether Dhammajyoti would be able to bring his idea to fruition all by himself. I was about to venture this opinion when he started talking about redefining his position with regard to the Western Buddhist Order. Suddenly hopeful that he was going to voice his determination to work in future with the Order, I pricked up my ears, but alas, he expressed only doubts about it. I felt sad, and rather frustrated, especially as he had done so much with which it would be good for the Order to connect. Surely, I thought, it would be of mutual benefit if we were able to work in harmony as fellow Order Members. At this point we strolled out onto the golden-sanded beach and watched the sun setting in a blaze of glorious gold over the ocean rim and setting every little cloud ablaze. Amazed at the sight, which inspired in me recollection of the Buddha Amitabha, our conversation came to a natural, if inconclusive end.

Dhammajyoti's van arrived just before dusk, so we were able to settle down for the night with our worries about tomorrow's transport dispelled. Next morning, after a hearty breakfast, we got ourselves and our few bits of luggage together and climbed into the pale green minibus. The driver-mechanic and three young lads, one of them a paraplegic, joined us. We were soon speeding along the Colombo Road, and Dhammajyoti resumed our conversation of the previous evening. He seemed impatient with my silences, and began to express himself more forcefully, attempting to redefine his position vis-à-vis the Order. I felt reluctant to speak just then about Order matters, because Siri, seated just behind us, was listening to our every word. Such, however, was the emotional intensity of the points raised by Dhammajyoti that it was impossible for me to hold back. He had evidently been feeling uneasy about his lack of Order contact. This feeling was now surfacing in the form it sometimes does - as self-generated doubt concerning the authenticity of one's Order membership. I did not doubt Dhammajyoti's commitment. But I could understand how he now felt.

It was all too easy, in isolation, to imagine that Order membership was simply an easy-going set of relationships in which nothing further was asked, nothing further encouraged. It also occurred to me that Dhammajyoti's defensiveness might be an indication of anxiety about participating once again in the life of the Order. Perhaps he expected censure, or even 'loss of 'face' for his several years of non-communication, though in point of fact, I'm sure everyone would have been glad to welcome him back. However Dhammajyoti now came out with what I had sensed for some time was on his mind: he confessed that he was considering offering his resignation to Bhante. I urged him to consider the matter carefully. I encouraged him to at least consider having Order meetings with me. If we could only do that, then everything could be resolved straightforwardly in due course, I said. But Dhammajyoti replied that he felt unable to do so since he would feel insincere. I responded that if he repeated what he had just said to me at an

Order Meeting, it would simply be accepted as a confession of his present, ephemeral state of mind, and respected as such. It would not provoke censure. Seeing that I could not help him out of his discomfiture, I urged him to write to Bhante to clarify his position. I added suddenly, however, that Bhante was less and less inclined nowadays to tolerate merely nominal membership of the Order, but immediately felt that I had said too much, and was not surprised to hear Dhammajyoti responding by saying that what I had said felt very much like pressure. He would prefer, he said, to leave things as they were, with us meeting on an 'informal' basis, and there I let the matter drop.

It was after mid-day when having been travelling for a couple of hours along the Galle Road, we entered the suburbs of Colombo. We stopped so that Siri could get off. He asked us to wait, however, and slipping into a nearby restaurant, soon returned with some vegetarian pasties. This was an expression of his usual generosity. It was also a way of preventing any awkwardness that he knew Dhammajyoti might feel at having to buy food, especially since we were now well after the witching hour when it was taboo for bhikkhus (though not myself, the Anagarika) to eat. Nevertheless I was grateful for my well-wrapped pastie, which I consigned for the time being to my bhikkhu bag.

Absorbed as Dhammajyoti and I had become in our own thoughts, it seemed only a short time later that we drew into the courtyard of the Jayasekaramaya Temple in the Maradana district of Colombo. I had for many years addressed copies of the Order newsletter to this place, and now at last I was about to see it with my own eyes. I had imagined it to be larger than it looked at first sight, but it was certainly grand by the standards with which I was familiar in the UK. Having had a chance to look around, I guessed that the roofed premises were at least four times the area of the London Buddhist Centre, and on a much larger site. And of course they had been purpose built, not converted for use as a Buddhist centre. The Jayasekaramaya, I saw, contained all the traditional elements of a Sinhalese temple complex. There was a stupa or *dagoba* standing in the open air, and nearby a Sima or convocation hall, with library above. There was an image-house with giant-sized images of seated, standing and reclining images of the Buddha; there was a separate shrine dedicated to the Bodhisattva Maitreya; there were extensive bhikkhus' quarters and a dining hall. There was a long bungalow-like residence for the 'Chief Priest'; and there was an annexe for 'meditating priests.' Finally, there was a very large hall used, apparently, as a kindergarten, and with various smaller rooms adjoining it. All the buildings were stoutly constructed and well-kept. They were tastefully arranged, I discovered, around two main courtyards on different levels which were joined by wide flights of steps. And everywhere beautiful trees and shrubs provided shade and colour and fragrance. The whole effect was highly pleasing, and the buildings were freshly painted. All this suggested to me that the temple was one of the many well-endowed and well-supported religious complexes in Colombo. Dhammajyoti told me, however, that there were only eight resident bhikkhus, which seemed a very small number indeed for the space available. I guessed that the Temple complex could have comfortably accommodated between five and ten times that number. But I am getting ahead of myself.

Immediately after getting out of the van, Dhammajyoti led me off to the *nayaka mahathero*, the Chief Priest. I was taken down a corridor of the Nayaka Thero's bungalow, and told to wait. From my vantage point I could see the flickering light and hear the sound of a television in a large room at the end of the corridor. We were not led to the inner sanctum, however, and were told by a junior bhikkhu that it would be 'more convenient' if we were introduced outside. As we walked back to the reception area, Dhammajyoti explained that the Chief Priest, once a meditator, no longer meditated. He was no longer a 'spiritual figure', he said, but nevertheless I should 'worship' him. Though not inclined to 'worship' anyone unworthy of worship, I prepared myself to go through the motions. I had no wish to embarrass anybody, much less still to arouse animosity. It only remained to see what degree of 'worship' was expected. Would I be required merely to bow, or to touch his toes? I had discovered that some Chief Priests were content with a little nod or a smile, while others expected nothing less than a prostration. After keeping us waiting a few minutes, the Nayaka Thero minced into the room with a curiously effeminate gait. This, I thought, spoiled the effect of a tall, slim and otherwise manly figure, and without further ado, I gave a quick bow of about one-third full depth. Dhammajyoti however whispered urgently behind my back: "Wait, wait!" So I did. The Chief Priest seated himself, and Dhammajyoti fished out a large handkerchief. Placing it on the floor in front of him, he got to his knees, placed his hands on the handkerchief, and touched his head on the ground at the elder's feet. This was evidently what I was expected to do. I had seen it done many times before by young monks before very much older monks. But it had never occurred to me to do this sort of thing except before Bhante or someone like Dhardo Rimpoche, for whom I felt genuine reverence. I had prostrated myself before Venerable Nyanaponika in his Kandy hermitage, but in that case also I felt respect for him; moreover I was prepared to discover that he was even better than I thought he was. But as for the Chief Priest of the Jayasekaramaya, so far I had no good reason to offer him a deep prostration. I therefore performed it with the mental reservation that this was merely a formal obeisance. Dhammajyoti then introduced me to him, and a stilted bit of non-communication followed. Although polite, the Chief Priest did not seem to be in the slightest interested in me, and so it was difficult for me to develop any interest in him. He was icily polite, but seemed to be totally indifferent to me as a person. He even asked a few standard-sounding 'questions to be addressed to foreign visitors', but the strange thing was that neither he nor Dhammajyoti, who often seemed to want to answer on my behalf, gave me a single moment to respond with answers. It was really quite unpleasantly bizarre and alienating.

The introduction over, I was then shown to the room assigned to me. It was clean enough but devoid of any signs of life or love. I prepared to settle down for the night, as I was beginning to feel tired after the journey. I opened the window of my room, and a few moments later a man in a blue uniform peeped in, and stood there watching me making my bed. I looked at him disapprovingly, at which he said "Security guard", smiled, and walked away from the open window. Wealth, and the recipients of it, evidently needed guarding. Then I began to feel rather sorry and sad about the whole series of circumstances which had led up to this state of affairs. I reflected that in this place there was probably little more than a token practise of the spiritual path, and the lives of the monks must be difficult in many ways. But for myself, not having eaten since before mid-day, I was now feeling hungry. I closed the window and devoured Siri's pastie. After this I visited the bathroom and found a huge bath brimful of cold water, perhaps intended for me. However, as I was feeling very tired indeed, I used only the wash basin, and shortly after, lay down for the afternoon siesta.

The next morning Dhammajyoti and I were up early, anticipating an hour's drive to the airport to meet Kah Thong. We breakfasted alone in a large dining hall big enough for perhaps a hundred bhikkhus. On one long wall of the room there was a shrine with a four-foot high, seated Buddha-image coloured reddish-brown and gold, and not unpleasing in appearance. The breakfast consisted of delicious red rice, cooked in milk and salted to just the right extent, and a plate of shredded coconut spiced with chillies. I took only a very small helping of the latter. I noticed that Dhammajyoti was enjoying his breakfast too; after taking a second helping, he urged me to take more, which I did. The only other person in the room was a 'temple boy' of about ten, whom Dhammajyoti told me would soon be ordained. He seemed a happy lad, judging by his ready smile, and leaning on a table nearby he was content to watch us eating. We made sure that our driver and three young companions had breakfasted too, and soon afterwards set off in the van towards Colombo Airport.

An hour's drive brought us to the small but smart Airport building, where we discovered we had nearly an hour to wait; Kah Thong's plane had been delayed. I suggested that we have a cup of tea, to which Dhammajyoti assented, and we sauntered up to the cafeteria. We found however that the price of a cup of tea was five Rupees - far more than the usual price - and thought again. Dhammajyoti considered the price exorbitant, so we decided instead to ask for a glass of water. A young waiter brought what we asked, and then, perhaps thinking there was the chance of earning merit, or perhaps out of genuine concern, he offered us a free cup of tea. We accepted it, though both of us admitted to hesitancy because it was not clear whether the tea had been offered through *sraddha* (Skt. Pali: *saddha*, faith) or because of the waiter's fear of what we might say to the management if he had not given us liquid refreshment when we so obviously needed it. I decided that it would have been foolish to refuse, and drank my tea with a clear conscience. Dhammajyoti too seemed to be enjoying his drink, and savouring the comfortable surroundings.

Dhammajyoti and I presented an appearance very different from when we had met twelve years ago in Christchurch, New Zealand. What, I wondered, had changed internally? Conversation, for some reason or other, turned to poverty, to our respective parents, and to their hopes for their sons. There being still some time to go before Kah Thong's arrival, we went downstairs and sat in some uncomfortable plastic chairs. Dhammajyoti dozed or meditated, I could not tell which, and I continued with my reading of *The Threefold Refuge*[60] Until it was time to go and meet our mutual friend. Dhammajyoti thought he spotted him first, and sure enough, a few minutes later Kah Thong emerged from the customs hall. He looked quite fresh despite his long journey, and greeted me with an only slightly hesitant, bright-eyed smile. He seemed pleased to see me, and I was definitely pleased to see him. Dhammajyoti's practical sense did not desert him, and after exchanging a few words of greeting, he went off to get a trolley for Kah Thong's luggage. So we were left alone for a few moments. Kah Thong asked me how I was finding things in Sri Lanka. I replied that I was finding them very interesting, especially as I had not been in a Theravada country before. At this point Dhammajyoti returned with a trolley in tow, and our conversation was broken off. We made our way to the van, and were soon speeding back again toward the Jayasekaramaya Temple.

I thought that Kah Thong was looking more energetic and 'awake' than when I had met him almost exactly two years ago in India. I was sorry not to be able to find out more about what he had been doing, since most of his subsequent conversation with Dhammajyoti was in what I took to be Mandarin Chinese. On our arrival at the Temple, it was Kah Thong's turn to be introduced to the Chief Priest, and to 'offer worship.' He did so quite unselfconsciously, and, perhaps, uncritically. Much to my frustration, however, I had no opportunity either then or later, to discover what he thought about anything. I remained as much as possible in visual rapport with Kah Thong, and I concluded that whatever he was thinking, he was finding his visit interesting. The rest of the day passed in a continual succession of visits, during much of which Dhammajyoti and Kah Thong were conversing in Mandarin. I resigned myself to taking a back seat and perhaps discovering through later correspondence what Kah Thong's impressions were.

We visited the Gangaramaya Temple, which, I had been informed by a reliable source, had been set up by a hyper-active young bhikkhu with keen business acumen and strong political connections. He had started his career by clearing a slum area occupied mostly by Muslims, and turning it over to the setting-up of small industrial workshops for unemployed Sinhalese. It was apparently a successful enterprise, though probably, I thought, with less than skilful political, religious and ethnic implications. We looked into the Gangaramaya Temple image-hall, which was huge and replete with images of all kinds telling the religious history of Lanka. Perhaps even more remarkable, in the entrance vestibule of the main hall was an image of Kataragama, the ethnic god of the Sinhalese. The shrine had been set up with loving care, and was immaculately clean and well-tended. It was lit with a mysterious, reddish-purple light which produced an almost hypnotic effect on the observer. The central figure, slightly larger than life-size, was of a quasi-human figure of indeterminate sex, with six arms holding various implements. Most remarkable of all, the face was finely sculpted, very human in character, and with the gaze cast slightly down. It was difficult to tell what exactly was the nature of the expression, but it held my attention very powerfully until I had decided what it was communicating. I came to the conclusion that the emotion it was communicating was either jealousy, or unrequited love. I felt the image was quite sinister, and had no place in a Buddhist temple. In another part of the temple complex we came across a group of bhikkhus sitting around reading newspapers and magazines. Unfortunately, far from conveying an atmosphere of purposeful investigation, they attitudes suggested nothing but sloth and torpor. In yet another part of the complex, in what appeared to be a study area, there were two groups of bhikkhus, one group sitting around a table listening to one obviously dominant speaker, whilst the other group lounged in elaborate boredom nearby.

Dhammajyoti invited us to see the library, and we were shown around it by a zombie-like bhikkhu who escorted us to the Temple library. It appeared well stocked with a wide variety of books on religious subjects, and many on business and scientific matters. There were no books by Sangharakshita to be seen. I did however notice a few Mahāyāna texts and commentaries. I did not feel inclined to ask questions, and in any case, Dhammajyoti was impatient to be off on the next step of our journey. Our next stop was at the Pali-Buddhist University of Colombo, where he teaches Sarvastivada, one of the early schools of Buddhism. Kah Thong and I were introduced to a few of his pupils, and to his Principal. The latter seemed to be a man who enjoyed an intellectual tussle, for I could not avoid entering into conversation with him. Kah Thong and Dhammajyoti excused themselves. The Principal was in fact difficult to communicate with although he spoke excellent English. This was because every now and then he would break out into a long Pali quotation to illustrate some point or other. But my Pali was not up to his Pali, and each time he fired off his bullets of text, I would have to retrace our words back to the original point of departure before commenting further.

I did manage to make a few points of my own. I suggested, for instance, that the Theravada could be looked upon as the phase of introspection, the Mahāyāna as the phase of service, and the Vajrayāna as the phase of realisation of Buddhahood. This began to intrigue him, but he countered by asking whether I thought the Tipitaka was incomplete. This was obviously a trick question. We began to explore the notion of the Mahāyāna as an expansion of the Theravada rather than an addition. But then Dhammajyoti returned and it was time to go. The Principal advised me to 'keep plugged in', and I wished him all the best and hoped that we would meet again. Though probably a dyed-in-the-wool Theravadin, he was a sight more lively than any bhikkhu I had met so far except for Dhammajyoti himself.

Our next stop was at the great Temple of Kelaniya, with its big 'grain-heap' style stupa and beautiful temple murals. The murals here were amongst the most beautiful I had ever seen. They were painted within living memory, in the 'Ancient Sinhala' style of religious painting. There was an abundance of ochres, with red, black and white arranged in beautiful flowing lines and masses. There was also a great richness of detail and diversity in characterization of the human figures. I quickly became fascinated by the scenarios, such as the arrival on the shores of Lanka of the Bhikkhuni Sanghamitta with the Bodhi sapling. There were also familiar and well-loved episodes from the life of the Shakyamuni, such as his address to the Kalamas of Kesaputta, and his tending, together with Ananda, of the bhikkhu sick with dysentery. Kah Thong got busy with his miniature video camera, the latest from Japan, whilst Dhammajyoti listened to a few words of explanation from our guide, the Chief Priest, before proceeding with a commentary in Mandarin in front of the camera for the folks back home.

We had as usual been introduced to the Chief Priest on our arrival at the temple. We had also been given the opportunity of 'worshipping' him. A man of middling height and middling girth, he was wearing very strong spectacles. A curious thing I noticed was that, try as I would, I could find no trace of light in his eyes. This gave me the impression that I was speaking to a machine. I was told that he was a B.Sc., a piece of information that only served to reinforce the curious impression that I was perceiving a particularly well-oiled piece of machinery, complete not only with the power of speech, but also of laughter. The Chief Priest, I was told, was a very clever man, who had added a great deal to the wealth and standing of the temple. After his praises had been amply sung, he began to show a mild interest in me. When I began talking about myself and the Friends however, I could not help noticing that Dhammajyoti began to get a little uneasy. He began to interrupt what I was saying. I was made to feel that I was approaching a taboo topic, and not wishing to provoke the local deities I became quiet. In any case, sunset was now flushing the sky with golden hues, and it was time to be moving on.

A fanfare of drums coincided dramatically with our exit from the temple precincts and contributed to our elation. We had seen so much beauty inside the temple; and outside too, there was beauty and a wonderful atmosphere of faith. Devotees sat all around a great Bodhi Tree in their hundreds, offering little coconut lamps, sticks of incense and bowls of flowers. And all the while the low murmur of chanting lifted one into a beautiful and timeless realm. The representation I had just seen of the great Acharya Buddhaghosha instructing the Mahavihara bhikkhus rose clearly before my mind's eye as we left. And I wondered whether he too had been witness to similar scenes of devotion on his arrival in Lanka.

Our last planned visit for the day was to the Vice-Chancellor of the Pali-Buddhist University. We entered the two storey building on one side of a broad avenue lined with magnificent trees and freshly painted with yellow ochre. Having announced our presence to a doorman, we were straight away led upstairs and introduced to the Vice-Chancellor. He was a bhikkhu, and immediately remarkable for his girth, which was comparable to some of the Brahmins I have seen in India. The Vice-chancellor would have won a silver, if not a gold medal even amongst them, I thought. Other comparisons too leapt to mind, one of them Orwellian: the Vice-chancellor, seated behind his large desk, a pair of heavy black managerial-style spectacles perched on his nose, reminded me of nothing so much as Big Brother. Those known not to be toeing the party line would surely quail in terror when summoned to his presence. Fortunately I was spared an inquisition. In fact I was almost ignored. Dhammajyoti quickly set about introducing Kah Thong, and this time at least I could understand much of what was being said. An ulterior motive soon emerged, for very soon, conversation turned to the subject of collaboration between the Vice-chancellor's group and Kah Thong's group back in Malaysia. There was talk of setting up parallel Buddhist studies in Malaysia using the medium of Chinese.

In this vein they continued for half an hour or more, much of it being recorded by Kah Thong on video. Eventually I began to feel rather bored, and finally protested as humorously as I could: 'But what about me?' Fortunately, everyone laughed. The Vice-chancellor seemed suddenly to perceive my presence, and addressing his remarks in my direction, began to open up a little bit about himself. He confessed that he was not at all well and suffered a lot of pain. He wanted to know if anybody could help him. I immediately volunteered: 'Well, I know just what you need. You should walk at least one mile every day.' The Vice-chancellor looked at me in mild astonishment and replied: "I can't do that." But I had not offended him in the least. It was simply that the idea of personal, physical exertion just did not occur to him. Shaking his head, he took a box from a nearby shelf and lifted out a curious device. Plugged into the mains, it gave forth a secretive little hum. The business end of it approximated to the size of a small apple, and could we were told be applied to the painful part of the body to provide instant relief. "It works sometimes," the Vice-chancellor remarked, in a rather disgruntled tone of voice. After this inconclusive demonstration, we were shown the Vice-chancellor's personal quarters, to which we were ferried by a large, brand-new car of Japanese make. At one end of his sitting-room was fitted an enormous side-board made of teak and housing a large colour television. Dhammajyoti, rather to my surprise, asked him how much it cost. The Vice-Chancellor tried to side-step the question by saying, "Oh, the wood was twenty thousand Rupees." Twenty thousand Rupees is about four years' wages at current rates for a Tamil tea-picker. The Vice Chancellor seemed to be living far indeed from the ideal of simplicity to which the true brahmacharin is committed.

The well-rounded Vice-chancellor continued to chat amiably throughout our visit to his quarters. In fact, he seemed rather disappointed when I told him, in reply to his enquiry, that I was returning that evening with Dhammajyoti to Jayasekaramaya Temple. A conversation then ensued between Dhammajyoti and the Vice-Chancellor about a seminar on the oneness of religions. Here I grasped the opportunity of saying a few strong words on the subject. Slightly to my surprise, I found that the Vice-chancellor agreed heartily with my sentiments. What a likeable man! He didn't seem like Big Brother at all, despite appearances to the contrary. It was all very confusing. As if to put me in my place, however, he went on to declare in confident tones that he had no doubt Dhammajyoti was the best man to speak at the forthcoming seminar. By this time, late in the evening, I was almost falling asleep, and so, I noticed, was Kah Thong. I was certainly in no state to challenge Dhammajyoti, even if I had wanted to, but in fact I was quite happy that he should have the laurels, if there were any. I was interested in only one thing: bed.

However, all was not over yet. We were still to see the Vice-chancellor's Library and Image-house. The library was a big one containing perhaps 20,000 volumes. There was no sign of any book by Sangharakshita, or any other Windhorse publication. I was exhausted, and began to protest that I was very tired and needed to go. Dhammajyoti whispered urgently into my ear: "I'm as tired as you are". To this I replied, "In that case you should go to bed." We did manage to get away at last, but hardly had we driven out of the gateway in our van when Dhammajyoti announced another visit. He said he just wanted to drop in for a few minutes to see another bhikkhu friend of his before returning. It would only be five minutes, he said.

The last person we visited turned out to be someone whom I had met once before. He was a bhikkhu friend of Dhammachari Vimalakirti[61]. The man was a Pali and Sanskrit scholar who was at one time, I believe, resident in Pune. However, I was in no mood to appreciate the renewing of our acquaintance. Immediately I entered the room and he cast eyes on me, he muttered as if to himself, 'How many precepts?' Evidently he had not remembered me although I had visited him with a package from Vimalakirti, and told him that I was an anagarika. Managing to stay composed, I ignored his question and sat down quietly while Dhammajyoti introduced Kah Thong. There then followed a scholarly conversation about a Pali root which Dhammajyoti wanted to investigate. Mercifully, after a few minutes of such talk, it was time to go, and I was able to savour the peculiar pleasure of having mastered, for a sufficient interval, my anger, my impatience, and my exhaustion.

Next morning I would have to leave early for Unawatuna, and before 5:00pm would have to be in Matara, even further south, to lead a meditation class for three or four hundred people. I did not want to be late or rushed. Before going next morning, Dhammajyoti let it be known that I was expected to say goodbye to the Chief Priest of the Jayasekaramaya, which I did accordingly, and with all possible grace. Though I was eager to depart, I was indeed grateful for the very pleasant shelter and sustenance with which I had been provided. However, just as I turned to go, the tall saffron-robed Chief Priest called Dhammajyoti over to his side and pointed out a newspaper article. I was then obliged to wait for several minutes listening to them talking in matter-of-fact fashion about a report concerning a German who had been sent to a Sri Lankan mental hospital. The man had apparently picked up one of the planks of his bed and beaten two fellow Lankan inmates to death. I did not understand why the Chief Priest had chosen to point out this unsavoury bit of news to Dhammajyoti just before he left. Was he trying to say that Westerners are dangerous people? Perhaps it was a shared interest in psychopathology.

Not a moment too soon, we left the Jayasekaramaya in Dhammajyoti's van, and after a few minutes the driver stopped near a place where I would be able to board a coach to Unawatuna and 'Samma Ajiva'. Having wished Kah Thong a safe journey and noted his address in Malaysia, I waved cheerio to Dhammajyoti and stepped out into the brilliant sunshine. Before long I had boarded a coach to the South, and the attractive prospect of a bhikkhu-less Unawatuna.

Only a few hours after my arrival at 'Samma Ajiva', I was off once again by bus to Matara. Siri had not been able to commit himself to being with me on this occasion, so immediately on my arrival at the Temple I was eager to meet my translator. After my frustrating experiences yesterday and my efforts to arrive on time at the Matara Temple today, I was in for further frustration. The seventy-five year old gentleman, though earnest and willing, had a difficult time understanding me. And on commencing the class, it was evident that everyone else shared the difficulty. It was disheartening to see the lack of comprehension on such a large number of faces. I experimented with 'projecting' myself much more theatrically than usual, and I found this compensated to some extent for the limitations of the translation. Luckily, many Sri Lankans can understand basic English.

I had arranged to meet Siri that evening in Unawatuna on my return from Matara, but he was not there. And the next day he did not turn up at the hotel until after seven o'clock in the evening. I felt so upset that I could find no words to say to him. It was likely to be our last chance of one-to-one communication for a year or more. And then, after only a few minutes, he left, and appeared equally briefly the next day in the restaurant, when he seemed bright and cheerful but was not available for one-to-one communication. This was the last I saw of him before his departure for Japan.

The three ten-week courses in meditation are now over. I have been presented with a touching show of affection in the form of gifts at Matara and at Galle. At Imaduwa they just could not believe that the course was ending. Siri is in Japan and I have had two letters from him already. He wants me to lend him £1,000 so that he can import two mini-buses and make a lot of money. If he can do that, he says, he will come back soon. I shall try to help him out. And you will be glad to hear that I have obtained a one-year extension to my residence visa..

I am typing this Letter in Nuwera Eliya, which means 'New Light'. It is an ex-British hill station set six thousand feet up in the central highlands and is refreshingly cool and invigorating. The late afternoon sun is shining warmly through my window, and the distant hills are swathed in blue-green trees and vegetation. It is surely one of the most fertile and delightful spots on earth. Lying in a saddle between precipitous hills, it soars over all but the very highest tea plantations. The journey up here by bus was breathtaking. Bend after hairpin bend afforded panoramic views first on one side and then on the other. The huge extent of the tea plantations is almost unbelievable. There are myriads of small bushes in the most inaccessible and precipitous places. The labour involved in planting every single one of those bushes staggers the imagination. They are hardy, long lived plants, and some of them are over a hundred years old. The new leaves of each one are plucked at not more than five-day intervals by bands of healthy-looking Tamil women. They certainly do not look underfed or ill-cared-for, though I am told that bronchial diseases are three times the national average amongst the pickers. This is perhaps because of the moist conditions, which rarely allow their clothes to dry properly. The Tamil population here is practically equal in number to the Sinhalese, and the Government is providing every possible incentive to persuade the latter to increase their numbers. Tension, exacerbated by national, ethnic and vested interests is unfortunately almost palpable in this area, which for this reason makes it a sort of marriage of heaven and hell.

I am staying at a house maintained by the American Peace Corps and VSO (Voluntary Service Overseas) workers, though the friends who invited me here are not in residence. The young men and women who are here do not seem a very happy lot, for some reason, though they have been friendly enough to me. But tomorrow, on Christmas Eve, I shall be off. I do not want to join in their festivities, which will include beer, roast pork and turkey. I shall have enjoyed the mountain air and scenery, and two days of comfort and relaxation under a warm feather duvet. The room, which I have entirely to myself, is vaster than any I have been in for years. And the food, though I have had to cook it myself, was prepared with excellent raw materials. Soon, however, at the appropriate moment, I shall be off to Kandy and from there to Colombo and Unawatuna, which is not without its compensations.

NOTES

59 *pirith*: lit. protection. The ritual chanting of certain verses from the Pali for many hours - often all through the night - usually by a gathering of senior bhikkhus in the Temple premises, is thought to impart much benefit to those who assemble to listen and open themselves to the spiritual influence of the recitation.

60 *The Threefold Refuge*: the transcript of a seminar conducted by Sangharakshita on the book of the same name by Nyanaponika Thera. Pub: Windhorse Publications 1984, Roman Road, London.

61 Dhammachari Vimalakirti: a skilled simultaneous translator of Sangharakshita's talks into Hindi and Marathi. Now, unfortunately, resigned from the Order

* * * * *

11   A Christmas Ducking

I report the first request to be made a mitra from a Sri Lankan who has not had any contact with the wider Movement. A Christmas jaunt very nearly ends in disaster.

IT IS ONLY TEN DAYS since I last wrote a letter for Shabda. I have been having a bit of a break before starting a new series of talks on the Noble Eightfold Path[62], in which I will re-present as much as possible of Bhante's teachings on this topic, with of course rather different introductions appropriate to the conditions here.

Two or three memorable things have occurred since I last wrote. Someone has made a request to be a mitra. This is the first request from a man who has had contact only with me and not with any other Order member or with the wider movement. So this has proved to me that it is not altogether impossible working 'by oneself' here. I must hasten to add that the young man in question also read *Buddhism for Today*[63] three times, so much of the credit for his request goes to Subhuti. Rohita, as he is called, told me that I was the first person he'd met who was able to show him the way, and that our movement was just what was needed in Sri Lanka. Not only that. Rohita, being an only son, is the sole inheritor, among other things, of a quietly-situated, 15-acre plot of land on which stands a two-storey house not very much smaller than the front and oldest part of 'Padmaloka'. This property Rohita wishes to donate to Bhante. However, I mustn't jump to conclusions, and whether or not Bhante will consider it wise to accept the property, I shall wait and see. And also, whether Rohita is accepted as a mitra will depend to some extent on Bhante and Devamitra, since I have no-one here with whom to 'check my perceptions.' So I shall not tempt fate and say any more about all this until the intentions, however good, become realities.

Siri Goonasekara wrote to me a few days ago from Tokyo. He has parted company with the man with whom he was going to start a new restaurant, and is now serving as a cook in a Sri Lankan restaurant in the capital. He says he wants to return to Sri Lanka before April. I feel pleased at the prospect of sharing his company and giving talks with him as translator once more.

I am feeling well, which may have something to do with a more regular yoga practice, something to do with becoming familiar with the customs and habits of the monks and laity, and something to do with the feeling that the presence of the WBO here is, however imperceptibly, beginning to have an effect. No doubt Anagarika Padmavajra's and Kamalashila's visits, I hope in the not-too-far-distant future, will help things along too.

On Christmas morning, just after I had finished doing some writing and wondering what to do next, an American Peace Corps Worker friend of mine asked me if I would like to join him and a few friends in a boat ride in Unawatuna bay. I assented, looking forward to a pleasant hour on the blue ocean, and set off with them. I was wearing, of course, my robes, my sandals and carrying my black umbrella against the glare of the sun which, being of such intensity, is liable to quickly produce sunburn on the unprotected skin of Westerners. We procured a boat of the usual fishing boat type with outrigger, and took to the water with a local fisherman at the leading oar and a sturdy Peace Corps man the trailing one. The sea was choppy, but not unduly so, I thought, for this type of boat. After about fifteen minutes rowing, we were perhaps a quarter of a mile out into the sparkling blue ocean, with a magnificent panorama of the coconut-fringed shore spreading to either side in a great crescent. At this point, however, the waves began to build up in intensity, and the front oarsman began to show signs of nervousness. He made it clear that he was going to turn back, and the boat began slowly to veer around. Then as it came broadside to the waves, a particularly big one approached. The wave did not swamp the narrow hull, which might not have mattered, since it was mostly solid timber which would probably have floated. What happened was that the crest of the wave lifted the hull higher and higher above the outrigger. We were poised for a moment at forty-five degrees to the horizontal. Of course, trying to save ourselves from being pitched out, we all instinctively braced ourselves by thrusting out our arms on the edge of the down side of the narrow hull, with the result that the now heavily weighted outrigger began to slide beneath the water. Slowly and gracefully, the boat then performed a somersault, and we found ourselves floundering in the choppy seas. The Peace Corps Men and the fisherman immediately clung to the boat and set about trying to right it, but it soon became obvious that it was going to be a difficult job. Seeing that they all seemed to be good swimmers, I had only myself to think about, and almost immediately found myself in a predicament. In ordinary circumstances I would have been in no danger, as I am not a bad swimmer, the water was warm, and no sharks are found in these areas. However, I had not bargained with the hindrance of soaked robes. I soon found that it was impossible to make any headway in the water with the robes clinging to me. In this condition I was of absolutely no help in righting the boat or, as the others were now doing, dragging it slowly to the shore. If I was to save myself and not be a hindrance to the others, I would have to dispense with my robes. However, there were quite a number of people standing on the shore watching what was going on. There was only one thing to do. I unwound my robes, working them into a heavy ball, and holding them in one hand, swam back to shore. After a vigorous swim I began to touch sand beneath my feet again, so at this point I stopped swimming and managed to wind my lower robe around me. In this way I walked ashore in comparative decency. There were quite a few laughs from among the onlookers. Some of them asked what I was doing out there - a question which I did not feel it necessary to answer.

Recollecting myself, I realized that my umbrella had probably plunged to the ocean bottom. My sandals had floated, however, and were later handed to me by the Peace Corps leader. The boat was eventually pulled up on the sandy beach, whereupon the dark, wiry fisherman demanded a hefty fee for extra labour due to the overturning of the boat, as he claimed, by the second oarsman. This demand was laughingly refused by my American friends. Now that everyone was safely ashore, I felt invigorated after my unusual exertions, though I needed a slightly longer than usual rest after lunch that day.

NOTES

62   The Noble Eightfold Path: one of the most important formulations of the Buddha's teaching concerning the spiritual nature of all human beings: the gradual development, through faithful Buddhist practice, in the direction of, and eventual breakthrough into, Transcendental Insight. According to this formulation, the path of higher human development consists in the cultivation and unfolding, sometimes in sequence, sometimes simultaneously, of a number of steps or stages. These are described as 'right' or as 'perfect' according to whether the stage being referred to belongs simply to the Path in its 'mundane', verbally-formulated aspect, or to its Transcendental actuality. The initial Eightfold Path is the clarification of spiritual vision, leading to the breakthrough of Perfect Vision. It consists of: 1 Right View 2 Right Resolve 3 Right Speech 4 Right Action 5 Right Livelihood 6 Right Effort 7 Right Concentration 8 Right Mindfulness. On the establishment of Perfect Vision, the Path of Transformation, otherwise known as the Transcendental Noble Eightfold Path begins. It consists of: 1 Perfect View 2 Perfect Resolve 3 Perfect Speech 4 Perfect Action 5 Perfect Livelihood 6 Perfect Effort 7 Perfect Concentration 8 Perfect Mindfulness. See: *The Buddha's Noble Eightfold Path - Buddhist Wisdom for Today*, Sangharakshita, 2007

63 *Buddhism for Today*, Dharmachari Subhuti, Windhorse Publications, 1983

* * * * *

12   Words and Music

The fewness of the words in this letter seem to suggest that I am very busy; inspired by some gifts from the West, I write to thank the donors.

I AM ALIVE AND WELL. The donation of the fifteen acres of land and two-storey building offered by a Friend is currently being considered by a lawyer and I have every reason to hope that in a matter of months there will be an 'officially recognized' TBMSG/FWBO-style base in Sri Lanka. Rohita, the putative donor is so keen to get things moving that he wants to get the place done up professionally at his own expense, but I have other ideas. I am overjoyed that Bhante, so far as he could see, thought I should accept the offer, and will do my utmost to transform my hopes into a reality.

Yesterday the latest issues of *Golden Drum*, *mitrata* and *Shabda* arrived all at once, and I am beginning the task of assimilating them. Once again I found the account of Suvajra's journey to India deeply moving, and feel that it will make an excellent book, with a bit of editing prior to publication.

This month has seen quite a stream of visitors passing through the 'Samma Ajiva' meditation room, and I have thoroughly enjoyed imparting the flavour the Dharma to them. Some of them I hope will turn up at our European centres in due course, and one or two even at our Indian centres. I am looking forward to meeting Gunavati[64] in a few days' time - it will be interesting to see what effect she has on the women here. Our office has been filled with the sound of music - beautiful, inspiring music, this month; thank you those who sent the cassettes to me, and the same goes for the inspiring pictures, particularly a photo of Chintamani's thangkha of Green Tara, which came with the cassettes. I am beginning to feel excited at the prospect of visiting India later this year. I will be consulting with Lokamitra about the best time for me to arrive and the outline of my itinerary once there.

NOTES

64 Gunavati: a Dharmacharini of Finnish origin, now deceased. She was a keen photographer. She subsequently resigned from the Western Buddhist Order and joined a Tibetan Order, under the auspices of which she became a nun.

* * * * *

13   Gunavati, Priests and Hermits

I give up eating pineapples. Gunavati, an Order Member from Helsinki, arrives. I am very pleased to see her, and she regales me with presents. Her presence at a meditation class consisting mostly of women proves a boon. My hopes for an early solution to the question of more suitable accommodation for a Centre is frustrated, and I am offered a Temple. Siri and I, Gunavati and a Friend, visit a hermitage deep in the forest.

I AM IN BETTER HEALTH than I was a month or two ago, due to the discovery that I am allergic to pineapples. So much did I enjoy the flavour of these fruits, and so large and juicy are they here, that I managed to hide from myself the connection between my eating them every morning and a recurring and painful sinus condition. Siri was more convinced of the connection than I was at first, and it was he who persuaded me to try avoiding them. With some effort, I have at last succeeded, and there has been a vast improvement in my health as a result. Now my mouth does not even water when I see and hear others eating pineapple. Two other things stand out in my mind this month apart from the small personal victory over the pineapples. First is a visit by Gunavati, and the second, frustration over the non-acquisition of the land that had been offered to us.

Gunavati was visiting Sri Lanka for the second time, and is thinking, she says, of settling here. This time she had decided to come for two weeks before returning to Helsinki to resume her job for a final two years before retirement. She arrived with the usual Northern European winter pallor, but otherwise in good shape. By the end of her two week visit she had acquired a healthy-looking glow. We had met at Galle railway station, where she immediately expressed her appreciation of what I am doing here. She then pulled out of her bag a framed photo and presented it to me; it turned out to be a head and shoulders portrait of Bhante in colour, and with hair almost short enough to pass muster here in ultra-conservative Theravada Sri Lanka. I was delighted with it. The portrait now hangs just above my head on the wall of my office, beaming its grace-waves towards me whenever I look it.

Siri chauffeured Gunavati and me back to Unawatuna in his rickety, fourteen-year old Morris Eight which he is fond of describing as a relic of the days of the old colonial masters. On being shown into my office, Gunavati pulled out of her bag further gifts - cassettes of music by Grieg, Smetana, Sibelius, Wagner, Vivaldi, Mozart, and Bach, and a copy of Bhante's recent book *Ambedkar and Buddhism*[65]. Some hours later, when I was alone, the music and the book vied for attention. I gave ear to Sibelius first, listening to a magnificent fanfare of his, and then got down to reading Sangharakshita's book.

This is not the place to give a lengthy appraisal of *Ambedkar and Buddhism*. I think it is one of Sangharakshita's best. It communicates vividly a wonderful impression of the extraordinary courage, dedication and vigour of the great Indian Buddhist leader, and also the development of his thinking about Buddhism. As a result of reading this book, I found a renewed and sharpened, better-informed feeling of disgust arising against the caste system and all its manifestations, as well as a heartfelt identification with the unnumbered millions of unfortunate people of Indian origin who have lived and still live under the inhuman yoke of Untouchability. More even than that, I felt an even more profound respect arising for the great Indian Buddhist leader himself. *Ambedkar and Buddhism* gives a lucid and marvellously uncluttered account of Dr. Ambedkar's extraordinary life and work, and of the thinking that led him to his epoch-making inauguration of the movement of mass conversion to Buddhism that took place on the Deeksha Bhumi in Nagpur on 14th October 1956, less than two months before he died. I saw, of course, that in addition to its inspirational value, the book was a compendium of invaluable information for more 'secular' students - for psychologists, sociologists, anthropologists, and even for politicians. Inevitably also, it communicated essential material concerning the Buddha-dharma itself, and so could have a profound effect on those students of politics or sociology who might not at first have been moved to investigate the Path of the Buddha.

Gunavati spent some time during her first day at 'Samma Ajiva' talking to Siri and to the two prospective women mitras, and we afterwards compared notes concerning them. It was really refreshing to have an Order Member here with whom to talk these things over, and often to have my own vision of the state of things here confirmed and augmented. The following day, Gunavati decided that she wanted to accompany Siri and I to the town of Matara in the south. She wanted to participate in our regular morning-and-afternoon meditation session at a rural Temple, followed by a Dhamma talk in the evening in the middle of Matara.

The assembly of the faithful at the rural Temple, as usual mostly middle-aged and elderly women, were evidently interested in Gunavati, and overcoming their habitual shyness, began speaking to her. It was clear that she was able to communicate with them in a way which was difficult or even impossible for me. Not that my communication is without effect; but those of my male friends who have tried to speak with elderly eastern women will perhaps know what I mean. They tend to put people in robes on a very high pedestal. Gunavati had chosen not to wear her kesa, and had seated herself unobtrusively among the other women when the Refuges and Precepts were given by one of the Temple bhikkhus. This latter procedure had been followed ever since my first visit to the temple, when I had declined to administer the Eight Samanera precepts. From my refusal on that occasion, it was perhaps assumed that I was incapable of giving any precepts at all, let alone the Refuges.

The seniormost bhikkhu of the Temple, after administering the Refuges and Precepts, then gives *bana*. He leans heavily on quotations from the Pali, and the women listen with expressions that communicate nothing so much as polite or even feigned interest, alternating with boredom or even puzzlement. Then, after twenty minutes or so of this, the elderly bhikkhu dries up, stops abruptly, and presumably thinking his work done, leaves without even a glance in my direction. The field is then left to me.

My task with the women at first was to persuade them that meditation could be enjoyable, and that they were not expected to sit motionless and in pain or semi-stupor for an hour. We started with five minute sittings interspersed with ample opportunity for discussion and advice concerning suppression of the hindrances. The topic of inspiration was also not neglected. We have by now, gradually worked up to forty-minute sittings, which most of them seem to find quite within their capability and surprizingly enjoyable. I am reasonably happy with these Matara Temple classes, but the most urgent work, I feel, lies elsewhere. I intend to discontinue my visits after the next and last session of the course and will once more turn my attention to the young men of Galle, whether at karate or the billiard table. Even that may not last long, however, if Siri and I find a place to settle in Colombo. It will probably be in the suburbs rather than the centre of Colombo, since property in the centre is expensive. I would also like to set up a country Centre where we can hold retreats and house a resident community.

The land and house offered to us by Rohita Hevasilian has not yet been conveyed to us despite his initial impatience to get things moving. It has become clear that his interest in Marxism is by no means over. This almost certainly means that his initial surge of faith and generosity is not going to be followed quickly by commitment. I do not think that he will withdraw his offer, but it is not going to be as straightforward as I had hoped. There is a now only a faint possibility that, by the time Padmavajra arrives, we will be able to accommodate him in something less ephemeral than 'Samma Ajiva', the South Ceylon guest house, Unawatuna.

Another offer of accommodation has been made to me; this time it is a small Temple. I made a quick visit to it, and found it neither very beautiful nor in an ideal setting, but not wishing to look a gift-horse in the mouth I stalled for time by promising to hold a retreat there soon. In this way I shall be able to have a really good look at the place before making up my mind about it. It is about three hours bus ride north of Colombo. So there are at least two possibilities for future accommodation on the cards now.

More recently still, Siri, Gunavati, myself and a friend of Siri's called Edirivira went on a little expedition into the backwoods. We went to visit two of Siri's uncles who are bhikkhus living in a forest hermitage. After a two-hour bus ride eastwards, i.e. inland, away from the coast, we arrived at a small village set amongst paddy-fields and coconut trees in the middle of the countryside and got out of the car. Before setting off on foot, we refreshed ourselves with *temilli* or king-coconut. This is the golden nut of a common variety of the coconut palm, ovoid and about ten inches in length. The tree grows everywhere, and the nut contains a deliciously refreshing, almost clear liquid with a faintly sweet taste. The top of the smooth, bright orange husk is first sliced off with a sharp knife and a small square piece excised from the pithy white surface thus exposed. Usually, the contents are under slight pressure, and there is a spurt of liquid when the incision is made. One then pours the liquid into one's upraised mouth. After this, the husk is split open and the soft white fleshy lining can be eaten. Though the liquid is often slightly warm from the sunlight, drinking it has a very pleasant cooling effect on the body which persists for an hour or two. As you can imagine, this is very welcome in such a hot climate. Moreover, the flesh of one coconut will also keep the pangs of hunger away for a couple of hours.

Thus refreshed, the four of us set off, with Edirivira, a middle-aged Ceylonese gentleman recently returned from Nigeria, bringing up the rear. The *āraṇya* or forest hermitage was located, judging by Siri's pointing finger and his brief explanation, somewhere in the thickly forested hills about four miles from where we had alighted. We had not gone more than a couple of yards out of the village when a man rushed out of a nearby house. Prostrating himself in front of me, he asked if we would come to his house and take some refreshment. However, having drunk *temilli* only a few minutes before, we politely declined, and making it clear we were grateful for the offer, continued on our way. We then began to pass through some delightful, almost deserted countryside. Paddy fields gradually gave way to forested hillside, and soon we were climbing a steep and narrow pathway through dense jungle. Siri forged ahead and I followed on his heels. The voices of Gunavati and Edirivira could be heard somewhere quite a long way behind. In fact, from a vantage point which revealed the path winding up from below, Gunavati could be seen slowly bringing up the rear.

I began to proceed more slowly up the path at my own steady pace, whilst Siri went on ahead out of sight. Gunavati and Edirivira were so far behind that I could no longer hear their movements. The silence of the forest grew deep and mysterious, and at one point the whole setting became so intensely peaceful and beautiful that I looked for a place to sit down in contemplation for a few minutes. I sat on a convenient softly rounded rock in the dappled sunshine, shaded by a clump of bamboos just listening, and watching a couple of large black and yellow butterflies flitting languorously here and there. There was not a single disharmonious element present to my consciousness, and I felt perfectly content, perfectly at ease.

Eventually the sound of voices began once more to impinge on my ears. This time I could discern not only Gunavati's and Edirivira's voice, but also a third, and a few moments later, sure enough, three figures hove into view. The third voice, it now appeared, belonged to the man who had earlier offered us refreshment. Perhaps feeling curious concerning the two Westerners, one moreover in orange robes, he had followed and caught us up, and was now carrying Gunavati's bag. For this she was evidently grateful. I looked more intently than before at the stranger's face, and noticed an unusual brightness and positivity in it.

After another ten minutes or so of walking - easier by now, since the path had ceased to climb - we emerged into a forest clearing which was evidently the entrance to the *āraṇya* or forest hermitage. It was flat, sandy-floored and neatly swept. To one side and slightly lower down the gently sloping hillside was a primitive-looking hut divided, we later discovered, into two. One side was the kitchen, and the other a little dining room where, we were later told, the resident monks accepted their food from the visiting *dayakas* or helpers.

Siri had arrived a few minutes before us, and was already deep in conversation with a small thin bhikkhu. They broke off their conversation as we approached and Siri introduced the brown-robed, shaven headed man as his younger uncle. I was surprised to notice, however, that there didn't seem to be much affection between them. Siri had already told me that they had not seen each other for more than a year. So I was a little surprised that there was not more of a show of warmth. Not that they were unfriendly, but something seemed to be missing from their communication. They were too polite. The small bhikkhu greeted me with a defiant glare, which I did my best to melt with a smile, not entirely unsuccessfully. Despite appearances, he soon showed himself friendly enough, enquiring whether we had had anything to eat. His apparent stoniness I therefore took to be evidence of some inner pain or conflict. Perhaps, I thought, it was the result of some penance that he had undertaken. Maybe he was performing a *dhutanga* which, in the absence of kalyana mitrata, was going to an extreme and inducing pain. Gunavati also later mentioned to me that he did not appear happy. When, after I had taken a delightful bath in a cool stream, I was invited with the others to rest in his room, I noticed there was no mattress. I also noticed an almost vertical board padded by a thin cushion inclined at a slight angle to the wall. This suggested to me that he was practising the thirteenth *dhutanga*, undertaking which one sleeps in the sitting position, never lying down. The bhikkhu spoke little English, and Siri was busy with other things, so it was not possible to talk about his practice with him. Having offered me a narrow but comfortable couch, the surface of which looked clean and unused, he left us to wait for Siri. There was a curiously oppressive atmosphere in the plain and unattractive room, and I felt quite glad to leave when Siri returned to conduct us to his elder uncle.

Siri had told me that he thought his elder uncle might be a Stream-entrant, and this thought was uppermost in my mind as we approached his solitary hut in the woods higher up the steep hillside. The door to the hut was wide open and I could see a small brown-robed body lying flat on the bed inside. Siri stepped just inside the door, and speaking softly, tried to rouse the man from his slumber. He woke easily and quickly, and sat upright on the bed. We could now see that his little old body was emaciated, and his face bore a slightly bewildered look. This was hardly surprizing, since he had probably not been warned of our arrival and had in any case been asleep. I felt like an intruder and moved slightly away from the door as if to leave, but Siri beckoned to me and so I drew nearer and stood quietly watching at the low doorway. The old man's mouth was toothless, and had it not been for his eyes, I might have concluded that there was nothing unusual about him. His eyes, however, were unusually bright, not, it seemed, with the light of fever or harshness of any kind. They had a sort of soft glow which seemed sometimes to come from within, and sometimes, curiously, to play outside and around his head. It was almost as if there were beings of light in attendance upon him.

Siri seemed to be shocked by his elder uncle's appearance, and bit by bit it emerged that the old man had recently suffered a stroke. Death's chariot had evidently swung low, but not taken him away. Siri translated his uncle's quiet words; he was saying that the *nimittas* – by which he meant the signs of death - had not appeared to him. He added that he thought he might live for quite a while yet. Gunavati's faithful bag-carrier, who had accompanied us, now stepped inside the hut and put his hand affectionately on the old man's shoulder. He didn't at first recognize the newcomer. But on being told by someone who stood in the shadows "It's your chief *dayaka*" he broke into a wide smile, obviously delighted, and clasped the man's hand. There was an almost palpable bond of affection between the two, so strong that it overflowed from them and enveloped all of us in its warmth. Gunavati remarked afterwards, in her delightfully soft-voiced English: 'That monk seems happy.' Even Edirivira, not particularly demonstrative since he had been recovering from a nose operation, was moved by the scene. He observed how lucky the old man was with such friendly people in attendance on him and how miserable old age must be for those who have no such luck.

After taking our leave and wishing the old man a swift and full recovery, we went to inspect the small and unpretentious *pujasthan* belonging to the hermitage. This, we found, was a small statue placed on a rough unpolished wooden table in the open air; it was a pleasant marble image of Shakyamuni about eighteen inches high. Large grey monkeys watched us from the trees above, and swung from branch to branch as we descended the path towards the dining-room. Brown rice and dhal, simple but satisfying, had been prepared for us, and large chunks of pineapple and papaya were offered for a second course. I took only a piece of papaya, which I found deliciously sweet and almost soft enough to melt in the mouth. After drinking some tea, we washed our plates and hands with water directed along a little bamboo trough from a stream chuckling its way down the hillside. We then inspected the remaining facilities of the hermitage. I felt that, all in all, it was a delightful spot, and thought it might do rather well for Kamalashila, if and when he comes here after his trip to India later in the year. On enquiry, we found that a kuti could be made available for him if he wished.

There was one more thing worthy of note to see before we left. It was the early beginnings of a large meditation hall, and consisted of no more than a wall about four feet high enclosing a rectangle of ground perhaps fifty by twenty five feet. Moreover, we discovered that our bag-carrying chief *dayaka* was the architect of this project: he was evidently not only friendly but highly industrious. He told us that he had personally carried innumerable loads of bricks all the way up the forest path, and done the building work with his own hands. Rather wistfully, he added that he did wish that he had some help to carry the bricks. I asked him whose idea the building was, and he said it was his own. He wanted to build a place, he said, where people could come and practice. It was an ambitious plan. Probably with no very clear idea of what was actually involved, he was undertaking the enormous task single-handed. Where the people would come from to fill such a large hall it was not clear to me. The *dayaka*'s largeness of heart, however, suggested to me that he might well be successful, and that he would be aided by the Bodhisattvas of the Four Quarters. His face was beaming with delight as he showed us his handiwork, which showed, I thought, something of the Bodhisattva spirit.

We retraced our steps towards the village, going back down the path by which we had ascended, noticing this time the spoor of wild elephants which must have followed not far behind us as we approached the *āraṇya*, and eventually descended to the paddy fields. Edirivira, whom I feared would be exhausted, declared that he felt as strong as an ox after our trek. Despite the physical exertion, we were indeed all in good spirits. We were stopped on the track into the village this time by another man, and gladly accepted his offer of coconuts. He promptly shinned up a palm tree in his back garden to fetch them, and with loving care prepared them for us to drink. After we had quaffed the sweet, cooling liquid, Gunavati took photographs of us with the man and his large family of mischievous-looking boys.

Back at the village itself we had to wait an hour and a half for a bus. In the meantime, the villagers had a good opportunity to look at us, and by the time the bus came, everyone was wreathed in smiles. It was Gunavati's last day in Sri Lanka, for a while at least. The others got off the bus at Unawatuna, whilst I proceeded to Galle with her to see her onto a coach and say farewell. Her visit seemed to have lasted hardly more than a moment, and I didn't have any very adequate words to say. I asked her to give my good wishes to everyone in Helsinki. I waved to her as she got onto the bus which would take her back to her hotel in Hikkaduwa, a popular tourist resort some fifteen miles north. And then she was gone. The next day she would be on the plane to Finland. I imagined the icy north, where the temperature would be unimaginably low for people accustomed to the equatorial climate of Sri Lanka. I was glad to notice that Gunavati had had a warm glow on her face. No doubt it was the result of all the tropical sunshine she had soaked up and which, with luck, would help her through the Northern winter in good health.

An image of Gunavati that remained with me for some time was her meeting with and talking to a middle-aged Finnish couple. They had by some extraordinary coincidence arrived at 'Samma Ajiva' within minutes of her own arrival. I listened to them conversing in Finnish, and when there was a suitable lull in their conversation, remarked: 'Finnish seems a very good language with which to convey kindness.'

The March issue of the Order newsletter arrived yesterday, and I have read it from beginning to end. I was very pleased to find a more extended account of my old friend Siddhiratna's adventures, which I kept, like a sort of literary lollipop, until last. But I found the most absorbing reports were those of Padmasuri, describing the ordinations of Jñānasuri and Vimalasuri, and Śrimāla's description of the same event. Although I had not had much contact with the ex-Mrs Labhane and the ex-Mrs Kharat during my four years in India, I had formed a very favourable impression of them both, and was delighted when I heard that they were going to be ordained.

NOTES

65 *Ambedkar and Buddhism*: Sangharakshita, Windhorse.

* * * * *

Adam's Peak

14   Wickramasinghe & Kirilov

This short letter records my anxiety concerning further atrocities by terrorists in Sri Lanka, my continuing efforts to find accommodation suitable for a Centre, and my interest in Martin Wickramasinghe, the Sinhalese Buddhist writer.

I HAVE BEEN SPENDING LESS AND LESS time giving talks at temples recently and paying as much attention as possible to those wishing to learn to meditate. I am also spending more time with mitras and potential mitras. This is partly from necessity. There have been atrocious happenings in Sri Lanka during the past month, as I think everybody knows. This has affected almost everyone I meet, making them depressed and irritable. I have managed, with some difficulty, to remain in reasonably (or unreasonably) good spirits (i.e. friendly ones). However, I am very much looking forward to seeing Padmavajra later this month, and to the unexpected but welcome visit by Devamitra in the not-too-distant future. Towards the end of the year I shall be visiting India - mainly Hyderabad and Sholapur - to meet Friends. I hope also to visit Pune, but exactly when that will be is not yet clear. My efforts to find a small place in Colombo for a community and Centre have not yet borne fruit, but it is only a question of time. The first offer of a house and land to the Movement has been unfortunately withdrawn. We are still investigating the small Temple which I mentioned in my last letter, and which we now know to be situated on about one hectare of land three hours north of Colombo by bus.

On the literary front, I was not at first very impressed by what little writings I had seen of Martin Wickramasinghe, a well-known Sri Lankan author now unfortunately deceased. However, I recently read his study *The Buddhist Jataka Stories and the Russian Novel*, which has raised him in my estimation. For instance, his exposition of the character of Kirilov in Dostoevsky's *The Possessed* is very interesting. In a praiseworthy attempt to demonstrate the similarities between certain Russian characters and the Bodhisattva, Wickramasinghe quotes Dostoevsky's Kirilov: "You're given life now for pain and fear, and that's where the whole deception lies. Now, man is not yet what he will be. A new man will come, happy and proud, to whom it won't matter whether he lives or not. He'll be the new man! He who conquers pain and fear will himself be a god. And that other God will not be."

I would also suggest that anyone who makes the effort to trace and read Dr. Beni Madhab Barua's *Ceylon Lectures,* particularly the one entitled

Buddhism as Buddha's personal religion, will be well rewarded. That particular lecture is even better than I had anticipated, and is of great importance in Buddhist philosophy.

* * * * *

15   An Order Meeting in Unawatuna

This short letter includes a verbatim report of an Order Meeting between myself and Padmavajra. Evidently I am very pleased to have his company in Sri Lanka.

PADMAVAJRA AND I MET in the comparative seclusion of his bedroom in the 'Samma Ajiva' guest house for a reporting-in session on 6th June. Neither of us had a great deal to say on this occasion, which was just as well because hardly had we finished when we were invited to a 'Dana' ceremony with about twenty local bhikkhus.

Padmavajra: "I've been here nearly a week and I'll be leaving in two days' time for the U.K. I got myself wound up here and thought I was dying. I woke up in the middle of the night and found that one of my arms was cold and numb. And then my legs began to get cold. Ashvajit very kindly looked after me for the rest of the night. I think he was right when he said that I was wound up because I'd had no time off for relaxation. These last six months I've had in India have been the most stimulating period of my life - very enriching. At times it's been very difficult, but very rewarding. I have benefited very much from them. I want my future to be in India. I'll be finding my way back there and aiming to arrive this December and staying for one year. Before that I'll be visiting Malaysia and Nepal to do a bit of work there. I've no reflections on Sri Lanka at the moment except to say that there are some very good people here whom Asvajit has got involved in activities. The mitras I've seen all look like good people - keen and bright. It will be good if they can keep in contact and keep up their practice. Asvajit is a good host and has looked after me well. I'm enjoying his company. Metta to all Order Members and salutation to Bhante."

Asvajit: "I am delighted to have Padmavajra here. It is very enjoyable indeed to find communication so easy [because of course] it's with someone from my own cultural background. But I have more in common with Padmavajra than culture, since I've got to know him better and better over a long period of time, and now I am delighted to see him as a fellow Anagarika. He wears his robes very well. It is very good having another Order Member here, not only to meditate with but also to share Kalyana mitrata not only between ourselves but also with mitras and Friends. Padmavajra's arrival has certainly brought a very pleasant extra dimension to our activities. I am sorry only that he is leaving so soon, and hope he will make it a habit to visit Sri Lanka from time to time. During the past month I haven't done very much by way of public activities, but I did give a talk and meditation class on Wesak Day at a big temple at Panadura at which there were about 500 faithful women and maybe a hundred middle-aged and older gentlemen, and quite a lot of youngsters."

* * * * *

The beach at Unawatuna

16   'Buddhist Rest', and the Cave of the Buddhas

Reflecting on my experience of the last few months, I experience a desire to retreat. I pass the bus station where a bomb explosion had recently killed more than a hundred people. Visiting for a second time "Buddhist Rest", the little Temple near Kurunegala of which I have been invited to accept the incumbency, I get to know something of Venerable Sumetta and his peculiar difficulties. We visit Dambulla and glimpse the glories of nature and of Sri Lanka's illustrious past, and the inexpressible wonder of the Cave of the Buddhas.

IT WOULD BE GRATIFYING to be able to give a connected and inspiring account of all of significance that happens in one's life. This is perhaps the function of biography - something to be undertaken in the mature seclusion of early (or possibly late) middle age, and with an appreciative, even an affectionate and loving audience. For the present, however, my Letters from Lanka, comparatively disconnected, variable in quality and with no more than - I dare say - a small and attentive audience, will have to do. Let me supply a few threads of connection, however. In the July Order newsletter there was a reporting-in from Padmavajra and myself. In June, there was a one-page Letter revealing (compared with previous letters) a withdrawal from matters external; and in May there was a five-page Letter expanding on How I could be working and How I am working Here, which was a question that someone actually asked. Not until I go back to the April issue of the Order newsletter do I find evidence of being wholeheartedly engaged with something more external - which is not necessarily to say superficial. That trend towards inwardness has continued, for the most part, since then, but there have been a few little scenarios recently which have excited my imagination in one way or another. So now here they are.

On the 7th May, Mr Francis and I set out from 'Samma Ajiva' for 'Buddhist Rest'. Mr Francis, a seventy-year old friend from Matara, well-versed in the Pali and instrumental in arranging my Dhamma and meditation classes in a temple near the town, had arrived the previous afternoon. Of medium height and willowy, his silver hair contrasting sharply with his dark skin, he might have been considered an attractive figure were it not for a large and disfiguring goitre. However, such things being of quite secondary importance, in his estimation, he had declined to have an operation, especially as he is able to eat and speak without any trouble. As it is the goitre lends him a somewhat pelican-like appearance; and like the pelican, Mr. Francis wears white, not of feathers, but the white long-sleeved shirt of thin cotton with stand-up collar and white sarong worn by the old traditional type of Sri Lankan Buddhist gentleman. This was the form of dress encouraged a hundred years ago by Anagarika Dharmapala, and is today usually equated with the status of Buddhist Upāsaka or lay-follower of the *sāsana*.

Jinasena, looking athletic in his blue western style trousers neatly pressed, and a western style shirt, completed the trio. The Brahma Kumari express was crowded as usual, but someone gave up the 'Reserved for Clergy' seat they were occupying, deferring graciously to my yellow cloth, and Mr. Francis and Jinasena crowded into a space large enough for one. We drew into the Fort (Pettah) Station, Colombo, just before 9:30am, and met, as previously arranged, Mervyn Nanayakkara, who is now a mitra. Mervyn is a few years younger, rather shorter and more squarish than myself. He greeted me as usual with his lightning-quick, slightly mischievous and boyish smile - a look so quick that it is difficult to tell who has seen who first, if indeed either has. Mervyn, an ex-flying school officer and free-lance journalist, was dressed quite nattily, also in Western style, so the foursome was now evenly balanced with regard to mode of dress, two being in Eastern, and two in Western cut.

The four of us then proceeded to the Bo-tree bus station where, only a couple of weeks ago, a huge car bomb had exploded in the middle of the rush hour, scattering human bodies and limbs everywhere in an orgy of destruction. More than a hundred people had died here. Attempts had been made to remove the last traces of the mess, but one didn't need to be a forensic scientist to read the marks, and feel the onset of nausea on noticing pitiful daubs of paint covering bloodstains all over the face of a nearby building up to the second storey, the buckled metal shutters over the shop fronts, and a big area of the road which seemed to have been recently dug up. One of our friends, a member of the hotel staff at 'Samma Ajiva', had been near the explosion at the fateful moment but, standing between two buses, had escaped with minor injury.

Fortunately, we didn't have to wait long viewing the scene of the recent horror, for our bus set off after a very few minutes in the direction of Kurunegala, a town about 95 kilometres north-east of Colombo. By mid-day and three hours of severely restricted, noisy and jolting movement later, we had arrived at 'Buddhist Rest'. Lying about the length of a cricket pitch away from the road, on a rocky slope overlooking fertile paddy fields and the ubiquitous groves of coconut palms, 'Buddhist Rest' is a Temple consisting of a *pansala* (from the Pali: *pañca sila*, meaning the five 'lay' precepts for skilful conduct of one's life) or teaching hall, with adjoining rooms slightly above road level. Much higher up lies the temple proper. This was reached by ascending a precipitous flight of about a hundred and fifty small, rough steps at the top of which stood a slender bell-tower.

Finding no-one about, we toiled to the top of the steps, where Jinasena gave the bell-rope a yank. It sounded out rather sweetly, rather like a melodious school bell saying ding-dong, time to change, ding-dong, play time, ding-dong, time for class. We inspected the tiny image house, and the nearby stupa still in course of construction. The base of the spire to the stupa stood at a height of about four tall men, and was surrounded by scaffolding.

Inside the image house was a six foot tall, seated Buddha-image in the traditional Sinhalese style, flanked by standing images of the two Chief Disciples. Our curiosity satisfied, we went outside again and surveyed the landscape. There was an exceptionally fine view over the surrounding countryside, almost unobstructed but for the overhanging branches of two temple-flower or frangipani trees with their little white, intoxicatingly fragrant blossoms. Far beyond the paddy fields, perhaps twenty miles away on a line of distant hills swathed in green palms, we could see another stupa, small but clear and white in the brilliant sunlight. Were it not for the road down below, we would have been in an ideal spot for meditation here. But the traffic was infrequent, and as a car hurried past, one could feel the mind grasping for the silence and then relaxing again. The perfect, deep blue dome of the sky, and the distant green wooded hills had a soothing and expanding influence on the mind, and one could savour the underlying, deeply peaceful *genius loci*.

I had been asked some weeks ago to accept "Buddhist Rest", and, in the light of previous experience, was very cautiously investigating. My contact with the present incumbent had been initiated many months ago, by someone who had replied to a newspaper article about the Friends, and who had come to stay at 'Samma Ajiva' for a few days. Aloy Prematilleke was cultured, urbane, and soft-spoken. He was about my own age, and with a very sophisticated mind. I was very open with him about my commitment to Buddhism, and he was, I thought, mildly shocked at my rejection of Christianity. We parted on affable enough terms, but I thought that would be the last I would hear of him. But a few weeks ago, after I had returned from India, he had written to me urging that I meet Venerable Doctor Sumetta, the incumbent of "Buddhist Rest".

Having made arrangements to visit, I arrived in Kurunegala by car ten days ago and went to the local clinic. Ven. Sumetta turned out to be a short, well-rounded bhikkhu just avoiding fatness, and fully qualified as a doctor in Western medicine. I could not understand at first what had caused him to pursue this rather unusual life-style, or combination of life-styles, which I imagined would be rather difficult to harmonize. Later on I discovered. But at first he told me simply that he was considering disrobing in order to work more effectively as a doctor, and that he wanted to add homoeopathic studies to his armoury of skills. He was fluent in English, highly intelligent, and seemed to find my company a great relief. I found it pleasant talking to him too, and came to appreciate his uncomplicated openness, or what I took to be so, and his evident trust in me. Having left the clinic and proceeded to what was evidently a pleasant little temple situated not far from the road a couple of miles outside Kurunegala, we spent quite a lot of time talking together, and little by little the truth emerged. Sumetta was involved with a woman, who was, he said, blackmailing him with suicide threats. Could I do anything to help? I was the very first 'priest', he said, in whom he had been able to confide. All the Sri Lankan bhikkhus would have written him off as a womanizer and shunned him, had he told them, but he wasn't a womanizer at all, he said.

Well, I was rather reluctant, as you can imagine, to become involved in such a delicate situation. But I could not remain indifferent, and eventually agreed to meet the woman. I had no idea what I could do, if anything, for her or for Sumetta, but thought that a bit of straightforward human communication might not do any harm. Sumetta accordingly sent one of his helpers off to fetch her, and after an hour or so, the car returned and out stepped a slight, pale skinned woman of not unattractive appearance dressed in Western style. She was introduced to me as 'Gita' by Sumetta, and took a seat politely to one side, whilst he sat on the other. The first difficulty was that Gita didn't speak English, and I understood very little Sinhala, so I had to rely very largely on Sumetta's own translation. But after a few minutes of talking with them, the message was all too clear: Gita intended to commit suicide if her wish to marry the man of her choice was frustrated. I tried to point out that true love was unselfish, and that there were many other eligible young men for an attractive and wealthy woman like her. But it was useless. We went on talking in this vein for a while, and then I began to be aware of another difficulty. Apart from the woman's intransigent attitude, Sumetta appeared, either consciously or unconsciously, to be 'reading her thoughts'. He was not, I suspected, translating simply what she said, but was making various additions and comments that purported to come from her, but which were probably his own thoughts. It was in fact impossible for me to tell, under those conditions, whether what I was hearing were his thoughts and feelings, or hers. Indeed, like the double helix of the geneticist, there appeared to be one organism rather than two, born from their sharing, willingly or unwillingly, a certain view of life. I terminated our talk and went for a walk outside. Later, whilst Gita was resting in his room, Sumetta told me that he had had an affaire with her six years ago, and soon after, she had begun to blackmail him. In order to escape her, he said, he had become a bhikkhu. But apparently it had not helped. Perhaps because she was a Christian, she had not taken his declaration seriously. And every month since his ordination, Sumetta told me, she had visited him demanding intercourse and marriage, and threatening suicide if he tried to refuse. I professed myself astonished at his compliance, and said that I didn't think he would be wise considering even for a moment, entering upon marriage with her. I told him that I was very much afraid that if he did so, he was likely to become bitter and resentful, and to feel that he had been thoroughly exploited. He seemed to take my point, but added "But what can I do?" Neither of us, of course, relished the thought of her committing suicide, and I agreed to have another go at talking to her. With Sumetta's help, I tried to teach her the metta bhavana, first stage, and part of her seemed to open to the practice. But I could see it was not enough, though it was all I could do for the time being. We then parted company. All this had occurred during my first visit to 'Buddhist Rest' ten days ago.

Now, on this second visit, another episode of the drama was enacted. While Mr. Francis, Jinasena and Mervyn were walking in the temple precincts, Gita and another woman, driven by a young man whom I later learned was Gita's brother, arrived in the temple car. Gita seemed emotionally distraught, tossing her head one way and another, but at the same time, curiously dull and listless, like an over-acting starlet trying to do a convincing imitation of a swoon. Thin and large-eyed, dressed in a simple skirt and blouse, she imploringly offered me a gift of sweets in brown paper bag. Then, appearing on the verge of collapse, she made a wobbly exit to Sumetta's room. Some minutes later, Sumetta, who had followed her in, emerged to inform me that Gita had swallowed eight Valium tablets some time before her arrival. Eight, he said, was far from a fatal dose, but was likely to keep her in a heavily-sedated condition for a day, and he would have to keep an eye on her blood pressure. He returned to his room, leaving me alone with the other young woman, the driver of the car having gone off to some other part of the building. She introduced herself, in good English, as Gita's friend Rosie. Rosie was even smaller and slighter than Gita, and with even larger, doe-like eyes. She seemed curiously unconcerned about her friend, and with astonishing frankness, said she had come only to see me. She wanted to know all about Buddhism, and was especially keen to visit India, she told me. I enquired, half-humorously, whether she wanted to be converted, then receiving no reply, in rather more serious tones suggested that she had better think rather carefully whether or not she was a Christian, and why. The answer came pat: her parents were Christians, but she was interested in Buddhism. Her large, doe-like eyes looked at me imploringly, whilst her mouth suggested mute suffering. I wondered whether she was completely vacuous, or whether she was trying to seduce me. I smiled at her in brotherly fashion and said Good, if she was really interested in Buddhism, and continued to be so, she might consider going on a Buddhist pilgrimage. But, I added, she should continue to ask herself if she understood the difference between Buddhism and Christianity. It appeared I had said the right thing, for she smiled, and became so absorbed at the prospect that she forgot to ask when we would be going. Not a moment too soon, Sumetta emerged from his room again and summoned me to another audience with Gita.

Gita was lying on Sumetta's bed, propped up on some cushions, and looking at the same time drowsy and sorrowful, as if to say "How can you not believe that I mean what I say?" Sumetta was looking a little puzzled, and wanted me to say something to her urgently. He whispered to me: "You must get her to promise you not to do it again." This was a bit of familiar counselling technique, but in fact nothing was further from my mind at that moment than to extract such a promise from the woman. And I thought that, even were I to do so, it would be worthless. My instinct or intuition, quite frankly, was rather to say that she could, if she insisted, do away with herself, but please not to take Sumetta with her.

However, there was something so compelling in Sumetta's manner, and in Gita's pathetic appearance, that I thought to myself "Well, it is what they both want, there's no point in my resisting." So I sat down quietly on the edge of the bed with Sumetta and said to Gita in a gentle voice, "You're not going to do this again, are you?" Sumetta translated, and at this, Gita's eyes opened and brightened, and she reached out and clasped my hand fervently and said "Oh no, I won't" (in Sinhalese). Sumetta seemed to breathe more easily and said to me, "Ah, now she's promised, it's all right." But I could not help thinking that everything was not all right, and that I had been party to a bit of second-rate theatre. But what was done was done, and an hour later, Sumetta drove off with the two women, Gita's brother at the wheel, saying that he would have to take her to the local hospital, as her blood pressure was getting dangerously low. The conditions tending towards marriage are continuing to accumulate, I thought to myself.

Later on in the day, Sumetta returned, to report that Gita had been put on intravenous drip, but was quite comfortable now and out of danger. I wondered whether the danger had really been averted. Much could be accomplished with eight Valium tablets, and reinforced with a bottle of saline!

The next day passed uneventfully, or almost. A few local scamps, eight or ten years old, turned up at "Buddhist Rest" saying they were interested in meditation, so I did what little I could with them. In the mid-afternoon, having recovered from the post-prandial stupor common to temples, I sauntered outside to view the paddy-fields, and watched a very thin, dark *goigama* (farmer) up to his knees in mud trimming the irrigation bunds with a mammoty (known more commonly in the Boy Scouts and the Army as a trenching tool). Wearing an absolutely minimal loin-cloth, he went about his business methodically and without pausing for rest so long as I stood there. Unlike farming people in other places, in Sri Lanka (at least in the Sinhalese parts), they occupy a respected place in the social hierarchy, being considered "high caste", and though usually lean and horny-handed, they look happy and healthy.

That evening, Mervyn, Mr Francis and I studied *Mitrata*, and after a meditation and Puja in the image house, went to bed and had a peaceful night's rest.

The following morning, Mervyn decided to leave. Ven. Sumetta, although he had earlier professed interest in our Movement and in meditation, had not participated in any of our activities, and I began to become suspicious of his offer to hand over his temple to us. I asked him to show me the title deeds of the land and temple, which he had said were in his name. Quite disingenuously, it seemed, he said they were deposited at the bank, and that he would send me photo-copies as soon as he could get them. Meanwhile, he continued to be the picture of friendliness, and suggested we should go for a little drive somewhere. He even suggested that we went that very evening to Anuradhapura - a journey which it was quite unrealistic to think of doing in one evening, and I said so. So Sumetta then suggested we visit Dambulla, where there were some beautiful caves. It was hardly an hour away, he said, and having seen some rather attractive pictures of the place, I felt eager to go, and concurred with his suggestion. "Alright", said Sumetta, "when I get back from the clinic at 4:00pm, we can go." Good, I thought, this will be very interesting for me and Mr. Francis (Jinasena too had by now departed) - and it will be an opportunity to try and find out whether Sumetta does really intend to hand over the temple to us.

However, at mid-day, not only Gita, but her mother and brother turned up, together with a small boy. It was evidently going to be a family outing. Having spent the afternoon preparing various fishy dishes for themselves and

one or two vegetarian items for me, everyone was eager to go by the time
Sumetta returned from the clinic. At 4:30pm we were off, all six of us
crammed into the temple car - a Volkswagen 'Beetle'. None of them had, they
said, been to Dambulla caves before, although it was only forty miles away.
Poor Mr Francis, of course, had been entirely forgotten in the others'
eagerness to go, and had to be left behind. I could not help feeling that the old
man was rather more deserving than the others, if only for the reason that,
being so old, he might not have a chance to visit the caves again. However,
he stoutly maintained that he didn't mind, and off we went without him.

   We sped along at a brisk pace as the sun dipped towards the West. The
miles flashed by, and the countryside grew progressively more beautiful. The
palms began to give way to huge deciduous trees casting a welcome shade
over the road, still oppressively hot even in the late afternoon. They had been
planted more than a hundred years ago by one of the more benevolent
Sinhalese kings, for the benefit of travellers, to provide shade and beautify
the countryside, which indeed they did. Some of them wore a crown of bright
crimson flowers, some, yellow. All were tall, mature trees with sturdy trunks
and branches holding elegantly aloft huge canopies of green leaves. The road
passed through the midst of what seemed to be a forest, and then through
plantations of spindly rubber-trees. Their slender trunks all leaned in the
same direction, bent by the prevailing wind, and each bore, near its base, a
little earthenware cup collecting the white latex dripping slowly from a spiral
cut in the bark.

   By the time we reached the town of Dambulla, the sky had already
begun to blush with the hues of evening, and parking the car in a big new
public car park empty but for ourselves and two or three other cars, we all
eagerly began our ascent to the caves. The way led up a long incline of bare
rock, like nothing so much as a solidified, grey-brown river flowing down the
hillside. And as we ascended, it was as if we were entering a pure land. Every
step we took revealed further reaches of a glorious landscape of great mature
trees, huge rocks and tree-covered hills, until it seemed that the hilly plain
stretched into the infinite distance before it met the blue dome on the horizon
immeasurably far away. And what colours and shapes the dome was now
displaying! The dome itself varied from the palest, most delicate, Chinese
willow-pattern blue at the horizon, to a deep, rich, almost velvety indigo at
the zenith. And within the dome were great assemblies of different clouds
ranging from little white fluffy bundles, to huge, blue-black elephants of
storm clouds. As we climbed higher still, the sun sank lower, and every
minute, every second, brought new and breath taking colours into view, from
palest primrose to deepest crimson. All around was perfect silence and peace,
and we seemed to be the only tiny figures present, made microscopically
small by the size and grandeur of the vast landscape.

   Having climbed perhaps a thousand feet above the plain, first up the
river of stone, and then up well-worn paths and flights of steps between huge
boulders, we arrived at the entrance gateway to the caves. It was a towering,
modern structure of no great beauty, in which a few young bhikkhus in their
resplendent orange robes were idling, oblivious, it seemed, by their careless
attitudes, of the beauty of their surroundings. The instant I stepped over the

threshold into the cave-precinct, I had the distinct impression that I was entering a mandala, where, more than anywhere else I had been so far in Sri Lanka, the Dharma had been practised. There was a profound silence, a deeply compelling, utterly arresting calmness and peace - a peacefulness which seemed to envelop me both from outside and inside, and which washed ones very bones with an unearthly purity and bliss and coolness.

We strolled from the precinct into the first cave, which was long and narrow, and contained a huge reclining Buddha-image. Actually, it was not exactly a cave, but a deep cleft in the rock formed by a huge overhang of the rocky mountainside. This enormous cleft appeared to extend along the mountainside for perhaps two hundred yards, and had been formed into a series of 'caves' by the construction of a stone wall which separated the overhung space from the broad and flat stone terrace running the full length of the cleft, and side walls which separated each 'cave' from the adjoining ones, and which afforded further magnificent views over the valley below.

The reclining Buddha-image, attractive though it was, did not satisfy my artistic sensibilities however, for apart from the cave being in a shabby-looking, unkempt state, the image more or less filled the space available, giving a cramped and overcrowded sort of feeling to it. So from here we passed quickly back out onto the terrace, which afforded us further magnificent views over the valley below and of the sky, now suffused with purple and gold.

We entered the next cave by means of a pair of very tall and narrow doors of heavy timber, and fitted with monstrous brass hinges and bolts; doors such as Don Giovanni or Faust might have contemplated, barring the entrance to Hell, glimpsing beyond them the glowing embers and hearing the muffled roar of flames. But passing eagerly through these doors, we discovered no infernal scene. Here the colours, as if echoing the sunset glory of nature outside, but raising it to a higher, transcendental level, were soft, muted golds, yellows, ochres, browns, reds, pinks and whites. Painted on all the visible surfaces of the cave were pageants of people and animals, birds and strange monsters, interspersed with figures seated in meditation. They covered every inch of the walls and ceiling of the huge cave into which we had stepped. This 'cave' was a continuation of the previous one, in fact it appeared to be the main body of the same great cleft in the mountainside, far deeper, longer and higher than the previous one containing the reclining Buddha.

Overcoming a sudden fear that the huge rock-mass above might collapse - for there were no pillars or supports of any kind within the body of the cave, we stepped further in towards the middle. The cave was evenly illuminated by carefully concealed lights, so that the walls appeared not so much to have light shining on them, but to be glowing with their own luminosity. I tried to form an idea of the dimensions of the cave, and as I did so, I began to experience one of the subtleties of the extraordinary space. Big it was indeed - one of the biggest such mountain overhangs I have ever been in - but as I tried to apply some sort of mental yardstick to this creation of art, I began to realize that none of the surfaces were plane, level, or parallel (with the exception of the outer wall, which one could easily ignore). Moreover, the seated Buddha images, ranged in a long line around the perimeter of the cave and facing towards the centre, varied in height, so though one might estimate the height of the image next to which one was standing, it was positively misleading to make any judgement concerning the dimensions of any other part of the cave based on the Buddha images in that part.

As we sauntered around in this magical place, a further subtlety began to reveal itself. The ends of the cave seemed to recede, the walls and roof expand, and the whole space grow unthinkably vast, one's own self becoming very small, just as we had experienced upon our ascent of the river of stone as the landscape 'expanded'. I began to look around with amazed delight at the scene. Here also was that beautiful, profound silence that I had sensed earlier, as if one was in the presence of a great and completely benign spirit. The Buddha-images, looking steadily and levelly ahead, began to occupy my attention. At first I had thought them a bit crude, almost pagan in character, and indeed, they did hearken back to that period of artistic and sculptural endeavour before the influence of the Greeks had made its mark on the East, or at least, in Sri Lanka. The seated images were big, some of them three or four times the height of a man, but unlike pagan images, of which I had seen many in India, and which are devoid of truly human characteristics, these were kindly, even, in some cases, humorous, and it was impossible to feel anything but the completely benign intention of the Will that had shaped these forms and placed them in their peaceful setting.

The sheer incommensurability, and the extraordinary silence, stillness and beauty of the cave continued to pour itself into me, and with my inner ear I began to hear voices deeply intoning verses of the Good Law Whilst I was communing with these, Sumetta broke in on my thoughts and invited me to come over and see something. Hesitating to be drawn away from those inner voices - though I could not have said whether they were in fact inner or outer, I followed him, and my eye was led to a crack in the roof from which fell, every few seconds, a drop of crystal-clear water, which, catching the light as it dropped, appeared as a sparkling jewel falling to the ground, where a great bronze pot stood to catch the riches. It occurred to me unbidden: "This is how one is purified", but again wresting me from my inner voice, Sumetta insisted on informing me that the water was collected and used exclusively for *Buddha-puja* in the great cave.

Walking once around the perimeter, I eventually came to a halt in front of a standing image, large and well-proportioned. The image was backed by a short section of richly-painted wall which rose to the ceiling, and on a sudden impulse, I walked around to see what was on the back of it. My curiosity was rewarded by the sight of a picture of a standing figure in bhikkhu robes and carrying what would have been anathema to many died-in-the-wool Theravadins: in one hand the figure held a vase of initiation from which protruded peacock feathers, and in the other, a mala! Returning to the front and making the standing image the focus of my devotions, as evidently many other visitors did, I made my offerings and recited the Refuges and Ten Precepts. My lighted stick of incense was quickly extinguished by a young monk who hurried up, perhaps because he wanted to protect the murals, or perhaps because he was impatient for us to go so that he could close the doors.

As we emerged, from the cave, without however leaving behind that profound, utterly peaceful silence, the tall doors closed behind us with a crash and a thud, and we found ourselves bathed in a glorious golden light radiating in millions upon millions of rays from the setting sun. The whole landscape was as if aflame in those golden rays, which appeared all the brighter by contrast with the dimness from which we had just emerged.

On passing, this time outwards through the gatehouse, I felt that the mandala had completely penetrated me, emptied itself into my consciousness; so much so that this cave, once entered, could never be left. Its completely benign influence would remain with me, I felt, to the end of my days. It seemed to speak of the heyday of the Ceylonese Sangha, of the Sāsana as transmitted by Arahant Mahinda, and before the tradition of meditation had been effectively lost and more trust placed in the letter of the Teaching than in its spirit and essential meaning. Perhaps even practitioners of the Mahāyāna - Bodhisattvas, or Siddhas of the Vajrayāna, had meditated here. However that may have been, such was the power of the cave that all of us were deeply affected by it, and in an intensely happy mood, we began our descent.

By ten in the evening we were back in 'Buddhist Rest', and the next morning Mr. Francis and I were up at four in the morning in readiness for the journey to Colombo and Unawatuna.

* * * * *

17   Hello from India

I visit to India from Sri Lanka at the invitation of Lokamitra. I cover much ground and am invited to give Dharma talks as well as to preside at other formal functions in many places.

ON TOUR OF OUR INDIAN CENTRES with Jinasena as my companion, I have visited and given talks in Pune, Ulhasnagar, Sholapur, Aurangabad, Wardha, Hyderabad Kolhapur, Ahmedabad, Gandhinagar, and various towns and many villages whose names I do not now remember. I have both supported and led retreats near Wardha, Sholapur and Igatpuri, and also in Ahmedabad. I have presided at two marriages and administered the Refuges and Precepts to the brides and grooms, but not married them. I was unable to entice any of them away with my begging bowl. I also performed a name-giving, and gave talks at two *punyanumodanas* or death-ceremonies. I have given talks at least once a day outside Pune, except during full days of travel and whilst on retreat - in all so far forty full-length talks and many shorter ones, including one in Pune on Sangha day which erred on the side of generosity timewise and could have been more concise. Barring the ups and downs of the stomach, inevitable it seems in India, I am bearing up and feeling invigorated by contact with enthusiastic Friends, mitras and Dhammacharis. Jinasena also looks inspired by his first departure from Lanka and contact with new Buddhists, and even gave a talk at one of the villages, which intrigued his listeners. We have had a very full ten weeks in India and are looking forward to another four or so, before taking the train to Trivandrum and the plane to Colombo.

I was very happy to see the pictures of the newly-ordained Order members in the October issue of Shabda. Special thanks to Devamitra and Gunavati for giving me a rare glimpse of myself through others' eyes. Incidentally, the Sinhalese Buddhist Year is reckoned as 2531; I was therefore intrigued to see that both *Shabda* and *Golden Drum* bear the date 2530. There is presumably a convincing argument for the discrepancy. Fortunately, we have a supra-national, secular date line.

As I am typing this letter, the teacher in the shrine room-cum-infant school next door is trying to teach her little charges to sing. The noise is rather loud, and erratic enough to attract my attention. The teacher doesn't seem very efficient. When I was at school the mistress there taught us first to sing the tonic sol-fa and only then, when we had learned to control the level and pitch of our voices, were we allowed to sing a tune together.

* * * * *

Ashvajit in Pune, India, wearing a blue Dharmachari shirt under his orange robes to distinguish himself from the bhikkhus

18   Inching into Colombo

The beginning of the second part of my sojourn in Sri Lanka has begun with homelessness. Together with my companion Jinasena, I have started searching in earnest for suitable accommodation. In addition to these letters, provoked by an acute sense of impermanence due to the parlous state of affairs in this country, I am also starting to write my memoirs.

HAVING ARRIVED IN SRI LANKA FOR THE SECOND TIME, after a three and a half month Dhamma tour in India, I am taking stock of the changes which have taken place. I feel well - physically stronger - and inspired by my contact with many Order Members. This country however is in an even deeper state of restlessness and anxiety than when I left. Whether the Government is really democratic is being brought more and more into question both by the media and by the gun. Also, more and more people, more and more readily, are expressing to me their dissatisfaction and disillusionment with the bhikkhus. On several occasions I have felt an almost overwhelming sense of disgust and a desire not to wear my robes, which of course tend to identify me with the bhikkhus. The hostile looks that I get from many members of the public in Colombo (some of them no doubt Tamils) needs all my metta to transform. On the other hand I cannot deny the personal friendliness, helpfulness and intelligence of at least some of the bhikkhus towards me. My visa depends at present on my wearing the robes, and it may be a long time before that will change. One thing I could do would be to wear the blue Dharmachari shirt under my upper robe, but it is so very hot and humid here that it would be unbearable most of the time.

During the past month I have been commuting once a week from Galle to Colombo, to lead regular meditation classes in each place. A strong feeling, not to say bond of affection has begun to grow between me and some of our friends here, and I can no longer feel, as I once did, with Jean-Paul Sartre, that "Hell is other people." On the other hand, I can still at times see a certain truth in the aphorism.

On the verge of taking up residence - turn by turn - in two different flats in Colombo, the respective landlords changed their minds and turned down my offer. So, accompanied by Jinasena I am still pacing the streets of the capital in search of accommodation. The YMBA Colombo is full of men who are neither young nor particularly Buddhist, so we have to ply the commercial market and resist the idea of taking up residence in a Temple. In the meantime we are the guests, to our great good fortune, of a very sweet old lady by the name of Florence who is an aunt of Mervyn Nanayakkara, one of our mitras. Refusing all payment, she has given me the use of a small room in her small flat. Jinasena sleeps on the floor, which I am not very happy about, and we are both provided with delicious food prepared by good old Florence who insists on 'doing' for us in the general spirit of service which I find amongst so many Sinhalese lay-people. The other occupant of the flat is Ranjith, Florence's son, who is, or was, a university lecturer. Having been subjected to no less than thirteen sessions of electro-shock therapy, and heavily dosed with tranquillisers, he was discharged as "incurably, atypically schizophrenic." Shortly after we met, I gave him a bit of a telling-off, and since then he has improved markedly. His drugs are down by two thirds, his garrulousness by half, and his depression to a mere fraction. I did what I did more out of a sense of self-preservation than any insight into his character, but it seems to have worked.

As well as searching for a flat as a temporary base in Colombo, I am following up a suggestion by Lokamitra to establish a Hostel there. This morning, Jinasena and I went to see a seven year old, twelve-roomed house on a quarter acre plot of land that would serve our purposes admirably. Even at the asking price of £18,500 (at present rates of exchange) it is an incredible bargain by any standards. We would be able to accommodate between ten and twenty young men and give them the benefit of a proper Buddhist training. I am becoming more and more enthusiastic at the prospect, and now have to turn my mind to fund raising for this, as well as giving due consideration to running costs and the implications for the Movement here. If any Order Members individually or collectively feel they could support this project financially, please write to me as soon as possible.

My Travel Letters (from India) are still unfinished since I have been living out of a suitcase since arriving, but I hope to send them soon, as I have had quite a bit of appreciative comment concerning earlier Letters. I am not satisfied with the work I have done on the seven *bhojjangas*, and without being able to refer to Bhante's comments on the subject in seminars, do not feel confident that the treatment is full enough. I am therefore putting that work to one side, and taking up the task of an autobiography. 'Memoirs' is probably a better word, being more concise and poetic, and truth to tell, more accurate. I hope that Bhante (and others, for that matter) will not think I am plagiarizing.

Thanks to everyone for the Kalyana mitrata I enjoyed in India; now I feel strong enough to cling to solitude for a while. Jai Bhim to that indefatigable campaigner Vimalakirti, to our young trail-blazer Shakyanand and to all the new Indian Dhammacharis.

* * * * *

19   'Rajgiri', and the Ramakrishna Mission

At long last, and with great relief, I find a base in the suburbs of Colombo. Boarding with Florence and Ranjit has tested all our powers of tolerance. The new premises are small and noisy, but a lot better than nothing. At least we are now relatively independent, and have a degree of privacy. I visit the Ramakrishna Mission, and find two Swamis, in a curious parallel to Sangharakshita's visit forty-four years previously. I begin to realize that the translation of dharma texts into Sinhalese is going to require not only a translator, but commitment. I pay another visit to Dhammajyoti.

WE AT LAST HAVE A TOE-HOLD in Colombo, this capital city of Sri Lanka, though not the capital city of Theravada Buddhism. Having secured a one-year lease on this two-room, kitchen and bathroom flat in the fragrant lee of a chocolate biscuit factory, the next task is to seek registration as an officially recognized charitable body with Bhante as Spiritual Adviser. The question of what to call ourselves here is currently under consideration. I have suggested Trailokya Bauddha Mahasangha Sahayaka Samithiya, since the word 'gana' does not enjoy the general currency here that it does in India. There is also a not unpleasing play in the initial letters TBMSS. Anyway, we shall see if there are any objections or better ideas than this in due course.

The flat here is one third, more or less, of a bungalow situated only a few yards away from a busy road. The other two thirds of the building are occupied by the landlord, his wife, an Alsatian dog of gigantic proportions, and two Burmese cats. The noise of the traffic is loud but not unbearably so. My tolerance to noise has risen markedly over the years, but I will not be tolerating this noise any longer than absolutely necessary, and intend to be moving into a larger and quieter place by the end of the year. In the meantime it will do. I was getting more and more exhausted and even ill-tempered tramping the streets of Colombo and this is the first place that we found that was not altogether unsuitable. By we, I mean myself and (mitra) Jinasena who is the other occupant of the flat. We thus form the nucleus of the New Society in Sri Lanka. We have already had several visitors since moving in on 25th February, and the atmosphere of the place is good and getting better. The name I have chosen - 'Rajgiri' - will be familiar to Indian Dalits as the name that Dr. Ambedkar gave to his home in Bombay. I hope that it will be worthy both of the associations with the Buddha and with Dr. Ambedkar.

Lokamitra has very kindly suggested I do another Indian tour, though how I am to follow his injunction not to criticize the bhikkhus, the gods, or Hinduism, I am not yet sure. I suppose I shall either have to do it indirectly or present my listeners with such a good, shining example of spirituality that I do not have to resort to criticism at all. Perhaps Vimalakirti will have something to say by way of advice for the next tour. Anyway, I look forward to it, whenever it will be.

I recently visited the Ramakrishna Mission in Colombo. Bhante speaks of the Mission in *The Rainbow Road*[66]. I had an interesting talk with one of the swamis there, called Samprajnānanda, and purchased a copy of Romain Rolland's biography of Sri Ramakrishna. Rolland's style is dreadful – though perhaps it is not quite so bad in the original French - with footnotes often more extensive than the text, and continually interrupting the flow of the narrative. Rolland does not stick to the point, and time and time again digresses with long stories about Ramakrishna's contemporaries. Having made allowance for these shortcomings, however, a picture of the modern Hindu saint who was the guru of Swami Vivekananda does emerge. I confess to having felt a mixture of fascination and horror at the unfolding of the story of Ramakrishna's life - a story tinged with not a little hysteria - and to wondering that people can place faith in the "I am God, Thou art God" credo. I encountered an example of this myself, incidentally, during a retreat a few years ago at Daund in India, during which I became severely dehydrated and had to seek medical attention. A young Brahmin came up to me whilst I was strolling about outside just after my recovery and said, with apparently perfect sincerity: "Thou art God". I did not feel at all happy with the implications of his words, and said: "No I'm not", a remark which did not appear to satisfy.

I found my way on foot to the Ramakrishna Mission, Colombo, and it was Samprajñānanda whom I met first. A middle-aged, somewhat severe-looking man dressed in ochre robes, he turned out to be more intellectually vigorous than any of the bhikkhus I have met so far here, though his mental attitude, I soon discovered, was rather rigid. The name of the other Swami to whom I was introduced I do not now remember, but I do recall how sharply he differed from Samprajñānanda. The second Swami appeared to be in his early maturity, well-built without being heavy or muscle-bound, and with healthy, shining and happy features. He looked a fine example of a yogi; I wanted to talk to him, but unfortunately I had arrived, he told me, at the time he usually performed his *pūja*. I was therefore left talking to the first Swami. In the midst of our conversation, a middle-aged American walked onto the veranda where Dennis Lingwood (before he became Dharmapriya and later, Sangharakshita) had sat forty-four years ago with Swamis Siddhatmananda and Vipulananda, and after listening to us for not more than a few seconds said with amazing directness and frankness: "Swamiji, you're so darned sure that what you think is right that you're just not listening to what that man (i.e. me) has to say." Which just about summed it up. The American, I later discovered, was a freelance psychologist interested in spiritual matters, and we exchanged addresses.

Based as I now am in Colombo, I am travelling South to Galle and Unawatuna for a two-night stay each week. I find the change more refreshing than strenuous. There is very little response to our meditation class in the town so far, but we are moving back to our old venue at YMBA Galle next week, after holding the class in two private houses without much success. We shall also be doing a lot more advertising, and perhaps things will improve. Siri, my chief translator, has been making plans to go on another long trip - to Australia, New Zealand, America and the U.K. However he has got into difficulties with visas, which is more disappointing for him than for me, and is now thinking of coming to join us in 'Rajgiri', where I think he would be an asset to the community. He wants to translate Subhuti's *Buddhism for Today* into Sinhalese, which is quite an undertaking, and he would need the support of the community to do it. He has already done the first draft translation of Bhante's *Going for Refuge*, which is now being checked for errors, omissions and amendments. However, I doubt that he will find himself able to leave his family for long. As well as being a good translator, Siri is one of the few people in Sri Lanka with whom I can be completely straightforward.

I dropped in on Bhikkhu Dhammajyoti recently and was pleasantly surprised to see that a large building had sprung up on the piece of land which he had purchased next to his Temple premises. I said not very long ago that I did not think he would have the means to do it; but I was not thinking then so much of financial means (although he has raised those with commendable swiftness), I was thinking of the support that he would need from spiritually mature individuals to make his project a real success. Be that as it may, the new building, I gather, will provide additional accommodation for his thirty-two young protégés, as well as a large meditation hall - not a Shrine room, Dhammajyoti insisted. He likes to reserve the term shrine room for the image house or *budugè* in which the very imposing, twelve foot high seated Buddha-image is kept. I could not help admiring the industry with which he is pursuing his aims, though I continue to have reservations concerning compulsory meditation for young boys, even in a culturally Buddhist context.

I am well, getting on with writing my memoirs, and sorry only that I will not be able to join the Order Members celebrating the twentieth anniversary of the Founding of the WBO. But we will have our own celebration here. I wish all Dhammacharis and Dhammacharinis a joyous 20th Anniversary Dharma feast, and rejoice in the inconceivable merits of all Order Members, and those of its extraordinary founder.

NOTES

66 *The Rainbow Road,* Sangharakshita, Windhorse Publications, 1997. The fist volume of Sangharakshita's memoirs of his early years in India, during which he meets various fascinating characters - some genuine spiritual teachers and others charlatans. See also: *The History of my Going for Refuge,* Sangharakshita, Windhorse, Glasgow, 1988.

* * * * *

20   A lesbian couple, and some reflections on 'Vipassana'

We acquire a new mitra, I sit in meditation throughout one full-moon night in Unawatuna, and I report my perceptions concerning the attitudes of many European men to my being in robes. I befriend two Austrian women and reflect on vipassana. Returning to 'Rajgiri', I feel pleased by the positive atmosphere but frustrated by the smallness of the premises.

I ARRIVED HERE AT 'RAJGIRI' - our new base in Colombo - yesterday in time for lunch. After having been up all night meditating with two Friends - a middle-aged German couple, in the beach-side *devale* (Hindu image-house) at Unawatuna, I felt surprisingly well. I had been in Galle ten days previously on my usual trip South for the regular weekly meditation class at the YMBA, and this had been followed - a couple of days later - by a weekend retreat or 'Bhāvana Camp' for men at an old Temple reputed to have been visited by Colonel Olcott. Madame Blavatsky was not mentioned by the residents of the Temple as having visited the place, though she had come with Olcott to Ceylon. We had a very pleasant yet quite intense retreat.

Mr. Thilakaratne, a Senior Officer of the Government's Co-operative agency in Galle, had his mitra Ceremony at a temporary shrine we put up in the Temple precincts. For study, we dipped into Colonel Olcott's *Buddhist Catechism*, whilst sitting in the sun-dappled shade of a delightful woodland grove of palms, areca, mango, and the fragrant Ma tree. We decided that the American Military gentleman had a rather one-sided approach to the Goal. One of the participants in our study group was the very lively, though somewhat dogmatic colleague of Mr. Thilakaratne's who had organized the retreat for us. Despite his dogmatism, however, I appreciated the presence of someone who was prepared to speak up and even chip in when I began to wander, apparently, off the straight and narrow. The Sinhalese as a race, I have begun to suspect, are intellectually very passive, and I really have to provoke them by saying something outrageous, or else wait for endless minutes, very often, in order to get any kind of response. They do not seem to be at all used to mental exercise, much less possessed of intellectual courage, with a few noble exceptions.

The Temple we found ourselves in was an old and quiet one, as unremarkable for its architecture as for its resident bhikkhus, who largely ignored us, as I have now come to expect. A young layman, resident for some reason or other in the bhikkhus' accommodation, became very interested in us however, and asked to be informed of our future activities, concerning which I was glad to speak. Hundreds of Christmas lilies graced the precincts of the Temple, thrusting their tall green stems bolt upright through the undergrowth, and each bearing three trumpet-shaped blossoms of a most delicate salmon pink.

Since I was due in Galle again on the Tuesday after the weekend retreat, I decided to stay in Siri's Guest House in Unawatuna, and it was during this extended visit that I met Samanera Kosia, who walked into the restaurant one day, and introduced me to the two German friends of his with whom I subsequently did a session of all-night meditation - on a full-moon night, actually. Never having done this before, I was at first reluctant to say "Yes" to the German couple's request. But then I thought, well, why not try it while I am still young enough, so I decided to go ahead with the all-night sit. I found it easier than I had expected - easier, for instance, than getting up to synchronise with the UK Order *metta bhavana*[67] sessions, which means getting up at one o'clock in the morning after having had, perhaps, two hours sleep. Perhaps the idea of 'unlimited' vigilance is more potent than 'limited' vigilance, after which one can 'crash out' after a suitably manful struggle. At any rate, I found myself able to rise to the challenge on that full-moon night, getting up to stretch my legs every hour or so then returning to my seat on the sandy courtyard in front of the small Hindu god-houses to the soothing accompaniment of the sea breaking on the shore only a few yards away, and aware all the time of the cool light of the full moon sailing overhead.

Samanera Kosia hailed from Surinam, and was of mixed Italian/Burgher descent. He had spent several years in India as a Shaivite mendicant before Going for Refuge with Ven. Balangoda Ananda Maitreya, one of the seniormost and most respected meditating monks in Ceylon. Despite his orthodox style, however, Kosia was by no means orthodox in behaviour, demanding various kinds of food in the restaurant instead of waiting, as is more usual for visiting monks, and accepting whatever is offered or placed in front of them. Furthermore, he said, he took no notice of people who criticised him for speaking to bikini-clad holiday makers. Well, he was less cautious than me, for all that I have no rule against speaking to them! Despite these aberrations, however, he seemed sincere in his meditation practice - at least he had one - and I enjoyed my brief communication with him. Unfortunately, two days before the projected all-night sit, Kosia received a call from his mother in Europe saying that his sister was dying of cancer. So now I had sole responsibility for doing the all-night sit with the German couple. I hoped the merit gained from the act would help Kosia's sister in some way.

During my longer-than-usual stay in Unawatuna, I made some more friends. This time it was two Austrian women. In fact this year I have been making more women friends than men friends - by chance, not by design. This is simply because more women than men from amongst the European tourists are interested in meditation. Not only that, I have noticed a disturbing phenomenon recently: an increasing number of European men are giving me the cold shoulder. This could be for several reasons. It may be that they perceive me as a 'European bhikkhu', and that this is abhorrent to their political sensibilities. It may be due to fear of homosexuality - they may perceive me as too 'forward' for decency, though nowadays I am very much aware of and on the lookout for the effect on others of my communication with them, and of the possibility of misunderstandings and reactions. It may be that they think that all bhikkhus are homosexual - a view commonly held here, it seems. Thirdly, I have found a number of men playing a game of indifference, or 'psychological imperturbability'; they play it so well, in fact, that I suspect they have become unconscious of the fact that they are playing it. Men with this syndrome are very clearly distinguishable from other male visitors to the restaurant, who are straightforward, friendly, and psychologically positive. I wonder whether this game - or mental illness, as it really is - is on the increase in Europe; none of the Australians and New Zealanders I have met appear to suffer from it. The women also seem to fall, very roughly, into two categories in this respect. There are those who seem to perceive me as an unavailable, undesirable, or uninteresting male, and those who perceive me as a potentially interesting individual. And I have been meeting quite a few of the latter category recently.

Two such women were Gertrud and Kristine, hailing from Innsbruck. They had already spent some four weeks on a "Vipassana" course at Rockhill Hermitage. They had been practising, very assiduously by their own account, the rise and fall of the diaphragm, and absorbing the instructor's - Bhikkhu Kassapa's - own particular brand of Sinhalese Theravadin pluralistic realism. The result was that this 'couple' (for thus it was abundantly clear they were), came to me in a condition of incipient neurotic alienation, a state from which I was able, fortunately, to relieve them without much difficulty. They then began to brighten up quite dramatically, and to display a quite unusual degree of positive emotion and a lively interest in the Dharma. In fact they both began to glow to such an extent that it was a delight to be with them.

I have been thinking quite a lot about 'Vipassana' recently, and am of the opinion that this form of meditation as it is practised in various places in Sri Lanka, - judging by the reports I have heard of those who have tried it - has a deleterious effect on the psyche of many of them, creating a split between the normally integrated conative and affective aspects of the personality. So deep has this split appeared to be in some of them that I have feared that sooner or later their state of evident neurotic alienation and depression would become habitual, with very unfortunate results both for themselves and for society. 'Vipassana' without true insight is positively dangerous, and those who teach it without the guidance of someone with genuine spiritual insight are irresponsible. Time and time again I hear of people or meet people who complain of being subjected to such teachings, and who have become rigid and depressed as a result. Fortunately, in the Triratna Buddhist Order, we are aware, through Sangharakshita's teaching, of the dangers of premature 'vipassana' practice, and can, if things have not gone too far, help the sufferer to correct the psychic imbalance previously set up. But many do not have such luck, and I can't help wondering what happens to them. Well, at least the Austrians Gertrud and Kristine clearly benefited from the Triratna method of meditation, and it may be that they succeed in making contact with one of our Centres in Europe when they return there later this year.

Our Wednesday Regulars' class at the YMBA Fort, Galle, shows a modest increase. I have even begun to think (not too seriously) of ways and means of 'taking over' their administration. How good it would be! But at present it would be more truthful to call the YMBA (Galle) the Young Men's Billiards Association, billiards being practised assiduously every day of the week by the young and not-so-young men, and meditation (with a few noble exceptions), not at all.

Something that I did this month that I have never done before was to go snorkelling in the Unawatuna bay. I was offered the gear by two men in their thirties, who were in the company of a young and very well-endowed 'topless' woman bather. I was passing by on my way to Rahula's meditation kuti, trying to guard the gates of the senses, when one of the men called out to me and asked if I would like to try some underwater swimming. Keeping my presence of mind, I said that I would be passing this way later, and if they were still there, I might take up their offer. When I came back, the men were indeed still there and the young woman had gone, so I felt free to try snorkelling without becoming distracted. Still a bit hesitant, I told them that I anticipated some difficulty swimming in my lower robe, but one of the men offered me a pair of orange swimming trunks to use. The colour decided it; I slipped into the swimming trunks and tried the snorkel, holding the mouthpiece lightly between the gums and lips and letting the breathing 'take care of itself'. I found swimming in this way an enjoyable exercise. Not only that, the colourful little fish swimming around the rocks and corals were quite fascinating at first. But the fishes' capacity for communication seemed rather limited, so after a while my mind began to turn to more interesting matters, and I left the water, dried quickly in the hot sun, and putting on my robes, took to the Seaside Kuti again to do some writing-up of my Indian Tour.

After the rather stagnant mood of Unawatuna, it was pleasant to return to the more lively atmosphere of 'Rajgiri', and to find Jinasena and Mervyn enjoying themselves together. Jinasena has become less moody since moving to Colombo, and Mervyn less depressed - even though he does not live here: he simply visits, coming on his moped from Panadura about half an hour's drive south. So I am beginning to feel that despite the obvious limitations of the place - the proximity to a busy road and a chocolate biscuit factory, the mosquitoes, the huge dog, and the lack of a garden, there are gleams of something else breaking through at times. I think an orthodox bhikkhu, if he came here, would have difficulty in understanding what was going on, if he could understand it at all. Having said this, I am looking ahead occasionally with an impatience which I find difficult to curb.

In response to my request for funds for a Hostel, Mahamati kindly wrote to me with a standard list of questions, which I was unable satisfactorily to answer there and then. So, it seems, there is a lot more preparatory work to be done yet. However, as I said in my reply to Mahamati, I did not feel that I had been culpably premature in my request, and would have happily and confidently gone ahead with the purchase of the proposed house for a Hostel, had I had the money. I confess to feelings of frustration, since I have just discovered that the house (or mansion, more properly, with its one-and-a-quarter acres of land) has recently been donated to the chief 'Vipassana' teacher of Kanduboda - the only other place, apart from Rockhill Hermitage, with anything approaching proper meditation instruction for ordinary people.

This teacher, I am told, was growing weary of his responsibilities at Kanduboda, left without putting anyone in charge, and is now making a nest for himself after the manner of the Temple Bhikkhus.

So anyway, the quest continues. Meanwhile, right now, I am happy to be alive, happy to be an Anagarika, happy to be a Member of the Order, happy that Urgyen Sangharakshita is well and that the Order is celebrating its 20th Anniversary in a few days from now. What a message we have to convey to the world; few if any others seem to have it.

Newly-framed pictures of Bhante, Dr. Ambedkar and Kuan Yin (thanks to Order Members in India) now look down at me from different parts of my room, as if reminding me to 'buck up', and a small Stupa of brass on the shrine gleams softly, as if to say that death can be as seductive as pleasure.

* * * *

21   Chula, Jayasuria, and the Rubber Plantation retreat

I am inspired by the natural beauty around Kandy, and by the work of a young woman with street children in the town. The YMBA (Kandy) do not seem keen to enlist my services. I enjoy a retreat in a mansion on a Rubber Plantation, and have a vivid dream about Chretien de Troyes.

IT IS NOT ORDER DAY HERE (or anywhere else so far as I know), but it is the day on which Shabda usually arrives, which invariably excites me. I am therefore writing 'in the heat of the moment' even whilst a vociferous young mechanic stands outside 'Rajgiri' admonishing the landlady in charming Ceylonese English concerning the internal combustion engine:

"The piston goes up and down the cylinder, Yes? And causes friction? So to prevent too much heat being produced, yes? OIL has to be supplied between the piston and the walls of the cylinder so that the piston can move smoothly up and down without the engine seizing up, yes?"

Brilliant, he's absolutely right. Couldn't have put it better myself. Now the woman will know better than to try to run her engine without oil. I always thought she was a bit of a dry old stick. Now they have both gone. Thank goodness.

It was lovely to find the first issue of Shabda addressed to 'Rajgiri' (thanks, Kulaprabha) awaiting me on my return from Kandy this morning. It was lovely to hear from Ajita, Sona and Subhuti, from Ratnaprabha, Aniketa, Vimalakirti and Aloka, and to see and feel so many members of the Order flashing and scintillating into this small haven in an otherwise Sangha-forsaken country. I left Unawatuna four days ago to go to Kandy, and rising early and taking the beach path to the bus stop I was rewarded with a glorious scene: a sky full of thunderclouds turned brilliant violet, a turquoise sea with white waves, and a magnificent, perfect rainbow poised over the sea. It seemed an archetypal vision, with everything pervaded by a clear light of the utmost intensity and brilliance. I thought to myself that whatever else it was, it was an auspicious sign for the New Year, which had been ushered in the previous evening with tom-toms throbbing far into the night. The journey to Kandy was hardly less inspiring, as the bus climbed higher and higher into the forested hills, and the emerald green paddy fields glinted far below, tier upon tier of ribbon-like terraces holding back a precious few inches of water. What a harmonious picture of man and nature co-operating. Where indeed did man begin and nature end?

I enjoyed myself royally in Kandy for three days staying in lone splendour in a small but salubrious hotel owned by a friend of Siri's. It stood high on a hillside overlooking the lake and the Temple of the Tooth. The morning after my arrival as I breakfasted, I could see emerging above a circle of forested hills around the lake, the topmost peak in Ceylon, piercing through layer upon layer of mist into a sky of utterly transparent, ethereal blue. And then, as the sun rose higher still, it glanced off the 22-carat gold tiled roof presented by the Japanese and recently erected by order of the Prime Minister over the old Temple of the Tooth. It had little enough to do with the Dharma, I thought, but it was certainly eye-catching. Sun shining on gold produces an intense and characteristic feeling. And the gold never tarnishes, nor does the sun - so long as it is the sun - cease to shine. And sitting in view of all this I was served delicious food upon tables of ebony. The cook himself was not exactly divine in appearance, but his culinary skill was evident, and he was friendly too. But something was missing, I felt. The feeling was a sort of loneliness; not that I needed company exactly, but that the experience, beautiful and refined though it was, was incomplete; even with the Anagarika robes, I was not able to communicate to anyone there even a reflection of the Dharma. So beautiful though the situation was, it was frustrating.

Later that morning, I walked into town. How easily everyone smiled, I thought. How confident they are, how mercurial and gentle the men, how soft and watchful the women. What need is there for meditation in a deva realm? Who would be interested, who would want to Go for Refuge? I went to visit Chula, a friend of Keerthi, our mitra in Kandy. She runs a school for deprived children, street children, children of prostitutes. She is the happiest person I have met in Sri Lanka. Her name means 'Small', and she is indeed diminutive, with an hour-glass figure dressed in the traditional white sari. When you speak to her, every fibre of her body seems to respond with delight, and her eyes become moist and dark and flash little points of diamond light. She is not however, just a pretty face. She knows what suffering is, but she herself feeds on joy. She is the efficient organizer, chief worker and inspirational force of this school. Her children adore her. Within her aura, time seems to stand still and happiness rules over everything. Since coming on one of our retreats at Rockhill Hermitage she has expressed a wish for me to start a meditation class in Kandy. She wanted to become a mitra but because she is working closely with Sarvodaya, the pan-religious movement started by Dr. Ariyaratne, I asked her to think about her true allegiance for a while. She thinks she will be able to find a suitable place for me to start Dharma classes, but has to ask the Sarvodaya administrator. After a talk and a cup of tea I left Chula and the smiling, ragamuffin children, and went in search of a couple of men friends.

I walked up a steeply-sloping lane lined with bushes from which protruded sky-blue trumpets of convolvulus and hibiscus of brilliant scarlet, past little houses nestling snugly into the hillside. Is there any place nearer heaven, I thought, as the morning sun raised a mild perspiration on my forehead. But despite the beauty of nature, I felt once again that something was missing. I was without a spiritual companion. To whom could I communicate my sense of Going for Refuge, or with whom could I share it? A solitary Going for Refuge, even if theoretically possible, would surely be a dry and unsatisfying thing, and I keenly felt the need of a companion to share in my own apparently ever-deepening Going for Refuge. But there was no denying that I felt so much lighter, more virile, more vigorous, in Kandy. Should I not try to build a Centre somewhere near here? With these thoughts in mind, I continued to search for my friends - two men working for "Plenty", a Canadian organization promoting Soya beans, whom I had met in Siri's Hotel - but they were both out, much to my disappointment. I left messages for them, and returned to McLeod Inn for lunch.

Next morning I went to visit the YMBA President at the substantial-looking and well-maintained headquarters building lower down the road from McLeod Inn. The administrative secretary, a Mr. Jayasuria, was a little bird-like man who greeted me politely and apologetically explained that the YMBA President worked full-time in an insurance office, in a place several miles out of Kandy, and could be seen only in the evenings. However, he said, the President had received my earlier letter requesting the granting of facilities for meditation classes, and my request would be considered in due course by the Committee which had not met for a while "due to the New Year". I asked Mr. Jayasuria if he was a member of the Committee, but he said no, being an employee of the organization, he could not be a member of the Committee. I felt that this was ridiculous and said so, pointing out that surely he, more than anyone else, would be in touch with what was going on here. But he merely smiled a little apologetic smile and shrugged his shoulders. However, I said, I did not want to interfere in his affairs, all I wanted was for him to put to the Chairman as clearly as possible what I was hoping for - which I proceeded to explain. Mr. Jayasuria listened sympathetically, and impressed me by taking notes. He promised to pass on what I had said. I felt I had an ally in him, but sensed also that in the Committee of the YMBA I was up against a conservative-minded power group who would be unlikely to respond wholeheartedly to a call for the practice of the Dharma.

I returned to Colombo to pick up the threads of our work there. Mervyn Nanayakkara was in charge of the arrangements for a week's mixed retreat at a rubber estate Mansion belonging to a friend of his, a Christian ex-Mayor living near Panadura. However, the owner was balking, so I had visit him to find out what were the difficulties. After I had talked with him for half an hour about our work, he agreed to let us hire the place as originally requested, which was fortunate, since we had already done some advertising for the retreat. But it was not enough and too late. Only three people turned up, apart from myself. A telegram came from Siri saying that he could not come. The house, though large, was furnished for a mere handful of wealthy occupants, and though we would have had difficulty in accommodating a large number of retreatants, there was room for six or eight more of our number. But there was no point in lamenting; there would be better organization next time, and for now there were four of us.

I enjoyed the retreat very much, finding that my meditation began to deepen quite naturally and easily. The early bath, taken with cold water from a well in the bright morning sunshine, was particularly refreshing. Then I began to encounter an area of pain which would not shift, and to realize that I am living under quite a strain at present, what with the relentless heat and weekly journeys, the inadequate accommodation, and the lack of Order contact. Though both Jinasena and Mervyn are developing, they cannot as yet supply that element of peer communication which is so necessary. I began to feel that setting up a meditation Centre in the Kandy, or some other hill area was really a must, and that it would be wise to regard "Rajgiri" more as an office and pied-a-terre in Colombo, rather than a place of residence.

The night after returning from the retreat (it had been six days, during which we did five hours of meditation each day) I had an 'Archetypal' dream in which a mediaeval knight appeared to me. His shining silver armour was covered with a red and greenish-blue surplice embroidered with a fleur-de-lys (or was it a bird?). I asked "Who are you?" and he said in a quiet, matter-of-fact voice: "I am Chrétien de Troyes". So astonished was I at his direct and clear response that I woke and sat up suddenly, my mosquito net collapsing on me. Chrétien had seemed actually to be there in front of me, as large as life.

Last Saturday was our first mitra Day, and we dedicated the Rajgiri shrine, meditated, and did some study of the Noble Eightfold Path. Despite its physical limitations, there is no doubt that our Centre is here at present. We have yet to make it official.

* * * * *

22   Where am I?

*I describe in some detail where I am based, for the benefit of those
without a large-scale atlas. I give a Wesak talk in Temple, and play the sitar
in Kandy. I do a series of radio talks, and contemplate being alone for a
while in "Rajgiri." Writing my memoirs assists my meditation.*

FIRST A POINT CONCERNING MY PRESENT ADDRESS, which I
have previously given as 31 Attidiya Road, Ratmalana, Sri Lanka. At the
same time I have also spoken of being 'in Colombo.' So some of you might
have been puzzled concerning my whereabouts, particularly if you wanted to
write to me. A glance at the map of Sri Lanka (previously Ceylon), reveals a
lozenge-shaped island tapering not quite to a point in the North, and the
application of a ruler and a simple calculation reveals that it is some two
hundred and sixty three miles in length, that is, along its major axis, which is
tilted a few degrees anti-clockwise of True North. The top end of the axis lies
in Kankesanturai, a coastal town near the mostly Tamil city of Jaffna some
ten miles to the South, and the bottom end in Devinuwera - the 'City of the
Gods' - which is Sinhalese-dominated. Two-thirds of the way down the left-
hand or Western coast of the Island, at the Westernmost end of the minor axis
of the "lozenge", lies the city of Colombo, and near the Eastern end of the
minor axis is the town of Batticaloa. Another application of the ruler and a
simple calculation reveals that at the minor axis, the maximum width of the
island is some 137 miles.

Now just as one might be hard put to it to define the limits of London,
or Bombay, so, on a smaller scale, it is not easy to say where Colombo begins
and ends. It is an urban agglomeration stretching ribbonwise along the coast
for about fifteen miles. From the Lighthouse near the top of Marine Drive,
which no-one would be disinclined to say is in Colombo, southward to the
district of Moratuwa, is about twelve miles. South of Moratuwa one would be
disinclined to say "this is Colombo." And north of the Kelaniya River, which
issues into the sea about three miles north of the Lighthouse and Harbour,
one would be equally disinclined to say "this is Colombo". The "ribbon" is
most densely populated towards the western side, which abuts the almost
mathematically straight stretch of coast line, and it gradually peters off to the
east into various suburbs and villages, eventually merging imperceptibly with
the paddy fields, palm groves and hills which characterize the countryside.
Many of the city streets occupied by the wealthy are straight and broad, and
often pleasantly tree-lined. Large houses - bungalows or two storied
buildings - with shady eaves, colonnaded porches and cool terraces, lie well

back from the road, and there is a uniformed guard posted outside, if not a soldier or two with a rifle or machine gun at the ready. In the areas of the "have-nots", the buildings degenerate into concrete dolls-houses and architecture without architects. Makeshift timber-and-corrugated-iron huts roofed with cajuns or woven palm leaves cluster together for comradeship in places. But the extent of these dilapidated areas is not so great (though pitiful enough), and never quite reaches the level of squalor found in Indian hutment areas, for instance. The shady presence everywhere of the cocoanut palm, and an abundance of flowers and greenery of all kinds manages to soften even the poorest areas into something which manages to convey a sense of cheerful simplicity. The general impression the casual visitor gets of Colombo is therefore of a prosperous, developing city, more than coping with its backlog of barbarism, and emerging into the bright but not harsh light of modern 'civilization', with a distinctly Western or 'International' style. It has in fact become a modern Eurasian city - something which Anagarika Dharmapala railed against a hundred years ago, and which must have been very painful to his discerning and far-seeing eye, and to his heart so rooted in traditional values. But today, those with the Dharma in mind must learn to tolerate, if not condone, the fate dictated to all cities by Western technological and secular society.

The Postal Service divides what it is pleased to call Colombo into fifteen Postal zones, arranged in a sort of distorted fan-shape around the lighthouse. But Ratmalana, from where I am writing, lies just beyond the edge of the 'fan'. It is not assigned a zone number. Ratmalana was, presumably, originally a village lying in comparative isolation about nine miles south of the Marine Drive lighthouse, but now it has been engulfed in the general conurbation, and there is nothing worthy of note to distinguish and separate it from the ribbon of development which continues a further three miles or so south to Moratuwa.

'Rajgiri' as I have named it - the name reminds me, amongst other things, of the Lama the All-performing King - is the annexe of a bungalow, modern and unprepossessing, lying a mere ten feet back from a road running eastwards from a point where it joins the North-South Galle road about a quarter of a mile from here. The area is a mixture of industry and housing, and as I think I have remarked elsewhere, rather noisy and polluted. Being unable to afford triple glazing and air-conditioning (though we do now have a fan), I started to look for alternative accommodation almost as soon as we arrived. But we shall probably be here for the best part of this year and 'at home' every Friday for Beginners' class.

Ratmalana is not, therefore, technically Colombo, but for all practical purposes it is. The postal description 'Rajgiri', 31 Attidiya Road, Ratmalana, Sri Lanka, is quite sufficient to locate me, but if you want to add "Colombo", that doesn't matter, it will not lead to confusion.

Last month has as usual been a mixture of pleasure and pain. Wesak has come and gone. I passed it enjoyably enough, and was invited, it so happened, to give a talk to the faithful at a village temple near Galle - the Tuwakugalawatta Purānavihāraya. I had befriended a young bhikkhu who had taken it upon himself to invite me there, so I turned up not altogether expectedly on Wesak morning. The High Priest however was evidently happy to hand over to me what he apparently regarded as a bit of a chore, presumably on the basis that any *sudu hamudru* or white bhikkhu was good enough for him. I did not disappoint him, and my talk and meditation class translated by Siri seemed to please everyone, particularly the chief *dayaka* or lay supporter, a Mr. Peiris, a charming, intelligent and sensitive man who I hope to meet again. He has I think more chance of gaining Enlightenment than either the Chief Priest or the young bhikkhu with his Pandit degree who invited me there, youthful and pleasant though he was. I would like to have celebrated Wesak with our mitras, and indeed, sooner or later, we must. But at present they are too scattered for that. At the end of my talk I was presented with a magnificent set of bhikkhu robes which I kept, thinking that Bhante might find them acceptable.

Other memorable events during the month were the magical appearance of Devamitra whilst I was travelling south to Galle on the train. Suddenly he was there, sitting on a seat on the opposite side of the gangway. It was some moments before I thought to myself that it was rather odd that Devamitra should be sitting there, and then he vanished. Later, we had a weekend retreat in a leafy *āranya*, or forest hermitage. Though the average age of the participants, 54, was somewhat high, the retreat was as enjoyable as usual. However, yesterday at 'Rajgiri', the average age plunged to about 30, with the arrival of two young men Friends, and I must admit it was rather refreshing.

I visited Kandy this month and during my first evening there had the opportunity of playing a Sitar - something that I had never dreamed of being able to do. It was not as difficult as I had thought to produce a pleasing sound. The following day I went to Peradeniya University to meet Professor Gunapala Dharmasiri. He is the author of *A Buddhist Critique of the Christian Concept of God*, and professed himself an admirer of Bhante - "One of the few people who knows, and practices what he preaches". I also managed to find a copy of the *Encyclopaedia Britannica* and look up a reference concerning Chretien de Troyes - the man whom I saw vividly in a dream recently, and which I reported last month. It was all very interesting, and it occurred to me that I should write something more about my relationship, whether real or imaginary, with this famous troubadour.

Yesterday I returned to Colombo and went to see, once again, Alec Robertson, the burgher in charge of the Sri Lankan English-language broadcasting on Buddhist matters. My periodic talks are, it seems, meeting with a positive response, and he wants me to give a series of four fifteen-minute talks on "Buddhism for Today". I will try to give Subhuti's book some publicity. Mr. Robertson, who speaks fluent English and Sinhalese, has developed a particularly mind-crushing style of conversation, acquired I imagine as a defence against Bhikkhudom, but this time I managed to hold my own rather well, and kept him in the Tushita Devaloka for quite a few minutes. He exclaimed delightedly afterwards "I do like these conversations - like being transported to another land for an hour." I hope I can do as well for the radio audience (all over South East Asia and India), and that some of them at least will not return to *samsara* for considerably more than a few minutes.

Siri, my chief translator, is about to leave Sri Lanka on a sort of world tour, first stop New Zealand, and Jinasena is off to India, so probably by the end of next month I shall be alone in 'Rajgiri' for a while. It will not, I imagine, be for very long: my days as a hermit are over, though I can quite happily enjoy my own company for a while. Living with other like-minded men is more difficult but more enjoyable and more conducive to insight.

Bhante's recently published books *The History of My Going for Refuge* and *The Religion of Art* arrived this month. There seems no end to Bhante's wonderful creativity. I am aspiring to authorship by working on my Memoirs. It is having a marvellous effect on my meditation, strange to say. I am not sure exactly why. I think it is because it gives me a good big 'object' to meditate on. Anyway, it is also helping me to see more positive aspects of what I had thought was a rather depressing, dissolute and worthless life up to the age of thirty. It is also helping me to work out some thoughts on Immanence and Transcendence.

I think that is all for now, except to thank Bhante for his picture post card of Valencia, his letter and note, and to say that I am feeling better now that the rains have started here and the temperature is down to something more comfortable. Best wishes to all Order Members and may you all have long and healthy lives.

* * * * *

23   India Tour 1987/88

In which I start my second tour of India with Jinasena accompanying me. The change of scenery and tempo of work, the appreciative audiences and company of Dharma friends have a tonic affect on both of us. Doing a dharma tour is not however a bed of roses. I preside at a marriage ceremony which, unfortunately, is not far short of farce. Jinasena and I visit the Museum containing the collection of artefacts which had belonged to Salar Jung, the Chief Minister of the Nizam of Hyderabad. Visiting a tiny vihara outside Hyderabad, I am impressed by a young and vigorous wife taking her drunken husband in hand. I am offered a meal of chicken curry, and taken to task for the mention of devas in the Buddhist scriptures.

THIS SECOND TOUR OF INDIA whilst I am based in Sri Lanka began - or at least, the planning of it began - when Bhante wrote, early I think, in 1987, suggesting that I might avail myself of some Kalyana mitrata towards the end of the year in India. Of course I was happy at the prospect of the Kalyana mitrata whether I was to be on the giving or the receiving 'end', a matter that seems more and more difficult to determine. Be that as it may, I anticipated correctly that Lokamitra would give me plenty of opportunity to contribute what I could to the growth of the Movement in India. With his usual efficiency he drew up a programme for me once I had decided to visit , and together we decided roughly when to start, though the exact fixing of the dates had to be left to me.

Lokamitra was also happy for me to bring Jinasena along. Jinasena is a healthy and relatively unattached 28-year old mitra, and would benefit from being introduced to an increasingly large aspect of the wider Movement; and travelling with a constant companion throughout the tour would I thought be beneficial for me too. On September 23rd, Jinasena and I arrived at Colombo International airport, and joined the group waiting for take-off. It was Jinasena's first trip outside Sri Lanka, and his first aeroplane flight. Much to his disappointment, the flight departure was after sunset, so there was little to experience except the curious shifts in "downwards" that are familiar to seasoned air travellers.

But I am anticipating a little bit. There were a few moments of anxiety at first when a mismanaged set of steps leading to the aircraft door lifted the door itself an inch or two. It then had to be checked to see if it would seal properly. The young, fair-haired European pilot, cheerful and matter-of-fact, ascertained that everything was all right, and finally closed the door and entered the flight cabin. Since we were seated in the front row, we could see right into the cockpit, where a whole barrage of instruments were aglow with green lights. Looking round and noticing that we were watching him, the pilot smiled at us, or rather, I think, we smiled at him, at which he got up and closed the cabin door. A few moments later we were advised to 'fasten our seat belts,' and we were taxiing out for take-off.

The flight was uneventful and two hours and twenty-five minutes after take-off the familiar and tension-relieving 'thud' of tires on the runway, followed by the roaring of engines in reverse thrust told us we had landed. The subsequent announcement that 'We have now landed at Bombay Airport' seemed unnecessary, but I suppose we might have landed somewhere else. Soon our passports were being checked. The Indian officers looked somehow familiar, and less formidable than on previous occasions. It occurred to me that having become accustomed to the grimness and darkness of Ceylonese faces (at least some of the more officious ones), by contrast and comparison the Indians looked lighter, both in colour and spirits. At any rate, the officer who checked my passport was really friendly, and having compared the pre-anagarika photo on my passport with post-anagarika photo on my visa, said "You looked better with long hair" - a remark which I found a refreshing contrast to the uncritical acceptance of everything 'monastic' by the ultra-orthodox Sinhalese.

Dhammachari Bodhisen, mitra Prakash and a couple of young men I did not recognise, met us outside the exit, and in a matter of minutes we were speeding along the highway in a bus which seemed as much in advance of Ceylonese bus technology as European buses had seemed in advance of Indian ones when I visited Europe a couple of years ago. We spent the night at 'Bhim Prerana' (Bhim's Inspiration) - the TBMSG flat in Bandra East, and the following morning took the Bombay-Hyderabad Express to Pune. I could not help noticing that on Bombay VT (Victoria Terminus) platforms one can now watch the latest inane product of Bollywood on colour TV every few yards down the platform. I also could not help noticing during the journey that new buildings were springing up faster than ever, but that, unfortunately, the slum areas also appeared more extensive and more hideous than I remembered them, especially in the Ulhasnagar area.

A friendly welcome awaited us at Pune station, where Dhammacharis Buddhapriya and Sudarshana, amongst others, quickly dispelled the sombre reflections of the journey, and we were escorted to Dapodi, which is now effectively a suburb of Pune, where Lokamitra was expecting us. The next and subsequent few mornings in Dapodi followed a similar pattern. Jinasena and I would walk from Sanghvi, itself a suburb of Dapodi, where Lokamitra has his office - called 'Madhuban' - across the river bridge. We would see the reflections of the dawn sky in the waters of the river, savour the coolness of the air at that time of day, and go and sit with the community members in Jeevak - the TBMSG Medical Centre, for meditation. Jeevak is currently being used as an administrative centre cum community centre, in addition to the function for which it was designed - a health centre and kindergarten, or *balwadi*. On the first floor of the Centre sits a brown-coloured Thai Buddha-image about four feet high, presented by some Thai bhikkhus, which provides a good big focus for the devotions of the community members.

After meditation, we would then make our way, in twos and threes, to the community house for breakfast. This involved a seven or eight-minute walk from Jeevak, along the main bazaar road, past a bust of Dr. Ambedkar, where public meetings are often held, and into the heart of one of the Dapodi slums. There, in one of the two small rooms (the other doubles as a kitchen), ten of us would sit and consume our breakfast, which usually consisted of *pohé* or fried rice-flakes, followed by sweet and milky tea and a tiny, sweet banana or two. Conversation would begin in desultory fashion, sometimes centering on the meaning of a word in Marathi, and soon break into laughter. Jinasena and I both began to feel that we were fortunate to be in the company of such a pleasant and wholesome community of young men. Their vitality and positivity were in marked contrast to the large companies of old women and children, and a few men, to which we had become accustomed in the traditional Sri Lankan scene. Jinasena remarked to me, after a day or two in Pune, that 'Indian Buddhists are more friendly and positive, they're more generous and open, than Sri Lankan Buddhists.'

I was asked to give a talk rather sooner than I had expected - at the *punyānumodana* ceremony for Dhammachari Shakyanand's 36-year old daughter, who had died of leukaemia. It was therefore with a curious mixture of feelings that I stood up before the little crowd of Friends - many of whom I knew well but hadn't seen for two years or more, and began to speak. Lokamitra spoke after me, and expanded on something I said about *karma* and rebirth - not that I had said very much, but I had forgotten what a difficult subject this is for ex-Untouchables. How sad, in a way, not to be able to offer consolation with that sort of reflection. The chief source of rejoicing in this case was that Shakyanand's daughter, although evidently suffering, had gone on meditating and being astonishingly positive and cheerful, right throughout her eight-year illness, which was a wonderful example for everybody.

After a few more days in Pune, Jinasena and I took a bus to Sholapur accompanied by Dhammachari Dhammodaya. Everything on the way seemed very familiar, almost comforting, and I found myself trying to shrug off the feeling that I had not been away for two years, had even not been away at all. In Sholapur itself we were met at the bus station by a group of a dozen or so mitras and Friends who were evidently very glad to see us. I was glad to see them too. Judging by the visible evidence, quite a lot of work had been going on in Sholapur during the past two years - no doubt both on the part of the Sahayakas and mitras, and by visiting Dhammacharis. The clearest evidence of this was the shrine room which had been built onto one side of the house belonging to Mr. Kadlak, one of our first and most ardent helpers. The dynamics of spiritual progress are such, however, that whilst Mr. Kadlak remained a Sahayaka, six other Sholapur Friends, less obviously devoted than him, had become mitras. But the centrality of actual meditation practice in our Movement was becoming clear now even to Mr. Kadlak, and he was taking valiant steps, it appeared, to remedy his deficiency in that respect.

A succession of programmes followed our arrival in Sholapur, and I was particularly happy to be able to make my own contribution to the celebration of the initiation of the Dhamma Revolution by Dr. Ambedkar on Ashok

Vijaya Dasami[68]. Later that evening, after the celebration, I found myself in a mitra's small house watching the national news on TV. I could not help feeling that it was utterly grotesque that no mention was made either of the great *Samrat* (Emperor) Ashoka, or of Dr. Ambedkar, surely two of India's greatest men, and whose memory was particularly connected with that day. Instead, platitudes were mouthed concerning the goddess Durga, who by some caprice was enjoying popularity that year, Mahatma Gandhi, 'the father or the Nation', and several other minor figures whose names I do not remember. Durga's name was being invoked in the cause of morality, which was no bad thing in itself, and I suppose if the Hindu pantheon is actually in process of being re-oriented towards the Dharma in the sense of morality, I really shouldn't complain, much less indulge in righteous indignation.

The other programmes in Sholapur were as usual, visits to various localities including shanty towns, notably the 'Forrest' district, thickly populated by Dalits. On my previous visit to the City, the large Vihara in this area had closed its doors to Dhammacharis of TBMSG, but perhaps because the Dhammachari in question was wearing robes this time, the ban was lifted, and I was able to give a talk there. I spoke, as on many such occasions, of the importance of Going for Refuge, and of the cultivation of Kalyana mitrata with Members, mitras and Helpers of the Trailokya Bauddha Mahasangha. Over the years it has become more and more clear to me that, well-intentioned though they may be, no one outside TBMSG really has a clue how to practice Buddhism or even how to inspire others to humanitarian activity without inter-group animosities. I really do hope that the efforts of TBMSG in this area will bear fruit, and further and more friendly connections be made with the vast number of caste-Hindu-oppressed members of the Indian populace.

I also took the opportunity whilst in Sholapur, of getting to know a little more about the mitras, and in addition to accepting their invitations to lunch and supper, I spent several hours talking with each of them. The lunch invitations I found less of an ordeal than on previous occasions, having become accustomed to even hotter Sri Lankan fare, and I was even able to enjoy myself, for the most part, though I took care to take very little of the hottest dishes, and to accept only about half the rice initially offered, putting the rest aside on an empty plate if necessary, which it usually was.

The tiny houses, often no more than tin sheds to which we were invited were always immaculately clean and tidy, and the food offered with great tenderness. That it is the poor who truly know generosity seemed here not so much a truism as a discovery which plumbed a dark secret of human nature. The rich are rich because in their poverty of spirit they cannot give, or cannot wholeheartedly give, whilst the poor are poor because, in their richness of spirit, they cannot withhold. One has to develop a strong stomach for Dhamma work in India, but I could not help feeling horrified by two of the huts in particular that we visited. Both belonging to mitras, they were not merely small, which according to a certain meme is beautiful, but miniscule. In one case, the place measured about an arm's width and a body length - a mere corrugated-iron corridor tacked on the side of a 'larger' hut, and situated on the piece of land that separated the latter from an open sewer. In the other case there was just enough room for two single, narrow bedsteads with a two-foot corridor in between and a two-foot space at the end far from the entrance, which served as the kitchen. Both these 'houses' were occupied by a man, a woman, and two children. Both men were well educated: a degree certificate hung from one wall. But their chances of getting decent jobs were minimal, because of the caste system. In the second of the two huts, a middle-aged man sat in the narrow space between the two beds whilst we ate, displaying a lower leg covered with the most horrible semi-liquid mass of eczema. I remarked with as level a voice as I could that perhaps he ought to see a doctor. I told him I didn't want him to lose a leg. He looked at me calmly, and said that he had been to several doctors but they had not been able to help him. He then pressed upon me a five-rupee note which, try as I would, I was not able to return to him.

The middle of our visit to Sholapur was punctuated by a journey to Aurangabad, Wardha, and Hyderabad. The bus trip to Aurangabad was a ten-hour one - long enough to travel from one end of Sri Lanka to the other - but we were still well within Maharashtra. Hour after hour, fields of sunflowers passed us by, and eventually, our backsides almost rigid with pain, we arrived at Aurangabad bus station. Just as we were leaving in a motor tricycle rickshaw, I spotted the diminutive Dharmachari Nagasena who had come to meet us, and we proceeded to the new hostel in Bhimnagar, an outlying suburb of the city. It was a joy to see the Buddhist flag flying above the single-storey building, and I silently rejoiced in the merits of Jyotipala, under whose tutelage the building had arisen. It was sited on an open piece of land with no other buildings near, and with a beautiful back-drop of mountains. Jinasena and I were shown into Jyotipala's room, which was simple to a fault, being graced by a large old upright-backed, yellow painted arm chair beside a small table, above which hung a photographic reproduction of the thangkha of Shakyamuni circulated by Dhardo Rimpoche, and in the middle of the opposite wall, a steel cupboard housing a small collection of Dharma books. Jyotipala was away on some mission of mercy, and we were looked after by a mitra.

Not long after our arrival, Dhammacharini Jñanasuri appeared, and she and Nagasena and I sat outside the Hostel in the glow of a beautiful evening sky, exchanging a few words before the Order meeting - my first for nearly two years, with the exception of my meeting with Padmavajra in Sri Lanka. The following day, Nagasena invited me to give a talk to an assembly of Sahayakas and mitras. He expected twenty people or so, who, he said, could be accommodated in the shrine room. If there were more, we could arrange things outside. So I set aside a couple of hours that day to prepare a talk. Just as I was beginning, a mitra called Inchikar turned up, with a barrage of questions for which he did not allow time for an answer before asking the next. However, as he seemed more interested in Jinasena than in me, we arrived at the mutually agreeable arrangement: he would show Jinasena around Milind College, where he is a 'professor' (i.e. teacher), whilst I would be left alone to enjoy the peace of Jyotipala's room and get on with my work.

That evening about a hundred people turned up for the talk, so we assembled outside. The weather remained clear and there was a beautiful full moon. I gave a talk about Sri Lanka, characterising Sri Lankan Buddhism as Ravana. I suggested that Rama had gone to Lanka and cut Ravana up into many small pieces, explaining that this was a poetic way of seeing the battle of Indian nationalism with Sri Lankan nationalism. However, Ravana was not destroyed so easily, and each of the small pieces of his body had now grown into a man clad in yellow robes. The audience laughed, and though I was of course being humorous, there was also, I suggested, truth in what I said. I explained that Sri Lankan Buddhism, insofar as it was merely ethnic, was a degenerate Buddhism – a Buddhism without meditation and without Insight. Most of the Sri Lankan monks did not practice meditation systematically if at all, I said. Often, I added, they were nothing more than Sri Lankan nationalism in thin disguise. I went on to speak of morality, regular practice and study, which would lead eventually to Insight and Stream Entry.

Nagasena translated clearly and faithfully what I said, so far as I could tell. He seemed very pleased afterwards, and I asked him what he thought about my talk. He replied that it was good. The following morning, after a delicious breakfast in the open air with the mitra who was looking after us, and also with some other friends, we left for Wardha. There were some hours of worry and delay after we discovered we had been misinformed at the bus station and got on the wrong bus. Luckily however, we were able to take an alternative route, later taking a train through the parched countryside to Wardha, and eventually arrived there at 7:00pm. A rickshaw to Bheem Nagar, named after Dr Ambedkar, completed our journey, and we soon located Dhammachari Vimalakirti, who was very relieved to see us, having been in a state of consternation when we had not arrived as expected. We were greeted by Dhammacharis Sanghasena and Manjuvir, the latter whom I was meeting as a member of our Order for the first time. I was as usual touched by Sanghasena's great, completely unaffected and natural friendliness and openness, and regretted not being able to converse with him more readily; his English was as limited as my Marathi. Manjuvir was bubbling over with talkativeness, whilst Vimalakirti was more reserved and statesmanlike. I felt a keen sense of pleasure to be with them both. Thus began our brief stay in Wardha, during which we were introduced to dozens of people and invited to their houses on every conceivable pretext. I quickly got an impression of a super-abundance of metta, and a keen and genuine interest in the Dhamma.

A retreat had been arranged for the weekend of our visit, and was attended by all, or almost all the men likely to become mitras. Vimalakirti led the retreat, and I led one of the study groups, with Manjuvir translating, so far as I could tell, very ably. The level of communication was excellent, and I felt that at least one of the men was not only ready to be a mitra but ready to be a member of the Order. The text for our study was *What Meditation Really Is*[69]. Not only was the study good; the meditation sessions were very concentrated, with hardly a twitch or stir amongst the twenty participants. Indians appear to sit so easily and comfortably in meditation, perhaps because they are used to sitting cross-legged almost since birth.

The day following the retreat, I agreed to give a talk in the evening to the Regulars' Class, which turned out to be relatively large, consisting of 250

- 300 men and women. There was an extraordinarily positive, almost festive atmosphere to the gathering. Once again I spoke about Sri Lanka, and with Vimalakirti translating, communication was straightforward and enjoyable. I felt that the Triratna Buddhist Community in Wardha was proceeding very well indeed.

Leaving Wardha, Jinasena and I went by train to Hyderabad on the first of two visits. The first one was short; we were to celebrate Ashok Vijaya Dasami, not according to the Hindu tradition, which places it on the tenth day after the new moon of September/October, commemorating Rama's return to his capital after slaying the ten-headed demon king of Lanka, but according to the immeasurably more meaningful Common Era anniversary of the Great Conversion inaugurated by Dr Ambedkar at Nagpur. On this occasion I had been invited to speak at the Press Club, and had in fact been billed as the Chief Guest. The hall was full to capacity - with about 250 people. The atmosphere however was strangely oppressive, and there was little evidence of celebration. I had been told prior to my arrival that several Judges were likely to be present as well as the Governor of Andhra Pradesh and various other non-Buddhist worthies. I had therefore prepared what I considered a low-key talk, designed not to excite Hindu sensibilities. After all, it was far from being my intention to stir up communal strife; rather I wanted to point the way that Dr Ambedkar had pointed, towards universal emancipation.

I had asked to be the last of seven speakers, having learned the hard way the consequences of not doing so, and I therefore steeled myself to sit through what I thought would be quite a lengthy period of boredom combined with a not very positive atmosphere. As my turn approached, the talks, having started entirely in Telugu, became longer and more English. Not only that, the general tone of them became more and more defiant and negative. I began to feel that whatever positivity there had been at first had largely evaporated, and also, that after the bellowings of these political bulls against the iniquities of casteism, my own talk would seem feeble indeed. However, I need not have worried. When my turn came, I found that I had an abundance of energy, and that the audience sat quietly and attentively. I approached the question of how to work as a follower of Dr Ambedkar today, and stressed the importance of adopting a positive attitude towards society, rather than a merely negative and destructive one, though there was no doubt much that needed to be changed. I ended by saying that Dr Ambedkar, in embracing Buddhism, had pointed to the importance of what might be called Bharatiya Culture, which was the legacy of Emperor Asoka. The moment I uttered the words, however, I sensed that this idea was completely new to most people. Perhaps my listeners did not feel that there was anything worthwhile at all in Indian Culture as such. For them, perhaps, Indian culture was synonymous with Brahminical culture, and therefore wholly evil and to be overturned. However, it was far too late in the evening to start extemporizing on the essential and universal value of culture, and in particular the values upheld by Asoka in his Kingdom of Righteousness, so I wound up as skilfully as I could by pointing to TBMSG as an exemplar of Dr Ambedkar's ideas and work and rejoicing in that. All in all, I thought I had not done too badly, having restored something of a festive atmosphere by extolling Dr Ambedkar's dream of a Buddhist India. There had been no sign of the Judges or of the Governor of Andhra Pradesh.

I discovered next day that my intuition concerning 'Bharatiya Culture' during the delivery of my talk had been correct: Mr. Bhalley, the penultimate speaker the previous evening, and well known amongst Ambedkarite Buddhists, before departing by train had announced to a little crowd who had come to see him off, that there was no such thing as Bharatiya Culture. Since Mr. Bhalley is in quite an influential position amongst Ambedkarites, this was rather unfortunate, and I resolved to follow the matter up with him. The evening after my appearance at the Press Club, we took our leave of Mr Rastrapal, the loquacious friend who made up to some extent for his lack of verbal restraint by providing accommodation for us in Hyderabad, and returned to Sholapur.

Upon arriving in Sholapur, after no more than an hour's rest, we were whisked off to a far-distant village for a programme that I had agreed to a few minutes before I had given the 'Forest' locality talk on my previous visit. We arrived in pouring rain, and a little crowd of bedraggled villagers turned up, looking, many of them, drunk or stoned. I did what I could in the circumstances, and then we retired for the night to a farmer's house, the front room of which was occupied by chickens and a calf. The journey there had taken twice as long as the estimate I had been given, so as a result, we did not get back to Sholapur the next day until well after the commencement of the Regulars Class, which I was supposed to be attending. In fact, it had nearly finished, and glancing into the shrine room as we passed the door, I noticed that the class was being led by Mrs. Shinde, a mitra whose virtues Devamitra extolled in the October '87 issue of Shabda. Mrs Shinde is an attractive middle-aged woman, unfailingly positive, who emanates an impression of irrepressible goodwill, as well as being intelligent and able to take the lead gracefully. I was rather surprised, nevertheless, that none of the other five mitras, who were men, had taken the lead, and did not discover the story, if there was one, behind their decision to ask Mrs Shinde to do so, or if, indeed, they had asked her at all.

By the time I had taken a cold water bath and recovered from the journey to the distant village, the Regulars' class was over, but the participants were eager to listen to a talk by me. I therefore spoke extemporaneously for about an hour, including translation, on the theme of meditation as the development of individualized consciousness. It was a strong talk, and everybody was pleased.

There followed the Sholapur meditation retreat, or *shibir* as it is known in Maharashtra. It turned out to be purgatory, if not hell. Whilst the general arrangements were tolerable and there were thirty-three participants, including myself, the venue was a school situated right next to a main road plied by heavy lorries with excruciatingly loud horns. Not only that, it was Diwali, or Dipa Wali, the Festival of Lights, which is chiefly notable for five days of almost non-stop fireworks, particularly firecrackers. Indian firecrackers have to be heard to be believed. You could be forgiven for thinking that armies were exchanging fire. And as if this was not already too much, near the school was a house which kept a large number of dogs that barked the whole night long. Most of the nights on retreat I was thus deprived not only of sleep but subjected to an atrocious cacophony practically the whole night through. During the last two days, practically every moment whilst I was not meditating with the retreatants or performing some other act requiring a vertical position, I lay flat on my back. The food, for some reason or other, I found totally unappetizing, and nausea lurked behind every mouthful I took. A few of the retreatants with less robust stomachs than mine vomited. By the end, it was as much as I could do to walk. The air was devoid of moisture and very dusty, and during the fourth day as I was clearing my nose, blood began to flow, though fortunately it did not persist. However, despite my state of near-collapse, I felt mentally light and bright. Nevertheless, I suggested that the organisers did not hold a retreat in that place and at that time again, but I suspected that they did not realize what an ordeal it had been for me. I think only Jinasena knew how ill I had become.

Despite all the noise, we studied the Mangala Sutta during the retreat, and my knowledge of Pali not being equal to a full explanation, I relied from time to time on the copy of the Seminar led by Sangharakshita on study of the Sutta, kindly lent to me by Lokamitra, and which I had myself published in the Ola Leaves series many years ago in Norwich. Dhammachari Aniruddha, a very friendly Order member from Pune, translated capably, and the friendly and indefatigable support of Amritabodhi and Vimokshapriya enabled me to lead the retreat, so people said, to their general satisfaction.

One of the more enjoyable things we did in Sholapur was to arrange an 'open' meditation each morning at 6.30am at 'Mr. Kadlak's Vihara' – the room set aside as a shrine room in our friend Mr Kadlak's small house - and the numbers attending gradually increased to twenty-five. It was very refreshing and inspiring to participate in these regular celebrations in the freshness of the morning, before the sun had become oppressively hot, and I began to anticipate them with relish. We left Sholapur happy to have renewed and deepened old friendships and to have made a number of new ones, and I was presented with a beautiful gold-and-white durrie or bedspread on our departure. Jinasena was given a blue shirt of silky material embroidered, as seems to be the fashion, around the buttoned opening. It suited him very well.

Then it was off to Hyderabad again. I did not like this to-ing and fro-ing at all, but it seemed to be necessary. We thought at first that we would be staying with Mr Rastrapal, the talkative and ebullient President of the Buddhist Society of India, Hyderabad, but rather to my relief, it was not to be. He had let his visitors' flat to someone else, and had arranged for us to stay at Ananda Vihara, Secunderabad, the 'twin' of the twofold city. Ananda Vihara was quite a large Shrine Hall by the standards of village India, besides which there was a comfortable 'Bhikkhu Nivas' or monks residence large enough for our purposes. The premises were maintained by the Barua family, originally of Chittagong, once part of India, now part of Bangladesh, and closely related to Mr Beni Madhab Barua, well-known to the Triratna Community via Bhante because of his *Ceylon Lectures*[70] in the course of which he speaks of the bhikkshuni Dhammadinna's spiritually positive exposition of the Buddha's doctrine of *paticca samuppada*[71]. I had befriended the Barua family (and they had befriended me) on my earlier visit to the Twin City.

Our stay in the twin city of Hyderabad/Secunderabad was in marked contrast to our sojourn in Sholapur. Instead of a seemingly endless round of visits and programmes, here our only duties were to visit a small number of old friends of Mr. Rastrapal's for lunch and supper. This, however, proved more arduous than I could possibly have imagined. Mr. Rastrapal's friends lived in what turned out to be the most far-flung parts of the city, and we would often spend an hour or more seated in a decrepit motor rickshaw rattling and bumping over potholed roads choked with traffic emitting clouds of poisonous and irritating fumes. And yet again, to my intense chagrin, I was subjected to Mr Rastrapal's loquaciousness. He would spend the whole journey engaged in a monologue of excruciating boredom. Although it was a monologue, however, he would check every few seconds to see if I was paying attention to him. I was several times reduced almost to desperation; never before had I met anyone, and I have met quite a few with this 'disease', who was quite so inconsiderate of the length and content of his address, the suitability of the place to deliver it, or the attitude of the person to whom he was speaking. It required the utmost self-restraint not to tell him simply to 'shut up'. His talk under those conditions was a form of torture, so that I usually arrived at our destination feeling exhausted. I considered being direct with Mr Rastrapal, but the 'right' moment never seemed to arrive, either in the rickshaw or later. Jinasena escaped the brunt of the verbal assault, as soon as he learned what to expect, by carrying a book around with him and opening it as soon as Mr. Rastrapal opened his mouth. I did not feel able, however, to escape in that sort of way. I did begin to wonder what was the cause of Mr. Rastrapal's neurosis, as it seemed more and more to be, but I did not get to the bottom of it. I suspected it had something to do with his wife.

Our days at Ananda Vihara, mercifully out of reach of the endless Rastrapal drone, followed a regular pattern. We would rise at 5.00am, and whilst Jinasena meditated alone, I would go and 'administer Pansil' in the Shrine Room to those of the Barua family who wished it. They were accustomed to bhikkhus, and I saw no reason to change the more positive aspects of their custom, especially as I saw to it that we meditated afterwards. I was pleased to discover that there was a particularly good atmosphere in the place - a sort of vibrant silence - which I had not noticed on my first visit some years earlier. I discovered that the Dalai Lama had visited the little Vihara not long before our arrival, so perhaps that had something to do with it. Whatever may have been the reason - and perhaps it was no more than the ideal conditions – it often felt as if we were absorbed in *dhyana*. After meditation, I would return to the 'Bhikkhu Nivas' next door for a further session of meditation with Jinasena before breakfast. It was a bit like a retreat, and I very much enjoyed the morning hours there. After my meditation with Jinasena, one or more members of the extensive Barua family would arrive, delightfully positive, cheerful and polite, and sometimes attractive too, and offer us breakfast. The food was prepared and served with real devotion, and it felt as if we were in the Tushita Devaloka. Jinasena made quite an impression on them. They marvelled that someone in ordinary clothes could be so meditative, and one of the more perceptive and forthright of our male visitors said to him: "You're like a bhikkhu without robes."

There was not only meditation and good food at the Ananda Maitri Vihara. There was also a small library, containing amongst other gems, a couple of volumes of Dr. Johnson's writings including his 'Rambler' series, and several translations and commentaries of and upon Nagarjuna. Nagarjuna had flourished about a hundred miles South of where we were situated - at a place called Nagarjunikunda, concerning which Sangharakshita has written a poignant poem[72] giving expression to his sensibilities on hearing that this ancient Buddhist site, intimately associated with the career of the greatest Mahāyāna sage, was threatened with submergence.

A diversion was provided, two days after our arrival in Hyderabad by the appearance of Mr. Narayanswami from Tirupati, East Central India. Mr. Narayanswami had several years ago been introduced to me by Lokamitra with the laughing comment that I could have him as my disciple. I was not at all sure that I wanted a disciple, especially one who had not even passed through the devotee stage, but I accepted the responsibility of keeping an eye on him. Mr. Narayanswami turned out to be of a highly emotional and ebullient temperament, his conversation liberally laced with hyperbole and literary allusions. After a short honeymoon period, during which I marvelled at so exotic a figure, I began to find him quite demanding. However, under the bluff exterior, I thought I did detect one or two small veins of precious metal, and began to regard our relationship, therefore, as a means of mutual purification. Over the last few years I have kept up a fairly regular correspondence with Mr. Narayanswami, and something a bit more akin to friendship has begun to emerge. The main difficulty is that he regards me as his 'master', though I have tried every conceivable way short of kicking him, to get him to see things in another light. But he is not easily shaken, and letter after letter of his to me begins with the most exaggerated hyperbole expressing his humble discipleship and my ineffable greatness. I get a bit fed up with it, but his persistence has really made me think. I wonder why he does it. Perhaps it is a case of my 'greatness' being dependent upon the degree of his humbleness.

However that may be, Mr. Narayanswami had been informed by Santosh Barua, the head, or one of the chief heads of Anand Maitri Vihar, of my imminent arrival. So my 'disciple' turned up in person to take my darshan[80] and imbibe the flavour of the truth at the feet of his beloved master. I was pleased to find the old rascal looking so well, and in fact, I thought, a bit more refined, and quite a bit happier, than when I last saw him. This would presumably be accounted for by his having done some meditation practice. Despite the fact that he had come all the way from Tirupati, however, Narayanswami did not spend very much time with me, and even when he did come and visit, he tended to get tongue-tied or resort to literary platitudes. But he did come for the morning 'sits' at the Vihara at 5.00am, and I could not but feel touched by the determination with which - though suffering from diabetes - the no longer young and now ailing man had come all that way. I hope that he gained some benefit as a result of his visit, and that I did nothing to encourage him to regard me as a great guru.

On our first visit to Hyderabad, I had been asked to perform a marriage, or rather, presiding at the ceremony, to administer the Refuges and Precepts to the Bride and Groom. This I have always agreed to do in India, considering that if the Buddhists cannot find a practitioner of Buddhism to officiate, they will find a Hindu one. But whilst Dr. Ambedkar had been keen to keep the marriage ceremony simple and unpretentious, this one, like many others I have attended, was a pompous affair that must have cost the parents of the bride a small fortune. The bride and groom were very tense at first, but after a few words with me they relaxed a bit. They both seemed to understand English quite well, and when the time came they repeated the Refuges and Precepts after me in a not unworthy manner. They were then left to the tender mercies of Mr. Rastrapal, who rattled through the duties of the bride to the groom and vice versa in a Telugu so fast that he himself barely had time to understand it. In fact he had to repeat himself several times because the respondents did not catch what he was saying.

But I have got a bit ahead of myself. Waiting for the marriage to begin, I have found, is often boring in the extreme, but this time I was introduced to a young woman who was studying medicine, and with whom I was able to carry on an intelligent and lively conversation which seemed to proceed quite naturally, as it were, from the superficial to the more profound. This was in contrast to my talks with a group of men to whom I was introduced later, and who seemed keen for my attention. There was a bullying Arya Samajist, who tried to pin me down to saying that one's position in life is the result of Karma; there was a rationalist Ambedkarite, who had nothing really to say and nothing he wanted to know, and there was a Christian ex-Untouchable masquerading as a Buddhist - I learned this later, merely perceiving at the time that he was more keen to talk about social work than about the Dharma (though the two are not necessarily separate, they are to some extent separable). Thus my time at the wedding passed not altogether worthlessly.

The groom turned out to be of one of the sons of a Mr. Tirupati, an old friend of Rationalist/Socialist, even Marxist inclination, who had translated both for me and for Lokamitra in times past. This wedding was if anything more pompous and lavish than the first one I had attended in Hyderabad. It sported two marquees, possibly 2,000 guests, and a band which was striking up some pop music as I arrived. My immediate inclination was to walk out in protest against such ridiculous and tasteless waste. However, mastering the impulse, I prepared myself for the not onerous task of administering the Refuges and Precepts. Furthermore, I thought to myself, Mr. Tirupati's son will have been well-primed by his father in the basics of Buddhism, and all these people will listen with interest and attention, and I shall be able to say a few words about Buddhism and marriage in the course of the ceremony. Not a bit of it. Not only did Mr. Tirupati Jnr. and his bride sound as if they were mouthing the Refuges and Precepts for the very first time, but Mr. Rastrapal took absolutely no notice of my few words to the assembly, in fact brushing them aside with a commentary of his own in rapid Telugu, followed by his chanting of various Pali verses in a strident voice whilst hardly anyone seemed to pay attention. In fact many people began to engage in conversation whilst he was chanting. Also, I could not help noticing, as I looked around, that a contingent of prosperous-looking men in European clothes were laughing and chatting amongst themselves in a spirit of defiance during Mr. Rastrapal's performance. I was told they were Brahmins. It seemed to be a case of Pali assertiveness versus Brahminical frivolousness. The whole thing was a ridiculous, ostentatious and ill-mannered show, and I began to regret that I was there.

After the Buddhist duties of marriage had been rattled through in Telugu, again too fast for decent comprehension, there was a frenzied rush to position necklaces, exchange marriage rings, bestow toe rings, offer garlands etc. etc. in which dozens of people were involved. And when all this was over, there were presentations of gifts to the bride and groom, during which a fat old Brahmin came up to them, sprinkling them with coloured powder and water, and reciting various verses in Sanskrit. It appeared that the Buddhist rites were considered insufficient and that the Hindus were now staking their claim over the almost totally passive couple. So much for the Rationalist-Socialist Buddhism of the Tirupatis, I thought. Actually, despite the amusing cartoon-like proceedings, and the undeniable riot of colour, I found the whole thing distasteful, and heartily wished not to allow myself to be levered into such a situation again. It was with a considerable sense of relief that I found that Jinasena and I were to be permitted to eat alone, and that no-one took any further interest in us. We soon left.

I gave three 'public' talks in Hyderabad - if my talk to the Barua family in their semi-private Ananda Vihar could be termed a public talk. The largest of them, attended by perhaps forty people, was at Siddharth Vihar, Bowenpally - a place that looked as if it had been quite a vigorous centre at one time, but now seeming to be dismally lacking in effective leadership. But there were a few young men in the audience, and I hoped that through the mists of Mr. Rastrapal's translation, some gleams of light would penetrate. At any rate, there was a really pleasant, friendly feeling afterwards, and several people came up to me to express their thanks.

None of the young men with revolutionary fervour whom I had met on my first visit to Hyderabad two or three years ago were in evidence, and although my present visit was not altogether without its entertaining side, I felt that the Dharmic impact was rather limited. What had happened was that I had been sandwiched between the 'old boy' network of Ambedkarite Buddhists on the one hand and the ex-Chittagong Baruas on the other. Whilst a marriage between these two contingents might have been something worth accomplishing, I had only succeeded in witnessing two wasteful worldly marriages. It all seemed to be a wonderful example of the vanity of human wishes.

One of the more enjoyable things that Jinasena and I did in Hyderabad was to visit the Salar Jung museum. In a vast, rambling, but relatively modern building erected specially for the purpose, was housed a huge collection of objets d'art brought together by the acquisitive instincts of Salar Jung when he was the Chief Minister to the renowned Nizam of Hyderabad, reckoned at one time to be the richest man in the world. This private collection was vast, comparable to some of the London Museums in extent, if not in uniformity of taste and value. The collection brought together sculpture, jewellery, porcelain, pottery, glassware, silverware, ceremonial dresses, silks, weaponry, oil paintings, watercolours, furniture, marbles, bronzes, toys and gaudy bric-a-brac in almost bewildering variety. Many of the pictures and much of the sculpture were of European origin, and with a decidedly sensuous bias. There were pictures of Salar Jung himself, photographic and painted, showing a dark, well-proportioned though somewhat small man with Moorish features wearing a slightly bored or disdainful expression, and surrounded by jet-eyed and fierce-looking retainers in elaborate warrior-costume and brandishing swords. None of the many pictures and photos of Salar revealed a smile. One of them showed him shopping in England, surrounded by a crowd of evil-looking English gentry. There was no doubt concerning Salar's wealth and power, and he was merely the chief minister of the Nizam. What then was the Nizam himself like? This speculation occupied my mind for a few moments without, of course, finding any resolution.

Extensive though the collection of Salar Jung's effects was, there was comparatively little of genuine artistic, as contrasted with aesthetic, value. Jinasena, judging by the time he spent looking at them, was impressed by the large oil paintings from Europe, of which he had probably never seen the like before. I enjoyed looking at the jewellery and at the jade collection, and at a bronze statuette of Alexander the Great. It was perhaps two feet in height, and impressed me with its portrayal of vigour and strength. There was no evidence, apart from his portraits, of Salar's own work and exploits, if indeed there were any. This collection, I thought, was the record of 'A glorious devil, large in heart and brain, / That did love Beauty only.....'[73]

Soon it was time to leave Hyderabad and its clear, cool mornings, its suffocatingly hot, dry, dusty afternoons, its pot-holed and winding byways and innumerable boutique-lined streets. We waited for two hours in the posh new ticket-booking hall at the main railway station, which had a system of lights showing on a screen how many seats remained on such-and-such a train on such-and-such a day. By the time we had worked out whether we had any chance at all of a ticket, it was time to present ourselves to the booking clerk - one of a small army of them - who, scanning his huge book with frantic speed, came to the conclusion that we could have tickets one day after we wanted them, which wasn't too bad considering that we had some slack before our next programme in Pune. Thus we could enjoy one more day in the company, at Ananda Vihar, of Dr. Samuel Johnson, for my part, and for Jinasena - Romeo and Juliet.

I was by this time feeling distinctly jaded by our lunchtime visits to part-time, occasional, partial, would-be, or even pseudo-Buddhists. The one worthwhile lunch-time visit we made, a far as I could see, was to a tiny Vihara miles outside the city. It had been set up by Ven. Ananda Kausalyayana, a bhikkhu acquaintance of Bhante's, though he had apparently not visited it for many years. On arrival we were surrounded by a very excited crowd of youngsters headed by a very personable and not unattractive woman, in, perhaps, her early thirties, and a programme was immediately arranged. After the days - it seemed more like weeks - of almost total lassitude, this was a welcome surprise indeed. We chanted the Refuges and five Precepts and the *tiratna vandana*[74], and I gave a talk, and a really good programme it was. Everybody was happy, light was everywhere. When were we coming again? Before we left, I was introduced to the leading lady's husband - a fat, drunken, coarse-looking man. The woman smiled a hard, bright smile at me. What could I do? I returned her smile, hoping that she would interpret it in the way I intended.

There was one more lunch to go. This time it was at the table of Mr. Tirupati, the father of the groom over whose wedding I had presided a week ago. After yet another typical rickshaw ride lasting the best part of an hour, and accompanied by the usual monologue by Mr. Rastrapal, we arrived at Mr. Tirupati's house. He greeted Mr. Rastrapal and Jinasena warmly, but seemed a bit diffident towards me. What had I done to offend him? We were joined by Mr. Premrao, an Advocate friend, who on an earlier visit had done much to help me, and concerning whom, I had remarked to Devamitra some months earlier, I felt very positive. So I thought to myself, this is good: two men who both know and understand me a little. I was ill-prepared for what followed.

A plate of chicken curry was shoved beneath my nose, but then, as if suddenly remembering something, someone hastily removed the pieces of flesh from my plate and gave me an additional plate of vegetables. After lunch, during which everyone but Jinasena and I partook liberally of the unfortunate chicken, accompanied by much sucking and smacking of the lips, I was more or less ordered to lie down on a bed, whilst the others retired to the next-door sitting room. An animated conversation ensued, the tenor of which was frivolous in the extreme, and prevented me from taking a proper rest. I eventually decided that after all, I was not really tired, and went to join the merry company. I sat quietly listening for a while, and the conversation began to falter. Then Mr. Tirupati chirped up with a question: "You don't really believe in devas, do you?" he said. Well, what could I say? I found, rather to my own surprise, that at that moment, whatever I might have thought or felt it wise to say, or had said at other times, I believed particularly strongly and passionately in devas. However, mastering myself as best I could, I put 'the case for devas' with as much diffidence and scepticism as I could muster, pointing out that such belief was far from obligatory, and that in any case, all beliefs were open to question in Buddhism. I might as well have fired a blunderbuss. My companions tried to make me eat every word I uttered, and I was given a lecture by all three of them, more or less simultaneously, on the falsehood, danger and foolishness of such beliefs, which were merely primitive superstitions. Poetry ceased to exist. Higher states of consciousness ceased to exist. Non-duality made no sense at all. All the Buddhist scriptures were to be selectively read. I was logically sat upon and rationally kicked and bludgeoned for an old-fashioned, out-of-touch heretic, and more or less ordered to toe the party line. For these rationalists, the devas did not exist, neither was it permissible for anyone else to see what they themselves did not see, even if the seeing was within inverted commas. Yes, of course I knew about the caste system and its deva worship. But in vain did I protest that Hindu devas were the philosophically untenable 'avatars of Brahma', whilst the Buddhist devas might be nature spirits, angels, or Bodhisattvas. But such things were an abomination to these men who had witnessed the ravages of the Hindu caste system, especially deva-worship. It was evidently useless to discuss with them, much less oppose them. But I began to wonder whether it was in fact possible to communicate Buddhism on a purely rational basis. No doubt reason can take one a long way, but sooner or later, imagination has to play a part. In any case, who had mentioned devas? I had not said a word about them in Hyderabad before entering Mr. Tirupati's house. It was all very unreasonable.

It was time to leave Hyderabad with its huge central lake, its vast promenade of Hindu worthies in bronze, its icing-cake Temple on the hill, its rationalists and its Baruas. Paradoxically enough, it was the rationalists who came to see us off. The indefatigable Messrs Rastrapal and Premrao kindly carried our luggage to the night train after a rickshaw journey of the most mind-boggling complexity yet, involving doubling-back, false turnings, and severe doubts whether either the driver or Mr Rastrapal had ever actually looked at the roads of the city, but had instead been directing themselves all along according to some sort of mass hallucination which approximated usually, with a bit of luck, to the city layout. Within a hair's breadth of Mr. Rastrapal and the driver engaging in verbal abuse, we arrived at our destination, I paid off the driver, and we were left holding our luggage and within sight of liberation. Once settled into our rationally-appointed seats, our helpers finally began to show signs of fatigue, and gratefully took their leave.

NOTES

67 Order *metta bhavana*: on the first Sunday of each month, at 7:30pm GMT or as near as possible to it, Order Members all over the world used to meet in Chapters and practice the *metta-bhavana* or development of *metta,* especially towards all other Order Members. It is a very inspiring practice, especially for those who for one reason or another, are not in physical proximity to a Chapter of the Order. I benefited tremendously from this 'telepathic' *metta* during my years of relative isolation in Sri Lanka. Nowadays, the Order *metta* passes round the world in a wave, being put into practice at 4:30pm on the first Sunday of each month wherever you are.

68 Ashok Vijaya Dasami : the occasion which Hindus call Dussehra or Dasara, also known as 'Victory Tenth', on which Hindus celebrate the victory of Rama over Ravana, the ten-headed demon king of Lanka. For Buddhists it is the celebration of the victory of Asoka over the forces of Kalinga and his subsequent conversion from conquest by means of war (*yuddha-vijaya*) to conquest by means of righteousness (*dharmavijaya*). For Dr. Ambedkar, the great Buddhist leader of post-war India, and his followers, it therefore symbolizes the victory of the forces of light over the forces of darkness. Ref: *Ambedkar and Buddhism,* Sangharakshita, Windhorse, 1986.

69 *What Meditation Really Is*: A lecture given by Sangharakshita in Auckland Town Hall, New Zealand on 13 February 1975.

70 *Ceylon Lectures*, Dr B M Barua, Sri Satguru Publications, Delhi, 1986

71 *paticca samuppada* (Pali) *pratitya samutpāda* (Skt.): the Buddha's doctrine, unique to his Insight and teaching, of conditioned co-production. It was formulated by him, according to the Pali, as follows:

imasmim sati, idam hoti, imass' uppada, idam uppajjati;
imasmim asati, idam na hoti, imassa nirodha, idam nirujjhati

(This being, that becomes, from the arising of this, that arises; this not being, that does not become; from the ceasing of this, that ceases.) - *Udana I,* i & ii, etc.

72   Nagarjunikunda : p.183, *Complete Poems 1941/1994,* pub. Windhorse, Birmingham, 1995.

73 *The Palace of Art*, Tennyson

74 *Tiratna Vandana*: Salutation to the Three Jewels. The verses traditionally chanted in Pali describing and saluting the characteristics of the Buddha, the Dharma and the Sangha. These verses are also very often chanted by members of the FWBO/TBMSG before a session of meditation or some other formal, spiritual practice in the shrine room. Being chanted in Pali in the traditional manner, they provide a very tangible link with the rest of the Buddhist world, and provide us with a reminder of the most basic, the most important things we hold in common with all Buddhists - our Going for Refuge to the Three Jewels. Ref: *Salutation to the Three Jewels* (the *Sangharakshita in Seminar* series), Windhorse, Glasgow, 1985.

* * * * *

View over the lake at Igatpuri

24   A retreat in Igatpuri

Jinasena and I return to Pune for a few days' respite, then journey to Igatpuri for a welcome retreat. Visiting Ulhasnagar afterwards, I am impressed by the work done by TBMSG there in transforming the consciousness of the Dharma practitioners. They are happy in an environment which Westerners would regard as hell. We tour Kolhapur district in the company of Dharmachari Shakyanand, and fail to arrive at a mitra meeting. We travel on to Ahmedabad, where we stay with Friends in the 'Triyan Vardhan Vihar'. Visiting a Muslim place of pilgrimage, Sarkhej Roza, I 'meet' Ahmad Khattu, the deceased Pir or Sufi saint. I give a talk on the occasion of Dr. Ambedkar's death Anniversary, and people are moved to tears. Travelling on to Bombay, we meet Kamalashila newly-arrived from England. Returning once more to Pune, we meet other Western visitors, and attend the Public Ordination ceremony of some new Indian Dhammacharis. Soon afterwards, Jinasena and I return to Sri Lanka via Trivandrum and its Art Gallery.

JINASENA AND I PLANNED TO STOP in Pune for a few days after our visit to Hyderabad. After that, we would be moving on to join a retreat which was to be held near the town of Igatpuri, best known, perhaps, for its proximity to the meditation centre of that name established by the famous 'Vipassana' meditation teacher S. N. Goenka. Of the day or days in Pune I now have no recollection, but I remember that our journey to Igatpuri took us via Ulhasnagar TBMSG Centre where we were both very glad to see Dhammachari Chandrasil once again, and enjoy his exceptionally charming company before our onward journey.

The train climbed higher and higher into the Western Ghats, affording more and more dramatic views down into the valleys as we proceeded. At Igatpuri itself we took an unbelievably overcrowded bus (even by Indian standards) and resigned ourselves to more than an hour of bumpy semi-suffocation before reaching the journey's end. I was exceptionally lucky since all my baggage was carried by sahayakas and mitras, who would not countenance my lifting anything. Whether this was because of my age or my supposed holiness, I do not know, but I was very grateful indeed for the help, as I wasn't feeling very strong after the Sholapur retreat and the Hyderabad lunchtime trips.

As we neared our destination, it became evident that we were approaching an area of quite outstanding natural beauty, and my spirits began to rise. Distant hills with ever more dramatic profiles stretched to the far horizon now purpling into sunset, and one particular peak was so precipitous that it resembled nothing so much as a huge finger pointing to the sky as if saying 'Excelsior'. If this was to be the setting for our retreat, the limited discomfort of the journey did not seem an excessive price to pay after all.

Dismounting from the bus, which disgorged a truly astonishing number of passengers, we now had a ten-minute walk to our destination as the last rays of the sun defied the onset of night. My companion on the walk was a diminutive and very talkative nineteen year old student of computer science, and whilst he confessed to feelings of gratitude - which I am sure were perfectly sincere - that he was able to attend such a retreat as this and receive instruction from a person like myself (what on earth had he heard about me, I wondered), I could not help noticing that his state of mind seemed to be one of nervous irritability and neurotic restlessness. The extraordinary colours of the scene now before us, now fast fading into night, seemed not to touch him at all, and I wondered if his study of computer science had rendered him insensitive to visual beauty. Our place of retreat was a government rest-house or Bungalow endearingly called 'The Chummery'. I shared a room with Jinasena and Dhammachari Bodhisen, who was now looking healthier than when, suffering from heat-rash, he had greeted us at Bombay Airport. Despite that, then as now, he was full of nothing but cheerfulness and good spirits.

The shrine was set up with loving care, and included as usual a photo of Dr. Ambedkar. After supper we dedicated the place, performed a Puja, and went to bed, but for several hours I felt uneasy and could not sleep. I was told later that one unfortunate man was suffering so severely from stomach cramps that a doctor had been called in the middle of the night to give him an injection to relieve his pain. After that, apparently, he had begun to recover. Next morning, I was up by sunrise, and able to appreciate fully the surrounding natural beauty. 'The Chummery' was situated near the shore of a huge man-made reservoir, and on the far side of the placid blueness of the water stood the range of mountains I had seen from the bus the previous evening. Now lit by clear morning light, they stood out in vivid detail against the pale blue sky, and were mirrored as if admiring their own beauty, in the clear still water. I stood transfixed by the scene for several minutes, and began also to notice and appreciate the coolness and freshness of the air. I had not breathed so easily since arriving in the East five years ago. In such a setting I thought, it would be was impossible not to have an enjoyable retreat, and in fact everyone seemed reluctant to go when the time came to leave. A request was made for TBMSG to assist in the work of the new Buddha Vihara in Igatpuri town, and 'to hold another retreat as soon as possible.' As usual, I suggested that some Dhammacharis were invited along to give talks and meditation classes.

The journey back to Ulhasnagar was almost, but not quite, as trying as the outward journey. This time at least we were stronger. The buses and trains were full to bursting, and everyone looked dazed. In fact, this sort of dazed or glazed appearance seems to be a more or less permanent condition of many Indians; it suggests to me an inner state of profound shock or neurotic anxiety. How they would benefit from a spell in the place we had just come from, and how remote the chance of them doing so in the foreseeable future! Back at Ulhasnagar once again we were able to savour the peculiarly calm yet 'energized' feel of the shrine room, impressive with its simple but effective design of a white Buddha-image backed by a large rectangular piece of blood-red cloth edged with a broad border of blue. And Chandrasil's sister 'Bhai' provided us with tasty food offered with quite exceptional tenderness and solicitude.

What is really amazing about Ulhasnagar and many of our other Indian Centres is that they are very small places indeed, set in the middle of huge shanty towns reminiscent of something out of a Dickensian novel. Noises, smells and fumes from a multitude of tiny makeshift workshops assail the ears and nose. It is not at all difficult to see the Buddhist centres set in these places as wish-fulfilling gems in a rubbish heap. Little by little, and sometimes remarkably quickly, they are radically transforming the lives of dozens, partially transforming the lives of hundreds, and at least touching and beneficially affecting the lives of thousands of poor Indians. They are bringing not only hope, not merely possibilities, not just good intentions, but really transfiguring those who are faithful and intelligent enough to utilize what is offered - and many are. And they bring to the practice of the Dharma a purity, straightforwardness and spontaneity which is a joy to behold. From what one sees, Dr. Ambedkar's idea may well be true that the Untouchables were descended from Buddhists who gradually became ostracized from the mainstream of social life by Brahminism. Though perhaps one shouldn't give too much weight to ties of blood, if those ties have served to preserve the Dharma, why should one complain?

Whilst in Ulhasnagar I took the opportunity of spending time with Dhammachari Silendrabodhi, getting to know him better, and was impressed by the clarity, sincerity and quiet determination of this small and gentle man with his thick-lensed glasses. We talked about the current difficulties with our Right Livelihood businesses, noticing how, once a mitra begins to be paid for doing a job, we are in a very difficult position if they do not continue to work in an inspired manner. Though they are totally dependent upon our Movement, they cannot be trusted to work efficiently, and may even endanger a whole project by sloppy work. The answer seemed to be to make sure we got the right kind of men in the first place, but that was easier said than done.

Our conversation took place on the steps of a rather dilapidated hall which had been used for a large meditation retreat recently. It stood within sight of a very ancient Hindu temple. In fact it was one of the oldest Hindu temples I recalled seeing. I guessed it to be between 1500 and 2000 years old, and it exuded an aura of incredible stillness and calm. How wonderful to be able to feel that connectedness with tradition, and how sad that there is so little in the West with which we can sense that millennia-long continuity.

Whilst at 'Gandhasughanda', meaning 'the savour of all fragrances', no doubt named in a moment of good humour, since the Ulhasnagar Centre stands in the midst of one of the most heavily-polluted areas in Bombay district, I followed up my intention to make contact with a local Sri Lankan bhikkhu, a friend of one of the last-remaining disciples of Anagarika

Dharmapala, Ven. Hapugoda Dharmananda, who had suggested to me before I left Sri Lanka, that I visit this bhikkhu. So Jinasena and I set off one morning to the 'Bhikkhu Nivas', which was within easy walking distance of the Centre. We were greeted outside the small building, set by itself near a Bo-tree, by a slightly-built, consumptive-looking man in orange robes who might have been 20 or 40 years old, it was difficult to tell. But the distressing impression hung about him that he was only twenty, and that already the juice had gone out of him. Jinasena spoke to him in Sinhalese and he became a bit cheerful, but it was rather dreadful and pathetic to see what the lifestyle of a bhikkhu was doing to this young lad struggling under his grubby, heavy robes into a distorted manhood.

I waited for what seemed ages, and not seeing the elder bhikkhu I had come to see, imagined him to be in some other part of the building. It was not until I finally gave up waiting and rather wearily walked out that Jinasena volunteered the information that the elder bhikkhu wasn't there - an unusual lapse on Jinasena's part, who usually tells me immediately what I need to know. Perhaps he thought I had followed their conversation in Sinhalese.

Our departure for Kolhapur, a city well known for its champion-wrestling, Oxford-educated Raja, was still a few days away. Now back in Pune, I took the opportunity, whilst in 'Madhuban', of dipping into the collection, complete and up-to-date, of Bhante's seminars. I read, in fact, as much as I could possibly digest, so that my mind could hardly have been further from Dapodi, its shanty town and houses so diminutive they might have been made for dolls. I felt in need of spiritual nourishment, and knew that the talks I was to give in the near future would be inspired by such reading. I would be returning to Dapodi in three weeks' time, and could then give more attention to the Sahayakas and mitras than I was able to give them at present.

But now it was time to go. Jinasena and I met Dhammachari Shakyanand at Pune bus station. Dhammachari Shakyanand is large. It is hardly any exaggeration to say that he is the Billy Bunter of the Movement. Despite his size, however, he is surprisingly nimble, and is also, when sitting, an inspiringly still, solid and upright figure. Not only that. He has an infectious sense of humour, and considerable powers of organisation, and the determination to start activities in Kolhapur, which is sufficiently far from Pune, his home, to establish that he is well and truly leaving it. Ever since coming into contact with him as a mitra in the Pune (Camp) class in 1982/83, I had been impressed by his good qualities, and felt a strong personal connection with him. I was very happy, though also slightly apprehensive, at the prospect of touring Kolhapur with him.

My apprehension stemmed from the fact that, such is Shakyanand's affection for me, and such his cunning, that if he can squeeze an 'extra day' out of me, he will - and I did not have an extra day to spare on this occasion. Our tickets to Ahmedabad - a night's journey north of Bombay - had already been booked, programmes arranged and so on, and if we missed that train, then many people would disappointed. So I didn't want to find myself in an outlandish village with Shakyanand, being told that the last bus had left and there was one more programme which it would be very wonderful for us to do, now that we had missed our connection.

Bearing all this in mind, I had checked Shakyanand's proposed itinerary as best I could, and intended to keep an eye on bus and train departure times at every step along the way. Not only that, I gave Shakyanand strict instructions to make sure that our programmes started on time. Knowing that I had asked him what was practically impossible, I therefore carried a certain amount of residual apprehension, small at the beginning and increasing as the mini-tour proceeded. At first everything went according to plan, except that on the way to our first stop, the bus collided with a horse, and when we arrived where I was scheduled to give the talk, an unfortunate woman had been knocked down by a lorry and died, so everyone was in a state of grief, and I found myself conducting a *punyānumodana* ceremony. But at least we had arrived more or less on time and departed according to schedule. Two programmes later, however, things began to slip. Our fourth programme had started late, as quite often happens, but according to the itinerary we were to stay in that village where I gave my talk that night. There was therefore apparently nothing to worry about, even though it was after midnight before I was able to finish my talk. It had previously been agreed that a sing-song of rousing Ambedkarite songs would conclude the programme, so, I thought to myself, in half an hour, or an hour at most, I shall be able to put my head on my pillow. After my talk, however, Shakyanand suddenly seized the microphone and began a speech of his own. I felt unable to walk out because of the disruption it would cause, and in any case, I had no idea where in the village we were to spend the night. By the time Shakyanand had finished speaking, I was fit only for bed, but the songs had not yet begun. I protested my tiredness, but was told that the singers would be offended if I left at that moment: I should stay to hear at least a few, and in any case, wouldn't they revive my spirits? Everyone insisted that I stay and listen, and so, as it seemed to mean so much to them, stay I did. But the night was cold, my clothes were thin, and I was extremely travel-weary. I listened, trying to husband every little flicker of bodily heat that I could. By midnight my nose was running and I had a headache. I could not stay up any longer. When there was a momentary lull in the proceedings, I got up and walked off into the night. Shakyanand and Jinasena followed me, and we were escorted by two young men from the pandal to the house where we were to stay. One thing, in fact, that had already impressed me about this mini-tour was the abundance of young men. Shakyanand's portly appearance, far from putting them off, seemed to attract young men; probably it was his humour and affectionate nature which endeared him to them.

We did not have far to walk, which was both good and bad: the young men's sing-in kept us awake for two hours more. The next morning we were scheduled to catch a bus quite early - 7 o'clock, I think it was. But to my puzzlement, no-one seemed to be in a hurry to get ready. Seven o'clock came and went, and in answer to my anxious enquiries was told "Don't worry, the bus comes along that road there (pointing to a place only a few yards distant) - and it hasn't come yet." One hour later, it had still not come, and my heart began to sink. We had rather a lot of ground to cover that day, and the following day we would need to be within a short distance of the city of Kolhapur itself, if we were to catch our train to Bombay and from there our train to Ahmedabad.

Without any explanation being offered to me, our little group walked to another part of the village where we waited for another hour. It was not unpleasant, actually, watching the life of the village - the strikingly healthy, elegant and gentle women in saris, carrying brass water pots on their heads, the dark, slim farmers in their white or scarlet pugrees, white shirts and dhotis[75]; the chubby children, naked but for little silver anklets and waistbands, playing in the dust. Then also there was the less pleasant side of life - here a bent old man, his body wasting away, there a deformed child, there a wizened dwarf, his face creased with a curious mixture of misery and cruelty, and yet through which also seemed to shine something else - a sombre, brooding, disinterested air akin to wisdom. Watching this village scene, through which trundled carts drawn by fine white bulls with strong, upward-curving horns, one could easily imagine oneself back in the time of the Buddha. Little, perhaps, had really changed. But our devotees were waiting for us somewhere! How were we to get to them?

It so happened that on our way to our present position, we had passed a Shaivite dairy farm, and whilst Shakyanand, for some reason or other, had stood hesitating at the entrance to it, someone had enquired of him what we were waiting for. Apparently he had then gone off and reported our plight to the dairy manager, for to my astonishment and delight, a car, apparently the dairy manager's own car, moreover driven by his personal chauffeur, now drew up near us and told us he had instructions to take us to our destination! I felt very grateful to the man for his solicitude, and his ability, it seemed, (unusual amongst caste Hindus in my experience) to overlook differences of religion. Or perhaps he had mistaken my orange for that of a *sannyasi*. I was certainly not interested in the religion of the car, and gratefully accepted the heaven-sent boon. It really was an act of generosity, for our destination was about an hours' drive away.

Since our arrival was late, the programme was even later, as all who know anything about India and Dhamma programmes know that nothing much happens until the guests arrive. What was more, it was nearly lunch time, and we were supposed to be lunching in Kolhapur itself! I wrote a note of thanks for the driver to deliver to the dairy manager, then turned my attention to the question of what to do. There was no question of leaving immediately - too many people had gathered; we were expected, though no preparations had been made for our talk. But really there was no question of the order of things. According to village custom, we simply had to eat. However, I managed to obtain a concession: we would have the programme first and eat afterwards. In this way, some time would be saved as food could be prepared whilst we were speaking. The alternative would have been to wait for a grand lunch, which would have to be followed by the inevitable afternoon nap, and risk that our programme would not materialize until nightfall, by which time we would have completely missed our next programme.

A large crowd began to assemble as a loudspeaker blared the announcement of a talk, and within half an hour or so, by some miracle, we had started. Not bad going, I thought. At this point, Jinasena begged me to give him a chance to speak. He had been studying my talks, he said, and now felt confident he could give one. I had some misgivings about this, but knowing that Shakyanand would edit-out or fill in as necessary as he translated, I agreed to Jinasena's request. His talk went well, if a little slowly, and I followed it up by expanding on his theme of the Dhamma being a boat (or raft). Then Shakyanand felt moved to speak too, and followed my address by quite a lengthy one of his own which went down very well. The now very large audience listened attentively and laughed at all the appropriate places. The trouble was, what with all this wonderful talk, it was already 2:00pm; Shakyanand, before I could say a word, had said we would have lunch here, and the good people of Kolhapur, whoever they were, were expecting us for lunch there. Eventually, after every one of us and several of the local dignitaries and helpers had been garlanded, we were led off to be fed. I refused to eat more than a handful, suspecting that we would have to repeat the performance again very soon. Shakyanand however, ate rather more than I had done, perhaps wishing to make up for my apparent ingratitude.

Now began our journey to Kolhapur. First there was a long walk, then a long wait. What to do? For the first time, Shakyanand began to look a little uneasy. Never mind about the second lunch, but wasn't there a programme arranged for this afternoon in Kolhapur? I stood there gloomily. Then, eventually, suddenly, magically, three motorbikes drew up and took us in relays about five kilometres further along the road, and deposited us at yet another bus stop. After another half-hour wait and a long bus ride, we arrived at Kolhapur at 5:00pm. Our host looked distinctly peeved, and not particularly mollified by our explanation. Not only was our specially prepared meal now cold, but twelve would-be mitras who had come in high expectation of listening to my talk, had left. I was extremely annoyed, but there was no point lamenting. I pointed out to Shakyanand the importance of giving mitra meetings priority over public talks, and of letting me know to whom I could expect to be speaking. Had I been told that the audience was to have been composed of mitras, I would have insisted on making our last programme a whistle-stop. I told everyone that I was extremely disappointed that the opportunity had been missed. Evidently the feeling was mutual, and having realized that, everyone calmed down and went upstairs to enjoy a meal which was excellent despite its temperature, and also had a friendly talk.

That evening, we left the town once more for a programme in the suburbs. It began to pour with rain. An outside meeting was impossible, but our friends knew of no hall that was available. What to do? I didn't want my talk to be a proximate cause of anyone's pneumonia. We managed to persuade someone to open his small house to us, and dozens upon dozens of men and boys crowded eagerly in. I felt inspired enough to give a very good talk. Shakyanand was really getting into his stride translating by now, and I felt very pleased that some real communication appeared to be taking place. At the end of my talk, people wanted to ask questions. Rather to my surprise,

Shakyanand was very reluctant to translate them for me. Perhaps he thought that, being a foreigner, I would not be able to give good answers, or else he was lacking the confidence to translate possibly difficult points. The questions were indeed tricky ones, but I wasn't going to be caught, and gave replies which seemed to please all but one man. What he wanted was confrontation, but I was not to be drawn in. I managed to start him thinking aloud, instead of reacting, then swiftly concluded the programme.

After a meal which I did not feel like eating, we returned for the last time to Kolhapur city centre, and boarded the night bus to Pune and Bombay. Shakyanand got off at Pune after the six hour journey, and so did Jinasena and I, but after a few minutes' discussion, we decided to re-board the bus and continue to Bombay. Thus it was that we arrived at Bhim Prerana – 'The Inspiration of Bhim (Dr. Ambedkar)', the block of diminutive flats in a multi-storey building constructed of dangerously thin concrete in Bandra. We took a wash and a much-needed rest in the sweaty mid-morning Bombay heat, and later enjoyed a simple but satisfying lunch prepared by a mitra, now Dhammachari Amoghaditya, who had volunteered to look after us.

The train to Ahmedabad left in the late evening, and I felt so relieved not to have missed the connection to the North that I enjoyed a peaceful night's sleep even on the wooden bunk as the train thrummed its way through the dark night.

Ahmedabad in the early morning is a not unpleasant sight, with a great variety of buildings both ancient and modern, humble and pompous, Hindu and Muslim. The city's name indicates its Islamic origins, and today even the casual observer cannot fail to be impressed by the jewels of architecture bequeathed to humanity by the architects of the Prophet. But now, sad to say, even some of those buildings which must be reckoned amongst the world's most beautiful, are showing signs of neglect and decay.

The very much extended, sprawling modern city of Ahmedabad lies on both sides of the River Sabarmati, once, perhaps, and maybe still, during years of more bountiful Monsoons, one of the great Rivers of India. On its banks lies one of the Ashrams founded by Gandhi, the 'Mahatma' and 'Father of the Indian Nation'. The ascetic simplicity of Gandhi's life-style is still capable of impressing visitors, but I saw little evidence of the dedicated *shramadana* movement that he inspired, or of that legendary spirit of opposition to social injustice that was supposed to have been his. His disavowal of casteism did not even convince the British rulers, and unlike Ambedkar, he completely failed to demonstrate to the Untouchables that he was rooting for them. Gandhi's Sabarmati ashram has in fact a somewhat neglected air, like that of a museum piece whose prize exhibit has been removed long ago, and through which middle-class and wealthy Indians and Europeans drift trying to discover the legend.

In the area known as Kankaria, in the midst of what, allowing for cultural differences, might loosely be described as a lower middle-class area, lies the TBMSG Centre. We were delivered to one end of the narrow street leading to the Centre by an obliging motor-rickshaw driver who had greeted us eagerly at the station. We walked past men, women and children still sleepy-eyed on their charpoys, and entered the gate of the TBMSG compound. It is a flat, rectangular area perhaps forty feet by one hundred and fifty, featureless but for a small clump of sparse bushes and small trees on one boundary, and we now began to notice that everything seemed to be covered with dust. This, we soon learned, was due to a three-year long drought in this part of Gujarat State. Beyond the walls of the compound could be seen various two and three-storey flat-roofed houses with numerous balconies, and at one end of the compound, stretching from one side to the other, lay a simple, low, flat-roofed oblong building which constituted the Centre itself. At the opposite end, in a corner, stood a tiny structure that later inspection showed was a toilet, next to which had been built a small water tank standing half in and half out of the ground, and fed by a single small tap.

This was Triyan Vardhan Vihar - which was to be a base for Jinasena and myself for the next three weeks. Noticing that the doors of the Vihara were closed, I wondered for a moment whether we should not have to go off in search of the key, but after knocking and waiting a few moments, we were greeted by Dhammachari Ratnakar, behind whom were discernible on the floor three or four bodies, apparently asleep, but which slowly began to move into action at Ratnakar's bidding. Soon a couple of them went off to get some breakfast for us, whilst the others made us feel thoroughly welcome and comfortable; we took a simple bucket-bath, tea was made, and breakfast arrived in the form of bread coloured brilliant orange accompanied by various kinds of fruit. The bread was palatable despite its colour, and the apples, chikus, custard-apples and bananas were excellent. I felt very much at home, and began to recollect the previous occupants and visitors to this place. Dharmachari Mangala, most notably, and perhaps Purna had come here when he was in the city as an Anagarika many years ago. Lokamitra would certainly have been here, and the present Chapter of Order Members also I knew quite well - Ratnakar, Bakul, Suman Dharmapal, and Varabodhi. During the next twenty days Jinasena and I were engaged in an apparently endless series of lunchtime engagements and evening programmes both within and without the city limits, sometimes crowded into tiny houses, sometimes in village squares accompanied by cows and dogs and chickens.

For the first few days at Triyan Vardhan Vihar, we were looked after by Dhamma mitra (now Dhammachari) Ratnapriya, and both Jinasena and I were very impressed by his friendliness and efficiency. I noticed that whilst he was around, everything went particularly smoothly, and that he never lost his smile. Ratnakar also came to visit us every morning before going to work - thus leaving me in no doubt concerning his appreciation of the Sangha-Jewel. The feeling was in fact mutual. We had some absorbing discussion concerning the translation of various Pali and Sanskrit terms, and I felt that Ratnakar had much of value to communicate. During one of our visits to Dhammachari Bakul's house for lunch, he taught us the positive precepts in Gujerati; it is always very much appreciated if you can repeat these in the local language when the Refuges and Precepts are recited.

Whilst visiting Suman Dharmapal's house I listened to the talk Bhante had given in Ahmedabad some years previously and was powerfully reminded of the need to define terms. In that tape-recorded talk Bhante had mentioned a visit he made to a Muslim place of worship a short distance outside the city, (he mentions it also, if I remember rightly, in his Travel Letters) and it is to a second visit that I made to that same place (called Sarkhez Roza) that we shall now turn. Having been once a professional Architect (according to the Royal Institute of British Architects an Architect cannot be other than professional) and having, though ceasing to be an architect in that sense continued to appreciate works of art whether in stone or any other medium, I had been drawn to this Islamic centre of worship by Bhante's report of it. In any case, sooner or later, I would probably have visited it, as it is much advertised in the guide books. In his Letter, Bhante gives his reason for visiting the place as being its architectural interest, and of course it would be odd indeed if a Buddhist was interested in an Islamic Centre per se. However, in the Letter, Bhante tells how, whilst visiting the place, he feels a psychic connection between himself and the Pir or Muslim holy man who is buried in Sarkhez. These two facts, each sufficient in themselves, to my mind, to warrant a visit, aroused my determination to go and see for myself. On the first visit I had gone with Dharmachari Mangala, and I had found the place not only aesthetically pleasing, but also imbued with 'a something' of a definitely psychic or psychic-cum-spiritual nature. On this visit to Ahmedabad also, I began to feel a sort of 'pull' towards Sarkhez Rosa, and justified a second visit with the thought that Jinasena would definitely appreciate the place.

Accordingly I took the bus out of the city to Sarkhez in the company of Jinasena and a mitra associated with the Ahmedabad TBMSG, and after half an hour's drive, the bus stopped at a nondescript looking place on the main road lined with the familiar crudely-constructed chai-shops and grocery stores. Just as I emerged from the bus, a very large, eagle-like bird glided mysteriously out of the blue and perched, as if coming specially to greet us, on a telegraph pole only a few yards away. We crossed the road and took the well-trodden dirt road leading to Sarkhez, and this time, hardly had we gone a few yards down the dirt-path when I began to sense that extraordinary presence which previously I had felt only within the boundary of the tomb itself. It was a feeling of being greeted by a man of truly extraordinary friendliness, peacefulness and warmth. I looked back at the telegraph pole, but the great bird had gone.

I walked on more keenly aware with every step, of that silent communion, but my companions seemed to be oblivious of it. In fact they soon started talking together. As we approached the collection of ancient and beautiful yellow-grey stone buildings with numerous domes, flanking one side of a huge artificial tank or lake, we passed a group of Muslims seated on the ground and talking animatedly together. Our Ahmedabad mitra remarked a few yards further on that they were talking about Islam and Buddhism.

We left our sandals at the gate of the main public area, and entered the first courtyard. To my continued amazement and increasing delight, that 'silence' now seemed to be coming from everywhere - out of the walls, the ground, the sky - it did not seem to be coming any more strongly from the building housing the tomb itself than from anywhere else. When, eventually, I reached the Tomb and entered it (the other two were either not interested; or subconsciously repelled), an attendant accompanied me inside and began to disturb the mysterious and wonderful silence by talking about the delicate inlay-work of the tomb canopy - and my rather curt reply did not succeed in curtailing his chatter. In exasperation, I walked out of the tomb followed by the persistent guide. Now he began to ask questions. Where was I from? What was my religion? I brushed these questions aside and asked him if he could tell me something about the Pir, and, at last pleased, the guide said, "Ah yes, there is a book." Having purchased it, together with two packets of incense, I was left in peace, but Jinasena and the other mitra seemed to be keen to move on by now, so I followed them out into the many-columned shade, across the courtyard, and out into the open air. We returned the way we came, past the Mulvis (were they Sufis?) who had been deep in discussion earlier, and who now smiled at us. We smiled goodbye to them, and I felt that I had for a second time 'encountered' Ahmad Khattu, the Pir. Or was it someone greater even than him whose presence I was sensing now outside the walls of the tomb?

One of our evening programmes outside Ahmedabad was memorable for the keen attentiveness of the audience. It took place in Viramgaon, outside the house belonging to the parents of the mitra who had accompanied us to Sarkhez (he is now Dhammachari Anand Shakya). The tiny house, one of a line on either side of an unpaved road or street in a poor area of town, was filled with pictures of Hindu deities and various colourful knick-knacks, but there was also a Buddha-image, which we set up on a table outside, using a brilliantly colourful sari as a drape, and we managed to produce a very attractive-looking shrine. Jinasena adorned it with a mandala of flowers, and soon people were gathering from all around and sitting waiting for us to start. Most of them looked like farmers with their wives and children, and I was told they were mostly Hindus, so I pitched my talk accordingly.

I spoke of there being two "histories" of India, one written by the Brahmins, and one written by the Buddhists. Strictly speaking Buddhism as such has no history, but without further elucidation the point was likely to be misunderstood. These two 'Histories', I said, did not always agree, but they could decide for themselves which was correct. But whichever was correct, I continued, one thing was certain: mankind today was more than ever one family, and for the future it was important to develop friendships with everyone, whatever their religion, caste or race, and for everyone to practice morality, without which there was no society, no co-operation. At this point, a large contingent of schoolboys arrived, and I went on to describe the teachings of the Buddha as the practice of the Middle Way. In this way I managed to keep everyone absorbed for a good hour and a half or so. Everyone was pleased, and there were requests to visit again, especially from the school boys, who were from a local hostel. We caught a bus back into Ahmedabad, and walked through the strangely silent streets of the sleeping city, past innumerable bodies sprawled in the open on string beds, on ledges and doorsteps, and often side by side with goats and cattle.

Another memorable programme (though it is invidious picking out some and leaving others), was the commemoration of Dr. Ambedkar's death anniversary, which was held at the TBMSG Vihara, and attended by quite a large crowd of Dhammacharis, mitras and Friends. Though I have come to appreciate Dr. Ambedkar more and more through studying his life and doing Dhamma work in India, and can therefore appreciate to some extent the sense of loss which his followers much have felt at his death, I was surprised at the depth of feeling which my talk evoked, and noticed many people close to tears. But though the occasion was a solemn one, it was evident from the people assembled that Dr. Ambedkar's spirit was as far from death as activity is from inactivity.

Following Lokamitra's advice, I sought to extend my Visa in Ahmedabad, and one day, accompanied by Bakul, and followed by Jinasena, I visited the Superintendent of Police. Displayed prominently on one of his windows, I noticed, was a sticker proclaiming 'Krishna ki jai' (victory to Krishna), so it was with a feeling of incredulity that I listened to Bakul speaking (in Gujerati) to the Superintendent about the *dhamma kranti*[76] (dhamma revolution). I wondered how the policeman was able to keep 'Krishna ki jai' and 'Jai Bhim' (Victory to Bhimrao Ambedkar) both going while he considered my Visa application. Perhaps both were equally irrelevant to him as he signed my papers. Perhaps he saw plainly that I wasn't a crook, which was all he chose to concern himself with, or perhaps he was a secret sympathiser with Dr. Ambedkar. At any rate, I was grateful to him for affording me an extension of my visa for three months. Jinasena and I had both been very happy in Ahmedabad; the peacefulness of meditation in the Triyana Vardhana Vihara in the mornings, the excellent breakfasts with which we were provided, the numerous friends who had visited us and whom we visited, all this had made our stay very enjoyable and worthwhile. Perhaps it hardly needs saying that most of our friends were from the poorest sections of the community - most of whom spend the majority of their days in menial toil under the menacing eyes of people who regard it as no business of theirs to assist their employees out of the conditions of semi-slavery in which they live.

Despite the extreme dryness and dustiness of the air (whilst travelling to Viramgaon I had remarked on the copper-coloured, hazy sunset which was reminiscent of some desert scene), I had remained in good health, and was just beginning to rejoice in the fact when our return journey to Bombay put an end to it. We had managed to obtain, through the good offices of Amritlal, an old friend of Bhante's, some tickets with sleeping berths on the night train, so I was not at all worried at the prospect of the journey. However, having settled down into a deep sleep, I was woken in the middle of the right by an intense irritation in my chest and a stench of unbelievable foulness in my nostrils. I and many others in the compartment were seized by a fit of coughing and sneezing. Since we were in total darkness, it was not possible to locate the cause of the foul pollution, but it was almost certainly the huge petroleum refinery which lies upwind from Bombay, and which we were now approaching. Luckily the train kept going - I do not know what would have happened if we had stopped there - but the effect on me of even a few minutes exposure to the poisonous stench was enough to bring on a sore throat immediately. My breathing then became congested and a severe headache ensued. These effects, together with bodily weakness, took several days to wear off. Jinasena, luckily, was not so badly affected, suffering no more than a fit of coughing. But what was happening to the people who had to work in the vicinity of that foulness, or in nearby Bombay when the wind was blowing from the refinery in their direction?

We arrived in Bhim Prerana to find Kamalashila, just arrived from the U.K. and Padmavajra, amongst others, and very glad we were to meet them. The feeling of Sangha which had begun to be apparent in Ahmedabad was present here in even greater measure. Kamalashila was resting, and Padmavajra was very much up and about. After a wash I felt lively enough to engage in conversation with Padmavajra, despite my sore throat and headache, now suppressed with a pain-killing pill. After lunch, Padmavajra lent me a collection of poems by Hart Crane, an American poet, and I wrote two not very good poems of my own - one about Kamalashila, sparked off by my observation of him during our first lunch together.

> Silent bearer of the Word,
> Quietly reassuring, softly urging
> Into the present, stillness.
> Measuring the depth of things
> Which move and decay and are empty.
> How sweetly your message
> Breathes itself into the city air
> From the world beyond all this.
> How sweetly sounds the song of your heart
> Into the noise of the city.
> How pleasing your appearance
> In a world of ugliness.
> How wonderful your truth
> In a world devoid of meaning.
> How bright your light
> In a world of darkness.
> How strong your affirmation
> In a world of negation.
> Would that all could witness your truth,
> Would that all could see the way
> By your bright light,
> Would that all could become strong
> With your unselfish strength;
> Would that your confidence,
> Born of the empty spaces,
> Could empty itself into the heart of all,
> Oh silent, lotus-like bearer of the truth.

The following morning, Jinasena and I set off for Pune on the now familiar train route, and for our last and longest stay in Pune on this occasion. We were led again to Madhuban, but quartered, this time, not in a nearby house, but in a largish room adjoining the Order Library and office. Other visitors from outside India began to arrive in the course of the next few days. Dharmachari Purna, and Gordon Wills (now Dharmachari Lalitavyuha) both come to advise on accounting and computing procedures, shared the room with us, and on quite a few mornings we managed not only to meditate together, not only to have breakfast together, but to begin to communicate something more than superficialities. Dharmachari Amoghachitta too arrived, thin but vigorous-looking, and then Mokshananda and Mokshapriya, whom I was meeting for the first time, trying to get over the curious feeling that I had already known them for a long time. Prakasha too turned up from his more solitary adventures (probably in the footsteps of Padmasambhava), evidently having thoroughly enjoyed himself, and exuding a sense of well-being and great friendliness. There was also a mitra whose name escapes me at present, who had been (and perhaps still is) an assistant of Kamalashila's at Vajraloka. And there was Bodhananda whose robust good health and smiling face impressed me deeply. It was good to begin to enter more deeply into communication with all these friends than I had been accustomed to for quite a while - to have the feeling that whatever one said, it would be understood, which I am certainly not sure of even amongst my English-speaking friends in Colombo. What if anything was even more pleasant was to find that my friends had something of themselves to communicate to me. They were used to a degree of openness which my Sri Lankan friends are only just beginning to discover is possible.

Soon I began to be invited to various places for lunch, and to give talks in the Pune 'localities' in the evening. The audiences seemed very happy to see me, as I was to see them, and one particularly memorable occasion was a question and answer session at the home of a mitra who was later to become Vimuktananda. Though some of the questions were of a very challenging nature, the whole atmosphere was so positive, and I felt so inspired by Dhammachari Vajirabuddhi, who was translating for me, that everything went off very well indeed. I had done quite a bit of Dharma study with Vajirabuddhi whilst I was resident in India, and it was a particular pleasure working with him now as a Dharma brother - one who had gone for Refuge effectively.

Dharmacharini Padmasuri arrived in Pune, and invited me to her lodgings at Parnakuti Society one evening. We had an enjoyable time, our talk ranging over a wide variety of subjects, and I was impressed by her vitality, which seemed greater than mine at times. I told her that I was beginning to feel rather moody - partly, I thought, due to finding myself in the company of a large number of people with whom I wished to communicate, but who all seemed to be going off the instant I made contact with them. This I found quite jarring after being used to the more or less continuous companionship of Jinasena for two whole months - a benefit for which I felt very grateful. I therefore began to look forward to some days of peaceful contemplation at our country retreat centre near the famous Bhaja caves in the near future, but first there were to be the Ordination ceremonies.

Jinasena and I caught a tightly-packed train from Dapodi to Malavli, the station near the ancient Buddhist caves of Bhaja high up on one of the hillsides. Hundreds of others were bound for the same destination, and there was an air of great excitement and happiness amongst the throng of people. I had almost forgotten how many people I knew, at least by sight, and they all looked really happy. Their Going for Refuge was evidently a joyous affair, and my moodiness began to disperse. Our feet seemed to be borne as if on wings over the warm fields towards the hills, and when we arrived at our retreat centre, the finishing touches were being put to the shrine by a team of busy people. I wondered if they needed any help, and discovering Lokamitra, asked him if he wanted anything done. He suggested that I went and sat down mindfully, which might, he said, encourage others to follow suit. And indeed, after sitting down as mindfully (and gracefully) as I could, I was very soon joined by several dozen Dhammacharis dressed in beautifully shining, neatly pressed blue shirts and white kesas, which had a very pleasing effect in the now hot morning sun.

It is quite impossible to adequately express in words the atmosphere of a Public Ordination. As usual, in this case everyone was in an unusually exalted state of mind, and such was the intensity of joyousness that tears came to my eyes on several occasions, especially when the new Dhammacharis, having made their ritual offerings to the Buddha-shrine, saluted the assembly. Kamalashila played his part very serenely and confidently, and Vimalakirti, who was sitting next to me, remarked at one point, referring presumably to the vase of initiation: "He is the only one who can pour".

After a delightful picnic lunch when the hundreds of visitors sat in little groups and shared all kinds of interesting fare, they departed and the Order Retreat began. I had not fully recovered my health even now, after the effect of the Bombay petroleum refinery pollution, and I had quite a struggle during the meditation sessions to remain calm and clear. I enjoyed listening to the talks, particularly Padmavajra's rendering of the story of Yasha's slippers, and when my own turn came, enjoyed speaking about Sri Lanka. There was also a "cultural event", in which the exuberance of the songs and humour, and sometimes the pathos of the sketches was truly remarkable. I particularly enjoyed a song by Bodhidhamma, sung with great sweetness and poignancy.

All too soon, it was time to leave, at least for me. Indeed it was time for all of us to leave Bhaja. Suddenly I found myself alone, taking to the path across the paddy fields, and a curious incident occurred within moments of my setting out. There were two bulls and a cow in the field just below the Centre entrance, and being quite used to these large-horned animals, I took no particular notice. However, as I proceeded along the narrow path, bag in one hand and yellow umbrella in the other, there was a bellow behind me and I glanced back to see the larger bull, a big black fellow, suddenly lower his head and give the other bull a terrific swipe across the belly with his horns, immediately raising a livid weal streaked with blood. I was startled by the suddenness and violence of the attack, but as it seemed to be taking place at a safe distance from me, turned and began to walk on, thinking I had better distance myself from this scene of rivalry as soon as possible. But a few moments later, a shout from a farmer on a distant hillock prompted me to look round again, and this time I saw the smaller bull rushing headlong towards me along the path. I instantly dropped my bag and flung myself off the path, umbrella flying to one side, and I just managed to prevent myself from slipping down a twelve foot drop as the crazed animal rushed past where I had been only a moment before. Unhurt except for some scratches and probably a few bruises, and making sure the young bull had disappeared from sight, I got up and, retrieving my bag and umbrella, resumed my journey.

In just a few days, Jinasena and I were back in Sri Lanka, having spent a day in Trivandrum during which we visited the very fine Art Gallery - a place worth making a detour to visit - which contains some remarkable pictures by the artist Nicholas Roerich. They provided a fitting conclusion to our tour of India.

* * * * *

25   Tarasri recollected, and thoughts for the future

I connect a vision of a rainbow over Unawatuna with the death of Dharmacharini Tarasri, and offer a poem. I continue to try to get TBMSG more established in Sri Lanka, but am not hopeful of early results.

I WAS SITTING IN THE OFFICE here the other day just watching my thoughts, with my eyes closed, and I opened them to find, as one might have expected, broad tropical daylight streaming in the windows. But the curious thing was, it seemed like night time - the world of my thoughts was so much brighter.

The thought that remains even now as bright as when I first saw it is that of a perfect rainbow poised over a turquoise sea and standing out in front of a violet sky - which is the 'vision' I reported in my May Letter to the Order newsletter. When I saw it one morning in Unawatuna it seemed so hypnotically archetypal that I could not help feeling there was some special significance in it. I attributed it at the time to a coincidence of natural phenomena and the effect on my mind of the tom-toms in celebration of the Tamil and Sinhalese new year the previous evening. It was only later that I discovered that Tarasri was at that very moment dying. Now as I recall that vision, my heart skips a beat, and I feel in contact with Tarasri, as if she had not departed from this world. I feel as if I have met her on the Archetypal plane, though I never met her in the flesh, so to speak. These were the words that occurred to me:

> Tarasri, your heart beats still,
> Your radiance flashes out,
> Out of the turquoise ocean you rise,
> The violet rain-clouds gather,
> The rain falls,
> Your colours glow in the firmament,
> Your laugh, your smile, death-transcending,
> Borne in the heart of compassion.
>
> And - who knows? Maybe even your fabled
> Likeness will appear one day to us
> Walking down the lane,
> Cap jauntily askew, and we will meet.

Tarasri in time reborn
From crystal tortoises and moon-hares; hello
Tarasri - here there is no beginning
And no end; only the coming
To perfection of your life,
Your greeting and rejoicing,
Your going and goodbye.

The rainbow fades. Rain
Falls, glistens tremblingly on leaves
And in the air
A marvellous freshness lingers.

I have been seeing more and more of the hill country recently, and have at last arranged a beginners' class in Kandy on Sunday afternoons at 4pm. I've also discovered, with mitra Keerthi's help, a small house not far outside Kandy with an adjoining hermitage and bamboo grove, which could be just the place I been looking for, for a small community. It could be so good I hardly dare think about it.

This month has been exciting and frustrating. My most notable failure was being likened, by a newspaper editor, to a Catholic Priest. Perhaps I was a bit over-zealous. I was feeling old and painful, and that there was no time to waste. That is when the harshness began to creep in. But besides, the Editor was thinking of young sweet-voiced, sweet faced monks, not of the Truth. No, I must not excuse myself - I was being harsh, using triumphalist logic. I must soften my ways.

Things here are, I feel, at last beginning to move, but oh so slowly. With regard to official registration, Bhante has told me that he has no objection to my registering as TBMSS (Trailokya Bauddha Mahasangha Sahayaka Samithiya), as it will be known here, since the word 'Gana' is not in current use. I have to find a suitable lawyer (attempts so far have not borne fruit) and then an MP who is willing to present a Bill in Parliament. That is the system here. The presence of the word Mahasangha, paradoxically makes me not unhopeful of a successful outcome to our application.

Prompted by Lokamitra, I visited Dr Ariyaratne of the Sarvodaya movement this month. I will be writing about that very soon. Last but by no means least, I am delighted to hear of our new Dhammacharis, recent 'graduates' of Guhyaloka, and to extend a warm welcome to them from Sri Lanka. How good, especially, to have an Ariyasingha in the Order, as well as all the wonderful bodhisattva-qualities now embodied, (at least to some extent), in our other new Dharma brothers. Sadhu, sadhu, sadhu![76]

NOTES

75 *dhoti* and *pugree*: *dhoti* : the traditional Indian covering of the lower part of a man's body: a long piece of white muslin or cotton cloth loosely draped so as to hang below the knees and carefully secured about the waist. *pugree* : a turban. May indicate the occupation or caste of the wearer.

76 *dhamma kranti:* the 'Revolution by means of Truth' (i.e. by entirely peaceful means). The name by which the contemporary re-emergence of Buddhism in India is known today, especially by followers of Dr. Ambedkar. For all Buddhists, Buddhism is not merely 'an alternative religion' - but the principial means of emancipation from suffering, the Path of paths. In the case of Indians weighed down the caste system, however, the choice with which they are faced is particularly stark: it is the brotherhood of Buddhism or the slavery of the caste system.

77 Sadhu! : a shout uttered three times on particularly auspicious occasions, in this case, to celebrate the Effective Public Going for Refuge of new Order Members. The word means something like "great", "wonderful", "hooray".

* * * * *

26   The Guru of Sarvodaya

Prompted both by Lokamitra and Siri, I visit Dr. Ariyaratne, the leader of Sarvodaya, the voluntary labour and self-help organization based in Sri Lanka.

I WOULD LIKE TO TELL YOU about a visit I made to Dr. Ariyaratne last month. Dr. Ariyaratne is the leader of an organisation, a very big and in some ways successful one, called Sarvodaya. Some of you may have heard about it, others not It is a pan-religious organisation and therefore, according to Ven. Nyanaponika for instance, not a Buddhist organization. However, whilst no great prominence is given to it, 'everybody knows' that the organization's base and pinnacle is Buddhistic. This, at any rate, is the popular view, and one, no doubt, that Dr. Ariyaratne would have everyone believe. I am myself inclined to view it as yet another 'alternative tradition,' in that, during my second meeting with Dr. Ariyaratne, which I mention later, he told me that he had summoned together the three leaders of the Theravadin nikayas (that's an indication of the power he has) and announced to them that henceforth he was not going to come to them for spiritual advice. I could not help applauding what seemed to be the action of an individual, if a rather ostentatious one.

However, it is clear from Dr. Ariyaratne's booklet 'Spiritual Awakening and Human Progress (in) Religious Co-operation - A Living Experience', that he does not distinguish essential Buddhism from its ethnic and cultural expression. He does not present Buddhism as a Transcendental Doctrine, and is therefore unable to utilize the full range of Buddhist thought and experience in his work. He is trying hard to think things out, and has done a lot of excellent social work. He applies the Dharma (or rather, a version of the formulated Dharma at the psychological level) with what, so far as I can see, is a limited amount of success so far. One of his basic *micchaditthis*[51] is revealed in the following statement (p.4 of the above-mentioned pamphlet): "I am sure all religions in their essence have teachings that go deep into the analysis of the human consciousness, mind, and thought-processes." No doubt this is what every pan-religionist would like to think, but there is little basis for it in truth. Such analysis, if it is undertaken at all, does not even remotely compare with the depth psychology of the Abhidharma.

Sarvodaya is said to have been inspired by the Gandhian Sarvodaya movement in India, and to have developed in Sri Lanka on a foundation of Buddhist principles. The 'movement' presents itself as not religious in a sectarian sense, though it is not made clear what this means. "It is founded on spiritual principles transcending religious barriers so that people belonging to all religions can work together for social, political, and economic progress. It has spread over 8,000 village communities in Sri Lanka, involving about 5 million people - nearly 20% of the total population. It has developed "fraternal links" with similar peoples' movements in other countries including Rissho Kosei-Kai, Niwano Peace Foundation and Life dynamics group in Japan." (from a publicity pamphlet).

Dr. Ariyaratne has been able to attract funds from a variety of European international funding agencies also, and the Sarvodaya budget this year is in excess of 10,000,000/= Sri Lankan rupees. Simply at the level of social work, the movement must be judged a considerable success by all ordinary standards. The 'secret' of its success is *gramdana* - the voluntary giving of labour for a limited period and limited objectives. This provides channels for the release of a lot of energy and enthusiasm in people, as I have seen, and certainly gets things done on the material plane.

On the question of "Transcending religious barriers", however, the question remains whether Dr. Ariyaratne is as successful as he claims. It is not at all clear to me that he has even been successful in transcending political barriers, for from time to time he appears on the President's political platforms, to the embarrassment of his workers in the South, which is JVP (Janata Vimukta Peremuna) country, where government rule is detested. Appeals, I hear, on the part of his workers and advisers to desist from public appearances with politicians, he has seen fit to ignore. He has been incredibly lucky so far in avoiding violent reprisals.

At the psychological level one must ask whether Dr. Ariyaratne has succeeded in cementing the allegiance of his workers. He makes much of establishing "rapport and confidence among workers." It is significant, perhaps, that he calls them workers, not brothers and sisters - the term favoured amongst the Sinhalese themselves, and used with a sense of great affection and solidarity. I have also met quite a few European Sarvodaya workers at the South Ceylon Guest House, Unawatuna, belonging to Siri Goonasekara, and have been consistently impressed in the negative sense by their low level of morale. I suspect this is a peculiarly European trait, but even so, one might have expected that Dr. Ariyaratne would have aroused the faith, confidence and enthusiasm of these people more than he has. In fact, far from helping them transcend religious barriers, he has, it seems to me, exacerbated an incipient sense of hopelessness and frustration and even cynicism amongst them.

Amongst the Sri Lankan, 'born Buddhist' workers of Sarvodaya, it is I think a very different story. So far as I can see from brief meetings with them, and watching them at work, they are much more positive, and even, like some of those working on Sukhavati, our London Buddhist Centre, in the early days, appear to be in a sort of semi-dhyanic state of enthusiastic and clear-minded absorption. Whether these men and women are able to transcend religious barriers I am unable to tell, but I have distinct reservations, knowing from my own experience how very difficult it is to transcend, even temporarily, thoughts and habits rooted in centuries of religious conditioning. What I think I have witnessed, in fact, is the functioning of a positive group with distinctive ethnic and cultural features. In fact the teaching of the True Individual[78] is markedly absent from those writings of Dr. Ariyaratne's that I have seen so far. His doctrinal stance seems to be that of a dogmatic denial of the existence of the self, which must surely create great difficulties for him when he finds that people look to him so much for leadership. There is, it seems to me, something missing from the good Dr. Ariyaratne's movement, and it is precisely that transcendental element which he sees, quite rightly, as being of fundamental importance, but which as I will explain appeared to be absent when I was face to face with him.

This meeting with Dr. Ariyaratne was my third. It was prompted, though not directly, by Lokamitra's request for information and literature about Sarvodaya. In following this up I was directed to the Sarvodaya leader himself, probably because I am a 'foreign monk'. The Sarvodaya HQ is situated in Moratuwa, which is only about two miles away from where I am based in Ratmalana. So it was a matter of a short bus ride and a half-mile walk to reach the Sarvodaya HQ - a set of well-constructed modern buildings of pleasant but unexceptional design, well shaded with trees and covered walkways and gay with a great variety of shrubs and flowers.

The first time I had met Dr Ariyaratne was eighteen months ago at Unawatuna, which he was visiting to inaugurate the work of a coir-rope producing team involving some of the village people. I had been reluctant at first to go along to the meeting, feeling that I did not have a sufficient connection with the affairs of the village, but Siri was very insistent, and much to my embarrassment I was given a place of honour, and so I could not now avoid a public meeting with the famous leader of Sarvodaya. Dr. Ariyaratne was already standing and speaking on my arrival, and the first thing that I noticed about him was his smallness of stature - almost diminutive but stocky, with a shock of long, greying hair. He was wearing the traditional white shirt and sarong of the Buddhist layman. His head was large, with a broad brow and not unattractive large eyes peering through Western spectacles, which from time to time he removed and dangled between his fingers. He sported a small moustache, which lent him the appearance of a banking-clerk. His manner of address was diffident and he spoke with a strangely high-pitched, half-choked voice, with his head on one side, giving the impression that he was under some considerable physical strain. At the end of his speech, which was in Sinhalese and closely attended to, he got a big round of applause from the villagers. He then seemed to relax, and I was introduced to him. He started speaking to me in Sinhalese, but soon switched to fluent English. Now at close quarters I could see clearly what I had sensed before - that he was indeed under some considerable strain or inner tension - perhaps he was suffering from some illness, which gave him a puffy and bloated appearance and caused him to breathe only with difficulty and his eyes to water. I immediately suggested that he should put his feet up and rest, because it was important that the 'helicopter' (of which he had been speaking, using it as a symbol of his movement) should continue to have a pilot. He seemed grateful for the suggestion, and we parted.

My second meeting with Dr Ariyaratne was some months later, when Siri and I happened to be passing the Sarvodaya HQ, and he suggested that we take a look in. Thinking that we would do just that, I agreed, but to my surprise and irritation, suddenly found myself being ushered into Dr. Ariyaratne's office and the presence of the man himself. This time, though he looked a little better, he still seemed blocked, and was smoking a cigarette. I noticed for the first time that his fingers were heavily tobacco-stained. Siri and I were courteously welcomed and asked to sit down for a few minutes whilst some business was being concluded, so I had a chance to collect my wits and to look around the office. It was without doubt one of the best-equipped offices I had come across so far in Sri Lanka. It was large, light and airy, well decorated and clean, with well-stocked bookshelves ranged around the walls. There was a comfortable reception and conference area, a computer, files, telephones, and a variety of not unattractive-looking items arranged in a decorative and artistic manner in strategic positions. It seemed to be a place where work was done and done with enthusiasm.

Not having been warned by Siri of the likelihood of seeing Dr. Ariyaratne in person, I had not come specially prepared, and now had hardly any time to think how to make the best of the meeting. Luckily, I had a copy of *Golden Drum* in my shoulder bag, and when Dr. Ariyaratne had finished consulting with his colleagues, and come over to ask what we wanted, I was ready. I told him that we had come to get to know him a little more, and to tell him about TBMSG/TBMSS. Dr Ariyaratne had apparently never heard of us, but appeared impressed by *Golden Drum* and by a Karuna Trust[777] newsletter which I also happened to have with me. He had not heard of Sangharakshita either, it appeared, for he simply nodded when I mentioned him. We spoke for about ten minutes, during which time Dr. Ariyaratne became more and more interested in what I was saying. However, our communication was interrupted when he suddenly asked us if we would like to take lunch - it was the traditional *dana*-time, 11:30am, when the lay-people present the mid-day meal to the bhikkhus. Siri and I assented, and I thought we would have the opportunity of introducing ourselves more fully, but we were disappointed. Instead of taking lunch with Dr. Ariyaratne, we were shown to a large refectory where there must have been nearly a hundred bhikkhus and a similar number of laymen seated at tables eating. I was of course nudged towards the bhikkhus and Siri towards the laymen, and so we took our separate meals, both of us, I suspect, feeling a bit frustrated. After lunch, we were conducted back to the office, where Dr. Ariyaratne asked me if there was anything else we wanted, and receiving a reply to the contrary, he courteously escorted us to the exit. He had a well-organized and impressive system, it appeared.

This third meeting, however, was rather more deliberate on both our parts. Having spoken over the phone, we were both prepared for a more open communication with one another than had been possible so far, and when I arrived at the HQ soon after 9.00am one morning, Dr. Ariyaratne was with me at Reception within a few minutes and escorting me over to his house which lay just a short distance away from the headquarters building. Waiting at the gate was his wife - a sturdy, homely-looking woman, who was holding a two-year-old ready for my attention. Giving them both a smile, I said 'hello' as I passed and followed Dr. Ariyaratne into the large house. It appeared to be typical, from what I had already seen, of the accommodation of wealthy Sri Lankan families. It was spacious and airy - almost a palace by Indian standards - and impressive even by comparison with the Wimbledon upper-middle class houses I had become familiar with whilst fund-raising for Karuna Trust some years before. None of this would have surprised me very much had I not read that "a Non-poverty, Non-affluent Society is the Objective of the Sarvodaya Shramadana Movement." (p.iii, Sarvodaya Shramadana Movement of Sri Lanka). On the other hand, I felt it was perhaps rather nit-picking of me to feel critical of a man who spent so much time and effort in the service of others, attending to the material welfare of his own family in a generous manner. Perhaps his wife had more to do with it than he had. We ascended several flights of stairs, went down a corridor, and entered Dr. Ariyaratne's private, third-floor room - an even larger and better-appointed one than the office only a short distance away. Here it was very quiet and the large array of books lining the walls was impressive, as was the double bed with a computer beside it. Squeezed into one corner was an elaborate shrine with half-a-dozen attractive Buddha-images placed upon it. Largest and uppermost was a simple white stone image, almost austere, and lower down, Thai images in bronze, in gold, and in green glass decorated with jewels. There was also a small Burmese image in marble. It was an impressive array, and I also noticed numerous photographs of a rather brutal-faced bhikkhu in a brown robe, with somewhat Western features but narrow eyes, arranged in strategic positions amongst the images. I was shepherded towards the shrine and Dr. Ariyaratne prostrated himself in front of it. So did I, whilst trying to ignore the bhikkhu looking out at me from his numerous vantage points.

The formalities over, Dr. Ariyaratne sat back on some nearby cushions and reached for a cigarette, whilst also inviting me to take a cushion nearby - an unorthodox procedure for a Theravadin. He didn't, however, seem at first to know what to say, neither did he give the impression of feeling easy saying nothing, so I took the initiative and started telling him why I had come. I had not got very far when there was a knock on the door and an attractive young woman entered at his invitation, carrying a brown glass bottle. Dr. Ariyaratne accepted it, whilst the young woman sat on the floor nearby, elaborately taking no notice of me. Rather more simply, I took no particular notice of her. Dr. Ariyaratne then took up a clear glass bottle which was filled with what looked like water. Holding his cigarette in one hand and the bottle in the other, he held the neck of the bottle under his nose, and then poured a few drops of the liquid into the woman's eagerly-proffered hands, and she bent her head to drink. Whether for my benefit or hers I could not tell, Dr. Ariyaratne then said "It's all right, it's only water." The young woman then got up and went out with a smile on her face.

I asked what was the liquid in the brown bottle the young woman had brought, and Dr. Ariyaratne said "Oh, she's one of my doctors, and every time she makes some massage oil she brings some for me and I do that for her." I wondered what, exactly, Dr. Ariyaratne had done for her. I wondered whether it really benefited the woman doctor to drink the water sniffed by the heavy smoker, or whether it reassured the heavy smoker to have an attractive and healthy young woman doctor drink water that had just been perfumed by his tobacco-laden breath. Putting my curiosity and slight disgust to one side, I returned to the question of the purpose of my visit, and began to talk about our movement, about Lokamitra and the work in India. I also put to Dr. Ariyaratne some questions that Lokamitra wanted me to raise, and presented him with the latest Aid for India and Karuna Trust newsletter. At this point he suddenly emerged from his previously rather sleepy state and seemed to become quite animated. In fact, after a few more minutes of talk, he said he would like to go and visit Lokamitra in India and see our work there. Furthermore, he got out pen and paper and wrote out the name of a big European funding agency that he thought would be willing to help us, and which I could pass on to Lokamitra.

Talk then turned to Sangharakshita, and I showed Dr. Ariyaratne some books by him. He showed even more interest, and said that he would like all of Bhante's books, and could I get them sent to him - he would pay for them. I agreed to do so. Our talk then turned to meditation and 'spiritual' matters. In answer to one of my own questions, Dr. Ariyaratne said that he meditated twice a day, and at this point he began to ramble on a bit. He said that during the last few months he had been feeling as if a god was protecting him, and he was trying to open himself more to the influence of what he called 'cosmic forces'. He then began to describe his own version of the mindfulness of breathing, at which point I said, very gently, that I knew it very well and practised it every day myself. I also said that his own vision of the cosmos was interesting, but suggested that he should be careful about thinking that a god was helping him - might it not be simply the result of his own past skilful acts? With this he partly agreed, but added "But that is what it seems like to me" - which was not a point which ought to be disputed, I thought. So then I pointed out that though there did seem to be powerful natural forces at work in nature, they were not enlightened, not the Dharma - the Dharma itself did not come from within Nature. On this point he appeared uncertain but said nothing.

I then asked Dr. Ariyaratne about his guru, who he said was the Burmese 'priest' depicted in so many places on his shrine. His name, he said, was Ven. Dhammajñānika Sayadaw. He proceeded to inform me that he was a Burmese monk with remarkable psychic powers who lived in the Burmese forest. This, my experience of Sri Lankan forest hermitages suggested, probably meant that he lived in a comfortable little bungalow in a park-like forest reserve, attended by a small army of devotees. Moreover, Dr. Ariyaratne said, he did not write any books or pamphlets, and did not give talks. He left others to do that. Oh, I said. I got up and looked closely at one of the pictures of the guru. His jaw was clamped tightly closed in an expression of repressed anger or frustration. His eyes, far from having the clear, open, sparkling and lightly penetrating, even slightly humorous gaze I associate with those having experience of the 'psychic' *dhyānas*, were almost obscured, as if trying to avert themselves from the camera's gaze. Hmm, I said. "Yes", said Dr. Ariyaratne: "He has very great psychic powers; I go and meet him from time to time in Burma."

We both sat down again, Dr. Ariyaratne having risen with me, and again I turned the conversation to India. I said that Lokamitra felt that we could learn quite a lot from Sarvodaya, and would it be possible for one of our full-time workers to come and work with him for a month or so? Dr. Ariyaratne seemed very pleased at the suggestion, and said yes, of course, and why not send him for three months. I added that Lokamitra was interested in any literature that was available about Sarvodaya, whereupon Dr. Ariyaratne got up, went over to one of the copious collections of books in the wall-to ceiling shelf near his bed, and pulled out quite a little collection of pamphlets and booklets which he presented to me. Having accomplished what I had set out to do, I expressed my thanks and started to go. Somewhat to my surprise, in view of his previously egalitarian behaviour, of which I by no means disapproved, Dr. Ariyaratne gave me a deep formal *anjali*[78], and I left, the good doctor following me to the exit and bidding me a friendly farewell.

NOTES

78   True Individual. A translation of the Pali term *ārya puggala* (lit. 'noble person'). A person who has broken at least the first three of ten fetters preventing one from gaining Enlightenment, i.e. (1) personality view - that one is born the way one is, and that this personality persists unchanged and unchangeable throughout life. (2) doubt and hesitation concerning the teachings of the Buddha sufficient to prevent one from getting down to actual practice and decisive reflection (3) superficial practice - 'going through the motions' of Buddhist praxis in such a way as to avoid, prevent or simply not to bring about radical change. Breaking these three fetters, one becomes a Stream Entrant, attaining the first level of true spirituality; in other words, the emotional, intellectual and spiritual state of someone who is truly - spiritually - an individual, a True Individual. The True Individual is sharply contrasted with the merely statistical individual who does not think and act for himself or herself but sheep-like simply follows the flock, the crowd or the group. See *Going for Refuge*, p16 ff, Sangharakshita, Windhorse Publications.

79   *anjali*: the traditional Eastern 'Salutation with folded hands'. It is the formal and universal gesture of respect there, made by holding the palms lightly together at chest level, and often accompanied by a bow, more or less deep, or a nod of the head. It has the merit of being almost impossible to perform without some measure of respect, mutual recognition and fellow-feeling.

80   *darshan*: lit. a 'view' or even 'vision'. To 'take *darshan*' means to have a really good look at someone, especially someone supposed to be of spiritual stature or worth. The idea is to try to see and appreciate directly, visually, what sort of person they really are. This good long look (not staring) at someone, far from being considered impolite, involves the belief that the person whose *darshan* you are 'taking' is more developed than you are. Respect for the person being contemplated in this way is thus implicit. Such a practice also implies the belief that spiritual qualities are in fact discernible, and that the observer has something of an artist's eye - the ability to appreciate visually, the nature of higher human qualities.

* * * * *

27   Kandy thoughts

Finding dharma work in Colombo arduous and frustrating, I retreat to the hills for meditation and reflection.

I

AM SITTING ON THE BALCONY of a small house with a beautiful view of the distant tree-covered hills and mountains. Birds are chirruping merrily in the trees nearby, and the sun is shining with its usual tropical intensity in a sky of purest cerulean blue. The house is perched on a forty-five degree slope near the top of a hill about a mile outside Kandy. It has been made available for my use by the generosity of Mr. Ananda Virasekara, a not-wealthy (he insists) but obviously quite well-to-do gentleman who occupies a large house further down the hill, and in whose back garden this small but sturdily-built smaller house I'm in is situated. It is surrounded by palms, and by papaya and jackfruit trees.

I feel as if I have reached a stage beyond which I will need some sturdy assistance from Sri Lankan Friends and mitras, and perhaps from other parts of our Movement. My money and energy are stretched to capacity. However, I shall be quite happy to base myself here until, with a bit of luck, the Movement in Sri Lanka begins to gain further momentum. This is not to say that I intend resting on my laurels, assuming I do have a leaf or two. I am currently holding, each week, beginners classes in Galle (two to six people attending), Colombo (forty-five to sixty attending) and Kandy (twenty to thirty attending) and have begun an advanced class (actually, a "mitra Request" class) in Colombo and Kandy, and with a bit of luck will be keeping up this programme for quite a while yet. The class in Galle, at the YMBA is poorly attended and more or less ignored by the Committee there, and I am thinking of withdrawing, which will leave me with time and energy to work more fruitfully elsewhere. In addition I am giving full-moon day talks in various Temples, as well as beginning to get involved in teaching a hundred and fifty so young Sarvodaya workers to meditate. Since things are indeed beginning to pick up momentum, I feel a bit of a conflict at the prospect of my India tour this year, but it will probably give me more inspiration and energy to carry on here in Sri Lanka afterwards.

It now appears that official registration of my 'group' as a Voluntary Social Service Organisation will be more straightforward than I had been led to believe, and I am calling a meeting next Saturday to pass the necessary resolutions and elect office bearers, etc. On the more obviously 'spiritual' side, Siri now having settled in New Zealand, and Jinasena in India, I am keen to encourage a new batch of people to become mitras. Of course I cannot ask them directly, but I can drop a few hints. At present I am sharing 'Rajgiri' with Indrajit, a Friend whose faith is more in evidence than his capacity to think and reflect. Despite this, with a bit of persistence, inspiration and luck, I am confident that there will be several requests in the near future.

Mahamati, the current Director of Karuna Trust, has written to me inquiring about my plans, and I shall therefore be outlining proposals for a Hostel. Proposals for the year are in any case required by the Registration authorities here. I had our first request for accommodation yesterday on behalf of a Tamil boy. I don't know yet whether I will be able to do anything for him. Other events this month have been two young bhikkhus becoming very interested in our work in Colombo. I had a stimulating session with them recently answering their questions.

* * * * *

28   A Crumb from Colombo

This is my last letter from 'Rajgiri', the small flat where I spent the best part of a year in the company of Jinasena, and in which we held meditation classes for those interested in becoming mitras. Though I make no mention of the fact, I am greatly relieved to be moving from the environs of the chocolate factory, the noisy road, and the landlord with the enormous dog.

I AM PREPARING TO MOVE to our new premises with the generous financial assistance of my mother and aunt, and the Karuna Trust, who are recovering tax on behalf of Trailokya Bauddha Mahasangha Sahayaka Samithya. Nor will I forget the words of encouragement and of caution from various other Order members. If things go according to plan, I shall find myself living in conditions which are palatial compared with those in which many of my Indian friends with families live. I have decided, however, not to take on the burden of purchasing the new place immediately, which would be more than I could do with an easy mind for the foreseeable future. It is a large British Colonial style bungalow, with eight or nine recently refurbished rooms, a large shady balcony, and about sixty years old. I shall be committing myself to a five year lease on it, with an option to purchase at the end of that period. This way there is a good chance of raising the purchase money less frenetically, or of moving out if for some reason or other it proves unsuitable. I say "we", but I do not yet know who will be forming the community with me. Jinasena is off to India for the second time in June and Indrajit, the Friend who is sharing with us at Rajgiri is a bit of a question mark. Evidently I am going to have to work to get together the community I want - it is not just going to fall into my lap.

I was pleasantly surprised one evening recently when Bodhiruci and his friend Robert arrived from the UK. They did not stay long since they had planned to go to the Maldives, and despite my entreaties to spend their time instead in South Sri Lanka and leave the money thus saved to the work of TBMSS, Bodhiruci told me that the Maldives were disappearing under the sea, and he wanted to see them before they did so. Meg Kayte, a mitra from the Croydon Centre, also called here and we had a good talk. So good, in fact, that she sent me recently, on her return to the U.K., a substantial donation for the 'Colombo Project', for which I am very grateful indeed. May she and whoever else contributed, receive and enjoy the just rewards of such an act.

One of the things I venture forth to do from time to time is to visit the new and second hand bookshops in the hot and polluted city of Colombo. I was delighted last week to find the three volumes of the *Digha Nikaya*, translated by Prof. and Mrs. Rhys Davids, on sale for a very reasonable price second hand. They were in almost perfect condition, apart from some rather irritating pencilling-in by a knowledgeable but inconsiderate previous owner. I purchased them there and then, spent a few hours cleaning them up with a rubber, and settled down to study them. Other books I am in process of reading are *Vanity Fair*, by W. M. Thackeray (brilliant, he is a great novelist) and Xenophon's *Education of Cyrus* (translated by H. G. Dakyns). I learned from the latter that the tally of men reckoned as Persian, not long before the fall of Babylon, was apparently a mere 120,000. Cyrus comes across as quite an interesting character, but unfortunately he enjoyed killing animals.

One blot on the horizon recently has been that a mitra has 'gone reactive' and started tale-bearing. The immediate cause of his reaction was disagreement with me over the question of whether one should ever criticize other teachers and other teachings. My answer was a qualified yes, his was a absolute no. So complete was the polarization that communication ceased, reaction set in, and within two hours he had packed his bags and left the community. This shocked the other mitras even more than it shocked me, but it was nevertheless rather distressing being on the receiving end of that sort of thing, even when there was no good cause for his reaction and his departure, and no substance whatever to the tales he then began to spread. The Regulars' Class consists at present mostly of girls and women. Last week two quite enthusiastic young men turned up. I hope they come again.

* * * * *

29   India Tour 1988/89 (Part I)

To my great relief I arrive in India on this my second visit from strife-
torn Sri Lanka. I travel from Pune to Ahmedabad and start a tour of the
Vidarbha district of Maharashtra, where there are many Buddhists. Visits to
towns and villages are filled with excitement, but travel over long distances
in the jeep is arduous. I meet a man with two wives but find them falling short
of conjugal bliss. I find humanity and beauty amidst the poverty of an Indian
village.

I ARRIVED YESTERDAY MORNING in Ahmedabad, and as I shall
probably be at out little centre (it is called Triyana Vardhana Vihara) in this
great city for nigh on three weeks, it seems that I have a chance of getting
well into the report of this, my second tour of India after having based myself
in Sri Lanka. There will then be comparatively little left to report when, with
a bit of luck, I get back to Colombo. By the middle of this year (1988) I had
already begun to think of touring India towards the end of the year when an
invitation from Lokamitra arrived at 'Rajgiri'. He informed me that Bhante
would be arriving in India in a month's time, and could I come to assist in the
lead-up to his arrival. The suggestion was that I should tour Vidarbha (the
Nagpur region). He also asked if I would give a public talk in Pune on Ashok
Vijaya Dasami. Since the situation in Sri Lanka was by then becoming more
and more unsettled, and spreading the Dharma was therefore becoming
increasingly difficult, Lokamitra's suggestion came as something of a relief. I
hastened to the offices of Air Lanka to book my ticket to Trivandrum, which
would be the least expensive route to Pune. Lest any of you should think I am
being, or was being melodramatic concerning Sri Lanka, let me sketch in a
few painful lines some facts.

During the past year, it is popularly estimated, roughly six thousand
people have become the unfortunate victims of political assassination. There
were daily reports of bullet-ridden bodies found with 'JVP punishment' or
something of the sort pinned to them, and on one shocking occasion I myself
saw a half-burned human corpse lying on tyres by the side of the road.
Everywhere, every day, there were groups of militiamen armed with rifles
and machine-guns at almost every street corner. There were stories of nightly
abductions by the police, and a Citizens' Committee of self-defence was set
up after people began to die in hospital of police torture and brutality, or even
in the police stations. Thilakaratne, one of our mitras, a responsible and
mature man and a Government employee, had his own story to tell on my
return to Sri Lanka: one morning, shortly after I had left for India, as he was

dressing, there was a commotion outside his house and a Government Jeep drew up, followed by an Army Jeep bristling with guns. Somewhat alarmed, he sent his wife out to enquire. She was informed that they had come to take him to a high-level Government meeting. Knowing that there were many JVP men in his village, Thilakaratne did some careful thinking: his life might be at stake. He sent his wife out again to say that he was suffering from diabetes, and could not come. (He does have incipient diabetes, so it was not untrue). After some hesitation and grumbling by the visitors, and further entreaties by his wife, the two Jeeps went away. Mr. Thilakaratne then completed his dressing, walked out of his house watched by a small crowd of suspicious onlookers, and made his way to the local clinic, where he persuaded the doctor to give him a letter admitting him to hospital in Galle. Many people must have been in such a predicament and, not being so lucky or resourceful as Thilakaratne, met horrible deaths either at the hands of the Police or from JVP militiamen wreaking their vengeance.

Emerging from Passport inspection at Trivandrum after the forty-minute flight northwards across the Palk Straits, I felt a wave of blissful relief wash over me. Everyone was so relaxed! Even though India was far from free of its own disturbances, it was such a vast country that it could absorb quite a few shocks without the majority of the populace going into reaction. The train journey to Pune was a long one. The frank curiosity of some of my fellow-travellers was however in pleasant contrast to the black-eyed reticence of the Sri Lankans in recent months. In reply to their friendly importunity, I told quite a few Indians who inquired that I did not regard myself as belonging to any particular nation or country, since firstly I was a Buddhist, and in Buddhism, universal brotherhood, which is contrary to nationalism, is encouraged. Secondly, I said, I had not lived in the West since 1982 and was in fact now just as much 'at home' with Eastern manners as with Western ones. Sometimes this rather lengthy reply evoked approval, sometimes an expression of blank disbelief. I eventually shortened my response to questions concerning my origins. I would say: "The world is my country", which amused almost everyone. After two nights on the train, I arrived in Pune and took a rickshaw to Dapodi. Everything was reassuringly familiar, and I was soon comfortably installed in "Madhuban", Lokamitra's Office and Order Library, by Raju his Assistant and Secretary. Lokamitra was 'out of station' and expected back in a day or two.

The next morning, whilst I was reclining on my bed with my back propped against a fat cushion, Lokamitra breezed into the Office, having just arrived from Bombay. Quickly surveying the contents of his in-tray and placing a few papers on his desk, he directed a few friendly remarks at me and left, promising to spend some time with me as soon as he could. I was very pleased to see him looking well and relaxed, and very happy to accept an invitation to supper at his house that evening.

It was delightful to be in the bosom of friendship again, but I was in India for a specific mission, and after a couple of days of rest and comfort I was off again. That night I was on a train to Akola, in Central Maharashtra, which would be the starting point of my Vidarbha tour with Dhammacharis Manjuvir and Sanghasena. Sanghasena had been, and still is, remarkable for

his vitality and pioneering spirit, and had for several years now been firing
the people of Vidarbha (the mythical 'Nagas') with enthusiasm for the
Dharma, for Bhante and for TBMSG. It had been planned that both
Sanghasena and I would speak at meetings, and that Manjuvir would translate
my English into Marathi. The arrangement worked very well, Manjuvir often
supplementing our efforts by giving a short talk too.

But I am leaping ahead. For two days after our arrival in Akola (the
other two Order Members had arrived by separate routes), there was
torrential rain. The roads were awash with torrents of water, but the rickshaw
wallas seemed to take it all in their stride, laughing and joking as they
struggled ankle deep in water through the floods. But trains and buses were at
a standstill, and this meant that our planned programme in the great city of
Nagpur - where there were probably thousands of Buddhists eagerly
awaiting our arrival - and which lay an hour or more away when the going
was good - had to be abandoned. I felt greatly disappointed and concerned,
especially since there was no means of getting in touch with our Nagpur
friends. Telephones and Telegraph lines were all 'out of order.' Not only that,
the Jeep that was supposed to have met us at Akola had not arrived, and
Manjuvir was beside himself with worry. Not only was the Jeep carrying a
large quantity of TBMSG publications, it was also the only practicable means
of visiting all the outlandish places it had been planned that we would visit.
There was little we could do but sit out the rain. Manjuvir's further attempts
at telephoning were fruitless.

Most of next day we holed-up in a hotel, where in a small but clean
room, seated on our beds, we held a meeting of the Order in comparative
comfort. We ventured out to a nearby cafe for breakfast, and lo and behold,
met the jeep driver - Dhammamitra Subhas Dolas, and a companion. If
Manjuvir was beside himself before, he was almost in a state of apoplexy
now, Subhas revealed that the Jeep had been left in a garage forecourt in a
town some miles distant, with sixteen lakhs of rupees worth of books in it. I
have rarely seen a mitra get such a dressing down. Subhas's head hung so low
that I thought he would collapse altogether. However, leaving to retrieve the
Jeep without so much as a cup of tea, he turned around and passed me, giving
me a wink and shrugging his shoulders, as if to say, 'Ah well, it's all in a day's
work.' Since we had now located the Jeep, we were at least free to make the
next move informed by knowledge rather than propelled by ignorance. We
decided to take a train (the rainstorm now being over), to Amaravati, where a
programme had been arranged for that evening. We eventually arrived in the
suburbs of the large town, and were there made to feel welcome and
comfortable in a way that, it seems, only the Indians know how. Upon
arrival, I had been presented with a beautiful, sweet-smelling garland of
small white chrysanthemums and roses of a most delicate pink. That evening
we spoke at a nearby hall to an audience of about five hundred, who had
assembled despite sporadic heavy rain. And despite the intermittent
electricity and intermittent thunder we managed to make ourselves heard and
received an enthusiastic ovation.

The next day, history seemed to be repeating itself, to some extent. The
Jeep had still not arrived. The rain, however, completely dispersed and a sun

of astonishing brilliance and intensity shone from a perfectly blue sky, turning Gawale Guruji's modest residence - where we were quartered in a very poor and down-at-heel area of town - into a sort of paradise sparkling with Jewel-laden trees and shrubs which had been tended with loving care wherever plant life was possible. As mid-day approached, the temperature in the little house rose to such a degree that everyone was immobilized. Still there was no jeep. After lunch and a snooze, Sanghasena and I sat and meditated in the midst of the hot hells. Manjuvir, unwilling to be still, went off to make another of his series of phone calls, and the afternoon wore interminably on. Manjuvir almost visibly giving off a cloud of smoke, returned with no news. 'What might have happened to those books?' he kept on muttering, and: 'How are we to visit our friends?' Another programme scheduled for that evening had to be written off, and the following day we took a bus to our next venue.

Our visit this time was to a new 'colony' or housing estate providing accommodation for power station workers. It was situated at no great distance from a monster of a Multi-megawatt solid-fuel power station with gigantic chimneys - they seem to be much the same world-wide - pouring its life-destroying fumes into the blue. After a rest in the local guest house, thoughtfully (or perhaps of necessity) equipped with air conditioning, we walked between neat rows of quasi-suburban mass housing to the community hall where there were more than a thousand people waiting to listen to us. I was informed in whispers that many of them were Hindus. This did not prevent me from giving a rousing talk on Dr. Ambedkar and Buddhism, which evidently everyone appreciated.

After a vote of thanks and the usual but nonetheless welcome distribution of garlands, we wandered off and apparently fortuitously, entered a house where someone was, we thought - although no-one seemed to be quite sure - preparing some food. Various hangers-on followed us in and plonked themselves down in front of me and started asking questions. Manjuvir got up as if stung, and taking me by the arm, more or less marched me out. 'These people haven't arranged anything properly, and now they want to ask a lot of stupid questions' he exclaimed. 'We'll return later to eat when they manage to get something together. We nearly always find that people want to ask stupid and reactive questions after our talks', Manjuvir went on, 'but we let them sleep on it, and the next morning they're usually in a much better mood and we can then have a sensible talk with them.'

We returned from our air-conditioned lodgings some time later to find that our would-be questioners, friendly or otherwise, had dispersed. We had started to eat a very late meal undisturbed when half-way through it, who should turn up but Sanghasen who had left us the day before at Amaravati. He had arrived in the Jeep with a new driver and Dhammamitra Jeune with a large sack of books. Subhas Dolas had apparently taken himself off, doubtless incensed at the dressing-down from Manjuvir. As for the latter, the black cloud which had been hovering around him for some days vanished miraculously.

Next day we drove to Brahmapuri, a township of narrow streets and closely clustered dwellings trying, perhaps, to afford each other shade from the ruthless beams of the sun. Hindu temples by the dozen poked their towers upwards, as if into the eye of Brahma. That evening, the programme, held in something like a town hall, with a stage at one end, was attended by nearly two thousand people, crammed in like olives in a clear glass bottle. The atmosphere was highly positive, and Manjuvir, Sanghasena and I all gave vigorous talks. The people laughed and clapped, especially at Manjuvir and Sanghasen, and large numbers of garlands were presented, mostly to me. Afterwards I said that Brahmapuri ought to be called Buddhapuri.

That night, for some reason or other, I was quartered, not with Manjuvir and Sanghasena, (or the others), but with a wizened old man (perhaps it was Brahma?) who insisted on sleeping close to me in the same small room. His presence was so stifling and constricting that, when his breathing had settled down to a steady rhythm, I took up my mattress and bedding and ascended to the roof, where I slept soundly under the canopy of stars. Next morning, the old gent, looking a bit put out, discovered me aloft, but appeared placated when I agreed to take breakfast with him.

Next day, the novelty of the Jeep began to wear off, and I began to realize dimly what I was in for as mile succeeded bumpy mile. Still, it was better than bullock-cart. We arrived in late afternoon at Jevatmal, at the Tilak Smaran Bhumi, before a very smart-looking audience. Influenced perhaps by the smoothness of the audience, I gave a very smooth-voiced talk, and was congratulated afterwards for my 'excellent manners and delightful personality'. I had not previously been at all conscious of these attributes, which now constricted my head like a sort of tightly fitting halo. One persistent young questioner asked me 'How is it that the Dhamma is so bright and the heart so dark?' Resisting the sudden impulse to beat the young cynic, I replied 'You'd better consult the dazzling darkness.' His wicked looking face emitted a pig-like grunt and turned away.

That night, I had very pleasant dreams, perhaps because I was given a comfortable bed all alone in a large room, prominent in which was a Buddha-bust of extraordinary sweetness backed by a fan of the most gorgeous peacock feathers. I had not been familiar with such luxury for many years. Next morning, during breakfast, a kindly-faced and intelligent-looking man whom I had noticed in the audience the previous evening, turned up to question me. He told me he was a doctor, and proceeded to ask me some questions about *karma* and *karma-vipaka*, which I answered to his evident satisfaction, while parrying some *micchaditthis* being proffered by my host.

After a very long, hot and bumpy journey, negotiated well by our excellent driver, we arrived at the town of Umarkhed, where we gave our talks on the maidan - a big open ground which might have accommodated ten times the number of people who actually assembled. We stayed at an old British-period Government rest-house on the outskirts of the town that night, and after breakfast the following morning half a dozen or more local dignitaries turned up and joined us on the verandah. I watched, amused, as they tried playing their various games with Manjuvir, plying him with questions that I could not help feeling that he attracted or wanted. However, he seemed to deal with them quite well, so far as I could tell with the limited Marathi at my disposal. One suave, middle-aged gentleman who ventured to speak to me in English, was anxious to tell me what a great religion Buddhism was, although he himself, he said, did not follow it. Thank you very much for telling us, I said, with meaning pointed enough, I thought. But he went on talking in the same manner as his opening gambit, apparently oblivious of the incongruity.

The game playing over, we settled our sore backs once more into the Jeep and departed for Karanje, a largely Muslim township, judging by the number of mosques and white caps in evidence. Karanje had appeared suddenly in the midst of a vast and arid wilderness after we had been travelling most of the day, and I for one was heartily wishing for the end of the hot and bumpy trail. Despite the ubiquitous signs of Allah, it was pleasant to stand on firm ground in a narrow shady street and savour the stillness and quiet. We walked a few yards from the Jeep along the street, turned left and passed under the arched entrance-way of our destination, which I was told was a hostel for boys. On the extensive playground inside, a wiry and strenuous-looking middle-aged man wearing white trousers and shirt and sporting a loud purple scarf flung carelessly around his shoulders, was directing a large crowd of boys who seemed to be really enjoying themselves in vigorous dance. There were some other men too, all looking healthy and happy. It was a very pleasant sight. Decorations were in evidence, and it became clear that we were expected and prepared for. Hardly had we stopped when the wiry man who was directing things blew a whistle and barked orders to some of the crowd to go off and get ready for the procession.

Asking to take a bath, I was shown to a large bare room devoid of any feature save a tap and a drain, and open on one side to the playground-courtyard. I took my 'bath' under the fascinated gaze of a troupe of gawping boys, and a couple of unselfconscious women. After this, the procession began. I was jammed beside Sanghasen into the seat of a particularly narrow cycle rickshaw, and off we went into town, preceded by a team of boys holding aloft tambourines headed by a band of drummers. We were followed by a much larger group of boys and girls, men and women, all shouting the familiar slogans: "Dacter Aambedkur-ki - JAI! Bhante Sangharakshita - VIJAY-HO, Bhikkhu Sanghassa-ki, VIJAY-HO (the latter slogan much to Sanghasen's annoyance, and he tried to stop it). All this, with occasional variations, additions and modifications, was kept up with amazing persistence while the drummers taking the lead worked themselves into an almost hypnotic, rhythmical beat and the tambourine-players leaped and whirled, rose and bent to the clash of hundreds of tiny cymbals.

At various strategic points in the town, the procession would come to a halt, the tambourine players form a large circle and the drummers take the centre. The drums would throb louder and louder, the tambourines work themselves into a sort of clicking and rattling ecstasy, the sound would subside for a few moments, and then we would move on as before. In this way the procession continued for about two hours. Having left the hostel under a canopy of glittering tinsel, and then returned the way we had come, the drummers gave a last climactic performance under the tinsel canopy at the end of which was written in bold letters: "WELCOME!"

After dismounting from the narrow rickshaw and stretching our cramped legs, and not forgetting to thank the rickshaw-wallah, Sanghasen and I were taken by Jeep to the house of a Mr. Meshram, where we were introduced to his two wives and partook of supper. Mr. Meshram's wife number one served the food. Wife number two remained inconspicuously in the background. After consuming the excellent meal at our leisure, it was time for the 'programme' in the School and Hostel grounds. About two thousand people had assembled, and in addition to being well-lit, the whole place was electric with expectation. Manjuvir opened with a brief introduction to Trailokya Bauddha Mahasangha Sahayak Gana, as our Movement is known in India, and Sanghasen followed up with one of his now familiar harangues, regaling the audience with all the tricks of rhetoric leavened with a vigorous mixture of humour and earnestness. Everyone was thoroughly warmed (if they had needed warming) by the time it was my turn to speak. I began by expressing gratitude for the exceptionally warm welcome we had received, and of admiration in particular of the drumming during the procession. This pleased everyone, and I then proceeded with a selection of well tried and tested themes connected with the life and work and Going for Refuge of Dr. Ambedkar, which was also very much appreciated, needless perhaps to say. Afterwards I was the recipient of a rather large number of garlands, several of them really magnificent, and I listened to a vote of thanks - in English, for the TBMSG programme which it was said was 'the best in ten years.' I thought this must be a slight inaccuracy - since TBMSG was hardly in existence ten years ago, and I was quite sure that the town had never seen or heard anything like Sanghasena's performance before.

That night we were taken to an ill-equipped rest house on the far side of the town. During the night a rat ran over my head, and I discovered next morning that in its eagerness to get at an apple I had put in my travelling bag, the aforesaid rat - or perhaps a brother rat - had eaten through the beautiful soft brown scarf which had been given to me by Mahadhammavir shortly before his death, and was one of my few prized possessions. *Omnia in terra mortuis imprimantur est.*

For breakfast we returned to Mr. Meshram and his two wives, and I was able to take a closer look at the menage. It was on the surface the picture of harmony. Wife number one served as before, and I noticed how keen and how discreet was her watchfulness. She seemed to take a special delight in serving, and in anticipating every wish of the guests - three Dhammacharis, one Dhammamitra, one Jeep driver and the purple-scarved hostel warden, to whom I had by now taken a particular liking. Not only was she watchful; she served with a swiftness and grace that was astonishing. Furthermore, she was no mere servant; she seemed to be self-possessed and humorous. Something however was missing or out of balance in her personality. Despite her apparent good humour, the occasional wrinkles on her forehead spoke of frustration and even anger. She was, it seemed to me, despite her apparent wish to serve, mainly angling for attention.

Wife number two was by comparison a little dormouse or hamster. Small and round, dowdy by comparison with wife number one, she was almost completely self-effacing. She seemed to be saying 'Don't take any notice of me, I'm just nothing.' After breakfast I asked Mr. Meshram if he had any objection to my taking a photo of him and his two wives. He had, perhaps unsurprisingly, no objection. I had hoped for a picture of triangular happiness, but not at all. Not one of the three would smile, and the resultant picture portrayed if anything, boredom. The one curious fact is that both wives went to put on spectacles for the photo - large and modern ones, of the sort that Germaine Greer might have approved. On leaving, as I got into the jeep, however, wife number one flashed me a smile of truly astonishing charm and brilliance, which, I could not help thinking, was the bait and the snare for poor Mr. Meshram, and the underlying reason, perhaps, for taking a second wife. Who could feel secure with one like the first?

The township of Karanje was followed by Washim, where the man in charge who greeted us had been, he said, a Captain in the Indian Army under the British. He was charming, but slightly eccentric in that he would neither shake hands with me nor perform the more usual *anjali.* Not that I objected to this: I simply noticed it. He had a certain seriousness or gravity about him which seemed to preclude anything so trifling as a physical greeting. Of the Washim programme I remember nothing; I think all of us were very tired. The next morning however, we were very much alive, and I was taken to a small vihara where I was requested to lead the Refuges and Precepts seated in front of a Nepalese-style image. This return of vigour did not last long, however, and the days' pummelling in the jeep reduced me to a state of nervous indifference to my surroundings. My energy, previously in abundance, began to drain away. The venue that night was in a village where some of Manjuvir's relatives lived. I managed to give a short talk, but the evening was chilly, and I went to bed feeling cold and restless. A crowd of curious villagers who had come to sit and look at me had to be sent away, since sleep was imperative.

The jeep relentlessly devoured the miles the following day, and by the time we arrived at our destination – I think it was Badnera - in the late afternoon, I was in no state to do anything but rest. Rather than travel even further, to a Government rest-house, I decided to accept the invitation of an old local friend to stay with him and his family of three daughters, who, although none of them were particularly pretty, were the very picture of politeness, gentleness and helpfulness. I lay thankfully on the bed I had been given, but soon found myself surrounded by a sea of faces gazing down at me. The locals had come to take my *darshan,* even though I was in a weakened state. I am not very keen on this sort of thing, and my first impulse was to tell them all to go away. But I suppressed it, thinking that, as I would not be giving a talk that night, it was after all my duty to try and be of service to them in whatever way was possible in the circumstances. So I sat up, propping myself against the wall with a pillow, and just looked at the visitors and they just looked at me. It was not unpleasant. After they had gone, I went to sleep in a very happy frame of mind and woke next morning feeling a bit better.

We participated in a very relaxed breakfast at which I remained as aloof as possible from the conversation. In this way I was able to watch Sanghasena answering questions from a small but very vociferous audience who had gathered around us on the upper floor of a small house which I thought might crumble under the weight of so many bodies. Sanghasen really excelled himself, I thought, speaking for long minutes on end with a combination of vehemence and humour which was astonishing for its smooth flow, its speed, and its perfect tone of conviction. The questioners were by turns stunned, entranced, inspired and delighted, and all questions finally came to a halt with everyone laughing, smiling, and really happy.

The next day was our last full day before making for Pune and the Ordinations to be conducted by Sangharakshita. We made a detour off the main road into a little village where we dropped off leaflets advertising the Hostel Opening by Bhante at Wardha, as we had done several times already at our previous venues. This time however, we stopped for rather longer in a tiny place of crude wattle-and-daub houses and a motley collection of villagers looking as if they had stepped right out of a film by Ingmar Bergman (though not, as in those rather sombre films of Bergman's, in black-and-white, but in incredible, vivid, luminescent colour). The lined, leathery faces of the old men and women and their smiling, guileless children, often with sores and scratches on their legs and arms, made a deep impression on me. This scene was even more characteristic of India, in a way, than its teeming cities, and if one ignored such a place, one would in effect be turning one's back on the greater part of India's population. There was no question of ignoring the villagers. We were asked to speak to an impromptu gathering. They obviously loved Sanghasena, who was well known to them. I gave a talk on Dr. Ambedkar's metta, and snakes. I am not sure exactly why the snakes came into it, but they did, and nobody seemed to mind.

By this time, my energy was beginning to come back in full measure, and with it a very intense bliss. Everything in the village appeared imbued with a quite extraordinary beauty, as if one was able to see with perfect dispassion the humanity and the brutality of such a place - the architecture without architects, the villagers and their simple village life, so deeply pervaded with basic ignorance, crudity and suffering, yet through it all shining also something else, some deeper, compassionate humanity. How much they needed the Dharma, and how little, it seemed, we could do for them at present.

* * * * *

30   India Tour 1988/89 (Part II)

*I inspect our nearly-finished Boys' Hostel in Wardha, and on a train to
Pune I discover the source of musk. I attend a public Ordination of nine new
Order Members presided over by Bhante, and introduce my old friend
Narayanswami to him. I follow Bhante's train to Aurangabad, then return to
Pune to give a public talk. Returning to Wardha, I meet Bhante near
Gandhi's ashram at Sevagram.*

I CONCLUDED PART ONE of this report with a sketch of a visit to a
village somewhere in Maharashtra - one of the dozens or hundreds that
Sanghasena visits regularly. The visit that I described brought to an end the
series of talks that we had been giving in so many places and to so many
thousands of people in the Vidarbha district, and feeling generally pleased
with the enthusiastic response (actually, I was more than pleased; I felt really
inspired by the faith of our audiences), began to turn my attention towards the
Public Ordinations which were soon to take place at Bhaja. News of Bhante's
arrival in India had somehow reached us, and the fact that we were no longer
separated by an ocean seemed to make his presence almost tangible already.
Soon we were on our way to Wardha - to our newly-established Centre there
under the Chairmanship of Vimalakirti.

We discovered Vimalakirti sitting in his temporary office which he was
renting prior to the completion of the new Hostel which would house seventy
boys from poor families. Vimalakirti was, it seemed, both happy and
unhappy at the same time: happy at the prospect of so many thousands of
people being able to benefit from Bhante's forthcoming visit, and unhappy
about all the difficulties and irritations that had arisen as a result of trying to
get the hostel designed and completed in an astonishingly short period of
time whilst also doing a thousand and one other things as well as being
concerned about his family.

Having once practised as an architect, I could well imagine the
problems that had occurred, and was not in the least surprised to find
Vimalakirti feeling irritable. I listened to his observations about the building,
plumbing my own feelings as we looked it over - a four-square, in fact almost
cubic building, by far the largest in the area, in imitation of the style made
popular by the French architect of Chandigarh, Le Corbusier, or 'Corb', as he
was affectionately known by his admirers. Unlike the Master Architect,
however, who evolved his plans through a functional response to the needs of
the client and the environment in which he was building, I could not help
feeling that in this case the Architect had tried to apply the Corbusier style as

a sort of cosmetic wrap-around, without having developed any empathy for the functions to be housed or the environment to be built in and sheltered from. It was indeed frustrating to think what economies might have been made and what opportunities for skilful design had been neglected. On the other hand, in defence of the Architect, and not forgetting all the others involved in the design, it was all very well to be "wise after the event". As I remarked to another Order Member, Bodhidhamma, some time later (he had also been involved in the design), whilst our ideas and imagination might remain infinitely flexible, at some point in time the poor Architect has to 'freeze' it all and turn the no doubt still-imperfect idea into bricks and mortar. I came to the conclusion that we had got a building which was by no means unprepossessing, and which in course of time we would learn to use efficiently, though a few modifications might be needed.

At noon next day, Vimalakirti, Sanghasena, Manjuvir and I took the train to Pune. We were accompanied to Wardha station by a group of friends, and quite a press of onlookers gathered around us. As we sat down in our train seats, Vimalakirti discovered that his purse had vanished: he had been pickpocketed. Luckily, there had not been a very large sum of money in it, but it seemed particularly ironic that a man so concerned to spend money wisely in the service of others should be the victim of a petty thief. As the train drew out of the station, I found that I had only one thought in my mind – 'Going to meet Bhante!' I began to reflect upon what use I could make, if any, of my meeting with him. Would I be able even to speak with him? Without having come to any conclusion, I took out from my bag a slim Seminar (entitled *Hedonism and Asceticism in the Spiritual Life*), and began to read.

Some time later, a flurry of activity in the corridor of the carriage caught my attention: an unusually healthy and happy-looking tribal woman was standing there with a large bag of something or other tied around her waist, and she was showing its contents to some of the passengers. At first glance, I thought she was offering some kind of fruit - globular and grey-coloured, but was rather puzzled by the excitement that handling the 'fruit' seemed to produce amongst the passengers. The woman offered one of the objects to Sanghasena, who was seated on my right, placed it in his palm, and closed his fingers around it. To my surprise, she then swiftly took hold of my right hand and rubbed the back of it against the back of Sanghasena's hand which was clasping the 'fruit'. Releasing her grip, she invited me to smell the back of my hand which had been in contact with the back of Sanghasena's. I did so, and found emanating from it a perfume of the most delicious, haunting and subtle sweetness. The 'fruit', Vimalakirti explained, was the gland of a Musk Deer, and the perfume, as the woman had so convincingly demonstrated, was not only intensely pleasurable but astonishingly penetrating. The whole of the woods where the Musk Deer roam, apparently, are pervaded by this scent at a certain season. The woman then asked me if I would like to make a purchase, but suddenly feeling revolted, I declined. What greed and cruelty would be necessary to make such a barter possible! The perfume, however, lingered on my hand for many hours, filling my mind with images of sunlit forest glades through which roamed the Musk Deer.

Early next morning we arrived in Pune, and I made my way, as usual, to Madhuban, where I found Purna and Shantiprabha in residence. I was very glad to see them both, and at the prospect of spending a few hours at least with them before we went our separate ways. They were in Pune to help inaugurate the high-powered computer which it had been decided would be needed by the office staff at 'Jeevak' to encourage greater efficiency. 'It will keep them occupied for ages', Purna somewhat enigmatically commented to me later. I had thought the point of a computer was to give you more leisure, but perhaps my ideas about computers are a bit simplistic.

There were other arrivals too. Mr. Narayanswami, my old friend from Tirupati, and his young acolyte Siddhamuni had come all the way from the East coast of India to witness the Ordinations by Bhante, and 'to Go for Refuge, at least to some extent', as I had suggested in one of my letters to Narayanswami. The vigorous old gentleman professed himself delighted to see me, though he was this time, I thought, a little more cautious and mindful than before, of what he chose to say. What he wanted, however, was clear enough. Having suggested to him that he come all this way, and he having done so, it was now nothing less than my duty to escort him personally to the feet of Bhante Sangharakshita where he could offer his *pranams*[80]. I had to point out that I could not guarantee to be able to do what he requested, but I would do my best. And of course, Mr. Narayanswami said, we will be going to Bhaja together tomorrow morning.

Wishing to avoid the huge crowd that would be converging upon Sadhammapradip, as our meditation Centre in the hills near the village of Bhaja was called, we took the early local train to Malavli, the nearest station to Bhaja. Even so we found quite a crowd of people travelling with us bound for the same destination. Amongst them were Dhammachari Nagasena and Dhammacharini Jnānasuri from Aurangabad. But such was their eagerness to get to Dhammadip and such was Mr. Narayanswami's slowness that little communication was possible before they had disappeared in the direction of the Centre by the little path branching off across the paddy fields to the right of the main track. The rice had already been harvested, and now only stubble remained on the brown, cracking earth. It was a beautiful morning; everything was brilliantly clear and still, as if just created out of the voidness. There were utterly delightful little flowers by the wayside, and in the distance the green hills and a sparkling waterfall cascading from the saddle between the precipitous slopes at the head of the valley. I found myself being drawn with increasing velocity towards Dhammadip, inadvertently leaving Mr. Narayanswami, his young friend Siddhamuni, and a third friend, Mr. Nagarale, behind. The truth was that, long before arriving in Pune, what was going on at Dhammadip had been attracting me like a magnet attracts an iron filing, or a candle flame a moth, and since alighting from the train at Malavali, the atmosphere of vibrant and mysterious peacefulness emanating from the base of the distant hill had become almost irresistible.

However, mindful of my duty to my three friends, I dawdled as they were dawdling, perhaps enraptured by the natural beauty all around them. I tried to determine what state they were in. Young Siddhamuni was evidently enjoying the marvellous freshness of the scenery that early September morning. Narayanswami however looked as if he was going to his execution, whilst Nagarale seemed chiefly concerned with the fact that my robe was getting mud-bespattered, so much so that when we reached a clear little stream, he insisted on washing the mud off both my legs and lower robe. As we progressed, the marvellous peace and silence that seemed to pervade everywhere grew deeper and deeper, and after the longest walk I seemed ever to have taken to Dhammadip, we arrived at the entrance, and the first thing I noticed was how much the trees and plants had come up since I was last there - evidence of the watering by so many devoted hands.

We soon saw a number of familiar faces, amongst them Dhammachari Chandrabodhi, who suggested that I 'go up' (to where, he didn't say), and have breakfast, and Lokamitra, who gesticulated from a distance and said something like 'I'll see you up there' (wherever that was). Thus it was that I began searching for breakfast, feeling slightly foolish since I did not know quite where to go except 'up'. So up I and my three friends went to the upper assembly hall, where there was no evidence of anything edible, but where, after a while, someone did appear with some food. Perhaps the first visitors had not been expected quite so early. Not that I was particularly disturbed by all this - I was more concerned, in fact, by the state of my body, which seemed curiously 'loose' - as if the agency that usually directed its movement had temporarily gone on strike. Whilst I was pondering the significance of this, Lokamitra strode up to me and said 'Bhante will see you now.' Since I had been informed in a letter of Lokamitra's that I was not to ask for an interview with Bhante at Bhaja, since there would be so many people with a prior claim wanting to see him, this came as a surprise, though certainly not an unwelcome one. As I rose to comply with the suggestion, I realized that I had no idea what I wanted to see Bhante for, nor had I made up my mind to ask him anything or tell him anything either. Never had I been so marvellously unprepared for so rare and valuable an opportunity, though an opportunity for what, I could not say either.

At this point, I feel tempted to draw a veil over what happened, though in fact nothing in particular happened. It is simply that words do not seem adequate to express my feelings, and even if I could, I would rather do it in verse. However, setting my compunctions on one side, I was very happy indeed to see Bhante, and found, as perhaps every Order Member has at some time or other, that I had very little I was able to say though there was a great deal that might have been said. I did not in fact say much about myself at all, except by way of reply to Bhante's gentle questioning about how I was feeling. I told him that I was feeling 'a bit febrile' (after all the travelling, I meant), and I then spent some minutes talking about the mitras in Sri Lanka. I lamented the fact that one had given way to parental blackmail, whilst another had fallen prey to his boss. After this, I 'dried up', a very unusual experience, for me, nowadays, and spent a few moments feeling a bit furtive and suppressing what seemed to be irrelevant ideas which kept popping up. I then asked Bhante how he was feeling, and he replied, with a slight smile: 'As well as might be expected,' and after a further short hiatus, said that he was now expected to take his bath, and proceeded to step down from the bed on which he had been sitting. Taking this as a cue for the end of the interview, I began to leave, but Bhante, perhaps sensing my slight disappointment, said in a kindly voice: 'We'll meet at Wardha, won't we?' at which prospect I suddenly felt unaccountably happy, and left.

Soon, people could be seen coming towards us across the paddy fields by the score, and I felt for an instant like getting as far away as possible, up into the hills. However, Jinasena, my good Sri Lankan friend, arrived just at that moment, and greeting me warmly, asked me what I wanted to do, so I had to be realistic. I decided that I would take a bath in the cool stream a little way up the valley, and Jinasena showed me to a suitable spot and left me there. After the bath, which was greatly refreshing, I felt very much better. On my way back I discovered Jinasena, who had been waiting patiently for me nearby, and he suggested that we go over to the retreat community building where I could meet the nine Order-members-to-be. Feeling a bit reluctant, but trying to overcome my unseemly reticence (after all, why should they not be pleased to see me?), I accepted the suggestion and walked the few hundred yards along the side of the paddy field and up to the community building on the hillside - the smallest and highest of the four buildings constituting the Retreat Centre at present.

Seated inside, each in a beautifully tailored, light blue shirt, were the nine new postulants, all silent and radiant, and I sat down in front of them. Someone, I think it was Chandrasil, encouraged me to say something, and I responded by saying how good they all looked, and how glad I was to see them. Then I told them a bit about Sri Lanka, and how important it was that they were Going for Refuge, especially since the central importance of the Going for Refuge was often not understood by the bhikkhus. It was vitally important, I said, that a true Sangha existed, for our own sake and for the sake of the world, and I felt very happy that they, having Gone for Refuge individually, would now, soon, be publically accepted as members of Trailokya Bauddha Mahasangha. Remarking that I was looking forward to hearing their names, and that it felt a bit strange speaking to them without knowing who they were, I took my leave and returned to the lower buildings, alongside a paddy-field, passing Bhante on the way going in the opposite direction, perhaps to say his own few words of encouragement or advice, or perhaps just to be reassuringly with them and saying nothing.

Reaching the Ordination pandal, a gaily-coloured tent erected over the shrine which was the centre piece of the event, and which was surmounted by a three foot high Buddha-image presented to the movement by some Thai bhikkhus, I was invited to join the other Dhammacharis and Dhammacharinis seated there like a lake of blue, and flanked by a small group of saffron-clad bhikkhus who had come to watch. My New Zealand friend Dhammachari Purna was in some anxiety concerning the recording equipment, and wanted me to use my own portable recorder to catch the proceedings on tape. For this I would have to be seated near Bhante, so in return, as it were, for agreeing to perform this very slight duty, I had the benefit of an excellent vantage point. From here I could see everyone's faces easily, and as I looked at the bhikkhus in their orange-brown robes and shaven heads - most of them quite young - they seemed to me to be much coarser in appearance than our blue-clad Dhammacharis. This had been my experience throughout my travels - that the refined bhikkhu is the exception rather than the rule. In fact, when I first arrived in Sri Lanka, I was quite shocked by the appearance of the members of the bhikkhu Sangha, many of them appearing to me like gnomes out of a fairy tale. Some of them looked like goblins and demons. They were, many of them, gross and corpulent, with heavy, fleshy features. Sometimes however they were very thin and wiry, perhaps with practice of austerities. There did not seem to be much of a middle way, if appearances were anything to go by. I had subsequently discovered, of course, that it is normal for many of the bhikkhus to eat very large quantities of the rich food presented to them by the laypeople, and usually including, often at the bhikkhus' explicit request, meat and fish. And since they do not take any exercise to speak of, the fate of most of them is corpulence.

The Dhammacharis-to-be seemed, in comparison even with the young bhikkhus now present, not only more physically refined, but more mentally alert. In fact, each of them seemed to be glowing and radiating in a way which must be familiar to every Order Member who has witnessed a Public Ordination ceremony. It was certainly a joy to behold. As I was reflecting on all this, there were cries of acclamation from the assembly, which now numbered perhaps five hundred people, ranged not only in rows under the tent but on the banks nearby in the already brilliant sunshine. Bhante appeared from the direction of the nearby building accompanied by Lokamitra. He looked very happy and very much at ease as he took his seat, and gradually the large audience grew quiet. A few people continued to walk around however, and Bhante remarked that it would be a real miracle if everyone sat down. But not everyone, it seemed, wanted a miracle. One could almost sense Mara fighting with Indra's net - the net that was descending, gently but inexorably, as golden threads of sensitivity and awareness extended themselves between people, in spite of the ongoing slight disturbances.

One by one the offerings were made, the Refuges and Ten Ordination Vows chanted, and the names announced: Smrtiraja, Abhayaraja and Vimuktiraja, Ratnasagara, Bodhisagara and Prasannabodhi, Vivekaratna, Vivekapriya and Vivekaprabha. I recognized them clearly now they were in front of me, and tried to commit their faces and names to memory - in some cases it was easy - for the Order metta bhavana. After the concluding threefold 'Sadhu!' which resounded from all quarters, and echoed strangely from the surrounding hills, the assembly began to disperse, and the BBC camera crew, who had been working away behind my seat during the proceedings, now dismantled their equipment. During the filming, I had been conscious of a larger audience, unseen, numbering perhaps tens of thousands or even millions, adding their presence, adding another dimension to the proceedings.

Now Mr. Narayanswami very much wanted to meet Bhante, and so, taking him by the hand, and closely followed by Mr. Nagarale from Visakhapatnam, we approached Bhante's door. Dharmachari Padmavajra emerged, and I asked if Bhante was willing to meet Mr. Narayanswami and Mr. Nagarale. Quickly turning around, Padmavajra disappeared and reappeared a few moments later to inform us that, Yes, Bhante was willing.

Narayanswami was at last ushered in, to his very great delight and excitement, and fervently grasping Bhante's feet, looked up at him with an expression of adoration. Mr. Nagarale was then invited in and performed a similar ritual. In the meantime, Lokamitra had also appeared, and perhaps feeling that Bhante would appreciate some privacy, ushered us all out, whispering into my ear that I should see that food was obtained for my friends. Mr. Narayanswami professed himself well satisfied with the meeting as I led him off and eventually found him and his young friend Siddhamuni places to eat. Having taken my leave of them, I breathed a little sigh of relief at having at last steered my old friend in the right direction. In parting from them I had received from Siddhamuni, though not from Narayanswami himself, an invitation to visit their hometown. I then went off to fend for myself. I found an unoccupied cushion in the building housing the community, where Jinasena had prepared a very palatable meal indeed.

That afternoon after the hundreds of visitors had gone, a Cultural Event was held in the upper assembly hall, with the usual stars in the ascendant. Dharmachari Dharmarakshita, who had translated many of Bhante's talks as a young man, was master of ceremonies. But before the billed performances, Bhante gave one of his own. He made a strong appeal for more friendship amongst Order Members, and more Kalyana mitrata with mitras. He opened up a vista of five hundred Dhammacharis within the next few years - all from India, and reminded us that he would like to see a Dhammachari in every village in India. He then took his seat, to a round of loud applause, and the stars did their thing, ranging from a heart-rending song from Bodhidhamma (well, almost heart rending, but saved in the nick of time by a mischievous little twist accompanied by laughter just before the end), to a pastiche in Charlie Chaplin style by Varaprabha, to a delightfully wistful melody on the flute by the heartening Chandrabodhi. There were some brilliant take-offs of country bumpkins by Siddhartha and others, enough to make everybody laugh until the tears came, and soon it was all over. Lokamitra remarked, in response to my words of appreciation, that he had not enjoyed it all that much, having seen it many times before, and that he had rather been hoping to see more drama. I remained impressed by the vigour and spontaneity of the performances.

Next day I followed some distance behind the main party making for Aurangabad, where at another of our Centres, associated with a Hostel started by Dharmachari Anagarika Jyotipala, our friends were preparing a big reception for Bhante. This was to be in the vicinity of the Hostel, only a stone's throw from Milind College, one of Dr. Ambedkar's educational brainchildren. Not long after my arrival at the hostel, whilst taking a rest in Jyotipala's spartan room, the Anagarika Jyotipala himself arrived and we did a bit of 'catching up' on the news. As usual I was delighted and happy to be in his company, and wanted to share my appreciation of a poem by Tennyson[173] with him. So he humoured me and listened attentively while I read *The Sicilian's Tale*, in which King Robert is deprived of his Kingship by an angel:

Nay, not the King, but the King's Jester thou
Henceforth shalt wear the bells and scalloped cape,

And for thy counsellor shalt lead an ape;
Thou shalt obey my servants when they call,
And wait upon my henchmen in the hall."

The Angel later restores the Kingship, having driven his message home:

And when they were alone, the Angel said:
"Art thou the King?"
Then, bowing down his head
King Robert crossed both hands upon his breast,
And meekly answered him: Thou know'st best!
My sins as scarlet are; let me go hence,
And in some cloister'd school of penitence,
Across those stones, that pave the way to heaven,
Walk barefoot till my guilty soul be shriven!

The Angel smiled, and from his radiant face
A holy light illumined all the place.
And through the open window, loud and clear,
They heard the monks chant in the chapel near,
Above the stir and tumult of the street:
'He has put down the mighty from their seat,
And has exalted them of low degree!'
And through the chant a second melody
Rose, like the throbbing of a single string:
'I am an Angel, and thou art the King!'

King Robert, who was standing near the throne,
Lifted his eyes, and lo! he was alone!
But all apparelled as in days of old,
With ermined mantle and with cloth of gold;
And when his courtiers came, they found him there
Kneeling upon the floor, absorbed in silent prayer.

Jyotipala smiled too, and commented 'That's what happens when you're deprived of your true identity.'

Preparations for Bhante's arrival were by this time well on the way to completion. I was alarmed by the incredibly loud racket being made by an electricity generator which was parked hardly more than twenty yards away from the pandal, and wondered whether Bhante would be able to make himself heard, but it was too late to do anything about it. The crowd was getting bigger and bigger; I guessed there were several thousand people. Purna came and sat near me and once more requested that I tape the proceedings; but this time it would not be possible to sit on the pandal. I would just have to go up to Bhante's feet as inconspicuously as possible, which would be very difficult, in light of the fact that I was one of the few people in the audience wearing robes, and operate the machine. There seemed to be some sort of delay, but eventually Bhante arrived looking somehow even more impressive than at the Ordinations - really regal, and took his seat. Garlands were offered and introductory speeches made by Dhammacharini Jnānasuri, who sounded a bit nervous, followed by Dharmachari Nagasena, who despite his small stature was a very confident speaker. These were the two seniormost Order Members in Aurangabad. Then at last Bhante rose to speak. By some miracle (I really could not understand how, because it was still running), the electricity generator's sound receded into the background and Bhante's voice spread a softening and calming spell over everyone and everything. His talk lasted just fifty-five minutes, including Vimalakirti's translation, but he managed to pack a great deal in. He concluded with an account of the Seven Bojjangas as the Teaching possibly most characteristic of the developmental model - which gave me encouragement to finish my own account of them at the earliest opportunity. Everyone was delighted with Bhante's talk, and all too soon he was being escorted away and surrounded by crowd of admirers and out of sight, though not out of mind and heart.

Next day it was back to Pune for me and a visit to the Aurangabad Caves for Bhante, where his visit was to be recorded on film. On the 20th October I was billed to give the Ashok Vijaya Dasami talk at Ambedkar Gardens, Pune, so that was where I went. I was an hour early getting in to town, so asked the rickshaw driver to take me to Manney's, the biggest bookshop in the city. I browsed quickly through the Reference section and through the Buddhist section, noticing a few Windhorse Publications books, but decided not to purchase anything there for Sri Lanka (books are so heavy!), and set off for Ambedkar Gardens where an audience of about three hundred and fifty people were very nearly settled for my talk. It was very much a family gathering, and I was pleased to see that quite a few of those present were known to me at least by sight. I gave the sort of eulogy of Dr. Ambedkar with which more or less everyone must have been familiar. It becomes more and more difficult to say anything about the Great Leader that is not known and appreciated already. But perhaps that is not the point, and it is the fact that a Western Buddhist, and one wearing robes, who was speaking to them, that gave the occasion extra significance for them. In addition to the eulogy, I laid stress on the importance of continuing to Go for Refuge more and more often and more and more sincerely, and the audience applauded warmly. I was presented with several garlands afterwards.

Then there was a hiatus of a couple of hours before the train for my next journey had arrived at Pune Station. Lokamitra's secretary Raju met me in the waiting room for a bit of last-minute communication. We had arranged to have supper together, but Raju's uncle had just died and so our meeting had had to be curtailed so that he could attend to the funeral arrangements. I was therefore alone for most of my long sojourn at the station. Finding myself alone on Pune station for a couple of hours, I decided to look for someone to talk to. A young man lounging horizontally on a bench on the opposite wall smiled back very openly to me, but then I thought, no, I don't really want to speak to anyone. But it was too late; the youngster bounced over, got into conversation, and started to tell me that he was a Hare Krishna devotee and had spent some time in prison etc. I said a few words about the advantages of staying free, and began to realize that I was more hungry than lonely. The Hare Krishna devotee did not want to eat, so I left the station for a solitary meal at the nearby Wonderland Hotel restaurant, where one can eat any quantity of well-prepared food one wants for a fixed sum. This is always an attractive proposition even if one is not ravenous. After an excellent meal and charming service I returned to the Waiting Room and found the Hare Krishna devotee had departed, rather to my relief. I dozed next to some German heavyweight backpackers with bulging leg muscles and hairy faces until it was time to descend to the platform and await the train. The only other person in the waiting room who had caught my attention was an unusually precocious girl of twelve or thirteen, who was, it appeared, discovering the joys and dangers of non-verbal communication. I thought of Nabokov and his definition of genius, and descended the stairs. By eleven p.m. I was on the train thundering through the darkness.

My arrival next afternoon at TBMSG's temporary Wardha office coincided with that of several other Dhammacharis, mitras and sahayakas, but not feeling very communicative, I made myself comfortable in a corner of the office and awaited developments. It was not long before Vimalakirti, who had been sitting at his desk apparently unconcernedly, suggested that several of us depart for Sevagram, where Bhante and Lokamitra were staying. I had no objection to that, but there was a further wait while everyone got themselves and their luggage together. I stood on the balcony of our temporary headquarters and looked at our new hostel a couple of hundred yards away. I watched a golden sun go down over the horizon, and noticed that our building now sported a coat of paint to make the legend 'Finished' slightly less incredible. A little girl on the ground down below was, with a small boy's co-operation, taking a peek inside his trousers. Then the Jeep arrived, and taking our luggage, the VIPs left for Sevagram.

As we approached the Sevagram Ashram and Hotel, the familiar, yet always delightful and slightly surprizing 'aura' of Bhante greeted us, and I began to turn my mind to the promised meeting. I felt that there were quite a few things concerning which I would like to unburden myself, and wondered where to start. I also wondered whether in fact such 'unburdening' would be the best use I could make of this rare opportunity. I began to feel slightly nervous.

NOTES

80   *pranam*: gesture of salutation, sometimes with the whole body. It can be anything from touching the feet of the person one reveres to performing a *panchanga pranam* - a prostration on the floor in which five parts of the body - forehead, hands and knees - touch the ground. The Tibetan Buddhists often perform a full-length prostration to objects or persons they revere most highly. In the Western Buddhist Order, the practice of visualizing and prostrating to whatever extent one is able, towards the Refuge Tree, the 'Tree' depicting the Movement's principal figures of spiritual veneration arranged around the central figure of the Buddha Shakyamuni, the first human historical Buddha, is encouraged.

* * * * *

31   India Tour 1988/89 (Part III)

I catch up with Bhante and listen to his talk to fifteen thousand people at Wardha. Escorted to Nagpur by two young men, I catch the train to Vishakhapatnam where I give talks to groups of desperately poor Buddhists. Travelling back west and south to Gulbarga, I lead a retreat there and encounter "the professor." I give a talk at the University of Gulbarga, and in a poor area of the City. I move on and lead a retreat in the city of Kolhapur. Having concluded the round of duties suggested by Lokamitra, I go to Sarnath, take a look at Varanasi, then set off on pilgrimage.

I NEED NOT HAVE WORRIED about my interview - rather an inappropriate word for a friendly meeting - with Bhante. It simply did not happen, as I feared it would not the moment I read Lokamitra's suggestion that Bhante and I meet at Wardha. Not that I have any inherent mistrust of Lokamitra's plans - they generally work out extremely well - but this one, for some reason or other, I mistrusted from the start. What happened to thwart it were two apparently unrelated events: first, on arrival at the Sevagram Hostel, I was told (by Bodhidhamma, I think), that Bhante had been suffering from a cold, or the 'flu, I forget which, and was still a bit indisposed. Whether he was indisposed to talk to me, I was not able to ascertain, but I decided unilaterally that I would not impose upon him, since the most important thing was that he should be well for his big talk the next day. So when, a few minutes after my arrival, a local farmer turned up asking me to give a talk at a nearby vihara, my sense of duty prevailed, and, Dharmachari Maitreyanatha having agreed to translate, we went off on the heels of the farmer, out of the hostel gates and down the road to the right.

The little group that gathered, after some time, in the small Vihara we had entered were rather passive, even unresponsive. Mostly men, probably local farmers, they looked rather dully at me, seeming not to know what to think or do, and not seeming to be completely happy to just look either. Perhaps they were hoping for Bhante, and they had got me. Perhaps they were stoned. When it seemed that the little group was not going to grow any larger, I started speaking. I told them the story of the Four Sights[81] and suggested that all Buddhists, all followers of Dr. Ambedkar, should try to realize the significance of the Four Sights in their own lives, and act accordingly. Which meant, I said, Going for Refuge as often and as sincerely as they could. Then followed my usual explanation of what it meant to Go for Refuge. Everyone maintained a rather stunned expression whilst I was speaking, and appeared not unpleased when my talk came to an end - whether because they were in a better state of mind than when they had first arrived, or for some other reason I never discovered - an unusual state of affairs in India, where people usually quite readily give evidence of their feelings of appreciation. Perhaps I had given a really bad talk! Next day, however, there did appear some proof of their appreciation. By the time Maitreyanatha and I got back to the Hostel late that night, it was bedtime. There was no question of having a talk with Bhante.

Next morning, after meditating, I sauntered out of the chalet which I was sharing with Padmavajra, amongst others, and started to become fascinated by the rose-garden which was by now splendid in the early-morning sunlight. I was thus absorbed when I noticed that Bhante was walking to and fro in front of his chalet. Lokamitra suddenly appeared, and with a "Hello Bhante, how are you feeling?" received a somewhat reassuring response. Encouraged by this I went over to Bhante myself, thinking perhaps I might have my talk with him after all, but he was not in conversational mood, and in fact, seemed rather deeply absorbed in his own thoughts. Feeling that I should not intrude further than I already had, I withdrew and returned to the rose garden. The roses had an elevating effect on my mind, especially a nearly full-blown one, white and tinged with pink, still sparkling with dew and emanating an exquisite fragrance.

After breakfast I went for a walk with Raju into the village lying half a mile or so down the road to the left as one walked out of the Hostel entrance. There was nothing very much to see: just a line of boutiques with rather shifty-looking youths in Western dress lounging around and small number of farmers in *dhoti* and *pugree.* As it was already getting rather warm, we bought cold drinks, or rather, semi-cold drinks, and having made the best of that, we sauntered back to the hostel where the farmer who had requested me to give a talk the previous day was waiting for me with the largest pile of bananas with which I had ever been presented. Accepting them with good grace, I wondered for an instant what I would do with them, but there was no lack of hungry mouths to feed. It was good to have some feedback on my previous night's performance.

Soon it was time for lunch. Though someone said Bhante would be taking lunch with us, he did not, unfortunately, appear. I took the opportunity to acquaint myself with the camera crew, headed by the film director who was called Bob, and who was visiting India for the specific purpose of making a film about Bhante. I was surprised to find how little the film crew knew about Buddhism, about Dr. Ambedkar and his followers, or about meditation. In fact they were less well-informed, it appeared, than I was at the age of fifteen. I therefore sowed a few seeds in as simple and straightforward a way as possible, and the crew appeared to want to spend more time talking with me. After lunch however, we all had various things to attend to, and our talk came to an end. There was not even time for a post-prandial snooze before the Jeep arrived to take some of us back into Wardha for the Hostel Opening ceremony, Bodhi-tree planting, and the Big Talk, so gathering our luggage we said farewell to Sevagram, its sleepy village, and the elegant simplicity but strangely gloomy inactivity of the deserted ashram of Mahatma Gandhi. At the TBMSG Wardha temporary Centre, there appeared to be nothing going on either, and feeling very tired, I decided to lie down and quickly fell asleep. Everyone was out on some business or other in connection with the big assembly that was gathering in a nearby field, so it seemed best to rest while I could.

I awoke feeling slightly uneasy, glanced at my clock and saw that it was time for the opening ceremony already! Getting up quickly, I walked as fast as I decently could, through a huge crowd numbering by now perhaps ten thousand, towards the entrance to the new TBMSG Wardha Hostel. Everywhere I looked there were people, but there in the distance I could see the Jeep arriving with Bhante and Lokamitra. But by the time I arrived, having traversed the remaining hundred yards pressed closely by people on all sides, it was too late to do anything: the red tape had been cut through and the Bodhi Tree planted. Bhante rose from a bending position, turned to me with smile and said "Got it?" presumably referring to a shot of the proceedings, since I had a camera slung around my neck. I felt crestfallen, but said "Yes", rather feebly, not wishing to disappoint: there were lots of other cameras around, what did it matter? I realized that I had done just what I criticised the Indians for doing: telling you what they thought you wanted to hear, rather than the truth. A moment later, Bhante was walking past me with Lokamitra, and Vimalakirti and a few others were hot on their heels trying to keep up. I brought up the rear of the little procession, and someone thrust a bright gold, red and blue rosette into my hands, as if granting me official status. Then we were walking through a long avenue of pleasingly sari-clad ladies waving lights and incense and showering us with confetti, just like a wedding, as we approached the pandal - a large, brightly-decorated stage on which had been set up a shrine complete with an image of the Buddha, a picture of Dr. Ambedkar, and many candles and flowers. It had been beautifully done. Bhante mounted the pandal together with Vimalakirti and Lokamitra, and I joined the little group of tape-recorder minders down below. This was my fate several times on this tour. It was as if someone was trying to tell me: "you haven't listened carefully enough before, so you had better listen while you still have a chance." However that may have been, in order to see Bhante and the proceedings from this position, I found that I had to crane my neck upwards at an angle of about thirty degrees.

And as I looked up, there was Bhante, and above him in a beautiful translucent blue sky was a flight of wild geese winging their way across the small fluffy pink clouds. It was quite a magical scene. The assembly appeared to be enormous. Seated figures stretched almost as far as far as the eye could see. It seemed that everyone was beautifully dressed, in freshly laundered clothes, and sitting for the most part peacefully and attentively. Counting a small section of the gathering and doing a quick calculation, I guessed there were at least fourteen or fifteen thousand people present. And near the front was a small group of young men in karate gear.

Bhante having made his salutation to the Shrine and taken his seat, which was one of several red-and-silver throne-like chairs of the type usually used for Indian weddings, he was ready to be garlanded. The first dozen or so devotees mounted the pandal and gracefully and reverently placed around Bhante's shoulders some large, brilliantly coloured garlands of flowers, and he seemed to enjoy receiving them; but as garland succeeded garland and the numbers coming to make their offering grew to hundreds and the discarded heap of garlands rose from the floor to Bhante's waist, they became progressively smaller and thinner, and were occasionally almost thrown at Bhante. Although he managed to maintain his decorum, I suspected that it must have been more and more difficult to really enjoy the activity, and that he was doing his duty because it meant so much to everyone. Fortunately, not long after this point had been reached, the offerings came to an end and the pandal was cleared of devotees.

Lokamitra rose and began to speak: his talk was translated in a very clear voice by Vimalakirti. The few wisps of cloud in the pale blue sky turned from pink to purple. Lokamitra's very long blue Dhammachari shirt or caftan looked much more like a sort of Mahāyāna robe, surmounted by his white kesa. I was reminded, for some reason or other, of a picture I had seen of Kuan Yin. He spoke of the enthusiasm for and the success of Dharma work in the Vidarbha area, and of the difficulties which had been experienced too. Bhante was to augment this point later on. And while Lokamitra was speaking, Mr. Barnham, the representative of the British High Commissioner in Bombay, arrived and climbed the steps of the pandal, to take his seat near Bhante. Bhante exchanged a few words with him across the empty throne-like seat between them and they appeared like two old friends exchanging pleasantries. Bhante seemed to be elucidating for Mr. Barnham's benefit some of the points that Lokamitra was making, and the High Commissioner gradually relaxed and even appeared to be enjoying the scene. Perhaps he had not been an honoured guest at such a gathering before. Lokamitra's talk drew to an end, and received a warm ovation. Now it was Mr. Barnham's turn to speak.

He had not come unprepared, and with Vimalakirti again translating with not a moment's hesitation, which must have been reassuring, he delivered a short speech, betraying only faint nervousness. He expressed his thanks for the invitation, and presented the High Commissioner's regrets at not being able to be present due to the shortness of the notice he had been given and his having to attend a prior engagement. He went on to say how glad he was "on behalf of the British Government, to have made a financial contribution towards this worthy project", and expressed his confidence that "the money was well-spent, by responsible people, and in a good cause." He too received a warm round of applause, and appearing mollified, sat down. For my part, I was interested to learn that Her Majesty's Government had found itself able to open its purse, and wondered whether there was now a 'Buddhist watch-dog' in Whitehall's corridors of power.

Now it was Bhante's turn to speak. His opening remarks, as usual, expressed his pleasure at being present on the occasion. He went on to say why a Hostel of the kind he had just opened was needed - that it was absolutely necessary because one needs places where students can work in a peaceful atmosphere, places where they can experience a certain amount of discipline and places where they can develop a sense of social responsibility. No one who has had any contact with the youth of today, especially in India, could have any doubt concerning the appropriateness of Bhante's words.

The main matter of Bhante's talk was a brilliant resume of his recently-completed *Ambedkar and Buddhism*. In little more than fifteen minutes (of his own words, excluding those of the translator), he took the audience on a swift guided tour of his already terse and highly concentrated presentation of the life and significance of the great Buddhist leader. I was deeply impressed that what might have appeared very well as a review in the pages of the Times Literary Supplement could be such an effective address to fourteen or fifteen thousand poor Indians. Though they were poor - many desperately so by Western standards - they were certainly not lacking in intelligence, and indeed, their quick responses to many of Bhante's points showed that they were more in touch with the essentials than many a Western audience would have been on the same subject-matter. Of course, Bhante was speaking on a matter very close to their hearts, so perhaps a comparison of this sort is invidious.

Bhante's closing remarks included a report that many people had been asking him to visit the Deeksha Bhumi - the site of the great Mass Conversion ceremony[82] in Nagpur. He said that he would be very glad to visit the Deeksha Bhumi - the Deeksha Bhumi was holy ground - but he was not prepared to go until all the Buddhists connected with it were working in harmony together. At this there was loud applause from the audience. They had received both a promise and a warning, and Bhante had, with a masterly stroke, turned the 'state of play' on the Deeksha Bhumi to the best advantage for everyone.

Bhante's talk lasted a minute or two under an hour, including translation, but he had managed to pack an enormous amount into it, without seeming in the slightest hurried. The vast crowd (though by Indian standards, this was not really a very big audience at all) began to disperse peacefully, and many of them began to make their way up to the pandal to 'take their leave' of Bhante - an almost compulsory gesture in the case of devout Buddhists. I would have liked to have done so too, since Bhante would shortly be leaving for the U.K., and I had no idea when I would be seeing him again, but time was getting on and I had to catch a train from Nagpur (still an hour or more away by bus) to Vaishakapatanam on the East coast in order to deliver my own short series of talks there. As luck would have it, I very soon discovered two young men who were going in my direction, and who kindly carried my luggage and relieved me of all further worry about how to get to Nagpur, and whether I could catch my train to the East coast. On the bus into the city I noticed a young man carrying a copy of *Ambedkar and Buddhism* prominently displayed for all to see, and overheard several remarks concerning the propriety of having Mr R. S. Gavai on the pandal. Mr R. S. Gavai is a politician prominent in the affairs of the Deeksha Bhumi who had at the last moment managed to ascend the pandal and occupy one of the few seats for honoured guests. Bhante, in his concluding remarks had made it abundantly clear for all with ears to hear, what his feelings were on the matter. What was not clear was whether Gavai was on the pandal at the behest of TBMSSG in any sense at all. I suspected that he had barged his way in, and that questions of this sort were rather academic. Nevertheless, they were being asked, and it was clear that many young people on the bus strongly disapproved. For them religion was one thing and politics another, quite separate thing. And who would dare gainsay them! At present, in India, Buddhism and *sila* are practically synonymous, and woe betide anyone who, wishing to participate in spiritual matters, blots his copy-book by unethical behaviour! However, the distinction between natural and merely conventional morality is often not clearly understood, so I have found it necessary to proceed with caution in speaking about such matters. However, I feel that the basic yearning of young Indian Buddhists for a sound ethical basis in the lives of their leaders and in their own lives is a very healthy one indeed.

By 3:00am next morning I was on my way to Vaishakapatanam, a big industrial city on the shores of the Bay of Bengal. I had visited it some years ago, before going to Sri Lanka. This time I had arranged to spend three days there, and gave three talks, the last of which, for some reason or other, went across particularly well. The reason, quite simply, was that I felt inspired to give of my best by the audience - mostly of desperately poor people who had been displaced some few years ago by the Burmese Government in a chauvinistic gesture of nationalist sentiment, and sent back to a barren hillside in Vaishakapatanam after having been settled for two generations in 'Buddhist' Burma, or Brahmadesh. Their faith in Buddhism must have been sorely tried, but here they were, looking for a raft to take them to the yonder shore. I aspired in my talk to give them bread rather than stones for their journey.

Mr. Nagarale, whom I mentioned earlier as having 'taken Bhante's darshan' at Bhaja after Mr. Narayanswami, is our chief contact in Visag (as it is known by the locals) and is beginning to lead meditation and Dhamma discussion classes, though he is not even a mitra. I hope the Indian Dhammacharis manage to take a closer interest in Visag and Mr. Nagarale, though it is a long way away from Maharashtra to provide Kalyana mitrata. Mr. Nagarale took care of my every need with great solicitude, even to the extent of offering me pocket-money, poor though he was. Of course I refused. I did however accept his insistent offer of a sleeveless blue shirt, since the weather was particularly hot, and wearing my long-sleeved shirt under my robes was becoming a bit of a torment.

From Visag I took a train to Gulbarga, a biggish town in Karnataka State, where I was to lead a *shibir* (meditation retreat). At the station, a large crowd greeted me shouting Buddhist slogans vociferously and surprizing the other occupants of the carriage. My travelling companions had, I think, previously come to the conclusion that the orange-clad Western swami sitting by himself was a somewhat doormouse-like holy man as obscure and useless as any other holy man one might see on a train. But whatever they were thinking, I for one was very happy to see such a turnout of friendly Buddhists, which augured well for TBMSG activities in the State of Karnataka

I was taken from the station by motor rickshaw to the retreat place, which was a spacious, single storey building enclosing a pleasant courtyard in a quiet area of the suburbs. The sleuth-like Dharmachari Dharmarakshita, my translator, arrived soon after me, having found his way by means of his miraculous 'nose' alluded to in Nagabodhi's book *Jai Bhim*. The way he is able to accomplish conjunctions on the slenderest of evidence is nothing short of miraculous. This time, apparently, Dharmarakshita had arrived at Gulbarga Railway Station, and enquired after the only person whose name he knew - a ticket inspector who happened not to be there. Whilst others might have given up hope at this point, however, Dharmarakshita just nosed around the station and eventually met a man who had heard someone saying that there was a sort of Buddhist meeting taking place in such-and-such an area of the city. And that, it turned out, was enough for him to find us. Not long after, Dhammachari Bodhisagara, who had been recently ordained in Pune, turned up too, though with the help of the exact address, and by this time quite a few local Buddhists had also arrived, eager to 'take my darshan', if not to converse with me.

The chief organizer at Gulbarga was a Mr. Mogha. The rather unfortunate name means something like ignoramus, and had presumably been given to one of his forebears by a census officer with a malicious sense of humour. Mr. Mogha was an exceedingly stout man with pouting lips and extra strong glasses who, despite his physical disadvantages, managed to convey an impression of firm, yet friendly and relaxed efficiency. He seemed in fact to be a natural leader, and I soon discovered that nothing could be accomplished amongst the Gulbarga Buddhists without him initiating it. He seemed to be not only the leader, but the virtual king of the Buddhists in the area, if Buddhists can have a king. Perhaps it would be more apt to describe him as a sort of Chief Minister, because, in spite of his apparently undisputed power, he always deferred to me, and was clearly not lacking in the quality of receptivity.

The retreat organised by Mr. Mogha went very well; there were twenty-three or twenty-four participants. The only thing to complain of was the food, which was almost inedible. Luckily, I was always left to eat alone, in a room overlooking an area in which there were several small pigs. They found palatable what I had found nauseating. I kept my energy up by eating the large quantity of apples and oranges offered to me each day.

I had not been in my room long after my arrival when a very boyish-looking, smooth-faced, smartly dressed man was introduced to me as 'the Professor'. Concerning the Professor, Mr. Mogha discreetly let it be known that he was very keen for me to 'effect a conversion'. But such a thing proved in the end to be impossible. The 'professor', I discovered, ran a number of schools for English tuition, and had been brought along to the *shibir* by Mr. Mogha on the pretext that he was needed to translate my talks into Kannad (the lingua franca of Karnataka State). The young, plump professor could hardly wait to help, and so I set him to work immediately, or tried to do so, on the translation of the Dedication Ceremony[83]. But although the smooth-faced young man could converse with me in perfect English, or at least, could carry on a perfectly correct monologue, when it came to translation it became clear that he could concentrate on no more than a few syllables at a time. His span of attention did not in fact extend to a single phrase, which made things very difficult. Time and time again I tried to bring his attention back to the meaning, and time and time again he would go dashing off on some long and pompous-sounding turn of phrase which I strongly suspected bore only the slightest resemblance to the simple English of Bhante's dedication ceremony. After a while, rather than accept the uncomfortable truth that he could not deliver the goods, the Professor began to cast doubt on whether I knew what I was talking about; after all, wasn't he the one who knew Kannad?   But strange to say, although I knew not a single word of Kannad, I was perfectly certain that the words he was using in translation were not what Bhante was saying, either literally or metaphorically. To prove my point, I asked him to translate back into English what he had previously given as the Kannad for a particular sentence. My intuition was correct. His re-translation bore no resemblance to the original English. I began to realize that I was dealing with a small, fat, exceedingly spoiled boy who had learned a few English phrases but never learned to discipline his mind, and who would only co-operate if rewarded with a sweet at frequent intervals. Proceeding therefore in this fashion, the 'sweet' being a very direct smile or word of praise at every seeming success, I was able to get the first half of the Dedication ceremony into something which I hoped was not too far distant from the original in meaning. But it was hard going, and we had not done the Positive Precepts yet. I asked the Professor if he could come early next morning, before the retreat was to start, and almost visibly swelling with pride, like a fat little mouse that has just discovered a morsel of cheese, the overgrown boy made his exit. The next morning, he came as promised, to give him his due, and using the same technique as before in an effort to sustain his concentration, we managed to set down on paper the five positive Precepts in Kannada, in the space of more than an hour. By this time, many people were waiting to meet me, so I was able to dismiss the Professor without offending him. As it was, he left with the parting comment - referring to my visitors within their earshot, and as if they had no knowledge of English – 'these people are uneducated, they don't know how to treat you properly'.

By that evening, everyone in Gulbarga who was going to take their Buddhism a bit more seriously than usual had assembled, the shrine had been set up, and we were ready to start. The Professor had temporarily suppressed his disdain for the other retreatants, and had steeled himself to 'translate' for me. "My translation of what you say", he said, "will be very impressive." "Don't worry", I said, "just say whatever I say." After a while he began to get the gist of my introductory remarks, but it soon became horrifyingly clear to him that some of the 'uneducated peasants' in the audience that he had so peremptorily written off were better translators than he, since they started prompting him and correcting him; and as their boldness and confidence increased, they were contributing almost as much as he was. At this point my talk ended, and I invited Bodhisagara and Dharmarakshita to introduce themselves. This they did in Hindi - the former's being somewhat hesitant and, by his own account, literary, whilst Dharmarakshita's was flowing and colloquial. But by now it was clear that quite a few members of the audience understood very well what was being said in two languages other than their native one. The Professor had taken a seat at the back of the assembly, and was looking very sheepish.

Next day's programme started well, and at 10:00am we commenced study of the Tiratana Vandana[85]. By this time the Professor had been reduced to a moody silence, and he listened with a curious mixture of pathetic eagerness and studied indifference to the unfolding of the Vandana, as translated by Dharmarakshita. By lunchtime the Professor had had enough, and he left the retreat, his Brahminical thread and all, without so much as a by your leave. "The food was too coarse", Dharmarakshita reported him as saying. With that, I had tacitly to agree. He had left another parting shot too, apparently. He was not satisfied with me: he wanted a 'Perfect Master'. Presumably he was so perfect that he could discern one. After the Professor's departure, the atmosphere lifted quite perceptibly, whether because of his absence or due to the effect of a bit more meditation, and the retreatants became happier and happier. I was impressed as usual with Dharmarakshita's vitality, remarkable for a man of his age, and with Bodhisagara's gentleness and friendliness.

The retreat ended beautifully, and the next day there were a number of programmes before I was to be allowed to leave Gulbarga. First there was a Bodhi-tree planting. Since it was in the grounds of Mr. Mogha's infant protégé, the Dr. Ambedkar Education Society (Gulbarga), I was happy to comply, and gladly participated in what was for me a novel experience, or perhaps I should say merely 'experience', since the hall-mark of all experience is novelty. I had never planted a tree of any kind before, and thoroughly enjoyed doing so. Before lunch, I was billed to address the Professors and students of the University. I had precious little time to prepare my talk, due to the pressure of prior engagements, and had to give most of it spontaneously. I spoke on Buddhism as the Path of the Higher Evolution, citing Dr. Ambedkar as an example of the kind of man the Higher Evolution can produce, and the talk went across very well indeed.

After my talk, the Chairman insisted upon a Question and Answer session, which I had been both looking forward to and dreading. I suspected that I might have some hostile questions to field. First, the Mathematics Professor, a bull of a man, leapt to his feet with the question "Why did you choose Infinity to designate the end-point of the Evolutionary process?" Inasmuch as Infinity contains all numbers, goes beyond all numbers, I said, the Buddha contains and goes beyond all the spiritual qualities and human qualities. He seemed happy with my answer, and ventured a little joke later about "the fascination of the Infinite." I was glad he thought it so. Another questioner was concerned about the 'transition from subjective consciousness to 'objective' consciousness', so here I gave a brief description of the Spiral Path up to the 'seeing' of the Three Characteristics, both negative and positive, and again the questioner seemed well satisfied. The Pali Professor asked a bit of a loaded question: "Was the doctrine of the Higher Evolution more Hinayanistic or Mahayanistic?" I replied that it partook of both; inasmuch as it was the background against which *samma vyama* (Perfect Effort) is realized, it could be attributed to the Hīnayāna, or to the Pali. Inasmuch as it was a vision of the Enlightenment of all sentient beings whatsoever throughout all space and time, it was Mahayanistic in flavour. Again, the Pali Professor seemed happy enough with my answer.

I was beginning to feel a bit pleased with myself when the Sanskrit Professor got up to give a 'vote of thanks', which turned out to be much more (or much less) than that. I noticed some of the students, who were devoted Ambedkarites, squirming with distaste at the highly questionable parallels the Professor drew between Buddhism and Vedanta. He did however say that 'he had heard many swamis speak on Evolution', and this was 'the best that he had heard'. At this point I regretted not rounding off my talk with some reference to the dangers of academic philosophizing, and the importance of countering this tendency by actualising the Higher Evolution by means of the *dhamma kranti* in one's own life. That would to some extent have taken the wind out of the Sanskrit Professor's 'It's all one' sails. He did not, of course, give me a chance to reply, and quickly wound up the meeting. I did in a sense make the last point however, over a cup of tea in the Staff Common Room afterwards, where all the Professors were gathered like eager boys for a bit of a lark. They all became strangely tongue-tied whilst I was drinking, but I did not chat to them. I left as soon as I could with one of the young men who had accompanied me, saying I had work to do, and wishing them all "Jai Bhim".

That evening I gave a talk in one of the Buddhist 'localities', the denizens of which are officially designated by the Indian Government as 'Scheduled Caste' localities, at which there were a large number of young people. I gave considerable emphasis to "what it is that makes us Buddhists", and overheard Mr. Mogha, who was chairing the meeting, say to a listener "very impressive" - which was quite pleasing to hear, since it is sometimes not easy to tell what sort of impression one is making. The evening ended with a sort of celebration supper, at which two rival Buddhist groups who had been contending for my presence were, if not reconciled, at least meeting together, and dozens of photos were taken, including one of me holding an extremely fat looking baby. Dharmarakshita and I caught the midnight train for Pune, feeling that our first tour of Karnataka had met with some success.

Two days later I was in Kolhapur with Dhammacharis Shakyanand and Manjuvir to give three 'locality' talks before a five day retreat. There were many more people in evidence here even than in Gulbarga, and everything went very well. Seventy-two people turned up for the *shibir*, which was held in a Hostel built around a large courtyard, near the middle of the spacious and pleasant town. There was also a 'Professor' on this *shibir*, who, like the Gulbarga Professor, seemed reluctant to be receptive. Dhammachari Aryasura, who had arrived with Dhammachari Vimuktananda from Pune, told me that he had really laid into the Professor during a study session, telling him that he did not think he was a sincere and genuine Buddhist at all - which, although, strictly speaking, an *ad hominem* argument, produced a sobering effect on the man. I spoke with the Professor too, avoiding the 'encounter' which he seemed to expect, and discovered that he simply could not believe that our Buddhist Movement was genuine and actually following the kind of programme of action that Dr. Ambedkar would have followed had he been alive. So I told him a bit about the range of our work, spiritual, educational, social and medical, and pointed out that the energy and inspiration for all that came directly from the process of Dhamma Diksha ('conversion by means of Dhamma'), or in other words, the Going for Refuge.

And the Going for Refuge, I added, was what we were doing at its most concentrated here on this *shibir*. With that I left him to his own thoughts. On the following days, the Professor began to change markedly, whether as a result of the combined efforts of the Dhammacharis on him, or because of his own spiritual practice, or both, and he began to shine.

We had periods of silence, and everyone, it seemed, got into the spirit of it. The walking and chanting was particularly effective during these periods, with seventy-three of us circumambulating the large courtyard, including even a blind man. The man participated by reaching up and resting his arm on Shakyanand's broad shoulder, and shuffling along behind. We divided into three groups for purposes of study, and Manjuvir translated for my group. He expressed considerable doubt whether anyone understood anything about the Dhamma at all, and thought that we should begin with something more basic than the *ti-ratna vandana*, which is what we were studying. Though in a sense I could see what he meant - the level of participation by the 22-strong group was minimal - I did not see what else we could do without becoming a sort of discussion group, and so we ploughed on. I regarded what we were doing more as a way of 'saying hello' and planting seeds for future germination, and did not consider it disastrous that not much reflection was going on. The talks by each of the Dhammacharis in the evenings were perhaps more instructive, and between these and the 'study groups', I considered that people had quite enough to think about and to delight in.

The morning meditation sessions, as well as the talks, were conducted in the courtyard, with a shrine attractively placed on a broad ledge mid-way along one long side of the yard - a ledge that the Dhammacharis sat upon also, and which afforded us a good view of the assembly. The mornings, by this time, were becoming decidedly chilly, especially for me after the Sri Lankan temperatures I was used to, and I was worried at first that everyone would catch chills. But as we got deeper into meditation, bodily discomfort faded into the distance, and by the end of fifty minutes, everyone looked as if they had begun to contact some inner fire. When the sun came up of course, the difficulty was very much the other way around, and it was a question not of stoking or contacting the 'inner fire' but of finding 'the cool cave'.

Towards the end of the *shibir*, there were 'interviews' for those interested in becoming mitras - I think there were twenty-five or thirty of them, fifteen of whom had already made their request to Shakyanand, and some of whom had been waiting nearly six months for a reply. The delay had been due to Shakyanand's illness, which had necessitated his return to Pune, and left Kolhapur without a resident Dhammachari, or even a regularly visiting Dhammachari. I was deeply touched by the faith and enthusiasm of so many of these young men, and wished there were more Dhammacharis willing and able to work with them. Kolhapur, or what little I had seen of it - both the town or city with its broad avenues and its environs stretched out on a range of broad hills fanned with cooling breezes - seemed a very suitable place to have a TBMSG centre, and clearly there was already a substantial response to our efforts there. Lokamitra, I know, is also concerned to do as much as possible for this area. The Kolhapur retreat ended with a talk by me to which outsiders were invited, and we concluded with a short Puja. Despite the sudden influx of people who had not been meditating with us, it all went off rather well. I spoke for one-and-a-half hours, which was longer than usual, though not for the three hours that Manjuvir, in all seriousness, apparently, requested. Perhaps he just wanted to tell me I was appreciated. Anyway, everyone seemed very pleased and friendly afterwards.

From Kolhapur we returned to Pune, to find Purna and Shantiprabha looking even more rested and relaxed than when I had seen them last. Part of the reason for this, I gathered, was that the computer that they were to have set up in Jeevak (our medical centre) had 'gone out of operation.' Purna told me it could not even be booted up which, whatever that meant, sounded very bad indeed. There was some hope, however, that rather than some intricate and intractable failure it might simply have been the main fuse, which, simple though it was to replace, was beyond Purna's mandate to touch without violating the machine's Guarantee. But what (presumably) was Purna's and Shantiprabha's misfortune was my good luck - the chance of that magical thing called Order contact in a freer format than the *shibir* had afforded. I was very happy to avail myself of this opportunity, and especially of discussing with Shantiprabha the economic dimension of setting up a Hostel in Sri Lanka, and what it would entail if funds were to be made available by Karuna Trust. Purna, I now saw, had benefited very much from his contact with the Order in the West, and I could not help feeling rather sad that he was going to the antipodes and married life, and that I would not see him perhaps for many years.

I had now completed what I had provisionally labelled 'helping Lokamitra' on this visit to India, and was about to start a short pilgrimage and visit another arm of the Movement. My intention was to go to Kusinagara and Lumbini, the scene of the Buddha's departure from and arrival in this world, respectively. This was to be followed by a visit to Dhammacharis Bodhananda and Amoghachitta in Kathmandu.

The train journey to Benares, or Varanasi, as it is known locally, was straightforward, and the train drew into the main station on schedule after a two-night journey. I let the crush of variegated humanity, now mostly speaking melodious Hindi rather than sturdy Marathi, ascend the steps to the exit, noticing how most people were well-muffled against the cold winter air that was now blowing down from the Himalayas. I weighed up whether to proceed immediately by bus to the nearest sizeable town to Kusinagara, which was Gorakhpur, sacred to the memory of the Hindu sage Gorakhnath, or to spend a leisurely afternoon and night in Sarnath to allow my nerves to recover from their jangling on the train. I decided upon the latter, having consulted the man in the travel bureau, and took a bus and rickshaw (reluctantly, since I always feel worried about the health of rickshaw wallahs, to that oasis of peace where the Wheel of the Law was first set rolling by the Buddha amongst the first five disciples.

The Maha Bodhi Rest House had been transformed since my first visit in 1983. Now it looked clean and well-kept; in fact it was sparkling white and with a small painting of Guru Rimpoche[84] on the West wall near the entrance. I was greeted by a wide-faced Tibetan woman, with eyes spaced so far apart that it was difficult to keep both in view at once. She told me with a smile that the caretaker was away for a few hours. Her English was fragmentary and my Tibetan non-existent, so further dialogue was difficult. I lifted my bags and made off in the direction of the Thai Rest House. Thinking however that I might still obtain a place in the company of the happy Tibetans of the Maha Bodhi Society Rest House, I called in at the office a hundred yards or so further down the road, and having received a polite greeting but no further assurance of accommodation from the Secretary (who was, I think, Sinhalese), I turned my attention to the somewhat portly Englishman sitting near his desk. He turned out to be the Englishman Bernard Betts, whom I discovered was in touch with Dhammachari Ratnaprabha, and who happened to be on pilgrimage with his family. One of the family, unfortunately, was not well, and Bernard had to leave to go and see a doctor, and so was not able to spend any more time with me, nor I with him. I smiled inadvertently as he performed the traditional *anjali* as we parted, and wondered whether he would do that in the West. Having said goodbye to Bernard, I walked on past the Sarnath Archaeological Museum to the Thai Rest House. I began to recollect my last meeting with the incumbent, Ven. Sasanarashmi, with whom I was on friendly enough terms after a previous visit.

By the time I got to the Thai Rest House it was nearly mid-day, the time when all good bhikkhus are well into their tucker, and sure enough, there was Ven. Sasanarashmi, as rotund as ever, seated at a smallish table with another senior-looking, well-rounded bhikkhu at his side, whilst at a lower, larger table sat three young and rather sheepish-looking bhikkhus. I was wearing my blue sleeveless shirt under my upper robe, since the weather was getting distinctly colder, and it must have been this which threw them all into a quandary. Sasanarashmi seemed to recognize me immediately, which was astute of him since when we had last met I was in civvies, and started to welcome me quite warmly, overcoming his surprise at my present appearance. But the senior bhikkhu at his side broke out with: "Are you a Buddhist monk?" to which I replied with a confident "Yes". Sasanarashmi's friendliness took precedence over the other's scepticism, by a narrow margin, and I was invited to sit at the upper table with the seniors. But for the next twenty minutes, during which I tried to eat my meal as calmly and mindfully as possible, my ears were assailed with a blow-by-blow account by the other elder bhikkhu concerning the superiority of the Thai Sangha and how I could not even be a Buddhist in their country. I said nothing and just went on eating, which had the effect of making the senior bhikkhu very uneasy indeed, and even more vociferous. Sasanarashmi tried to calm him down, but without much effect, and perhaps in embarrassment got up to leave the table, telling me to take my time and help myself to whatever food I wanted. The senior monk now saw fit to discontinue his inconclusive diatribe, and got up to follow Sasanarashmi without so much as a glance at me. Perhaps he felt he had made his point and proved what a thoroughly superior bhikkhu he was. I finished my meal quietly, being now able to enjoy the taste of the food. It was good.

Afterwards I was invited by one of the younger monks to quarter myself in his room; the prejudice of the senior one evidently did not extend to him, at least, I was thankful to note. The young monk made me comfortable on a bed beside his, apologising for the lack of a room for me in the spacious premises. "We have a big party of Thai tourists here", he said. He seemed a sensible man, and I soon discovered that, despite his youthfulness, he was the Chief Monk or abbot at a Temple housing a hundred bhikkhus. He showed me some photographs of it. There was clearly no lack of money where he came from. He went on to explain that he practised *anapana sati*[85] but could not devote as much time to meditation as he would like since he had so many duties to perform. But here, he said, he was able to do a little practice. I had not mentioned anything about meditation, so he must have been assuming that I was one of those Western monks who actually practice, and of course, he was right. I also noticed that his manners were very pleasing, and that, even though it was his room I was sharing, after going out and returning some time later, he would always announce his arrival by tapping on the door before entering. Whilst the motivation for such a discipline could be questioned, it served to establish immediately a sense of fellowship and non-identification with one's present surroundings, and I quickly began to feel on friendly terms with him. We talked a little about the Dhamma, and as I have now heard so many bhikkhus say, he told me: "You Western monks are new to Buddhism but you know more about it than us." For my part, I wished that I did not project the image of a know-all quite so readily, since I wanted to learn as much as I could from him.

After a much-needed rest, I awoke in time to go for a stroll before sunset, and as I walked past a door at one corner of the quadrangle of rooms, who should emerge but bhikkhu Gurudhammo, the young bhikkhu who had accompanied Dharmacharini Anjali, John Bloss and myself to Buddha Gaya in 1983. He was as happy to see me as I was to see him, and greeted me like a long-lost brother. After the initial delight of meeting was over, however, and he had invited me into his room, I saw sitting on the floor with her back against a wall, a young Burmese or Thai woman with rather coarse features. She gave me a surly look and said nothing. Gurudhammo offered me no explanation of who she was or what she was doing there, and I forbore to ask. Not only was he not forthcoming about her, but to my disappointment he had nothing to say about himself either, which considering it was five years since we had last met, was a bit strange. He seemed pleased, however, that I now wore robes, though he did not seem at all clear what an Anagarika, even an orthodox one, was. Apart from this he found nothing to say to me, and after a few minutes I rather sadly took my leave and said I would see him again when I returned from my walk. Leaving the quadrangle, which consisted mostly of residential accommodation, I could hear a group of bhikkhus chanting in the meditation hall on the first floor. It was very melodious indeed, and the most positive aspect that I had come across so far of the communal life of the Thai Rest House.

I slept soundly that night, and rose to meditate as usual about five o'clock next morning. My roommate rose too, and after his ablutions sat down, as I half-expected, after what he had told me, to meditate. But in fact he started chanting what sounded like a Pali *sutta*, in a very low and melodious voice, and went on in that way for the whole fifty minutes of my sitting. Breakfast time came, and I thought for a moment of the senior bhikkhu. I had no wish to endure another of his tirades. However, the matter had been 'solved' by my being relegated to the lower table with the younger monks, and though the senior bhikkhu again wasted a lot of breath in needless talk, at least it was not directed against me this time.

After breakfast I went for a walk around the Sarnath ruins, taking in the great stupa and the Mulagandhakuti Vihara [86] on my itinerary. There was hardly anybody around. There was a man touting photographic slides, who gave up after I had twice politely declined to buy his wares, and the third time told him to leave me alone. There was an old Tibetan lama, or *gelong*, sitting amongst the ruins chanting his mantras and telling his beads, and I felt intensely sad. So many ruins. He did not seem sad at all; his chanting was vigorous and joyful, and the melody of it remained in my heart as I walked towards the stupa in the still-cool morning air. There were some Tibetans briskly walking around the stupa telling their malas, and a few curious lookers-on. I walked down the avenue towards the Mulagandhakuti Vihara and a strange sight greeted me. When I had been here in 1983 there had been a beautiful green lawn on which I had seen, rather to my consternation, a little group of Hindu women tearing up the grass with rapid furtive movements. I had assumed they were either weeding, or else picking grass for their cattle, in which case they would soon be chased away. Now, as I looked, there were perhaps those self-same Hindu women again, this time accompanied by a small group of men who seemed to be directing them. But this time there was a difference: instead of the beautiful green lawn there was simply a big open space entirely covered with dusty earth and huge piles of dried-up grass. The time had come, so far as I could see, to dismiss the park-keepers and their female assistants on a charge of incompetence. But whether this would be done, with the Chief Bhikkhu of the Maha Bodhi Society now resident not in India but in Sri Lanka, and the local Hindu community laughing up their sleeves at the inability of the Management Committee to prevent cows grazing the lawns to destruction, I had my doubts. I approached the entrance to the Vihara, intending to study the magnificent murals which I knew were inside, depicting scenes from the life of Gautama the Shakyamuni, and as I did so I noticed a number of youths lounging on the steps of the Vihara as if they owned the place. They directed at me looks which were a mixture of insolence and bare-faced contempt. Although I have met far worse looks in village India and been none the worse for it, this sort of thing was rather unexpected and slightly disconcerting here in this sacred place. I changed my plans about going inside, and instead approached and circumambulated the statue of Anagarika Dharmapala. After that I returned to the Thai Rest House.

Sarnath, which had meant so much to me on my first visit, now provoked feelings of frustration and sadness. Something needed to be done here! I decided to leave after lunch on the next leg of my journey - the first part of my pilgrimage proper - since I had come to Sarnath only on impulse this time. I said goodbye to my room-mate, thanking him for his kindness, and he said I was welcome to stay at his temple in Thailand at any time. I said goodbye to Gurudhammo, who exclaimed that he would be seeing me in Kathmandu and in Poona, but I had my doubts. I said goodbye to

Sasanarashmi, who told me frankly and disarmingly what I already knew, that there was nothing going on Sarnath but eating and sleeping, and set off down the road.

Varanasi seemed almost welcome this time. On my first visit in early 1983, I had detested it and mistrusted the crowds. This time, though I am no more a lover of crowds than before, I felt the throb of activity as a not unwelcome contrast to the sloth and torpor of the Rest Houses at Sarnath. I made for the Burmese Rest House, not far from the Railway Station, and arrived to find a little group of wretchedly poor-looking Tibetans were begging to be given some space. We were all directed to a large room with space enough for all of us. I tried to speak on the Tibetan's behalf with the bhikkhu in charge, who was an intelligent man speaking good English, but he pointed out that they wanted to settle for several months whilst selling their knitted clothing, and that was not what the Thai Rest House was intended for. I could see his point, but could not help feeling sorry for the Tibetans, deprived of their homeland, with nowhere to rest their weary legs and backs. They smelled of weeks of toilsome travel in the plains of India with no baths. As I turned to go to my room, they twinkled their eyes at me without the slightest suggestion of ill-will.

Later, as afternoon changed into dusk and the dusk into twilight, I went shopping in one of the nearby markets. It was getting colder day by day, and I was heading for the North. I needed warmer clothes. I purchased a warm woollen vest and long-johns, and a very heavy pale orange blanket which I thought would keep out all but the bitterest cold. It proved to be an excellent purchase, not only that night, but on many subsequent occasions. On my way back, along a road thronged with people on their way home, out on a shopping spree, or just taking a cup of tea and watching the crowds go by, I dropped in at the Burmese Rest House. The Tibetans, I found, had been accommodated there in two tiny rooms - hardly more than storage sheds for junk, at the bottom of the garden. I went to see whether they had a pullover to my liking, but discovered that, far from selling Tibetan hand-made articles, they were peddling cheap factory-made material from Taiwan, Hong Kong and Japan. I did not buy anything, and wandered away feeling a little bemused. I went to examine the big central building of the Burmese Rest House, which turned out to be an Image House. Clearly a lot of money had been spent in erecting the finely-detailed and well-built edifice. High quality reconstructed stone (or possibly, marble) had been used for the shrine room itself. But the shrine, though it could have been an inspiring sight, was in a state of neglect, and evidently was hardly ever used. I tidied up a bit, offered a stick of incense and a candle (there were no flowers available), chanted the Three Refuge and Precepts, meditated for a while, and left for my own quarters in the Thai Rest House.

Early next morning, before sun-up, I walked to the bus station and took a bus to Gorakhpur, settling back in my seat to watch the countryside slip by. My thoughts had come to a standstill. I was content to let them be like that for a while. By early afternoon I was in Gorakhpur. After taking lunch in an open-air restaurant, I made enquiries at a Travel Agency about buses to Kusinagara, and in answer to their queries told the young men there that I was heading for Lumbini and afterwards, for Kathmandu. Unfortunately this was just what they were waiting for, and hardly had I realised what was happening when I was whisked away on a rickshaw to have my Visa photos taken (which was in any case necessary). What was far from necessary was that I was issued with a through-ticket to Kathmandu, including a booking at a Hotel on the way, at three times the price I need have paid, as I discovered later. Fortunately, I was not down to my last penny, but it was a bit annoying all the same.

I waited what seemed an interminable time for the bus to Kusinagara (or Kasi, as the locals insisted on calling it), and was able to see no information at the bus station about its likely time of arrival. I was offered the chair usually occupied by the Information Officer, in front of the "enquiries" grille, which put me in a peculiar spot as various other travellers came up for enlightenment. I smiled at them until they went away, and watched a cow sampling banana skins outside the door. After about two hours the Kasi bus arrived and there was a frenzied rush for seats. It seemed that some people had tickets whilst others had not. One of the two bus conductors glared terrifically at everyone and said something which I did not understand, but which sounded like "all those without tickets, get off." I made up my mind not to budge. Sure enough, the conductor was calling people's bluff, for although some people did get off, thus making the bus a hundred percent overcrowded instead of a hundred and fifty percent, as soon as we started on our way he began to sell tickets. Or had I got it wrong? Perhaps he had said something completely different, and I had spent several minutes thinking I was seat-jumping, quite needlessly. Anyway, I sat glued to my seat, and got my ticket. After an hour and a half's bumpy ride during which the road seemed to get worse and worse, I got off at the junction just outside Kasi and asked the way to the Mahaparinibbana Temple. Evidently the locals did not like bhikkhus, for no one gave me a civil reply or attempted to help me. Picking up my bag, I walked off slowly down the road in the direction which, I thought, was the likely one. A bicycle rickshaw-wallah pulled up beside me after I had been walking only a few minutes, and I thankfully clambered in and said "Rest House", which was enough to get us started. I was on the lookout for the place where Bhante had received his Sramanera Ordination, but I was not sure of the name, and we passed a number of buildings before I began to wonder where I was being taken. I looked at the rickshaw-wallah and said "Where?" "Tibeti Temple" he said, laconically, and that was that. A few minutes and Ten Rupees later, we had arrived at the Tibetan Temple, situated in almost featureless countryside, but with a few welcome trees growing around it, silhouetted against a pale blue sky as the sun was going down. Not far away I could see a hemispherical stupa-shape with a threefold honorific umbrella surrounding it. Perhaps that is what I am looking for, I thought, and walked into the Tibetan Temple.

The Tibetan Temple consisted of a two-storey rectangular block adjacent to a single-storey L-shaped dormitory block, and near a *chorten*[87] that appeared to be of recent origin. A tall Tibetan in neat trousers and shirt came to greet me, and offered me a room for twenty-five Rupees, which I was glad to accept. His straightforward, business-like approach was so refreshing and reassuring after the Hindu one I had met so often, which always left me wondering: "what's he after now?" I was shown to a neat, clean and spacious room, and thankfully set down my bags and lay back on the bed, too tired for the time being to do anything else, and reflected on the day's journey.

As the bus had drawn away from Varanasi that morning, and my mind had relaxed, freeing itself from all ideas of duty to the Movement and 'helping Lokamitra', good and enjoyable and worthwhile though all that had been, I had more or less deliberately set my mind in the mood of "death, death", and just watched. The countryside had grown more and more beautiful, until I began almost to gape in amazement. At first I could not say exactly in what the beauty lay, but I eventually decided that it had something to do with the complete absence of anything factory-made or industrialised. As town succeeded town and village succeeded village, I began to feel, if the expression were permissible, that the landscape was touched by the Hand of the Creator. Everything that I saw, every person, article of clothing, face, doorway, seemed as if painted by a master-artist. Everything was in perfect harmony with its surroundings, down to each minute detail. Each aspect, each part unique, yet part of a magnificent, ever-changing, impersonal process. A feeling of immense gratitude for the earth and its beauty sprang up in me, and I could hardly hold back the tears. "Rarely, rarely comest thou, spirit of delight ...." How harsh and brash and crude seemed, in retrospect, everything modern man has devised, compared with what I was now seeing.

NOTES

81 The Four Sights : Prince Siddhartha, the Buddha-to-be, whilst following up his quest for knowledge, left his palace one day and encountered Four Sights - seeing them as it were for the first time: a sick man, an old man, a corpse, and a wandering holy man whose bearing was serene and peaceful. Seeing these and their implications for his own life had a tremendous impact on him, and he eventually left his palace, his wife and child in quest of the Enlightenment, for his own sake and for the sake of all that lives, which the bearing of the wandering holy man had seemed to promise.

82 The Mass Conversion: the ceremony held on the Diksha Bhumi (Conversion Ground) in Nagpur on 14th October 1956. Dr.Ambedkar had his personal, individual Going for Refuge to the Buddha, Dharma and Sangha formally witnessed during this ceremony by the bhikkhu U Chandramani Mahathero, (who was the seniormost bhikkhu in India and also happened to have been Sangharakshita's Preceptor). Dr.Ambedkar then administered the Three Refuges and Five precepts, together with twenty-two *pratignas* or vows intended to ensure the continuance of Buddhism in India, to his audience of 400,000 followers, who thereby formally constituted themselves Buddhists in the traditional manner. Ref: *Ambedkar and Buddhism*, Sangharakshita, Windhorse, 1986.

83 Dedication ceremony: a ceremony composed by Sangharakshita in simple and elegant English, commonly recited whenever a new meditation shrine is set up, or when a new group of people come together for a spiritual purpose. Ref: *FWBO Puja Book*.

84 Guru Rimpoche: 'Precious Guru'. One of the appellations by which Padmasambhava, the great yogi and Tantric Guru of Tibet, is known by his devotees.

It is said that he was successful in establishing the Dharma in Tibet whilst his predecessor the saintly Santarakshita was not, because he was able to subdue and convert the local demons. Sangharakshita, and through him the FWBO/TBMSG, has a strong connection with Padmasambhava since several of his teachers belonged to the Nyingmapa School of Tibetan Buddhism, which traces its lineage back to Padmasambhava.

85 *anapana sati*: mindfulness of the incoming and outgoing of the breath. The practice taught in the FWBO/TBMSG to all beginners in Buddhist meditation, and which is continued with ever greater subtlety throughout one's spiritual career. (See also note 30). It is instrumental in bringing about the harmonious integration of all the psycho-spiritual factors constituting the happy, healthy human being.

86 Mulagandhakuti Vihara: The beautiful Temple erected near the ancient stupa or burial mound commemorating the first 'Turning of the Wheel of the Law' in the Deer Park at Sarnath (Isipatana) for the benefit of the five erstwhile ascetic companions of the Buddha, and 'for the benefit of gods and men'. The Temple was set up by Anagarika Dharmapala with the generous financial assistance of Mrs Mary Foster his American benefactress. Inside the Temple there are beautiful murals, painted by a Japanese artist, graphically depicting scenes from the life of the Buddha and his disciples.

87 *chorten*: a Tibetan-style stupa or burial mound of elaborate design and profound cosmic symbolism. cf. *The Legend of the Great Stupa*, Keith Dowman; *Five Element symbolism and the Stupa* – a talk by Sangharakshita available from thebuddhistcentre.com

* * * * *

32   Kusinagara, Lumbini, and Kathmandu

I visit two great places of pilgrimage, travel on to Kathmandu and meet many old friends. I disrobe - in body but not in spirit, and suffer hallucin- ations. Plunging back to the plains of India, I pass the birthplace of Shantideva, give some dharma talks, and return to Pune. Sent on an errand of mercy to Agra, I visit the Taj Mahal and the Red Fort, as well as befriend- ing some local Buddhists. A Dharma tour of Nagpur is arranged for me, and after returning westwards to Pune for an Order Convention, I make for the South of India.

I WAS ROUSED FROM MY WAKING DREAM by a tap on the door. The tall Tibetan had brought me some water and was asking me if I wanted a cup of tea, to which I heartily assented. He also showed me the washroom and toilet, and whilst he did so, I saw a middle-aged Lama walk past. Returning to my room, I savoured the tea that was brought a few minutes later, and then taking my towel, went for a wash. As I approached the washroom, the Lama appeared out of the shadows with a bucket of water and a smile. How natural, how simple, I thought. I asked him his name: "Lama", he said, in a deep voice. "Lama what?", I said, intending to be friendly. "Lama Guru", he said, in a voice even deeper, and walked off.

The next morning I was up well before sunrise to meditate and to visit the Mahaparinirvana Temple and "Bhante's Temple", wherever that was. Just as the sun was beginning to disperse the dew, I took the path to the first of my venues. There were few people around, just a couple of tourists in track suits, and with a Mongolian slant to their eyes and cameras slung around their necks. As I drew nearer what I could now see clearly was the Mahaparinirvana Temple, passing ancient foundations and stupas, some still standing in their entirety, some now little more than bare outlines on the ground, it became clear that I had been preceded by a party of Thai pilgrims, who were already crowding the area in front of a reclining image of the Buddha and making quite a lot of noise into the bargain. I began to circumambulate the Temple and the Stupa situated at the back of it, and wishing for respite from the crowd, I stood for some minutes in the lee of the ancient stupa, now reconstructed, as I gathered from a guide book. I savoured the atmosphere, whilst gazing at the numerous small stupas behind the main stupa: here too, some were complete, some no more than bits of bases; all was deeply peaceful. In the midst of my absorption, some Japanese visitors hove into view with clicking and whirring cameras, and a bit reluctantly, I came to the conclusion that things were not going to get any more peaceful at this time and place, and I had better move on. I completed my circuit of the stupa and Temple, returning to the steps in front, where a young bhikkhu who seemed to be attached to the Thai party was sitting. As I approached, he said to me without preamble; "Is Bhante Sangharakshita still in India?" "No" I said, startled, thinking that he must be psychic (though there could have been other explanations), and rather hoping that an intelligent conversation would ensue. But unfortunately the young bhikkhu showed no further interest in me, so I wandered off, deciding to take a look at the stupa marking the site of the Cremation of the Buddha's earthly remains, and then to look for the Temple where Sangharakshita, or rather, Dennis Lingwood as he was then, had formally 'Gone Forth' for the first time as a Samanera, in the presence of the Bhikkhu Sangha. As I left the vicinity of the Mahaparinirvana Temple, the sound of sweetly melodious chanting rose in waves and faded into the silence.

It was more than a mile to the Cremation Stupa, and on the way I stopped for a few minutes to take a look at the so-called 'Indo-Japan' stupa with the three-tiered honorific umbrella that I had seen the night before, looming in the distance. It was a brick-faced structure, strictly speaking not a stupa at all, but a meditation hall and shrine within the upturned "bowl" of the stupa. Clearly a lot of money had been lavished on it, but there was no sign of activity, and no atmosphere of meditation, so I left after a few minutes, noting the fine workmanship of the doors, done in the way it seems only the Japanese know how.

The only person in evidence when I arrived at the Cremation Stupa was a gardener. For a while, all was peaceful. I sat and meditated, until another party of Thai pilgrims caught up with me up and began circumambulating the stupa, led by a bhikkhu utilising a portable tannoy to explain the unnecessary to the unhearing. I got up and made to leave, then it suddenly occurred to me that I might make use of the Thai party. Their bus had drawn up nearby, so I went and asked the Indian driver if he had room inside. He indicated that he had, and that I would be welcome to come to Lumbini with them, as far as he was concerned.

I approached the young bhikkhu who had asked about Bhante, and he said I had better ask the leading bhikkhu (the one with the tannoy). I asked him if he could spare a seat, and he referred me to the leading *dayaka* or helper - a young rather brutish-looking man attired in a track suit. He looked at me through the narrow slits of his eyes and said "You Buddhist?" to which I replied "Yes". "You not Thai", he said. "No", I said,

"British?" "Yes", I said. "Our party Thai", he said, adding "All Thai passport", apparently as an afterthought. I smiled at him. "You cannot come", he said. And that was that. I walked off smiling to myself, and was overtaken by the bus some minutes later as I walked back to fetch my bags and take the far less luxurious public bus to Gorakhpur, Sonauli, and Lumbini. I had not proceeded far down the road before I discovered the place where Bhante had received his Samanera Ordination, which I might have missed had the Thais given me a lift. I had reason to be grateful to the brutal-faced Thai *dayaka*.

The 'Arakan Burmese Temple' was on the way back to the Kasi-Gorakhpur crossing. It was set well back from the road, and looked a bit run-down, but I noticed a fairly recently-painted sign saying "Please observe noble silence." Taking advantage of that, I walked in without saying anything, passing single-storey dormitory-like accommodation on either side, and approached a four-square two storey building. There appeared to be no-one about, so I took the staircase with a sign saying "To Sima" (an Ordination or Convocation hall), and mounted the steep, narrow steps. At the top there was a square, airy room with a lofty ceiling, and on one side, a not unattractive Burmese-style Buddha image in *bhumi-sparsa*, flanked by a shrine commemorating U. Chandramani Mahathero. I thought that this was probably the place where Bhante had received his Samanera ordination. I made an incense offering, chanted the Refuges and Precepts, and meditated for a few minutes in the peaceful and vibrant atmosphere, despite the rather neglected state of the little shrine. Time however began to press, and after a few minutes I got up and left.

The bus from Kasi to Gorakhpur was the most flexible I have ever ridden on. What amazed me most was that the windows did not shatter with the flexing of the body of the bus. Perhaps the glass was in fact the main source of stiffness and strength. Miraculously, we arrived in Gorakhpur, and after collecting my ticket to Sonauli, the border-town on the India-Nepal border, I caught a bus which I was glad to see was much sturdier than the one I had just left. Evening purpled into night, and I drew my blanket around me as it was growing distinctly chilly.

The Indian border Official at Sonauli asked me why I was not staying on the Indian side that night. Not wishing to offend him I said (truthfully) that I had a place booked on the Nepal side, and he let me go. The police on the Nepal side were very friendly and told me to come again in the morning. I was out of India and in the Himalayan, Hindu kingdom of Nepal. The rest house to which I had been assigned by the over-charging Indian touts was a scruffy but friendly place. In fact I was immediately impressed at how much more friendly the people were than on the Indian side. They were responsive and lively, and though perhaps the friendly attitude did not come from very deep, it was much to be preferred to the suspicious responses I had come to expect on the Indian side of late. There were a number of Europeans with snow-burned faces, going in the opposite direction, and with deep, far-away looks in their eyes. The hotel manager - though the place looked more like a hostel - was eager to know why I was a Buddhist, and why was I not a Hindu? I told him that Buddhism regards all men as equally brothers, and furthermore, there was no caste in Buddhism, I said.

He did not seem to appreciate the point of what I said, but remained friendly enough. A wandering sadhu came into the restaurant at this point, moving from table to table and applying a spot of powder on the foreheads of the faithful and accepting alms. I declined to be made holy in this way, or to offer alms to someone engaging in the propagation of error.

The next morning I was up just as the light began to appear in the sky, and ascended to the flat roof soon after sun-up. In the distance were the Himalayas, pink and magnificent, distant though they were. After breakfast I visited the police, who were helpful, and the bank, which was not. In fact I was obliged to cajole every bit of information I needed out of the bank clerk, and I began to suspect that he took a special delight in rattling people by mystifying them. I had to go back and forth from the bank to the police no less than four times before every bit of paper and every signature was to his approval. I eventually told him, in loud words, exactly what I thought of him, which rather shocked a number of bystanders, and was probably a bit unskilful. The clerk however was unruffled. "I am here only to help people", he told me disdainfully. He was about the most unhelpful public servant I had ever come across. Not to mince words, he seemed to be a particularly vicious kind of bureaucrat, taking delight in giving me insufficient information. Nevertheless on my fourth encounter with him I told him that I should not have spoken loudly to him, and hoped that he would forgive me. "I am here only to help you", he replied coldly, once again, and that was that. I had got more or less what I needed, at last, and presumably he had got what he wanted, so I could go, ten Dollars and some hundreds of Rupees (Indian) the poorer, and with a small pile of bright-coloured Nepali banknotes in my hand.

A local minibus took me most of the way to Lumbini, the birthplace of Prince Siddhartha, the Buddha-to-be. I was the first passenger on, but was soon followed by a crowd of the most wonderfully colourful healthy-looking people imaginable. I thought to myself that if I was in the position of being able to choose my birth-place, I could do a lot worse than this locality; in fact, I thought that I could hardly do better. What miserable specimens, I thought, were most Westerners compared with these sturdy sons and daughters of the soil, secure in their strengths and faithful in their allegiances, confident in their clothing painted as if by an Eastern Vermeer. On the other hand, would one come across the Dharma, say in the form of the Diamond Sutra, or in the form of some other transcendental influence tending towards Enlightenment, in a place such as this? Unattractive though it might seem, I thought, one would be far more likely to meet some such influence in the tenements of Worli[88] or the hutments of Ulhasnagar[89].

The bus stopped at a road junction. "Lumbini", someone said laconically, and off I climbed, together with another young man, a Nepali in Western dress who told me he was going in my direction. We took a side road, dusty. un-made-up, and undistinguished by trees of any kind. My companion made a few desultory remarks, and so did I, but neither of us was really interested in communication at that moment. As we trudged on, I became aware of that deepening of the atmosphere which I have felt at each of the other three main places of pilgrimage, and as this happened, I began to feel immensely sad. I thought to myself "Now there is nowhere else to go on pilgrimage. This is the last time I shall ever have the luxury of this experience." Accompanying it also, however, was a more subtle feeling of relief - that there was now nowhere else to go but 'inside'. I was so deep in these thoughts that it required a considerable effort of will to pay attention to the landscape, and to speak to the guide-book seller who now appeared in front of me as we approached the entrance to the Grove. There did not seem at first to be much of architectural interest, and I felt glad. There was not anything to detract from the natural simplicity of the place and its peaceful atmosphere. There was a small pool or tank, with a few ducks swimming in it, a grove of a few fine oak trees with low-spreading branches, and an Asokan pillar of the now familiar type, highly polished, of pale pink stone, leaning at a bit of an angle and telling the reader of ancient characters that this was where Maya Devi, the wife of King Suddhodana, had been delivered of a baby boy, Prince Siddhartha. It all felt very homely and peaceful, and I sat down and enjoyed the quiet for a while. There were an insignificant number of other tourists in the grove itself. The idea of establishing "an international pilgrimage Centre" here, complete with a whole campus of buildings, as was currently being planned, seemed like sacrilege in this peaceful place.

Rising from my reflections after half an hour or so, I went in search of food and discovered the Theravada Temple. On entering the main hall I found myself witness to the closing remarks of a refined-looking Theravada bhikkhu addressing yet another group of Thai tourists and a small company of bhikkhus. I hung around afterwards, and got talking to the yellow-robed man who had been addressing them. I discovered to my delight that he was from Palpa Tansen, and had met Bhante. He asked me if I had eaten, and discovering that I had not, immediately offered me food, which I gladly accepted. I was offered the remains of the 'dana' brought by the Thai group, and it was very good, apart from a heavily spiced meat dish which I put to one side.

Having eaten, the refined-looking bhikkhu from Tansen, who was very bright and friendly, asked me about Bhante's health, concerning which I reassured him as best I could. He then asked me how I was getting back to Sonauli, and hearing that I had no transport, stood up immediately, and taking me with him, introduced me to the Thai group who were relaxing in the adjoining main hall of the Temple. He asked them if they could give me a lift, and this time the answer was "Yes". After some minutes in earnest conversation with an older, well-educated Thai gentleman who told me he had been a bhikkhu but had forsaken the Dhamma for politics, we set off. We walked past the entrance to a Tibetan Gompa, outside which were sitting a happy-looking group of young purple-robed *gelongs* or bhikkhus. They looked with intense curiosity at me as I walked by and boarded one of the two luxury coaches carrying the Thai party. It was quite the most comfortable seat I had sat in during the whole of my India/Nepal tour. But I was not left to my thoughts and reflections for long. Strange once again to say, the little man sitting just behind me happened to be another friend of Bhante's. He had been "the little monk" at the Hampstead Vihara when Bhante first came to the UK from India, but had now disrobed and married, and was lecturer at one of Thailand's Universities. We hardly had time to exchange more information than this, when the coach, which had been breezing through the countryside faster than I had imagined, dropped me near the Indian border and disappeared into the distance in a cloud of dust.

I spent the afternoon in Sonauli drinking endless cups of tea and meeting some of the European tourists. Appearing perhaps as something of a tourist attraction myself, I soon found myself of absorbing interest to a little group of them. That evening, a very large contingent of tourists were due to arrive at the Hotel, and I was moved from a light and airy room at the top of the building to an airless and lightless one at the bottom. Still, I would be off good and early, before anyone else next morning, I thought. And so it was. I rose after a brief sleep, and the sun was just rising as I boarded the bus to Kathmandu. The dawn colours in the foothills of the Himalayas are quite beyond the power of words to convey. See them, see them if you can! I drew my heavy blanket close around me as the bus picked up speed. It was very cold.

For a large part of the journey we followed the gorge of a large river, the road skirting perilously near the deep blue-green, swirling waters, and sometimes winding precipitously hundreds of feet above it. I felt strangely excited at the prospect of seeing Kathmandu. But I had to wait a long time to satisfy my curiosity. We journeyed the whole day and evening, always climbing, until the road eventually levelled out, and there in the distance, and to my surprise, were the twinkling lights of what appeared to be a large and modern-looking city nestling in a vast plain between hills which led even higher towards snow-covered peaks glistening in the moonlight. The bus drew up somewhere in the centre of the city, and having dismounted with my bag, I found myself surrounded by a group of hotel touts. I knew which Hotel I wanted, however, and was lucky enough to find a young guide to take me there in a taxi, though he narrowly escaped being punched by one of the other touts.

The Hotel Asia, Thamel, in the tourist sector of the city proved to be a suitable enough place for me, and Dharmacharis Bodhananda and Amoghachitta had found it was a suitable place for them. It was particularly good to see Amoghachitta's cheery face, which was somewhat more fleshed-out than when I had seen him in India. In fact he looked fit and suntanned, and as if he had been enjoying himself, and he invited me into the top-storey room that had been rented for use as a Triratna meditation centre. But he had a point to put to me almost immediately. Whilst making it clear that he was happy to see me in robes, he did not know, he said, whether I really understood the situation here. He did not want to give the impression to the many Europeans who came for meditation classes that here was the 'secret lama' of the FWBO - such a message would contradict the one that he and Bodhananda were already putting out - that the FWBO had no 'lamas'. And so - would I mind disrobing? I thought about it for a bit, and did not feel certain enough to act immediately, so Amoghachitta, noticing my hesitation, suggested I speak to Bodhananda in the morning. And there we left the matter.

That evening I went for a stroll in the Bazaar, the network of tourist-oriented streets and shops nearby. It was extraordinary to see such a wealth of beautiful, colourful objects, religious and semi-religious, and to see so many Tibetans, all telling their rosaries. What I saw began to affect me in a curious way: I began to feel almost in despair by what I saw, but part of me was at the same time enjoying it. The part of me almost in despair was revolted by the commercialization of the religious art, and the part of me that enjoyed it was an undiscriminating, purely sensuous aspect of myself. I tried to let these two parts co-exist in me, but it became increasingly uncomfortable as time went on. I began to feel hungry, and to want to escape from the jumble of impressions. There were lots of good restaurants to choose from, and after taking a cautiously light supper, I returned to my hotel room and a comfortable bed.

Next morning I took breakfast with Amoghachitta on the roof of a nearby hotel, in air that would be have been chilly had it not been for the warming rays of the sun, which was already well above the horizon and in a clear blue sky. It feels so good here, I thought to myself: no wonder Amoghachitta looks so healthy! After eating a bowl of porridge to settle a delicate stomach I returned to the Hotel Asia to find Bodhananda there with his bicycle, looking if possible even more healthy than Amoghachitta. We were very glad to see each other. We aired the question of disrobing and Bodhananda told me that Bhante had made the point that if the Anagarika robes were worn by us in Nepal, that might imply adverse criticism of the Vajracharyas (who were not celibate). The argument did not seem completely convincing to me, but I did not want to gainsay Sangharakshita's anthropological knowledge, or to confuse the Europeans. I therefore decided to comply with the suggestion to 'disrobe' and temporarily adopt the appearance, if not the lifestyle, of a Dhammachari plain and simple. I went off to buy a pair of trousers.

A couple of hours later I was stepping out of my room in a sandy-coloured pair of trousers and a blue long-sleeved Dhammachari shirt. I felt very light and easy, and for a few minutes, as I looked at the people about me, I felt curiously voyeuristic, and as if I was in drag. The hotel manager looked at me and smiled. He did not seem in the slightest perturbed, and neither of course did anybody else.

I went for another walk and window-shopping spree, and a very curious thing began to happen. Whether it was the effect of the altitude, or the sudden change of style, I could not tell, but I began to have a quite, indeed a very disturbing experience. It might have been due to the cumulative effect of the extraordinary multiplicity of brilliant images and colours. But it was as if my visual field completely separated itself from the other part of my mind. What I usually identified as 'myself' wanted simply to walk straight down the street, not taking any particular notice of anything, in the way I often did, but the effect of what I was seeing had such a powerful influence that I seemed to have lost control of my eyes, and I was seemingly 'taken over', at least visually, by the images. They seemed to crowd in upon my mind in a chaotic and unwelcome fashion. Not only that, the images seemed to detach themselves and to become confused with the human faces that I was seeing, so that it was as if I was looking into a particularly fascinating and disturbing kaleidoscope - except that in this case it was not possible to put the device down. After fifteen or twenty minutes of this, during which it became more and more difficult to keep walking in a straight line, or even to consider where I might be going, I began to wonder whether I was suffering from detached retina, migraine, brain damage, or was prematurely precipitated into the after-death Bardo. Avalokiteshvara and Tara, Manjushri and Vajrapani, Hevajra and Kalachakra, and other images which I could not name, alternated and interspersed themselves with the faces in the street, which were already quite extraordinary enough. I began to experience nausea, and immediately tried to find my way back to the hotel before I became too ill to do so. Somehow I succeeded in finding my way back, and having rested for an hour or so, I meditated and began to feel very much better - in fact in a highly elated sort of mood. I did not however, this time, make the mistake of going out, but sat quietly enjoying myself in my room.

That evening I had arranged to meet Duncan, a young Englishman I had met in Sonauli, to have supper with him. Luckily, I had recovered almost completely from my experience earlier that day by the time we met, and I was able to walk perfectly normally to a Chinese restaurant. Duncan did not seem to find it odd either that I was now in civvies, whereas when I had first met him I had been in robes. I suppose from a Western point of view, it would not seem anything but normal; after all, non-conformist ministers of religion (with whom however I feel nothing in common) change regularly from formal to informal garb and back again.

Duncan and I had a long and earnest talk, and I found that he was particularly interested in my 'Hostel Project' in Colombo; he felt that he had a special connection with me, since he worked in the field of youth welfare. Although I might have taken him to task on his perceiving the Buddha as a glorified welfare worker, I refrained from doing so. For several years, apparently, Duncan had worked hard in his chosen field of welfare work, and was now taking a sabbatical. He was proposing to travel for many more months across Asia before considering what to do next. We exchanged addresses - or rather, I gave him mine, since he did not know where he was going to be from one day to the next.

Next morning I had arranged to visit the famous Svayambunath Stupa with Bodhananda, and hired a bicycle for the purpose. Cycling through the narrow streets after Bodhananda was exhilarating, and not the sort of thing I had been able to do for several years, since in Sri Lanka a monk just does not ride a bicycle, even though bicycles are not forbidden in the Pali. It was great fun, though the strenuous exercise in the thin air sent my pulse racing and caused my lungs to labour for air. I loved Kathmandu, and wished I could stay longer and explore its mediaeval buildings, fascinating images, and get to know its delightful people. Probably, however, like all cities, I would have tired of it eventually. But for this morning, the streets were filled with magic, and the prospect of seeing the great Stupa with the Eyes made me eager with anticipation. But before mounting the hill upon which the stupa was built, we had an interview with Mr. Vajracharya a headmaster, in whom Bodhananda was taking an interest, and to whom he wanted to give the copies of the ILEA educational material for young Buddhists (and no doubt older ones too) that I had brought from India. I had been studying some of it in my spare moments and thought it might be suitable for use in Sri Lanka, but that's another story. At any rate, Mr. Vajracharya, a portly man disinclined to smile, was interested enough in the material to want to keep it for a while and study it, which Bodhananda was happy for him to do. Mr. Vajracharya had a very high opinion of Bhante, it seemed, and I got the impression that he exercised a very beneficial influence on his pupils; if he lacked the definitely spiritual dimension of Dhardo Rimpoche, he was a man who seemed to have a firm and clear grasp of essentials, and would not allow his pupils to entertain any *micchaditthis*.

Having said goodbye to Mr. Vajracharya and chained our bicycles not far from the school entrance, Bodhananda and I walked slowly up the steep hill on the top of which was built the Svayambunath stupa. Both Hindu and Buddhist influences were at work here, and it was not clear which had the upper hand around the skirts of the stupa itself, which seemed to look down with an air of faint disapproval upon everything beneath its all-seeing gaze. Bodhananda and I found a comfortable spot near a soft drink shop and drew a liquid of chemically-concocted sweetness through our straws whilst we debated the question of rebirth. As we did so, a very curious realization began to dawn upon me, which I may relate upon some other occasion. But now, events are beginning to overtake this particular literary effort at least, and I must draw a few remaining threads together and conclude this report of my India Tour 1988/89.

I spent a week in Kathmandu in all; it was a very enjoyable and worthwhile week, especially in the company of Bodhananda, Amoghachitta and Aryachitta. The latter had located us after an itinerary on the Indian plains, and joined me in my hotel room where we both rejoiced in the unmistakable presence and vigour of the Order in Kathmandu. It was very refreshing. It was also refreshing to be within sight of the snow-peaks, and to be reminded of those cool and vast regions of silence where dwells the Abominable Snowman, despite every attempt of 'civilized' man to hunt him out.

It was time to leave. I boarded a bus late one evening with Aryacitta's cheery farewell at my back, and plunged back down to the plains of Northern India. I had a few hours' pleasant interlude in New Delhi, where I visited the famous Red Fort and purchased a well-fashioned vajra which now lies near a small image of Vajrasattva on my personal shrine. And after New Delhi there was a surprizingly comfortable train journey to Ahmedabad, in the company of a young American couple who seemed at once both interested and faintly disturbed by my presence. I did everything possible to make myself as agreeable as I could (and I can be very agreeable when I want to) but the flower of friendship does not really blossom in the hot-house atmosphere of newly-wedded felicity, which is so forgetful of itself that it may be many years before the partners try to build, perhaps together but within their own individual hearts, on the firmer foundations of the only fort worth building.

Eighteen days I spent in Ahmedabad while the hole in the ground on which our new TBMSG hostel is to stand grew larger. Apart from meeting many old friends and giving the usual Dharma talks in and about the City, I was taken by car, accompanied by Dhammacharis Bakul and Ratnakar to Saurashtra. This great plain West of Ahmedabad is vast and perfectly flat, almost devoid of any features, and it is the area in which the great Acharya Shantideva was born. We had passed through the village of his birth, and had proceeded an hour or more further on, when out of the unrelieved monotony of the completely flat and featureless landscape emerged a single prominence: a conical hill with a fairy-tale building at or near the top. We parked the near the foot of the hill and went up to have a look. We climbed, little by little, hundreds of feet above the plain, and dozens of rock-hewn caves began to reveal themselves. In fact, to my astonishment, I saw that this place at one time must have been a huge monastic centre, comparable in size to Ajanta, though perhaps less opulent. Unfortunately, because the caves had been so completely despoiled, absolutely nothing of the magnificence that had surely been there remained. There was not a single image, no painting, not even a pillar to be seen anywhere. All the decorative features had been destroyed. Only huge holes - and some of them really were huge - with their smooth floors, remained in mute evidence of what had been before the Muslims came and settled in the town beneath the hill and did their 'cleansing' operation. But what was the building at, or near, the top? The view here was magnificent, stretching as far as the ocean and revealing the strategic importance of this unique spot. The present building was a Jain temple, constructed on or around what had almost certainly been the chief building of the old Buddhist monastic centre. Though the new Jain architecture was not displeasing, and though its curious metallic images sat there in defiance as it were of Islamic iconoclasm, I could not feel happy that nowhere was the Buddhist origin of this wonderful place acknowledged. A couple of Jain monks eyed me up and down in rather surly fashion, but as they showed no inclination to communicate, we proceeded to the topmost parapet of the building, admired the view, and took a few photographs. After this there was nothing to detain us and so we continued on our journey to Bhavnagar.

The highlight of my visit to Bhavnagar was a talk I gave in a Hindu ashram to a group of people who claimed descent from the original Koliya clan, who were said to be related to the Buddha through his mother. The audience was unusually receptive and appreciative, and presented me, after my talk, with a thick tome in Gujerati concerning their history. This book I presented to Dharmachari Bakul for the TBMSG library in Ahmedabad. It made it so much easier to give a good talk seated comfortably in a well-lit, pleasingly-designed and quiet ashram, instead of, as I have often done, standing at a cross-roads, or in a village square, or in a dusty, ill-kept village hall, with cows and dogs and cars competing for attention. Though I may have given a more connected talk than I have sometimes been able to give, I suspected that the effect of it, being to a group well-entrenched in their own beliefs and practices, would have been rather less than had I been addressing an audience of ex-Untouchable Buddhists. Still, it was comforting indeed to sit in an aesthetically pleasing place, to be able to see and address the audience with ease, and not to have to counter the effect of the usual distractions.

After a day in Rajkot, a singularly depressing city in which hardly a building appeared to be more than thirty years old, and with trees few and far between, we presented a successful early evening programme to a small group of Buddhists, and afterwards, as it was growing dark, made our way to a little hotel near the bus station, making plans to depart early next morning. A high-caste Hindu came to see me to ask questions; he seemed concerned chiefly at the absence of a Buddhist bible, and was perhaps really searching for the source of Buddhist 'authority'. He went away, seemingly satisfied, having purchased some of our TBMSG publications, and having impressed me with his intelligent and apparently sincere search for knowledge.

Back in Ahmedabad, I enjoyed my last few days mostly in the company of Dharmachari (Chula-) Ratnapriya, whose infectious goodwill was, I found, a great source of delight. Recently ordained at Bhaja, he was now looking after a hostel of sixteen or so young boys, and to all appearances doing it with great success. He had, I was told, gone out and selected the boys himself, and a happier group of young chaps it would be hard to imagine. His choices seemed truly inspired. On my penultimate day there, Ratnapriya asked me to conduct a day retreat for the boys. They all meditated; one afternoon I had found them all sitting in half-lotus, apparently deeply absorbed, and being led by a twelve-year old sitting confidently erect at the front. I really began to wonder at the advantages of being born in a country where yoga is traditional. The retreat was very enjoyable, and using the question and answer method, I was able to discover that the boys were more capable of thinking than the more 'Senior citizens' whom I am accustomed to 'instruct.' It was a real tonic to find the Dharma being propagated so successfully in Ahmedabad.

That evening I was given supper by an old gentleman called Laxmibhai, a builder by trade, his son, and his grandson Dharmendra, who also presented me with four small Buddha-plaques or plaster casts. The ancient builder and the young artist between them spanned a momentous period of India's history, and it was truly fascinating seeing what the world had made of both of them. By 8.15pm I was on the train to Bombay, and by mid-morning the following day, I was in Pune.

There was a last round of programmes and invitations to supper either side of the Order Convention, and before my departure for the South and Sri Lanka, including an evening with Dharmacharini Padmasuri. I did more talking than usual and confessed a few things which seemed to mildly shock Padmasuri. She seemed so much more cautious than me about her effect on others. I felt a bit like an ungainly bull for a few moments, and in retrospect resolved to take a bit more care in my communication with others, if I could do so without inhibiting myself. A surprise came shortly before the Convention. Lokamitra asked me to visit Agra and to collect some goods which had been delivered there from Singapore. I went. It was bitterly, astonishingly cold. Even my heavy blanket hardly kept me warm. I made friends with some Buddhists who wanted me to come again, and was offered the incumbency of a Retreat Centre in Vaishali by Bhikkhu Kaundinya, who was appreciative of Bhante. I took some slides of the Taj Mahal, which was stunningly beautiful, and the Red Fort, which is an extraordinary mixture of the bizarre and the magnificent. I visited Mathura and its museum of exquisite red sandstone images of the Buddha - mostly damaged, sad to say. I detested the city, which was unusually filthy even for an Indian city, and felt ill. Laden with the goods that Lokamitra had sent me to collect, I caught the train to Wardha. The carriages were mislabelled and I could not find my seat. Luckily some soldiers befriended me and gave me one of their bunks. The ticket-collector was very rude when he discovered me in the early hours of the morning, but I was past caring, half frozen and heavily loaded as I was. But I was happy that I had been able to accomplish my task.

The Sanchi Stupa floated by on the dawn horizon, but I was far too laden for a jaunt, though I could have got off at Bhopal Station. I looked around almost expecting to see gassed victims; I was not in a particularly rational mood. The platform was curiously deserted - most big Indian stations are crowded with a whole society of platform-dwellers. The train was five and a half hours late into Wardha. I always seem to be late when going to meet Vimalakirti, but I was glad to be there, even though I did seem to be going around in very large circles. At this point, the recollection surfaces that my literary companion on this journey was John Wain, the author of a very fine biography of Dr. Johnson which is not only a faithful re-presentation of well-known material but full of interesting observations and anecdotes of the biographer's own. I felt continually grateful for Lokamitra's kindness in lending it to me. But now I was in the company of Vimalakirti who had said "You can do anything you want" when I asked him what I could do in Wardha this time.

It turned out that a tour of Nagpur had been arranged for me, whether I liked it or not. I did like, as it happened, though my health was getting rather run-down by now. One of my ears had begun to go 'pop-pop' rather irritatingly, and I felt continuously feverish, though not badly enough to incapacitate me. I felt curiously elated that I could ignore, at least to some extent, my physical condition and get on with the work of spreading the Dharma.

Nagpur accorded me a very warm welcome, and I was absolutely delighted to meet so many enthusiastic young men. I gave a particularly good talk, I was told, in Maitri Buddha Vihar, where I spoke on 'What is Buddhism?' In fact, all the talks went well, it seemed. Panchbhai, an old friend of Bhante's, translated for me when eventually Dhammachari Vivekaratna had to leave, and one morning, with Panchbhai translating, I gave a three and a half hour question-and-answer session which everyone appreciated. On the fourth day, after having given in Nagpur programmes in each of the main directions of the compass, I returned with Vimalakirti to Wardha and prepared for my last journey to Pune on this visit to India.

Of the Indian Convention itself I will say very little. Unfortunately I was too physically exhausted to enjoy it very much, though one evening I was sitting with Lokamitra after supper and he remarked on how friendly the atmosphere was. It was, in fact, very friendly indeed, and it did the heart good simply to be present in such a 'field of merit'. I went for a long walk and talk with Padmavajra, who had just disrobed, but we said very little about that. We were both quite talkative, if anything Padmavajra slightly more so, though I do not now recall what we talked about. All too soon the Convention was over, and I was being precipitated, though willingly, towards the South of India (Bangalore) and Sri Lanka. On my last journey to Pune with Vimalakirti, the following poem occurred to me. Though not very good as a poem, it does indicate the mood of optimism that I was feeling through contact with the Order in India.

I saw in my mind a building

Rising from earth to heaven.
Its walls were smooth, its windows clear,
And storeys there were seven.

I saw in my mind a building
Of broad and spacious plan
Its walls rose sheer into the sky,
Its tall spires I did scan.

I saw in my mind a building
Within which light did play.
Moon and stars into it shone
And the glorious sun by day.

I saw in my mind a building
Which ever higher rose
And as storey succeeded to storey
The base yet wider grows.

I saw in my mind a building
With windows of coloured glass
And doors of polished woodwork
And fittings of shining brass.

I saw in my mind a building
Standing atop a hill
And paths from all directions
With men did that edifice fill.

I saw in my mind a building
Its doors were open wide
To rich and poor and young and old
- for all it did provide.

I saw in my mind a building
The gates of which gave out
Teams of men and women
Answering to mercy's shout.

I saw in my mind a building
Within whose ample walls
Music and Art and Poetry
Inspired the hearts of all.

I saw in my mind a building
Which did humanity house,
And all who entered in its gates
Did make there faithful vows.

That building which my mind did see
So airy and so fine
Is founded in the heart of man,
And lasts till the end of time.

NOTES

88   Worli: a particularly poor suburb of Bombay where most of the inhabitants are ex-Untouchable or Scheduled Caste members. The place where Sangharakshita addressed a big gathering of Dr. Ambedkar's followers in preparation for the Mass Conversion (see above), explaining to them, at Dr. Ambedkar's request, the meaning of conversion in Buddhism.

89   Ulhasnagar: a new town outside Bombay having a population of perhaps ten million. It is almost entirely a huge slum, with many hutments made of rags and corrugated iron vying with chemical factories for space. The atmosphere is so polluted that the eyes of Westerners unaccustomed to such conditions water and their throats become sore. The pervasive smell of chemicals and refuse is indescribable. In the midst of this vast area of Dickensian ugliness there is a TBMSG hostel for young men called 'Gandha-sughanda' - the smell of all delightful smells - i.e. the perfume of the Dharma.

* * * * *

33   On my way to Serendib ....

*My return to Serendib, as Sri Lanka was once known, is interrupted by
a brief sojourn in Bangalore, where Sangharakshita's first edition of* A
Survey of Buddhism *was published. I am given the task of communicating
the Dharma to a hundred little boys. At Ven. Buddharakkhita's Maha Bodhi
Society premises in the city, I meet Ven. Sanghasena, the bhikkhu from
Ladakh.*

THE AIR INDIA FLIGHT FROM TRIVANDRUM was late in taking
off and delivered me to Katunayake (Colombo Airport) three and a half hours
behind schedule. I would not have been concerned for my own sake, but I
knew that poor Jinasena would have to wait all that time outside the airport
building. Then we had to wait an hour for a bus, which got us into Colombo
by 11.30pm, There were no buses to our flat in Ratmalana; we eventually
thumbed a lorry lift which got us to 'Rajgiri' by 2.00am. Everything seemed
to be peaceful in the city. But I am getting ahead of myself. Quite a lot
happened before I got back here.

Bangalore had been a quite interesting interlude during my return
journey. There was no one to meet me at Bangalore railway station, though
the school office responsible for arranging my visit had, I was led to believe,
been informed that I was due to arrive, and by which train I would be
arriving. I tried to contact a Mr. Bycolape – concerning whom Bodhidhamma
had spoken to me on the telephone earlier - but the station telephone was out
of order. On a sudden impulse, I enquired about the Maha Bodhi Society of
Ven. Buddharakkhita, Sangharakshita's companion in Going Forth from the
household life, and was told it was not far away. I hired a rickshaw to take
me there. Several lights were on, and a guard dog started barking loudly. But
despite my entreaties both loud and soft for someone to let me in, no one
answered the gate. Since it was 11.00pm and I was very tired, I decided to
take a hotel for the night.

Next morning I contacted 'Mr. Bycolape' from my hotel telephone. He
sounded rather strange, but offered to contact Mr. Shivalingaiah for me (our
other contact whom I had tried unsuccessfully that morning to telephone).
Only a few minutes later, Mr. Shivalingaiah phoned me and I felt I was
speaking at last to an ordinary human being, and a friendly one at that. He
came to collect me in his car about mid-day. He was sixtyish, greying,
handsome, and dressed in trousers and check jacket. I formed a favourable
impression of him during the subsequent five days; he seemed to be a
philanthropist of sterling quality, though his interest in party politics could

distract him from the Dharma. He had been Chief Engineer of Karnataka State, and was currently President of Deena Seva Sangh (the 'Social Workers Brotherhood'). He was an efficient and likeable man with a flair for administration of social services. He did not meditate, so far as I could ascertain.

During my stay I was shown three of Deena Seva Sangh's hostels for young people. Two of them were very clean and impressive: one boys hostel, the other for girls. The third was a bit scruffy, which Mr. Shivalingaiah immediately noticed, remarking that he had doubts about the Warden. I was taken on the first morning, after having a look at the State Legislature and Secretariat building, which was a truly magnificent neo-colonial palace, to meet 'Mr. Bycolape', who turned out to be a seventy-year old bhikkhu incarcerated (more or less literally) in Deena Seva Sangh's School for two hundred underprivileged children (most, if not all, boys and from Scheduled Caste). 'Mr Bycolape' was sitting in a large throne-like chair when I met him, and looked a dark and imperious man. His proper name, which he had failed to communicate sufficiently clearly to Bodhidhamma, was Bhikkhu Lokapala. Later impressions somewhat modified my first, without radically changing it. I discovered that he was an honest-to-a-fault one meal a day vegetarian: incredible! The first Eastern bhikkhu I had discovered following such a regime. He used to be an officer in the Indian Army. He claimed to have seen active service, but did not tell me any details. He used to do two mile runs every day, and was still very fit. He slept only three hours or so at night, and practiced meditation. His movements were very steady, but rather tightly controlled. He used to be at Buddha Gaya with Ven. Jnanajagat. Mr. Shivalingaiah had got to know him there and begged him to come to Bangalore. He had eventually given in, and had been installed in a largish room at one end of the school (which is part boarding, part day students). He seemed to be a courageous and basically kindly man, but very conceited about his Bhikkhuhood. He demanded that everybody treated him "as a bhikkhu should be treated" - that things should be offered to him in a special way, etc. He often imposed himself on visitors in this way, breaking up the natural flow of communication, and it did rather get on my nerves. Other people however - even Mr. Shivalingaiah - seemed to like this treatment, as if they actually wanted someone to boss them around.

When one morning Lokapala began undermining Dr. Ambedkar in answer to the questions of a visitor, I considered that he had gone too far, and pulled him up sharply. I said that although I did not regard Dr. Ambedkar as a fully enlightened Buddha, he was a very great man indeed, in fact a modem bodhisattva, and that he (i.e. Lokapala) had no right to criticize him in that way. To my surprise (and his credit), Lokopala swallowed the criticism without, apparently, reacting. Sometime later, however, again, rather pointedly I thought, in front of me, Lokapala told a devotee: "Never say Jai Bhim to me. Bhikkhus are not to be addressed in that way." I said nothing this time. I could see his good qualities while deploring his bad ones - his conceit and Theravadin insistence upon meaningless ritualistic modes of address and handing-over of requisites. One reason why I felt all this so keenly was that I was obliged to share a room with him, and this room remained my base during my stay in Bangalore.

On the more positive side, I discovered that Lokapala had learned to speak Kannada passably well in only two months. Moreover, according to Mr. Shivalingaiah, the school had been unruly before his arrival, but now everyone was well-behaved and happy. The boys - or at least, the boarders, - and I did not see much of the girls, did indeed seem happy. The boys would come into the Shrine room, which was Lokapala's room, at 6.30am to sit and chant. Lokapala's chanting was lengthy and highly eccentric, a bit like a sort of male Joanie Mitchell. He would chant the Ti-ratna Vandana followed by *Buddha-puja*, all in a curiously high-pitched (but by no means unattractive) American country/folk style. He would conclude, after five minutes of 'Just sitting', by chanting a blessing. This was a thoroughly orthodox rendering of the well-known verses beginning with the words: *bhavatu sabba mangalam*[90] followed by "*te-er-a mangalam, te-e-rer-mangalam, te-er-a mangalam, oh-oh-ye*" - chanted very, very slowly, from the pit of his stomach, like an old man breathing his last. At this point, to prevent themselves from falling asleep or else breaking out into laughter, all the boys would shout Sadhu![76] and immediately afterwards troop out. This performance was repeated every morning and evening at 6.30, morning and evening. After the five minutes 'just sitting' in the evening, Lokapala would say a few words in Kannada. Since my Kannad was at the "intuitive" stage I could comment on his instruction, but everyone seemed very happy the school. Not only that, Mr. Shivalingaiah and Lokapala had really got the bit between their teeth as far as the Scheduled Caste community was concerned. They were getting together funds to build a big meditation centre and administrative office on five acres of land which they had secured for themselves, and which could become twenty acres, all situated inside the University of Bangalore campus. Mr. Shivalingaiah was evidently a highly influential man now backed with the bhikkhu sangha's authority in the shape of Ven. Lokapala.

Mr. Shivalingaiah was also impressed with me, I think, and somewhat curious. He appeared to regard me as equal in holiness to Lokapala, but from me of course he got answers to his questions; from Lokapala he appeared not to expect any answers. He began to ask my advice - or at least my opinion, on various things, and invited me to come and live in Bangalore as soon as possible. I pointed out that I had my own plans for the future and suggested that he should try to improve his contact with Lokamitra. I also suggested he send some of his boys, as well as Lokapala, to Pune for training. I had asked Mr. Shivalingaiah to arrange a talk, thinking that it would be a good opportunity to communicate some Buddhism to the boys. Instead, I was taken before a meeting consisting almost entirely of middle-aged, middle-class matrons, who I was told were teachers and associates of the Deena Seva Sangh. A more unresponsive audience it would be hard to imagine. I gave an impassioned talk that appeared to leave them almost entirely unmoved. Afterwards they all departed without a single question, though I had invited them, and without saying a word to me. The few men present hung around for a bit, and one old gent took a liking to the beautiful pink rose with which I had been presented, taking it from under my nose. During the very good meal afterwards, I overheard one of the few younger men saying: "You know, that was a really inspired, spontaneous talk of Ven. Ashvajit's - we really should have tape recorded it." It made me feel a little better after the shock of apparently getting no response whatever from the audience.

One morning I had quite enough of being imprisoned in the school with Ven. Lokapala, and went off by myself, first visiting the Maha Bodhi Society, and then exploring further afield. At the Maha Bodhi Society premises, who should I meet first but Ven. Paramshanti, the little old bhikkhu who had based himself for a while in Bhaja trying unsuccessfully to set up an alternative retreat centre to our own. He looked very different here: relaxed, very much in his element and fortunately, in a non-reactive state. He was pleased and excited to see me, and twittered away like a little bird, mostly in Marathi, much of which I did not understand. After I had extricated myself from him, I met Bhikkhu Sanghasena, the Ladakhi disciple of Ven. Buddharakkhita, Bhante's companion in Going Forth from the life of the householder to the homeless life. By comparison with Lokopala, Sanghasena seemed all light and wisdom; he was so friendly. I felt myself almost lifting off the ground with happiness at finding someone so spiritually positive. It was quite clear who was in charge of the Vihara while Ven. Buddharakkhita was away in America for treatment for diabetes.

Sanghasena and I got on very well. He seemed to me to be a quite an exceptional man, charming and intelligent, with no 'Theravada airs'. He was currently looking after, with the help of three young monks, a group of thirty or so young Ladakhi boys, but did not want to stay in Bangalore. The food and climate were getting him down, he said. He slept poorly at night and his digestion was in a ruinous state. Perhaps as a result of all this, he was very much taken with the idea of doing a two-year solitary retreat back in Ladakh. Alternatively, it may have been that Buddharakkhita had planted in his mind ideas of developing psychic powers, or something of the sort, though to give Sanghasena his due, he explained his wish in terms of "reaching the highest possible point in meditation". In response to Sanghasena's questions concerning ordination in the Western Buddhist Order, I told him about our ordination process and he asked how he could work with us. He began to call me Bhante, and then invited me to Leh. I told him that I did not know whether I would be able to come, though I would if I could, but in any case encourage our Dhammacharis to visit the area.

As for Bangalore city itself, I found it a very attractive place. It is the most attractive city I have seen so far in India. I think it would be an excellent place to start TBMSG activities, what with its population of three million, including 500,000 Scheduled Caste members, and its strategic position in the South of India. I felt well pleased with my India tour this year, having enjoyed it even more than last year - partly due to my relying on basic material in my talks, which were with one exception I have mentioned, well received, and partly due to seeing so much inspiring growth in our Movement. I very much appreciated the short time I was able to spend with Lokamitra, and felt more and more happy with our deepening friendship.

NOTES

90   *bhavatu sabba mangalam*.... : the opening words of an ancient traditional verse invoking the blessings of the Buddha, Dharma and Sangha upon the recipient: "May all blessings be yours...." See: *Puja Book: The Triratna Book of Devotional Texts*, Windhorse Publications

* * * * *

34   A last leaf from 'Rajgiri'

Back in Sri Lanka, I am evidently not finding things easy, and already looking forward to leaving again. This is my last letter from 'Rajgiri', the small flat where I spent the best part of a year in the company of Jinasena, and in which we held meditation classes for those interested in becoming mitras. Though I make no mention of the fact, I am greatly relieved to be moving from the environs of the chocolate factory, the noisy road, and the landlord with the enormous dog.

LAST ORDER WEEKEND I WAS *EN ROUTE* TO COLOMBO from Bangalore, South India, where I had spent a last few days before leaving the sub-continent at the end of my tour. I am now sitting alone in "Rajgiri" on this beautiful March morning, thinking of you all; all over the world, and not least, of Bhante in "a cottage, somewhere in the U.K." I wrote recently to Bhante saying that I had been trying to imagine a future without his immediate physical presence, and wondering how the Order will be then. I could not help remembering that I did not have Bhante's 'seal' to carry out ordinations, as indeed most of us (Order Members) do not. Human nature being what it is, it is possible to imagine a number of scenarios. Basically, however, they all boil down to the possibility of less than perfect harmony and consensus amongst those Order members whose power, intelligence, goodness, charisma, or sheer persistent hard work, have enabled them to reach positions of real influence. The possibility of harmony being well established and flourishing would be assured, I added, if every Order Member saw himself in true perspective and always acted with real goodness.

Some of you may have received a 'circular' from me recently in an effort to raise funds to move into and purchase a place I have been offered in Colombo. I hope you will all forgive my importunity. Thanks to those who have responded positively i.e. with actual cash or words of encouragement. I have enough now to move in, but I still need £21,000 more over the next seven years or so, so do please keep asking yourselves whether you can help to establish a Centre in Sri Lanka. I intend to use the property - a nine-room bungalow in late 19th Century style - for a community and for public classes, in addition to the Wellawatte Temple where meditation classes are once more building up in numbers. One day you may reap the benefits of your generosity.

Things are returning to something approaching normality after the horrifying events of the past year. I hope it will not be necessary for me to comment further upon the endemic, sporadic terrorism which seems to continue not only in Sri Lanka but in many other parts of the world, except to say that there seems to be something in some members of the human species at least which needs to be actually destroyed, extirpated or subjected to catharsis, before peace can ensue. The language of self restraint seems too mild when referring to someone who has not only gone so far as to lay his (or her) hands on a gun, but in the second place refuses to lay it down or stop using it when it becomes evident that no-one else has one. Can metta do very much where there is so much incipient hatred? I do my best with the young 'rambos' I see every day here, but I suspect that something more is needed if they are to vanish off the streets. These disfiguring features apart, life in Sri Lanka could be rather better than the picture painted by the media would have us believe, at least in the South, and I look forward to the time when foreign visitors return in large numbers to the island. I was touched to find that during my absence in India, there had been many foreign visitors to Unawatuna asking after me. One can quickly build up a reputation in a place like this. Unfortunately, none of my admirers left any messages saying how I might contact them.

The new President of Sri Lanka, Mr. Premadasa, is now also self-appointed Minister for the Buddha Sasana, the State-ruled organisation that seeks to regulate the behaviour of the bhikkhus. Bhikkhu Walpola Rahula reportedly regards this as "A challenge for the Mahasangha". I have not so far found out further details, but in general we all know what can be the result of conflating Church and State, as Mr. Rushdie has recently discovered to his cost.

I am at present less than happy concerning a number of things apart from censorship. One: my not having yet produced a book. Two: the lack of young men taking an active interest in the spiritual life here. However, there is much to be getting on with. My chief task for the next few weeks is moving into our new Community-cum-Meditation Hall. With regard to the Order, I am a bit disappointed to read that two Anagarikas have disrobed recently. On the other hand, it increases my determination. An outer difference must make an inner one in this case. My life style since taking the anagarika precept does more clearly and adequately reflect my aspirations, and assists in my successive approximations to the Ideal. I only wish I had taken it up earlier in life, having found it so helpful. So three out of five male anagarikas disrobing within a comparatively short interval makes me wonder what is happening. Does it mean that wearing the robes (or even simply the yellow kesa) produces insupportable tensions? Does it mean that the projections of others onto the robe wearer (the 'power' aspect of the robe), is so problematical that it cannot be dealt with in a common-sense manner? Does it mean that negative projections are so bad that wearing the robe becomes just too painful? Or is it simply the 'gravitational pull' at work? The greatest difficulty surely, is guilt and the tendency to rationalise away the uncomfortable knowledge of one's own imperfections. One's self-image is all too easily tarnished, so one's belief in the possibility of leading the 'pure life' may be shaken. But the knowledge of one's ethical imperfection can act as a spur to even greater rigorousness. For without the direction or re-direction of conduct in the light of objective criteria, how would it be possible to weaken one's neurotic dependence? Without the actuality of sexual restraint there would be no escape from the tyranny of the orgasm, and from the neurotic sexual relationship. Without the objective criterion of abstinence from sexual activity, where would one draw the line? Going after pleasure directly is like seeking sustenance from a mango stone. Seeking pleasure indirectly through work, meditation, kalyana mitrata, yoga, study, the arts, and in many other ways that will spring readily to mind, is a source of nourishing and innocent delight.

I am very much looking forward to meeting everyone at the Order Convention in the UK soon, and I hope that I shall be able to deliver a talk there about Sri Lanka and its 'Buddhism'.

So here I am preparing to move to our new premises with the generous financial assistance of my mother and aunt, and of the Karuna Trust. I will not forget the words of encouragement and of caution from various Order members. If things go according to plan, I shall shortly be 'living in conditions which are palatial compared with those in which many of my Indian friends with families live. I have decided, however, not to take on the burden of purchasing the new place immediately, which would be more than I could do with an easy mind for the foreseeable future. It is a large British Colonial style bungalow, with eight or nine recently refurbished rooms, a large shady balcony, and about sixty years old. I shall be committing myself to a five year lease on it, with an option to purchase at the end of that period. This way there is a good chance of raising the purchase money less frenetically, or of moving out if for some reason or other it proves unsuitable. I say "we", but I do not yet know who will be forming the community with me. Jinasena is off to India for the second time in June and Indrajit, the Friend who is sharing with us at Rajgiri is a bit of a question mark. Evidently I am going to have to work to get together the community I want - it is not just going to fall into my lap.

I was pleasantly surprised one evening recently when Bodhiruci and his friend Robert arrived from the UK. They did not stay long since they had planned to go to the Maldives, and despite my entreaties to spend their time instead in South Sri Lanka and leave the money thus saved to the work of TBMSS, Bodhiruci told me that the Maldives were disappearing under the sea, and he wanted to see them before they did so. Meg Kayte, a mitra from the Croydon Centre, also called here and we had a good talk. So good, in fact, that she sent me recently, on her return to the U.K., a substantial donation for the 'Colombo Project', for which I am very grateful indeed. May she and whoever else contributed, receive and enjoy the just rewards of such an act.

One of the things I venture forth to do from time to time is to visit the new and second hand bookshops in the hot and polluted city of Colombo. I was delighted last week to find the three volumes of the *Digha Nikaya*, translated by Prof. and Mrs. Rhys Davids, on sale for a very reasonable price second hand. They were in almost perfect condition, apart from some rather irritating pencilling-in by a knowledgeable but inconsiderate previous owner. I purchased them there and then, spent a few hours cleaning them up with a rubber, and settled down to study them. Other books I am in process of reading are *Vanity Fair*, by W. M. Thackeray (brilliant, he is a great novelist) and Xenophon's *Education of Cyrus* (translated by H. G. Dakyns). Did you know that the tally of men reckoned as Persian, not long before the fall of Babylon, was only 120,000? Cyrus is quite an interesting character, but unfortunately enjoyed killing animals.

One blot on the horizon recently has been that a mitra has 'gone reactive' and started tale-bearing. The immediate cause of his reaction was disagreement with me over the question of whether one should ever criticize other teachers and other teachings. My answer was a qualified yes, his was an absolute no. So complete was the polarization that communication ceased, reaction set in, and within two hours he had packed his bags and left the community. This shocked the other mitras even more than it shocked me, though I found it rather distressing being on the receiving end of that sort of thing, even when there was no good cause for his reaction and his departure, and no substance whatever to the tales he then began to spread. The Regulars' Class consists at present mostly of girls and women. Last week two quite enthusiastic young men turned up. I hope they come again.

* * * * *

35   Some reflections on starting in our new Centre

This letter tells of my move into our new Sri Lankan Centre, which I name "Tushitaloka" - the Place of Contentment. It also tells of my feelings on hearing of the disrobing of three Anagarikas in our Movement. In retrospect, I could have been more forthright about this: I felt disturbed, thinking that the spiritual health of the Movement depended to a greater extent perhaps than we might have been prepared to admit, upon the aspiration to observe complete brahmachariya by significant numbers of Order Members.

THIS IS MY FIRST LETTER FROM OUR NEW 'CENTRE' - the inverted commas being in deference to, but not necessarily in agreement with, the prevailing opinion that a Centre is constituted by a minimum of three Order Members working together. However, with the aspiration that soon there will be at least those three Order Members, I am now getting more deeply into things here than before. We have registered our Council of mitras and Friends here under the name of Trailokya Bauddha Mahasangha Sahayaka Samithiya, or TBMSS. The word 'samithiya' has been used rather than 'gana' (as in the Indian sister associations), since 'gana' is not a word in currency in Sri Lanka. Otherwise, for the sake of simplicity and solidarity, I would have used the same title that we use in India. We have also acquired on lease, and with a purchase option, very much more substantial premises than our previous place, and opened a Bank Account in the name of the TBMSS.

Our new 'Centre', then, or the building embodying and containing its corporate existence, is a sixty-year-old British colonial style bungalow, slightly pretentious, perhaps, for some tastes, with six neo-classical Greek columns inside and eleven of rather more eclectic style outside, supporting the verandah and large porch. We have no gouty colonel chairs as yet. There are, or will be, thirteen or fourteen rooms, including the minor ones and the kitchen, which is yet to be built. There is space enough for quite a few people, whether Order Members, mitras, Sahayakas or Hostel boys - the building is technically a Hostel. But I am in no hurry to fill it, and will proceed with caution when taking on prospective community members. I want people who are sincere and actually or potentially able to help in the foreseeable future. The rental for the premises comes from a Covenant from my parents and one of my mother's sisters, but clearly this will not last forever. I am therefore turning my mind to fundraising to cover payment of rent, for future purchase, and for the support of a small number of Hostel boys.

The bungalow which is our Centre or Hostel is situated just outside the municipal boundary of Colombo City, in a relatively quiet area of the suburbs, and within a hundred yards of the local Buddhist Temple. I am on friendly terms with the bhikkhus, who were at first beside themselves with anxiety lest I start a rival temple.   In a sense, perhaps, they were not completely outside the mark, but I managed to reassure them, and I hope that we may even be able to co-operate to some extent. By and large and in the main, I feel happy to be here, and confident that good progress can be made towards the next stage, whatever that might be.

Now for something completely different. In my last Letter I said that I was a bit disappointed that two (and now, I hear, three) Anagarikas had disrobed, and added that "It doesn't do much to warm the heart." One recent letter to me however, put it to me that I was "a bit concerned" about the decreasing ranks of Anagarikas. Whilst this is not entirely untrue, it is not completely true either: whilst I do think that periods of brahmachariya are essential for the well-being of Order Members and the Movement, speaking for myself, I feel quite happy to continue being an Anagarika even if nobody else does so.

When I took the Vow of Celibacy, I did so because I considered it to be the best course of action for me whilst in India and for the foreseeable future. I was not at all concerned whether other Order Members were going to follow my example or not. So I do not feel elevated or diminished by the voluntary disrobing of three Anagarikas. The important thing for me at the time of the Vow-taking was that I had been deeply inspired by Lokamitra's highly effective period of brahmachariya, and considered that the life-style of an Anagarika would also help me to work more effectively in a traditionally Buddhist context - would help me to deepen my going for Refuge in that context, and help me to help others. Incidentally, contrary to the reported experiences of others, I did not find any access of alienation upon donning the robes; in fact, I immediately felt quite comfortable in them, and if anything - though this might be hard to credit - less self-conscious in the negative sense than before. Perhaps it was because I had already become more authentic in my life-style.

* * * * *

36   A Note

Matters seem to be rising to a head, I am not clear why. Am I going to be able to continue after nearly four years' residence in Sri Lanka?

OVER THE RECENT ORDER WEEKEND, and for a week since, I have been suffering from a particularly unpleasant form of 'flu. I have also been bad tempered, so this has put me in a mood of rare desperation, though disaster of whatever kind has been avoided. Generally, I feel I have been right up against the reactive mind, both in myself and in others, and sometimes barely preventing myself from becoming reactive. The prospect of 'going reactive' is all the more alarming because there is no-one here to help restore me to a healthier state. I have been trying to recollect the Order more vividly and do more spiritual practise.

Various people outside the movement are accusing me of homosexuality, whilst some inside it are saying that I 'use anger' and am 'non-receptive.' I find it difficult to listen patiently to these accusations, and to so many *micchaditthis* - false views - or to listen sympathetically when what is being communicated is one reaction after another. I need a solitary retreat. Maybe I will be appreciated in my absence, and my sense of humour return.

I am flying to the UK via Moscow: it is the cheapest flight, and besides, there is a guided tour of Moscow included. I very much look forward to seeing you all at the Order Convention.

* * * * *

37   A Two Month Visit to the UK

My visit to the UK shortly before returning once more to Sri Lanka shows my interest and delight in Art and Culture - a side of myself which I have been obliged to neglect. I meet my parents and sister and experience very keenly my love for them, and their impermanence. I also experience a high degree of harmony with my brothers in the Dharma. It is with very mixed feelings that I return to Sri Lanka.

I WANT TO GIVE YOU SOME IMPRESSIONS of the last two months. These impressions will be sketchy, but they will I hope serve the purpose. I had departed from Katunayake airport, Colombo looking forward to my visit to the UK. Whilst approaching Moscow I had noticed that the fields, far from being huge rectangles, as I had imagined they would be, forced into regularity by Communist reason, were in fact the most beautiful organic shapes, rather like pieces of a jigsaw interspersed with bands of forest, woodland copses and hedgerows, so that it appeared impossible to tell from the air where one field began and another ended - a beautiful simile, I thought, of mutual inter-dependence and the co-operation of Man with nature. I did not see very much of the Russians themselves, or their capital city, unfortunately, since I happened to be having lunch when the Tour Bus departed, and no announcement had been relayed to the dining area. Tourism apart, I got the impression from the staff on the aircraft, and the few ground staff I met at the airport, of cheerful efficiency and solidarity, simplicity and directness which seemed to have dispensed with the artificial politeness and 'niceness' which vitiates, or has vitiated British society in the past. They seemed like rough gems, the Russians.

The plane touched down in the evening at Heathrow Airport, London, on Dharma Day (Tuesday 18th July), and I was met by Dharmachari Danavira. He looked quite a bit older than I remembered him: matured, perhaps, by fatherhood and no doubt by father Time, but in good health, and with a twinkle in his eye. I told him I could hardly imagine a more suitable person by whom to be greeted after a long absence - easy-going and communicative, but not to the point of garrulousness. London looked clean and sparkling as we drove through it late in the evening. The streets seemed narrower than I remembered them, perhaps because of the unaccustomed height of the buildings on either side, so that it seemed to me as if we were driving through a series of canyons.

It was good to arrive at 'Sukhavati', to find it reassuringly familiar and offering rather more comfort than I for one had been used to for the past seven years since leaving the U.K. I was soon settling down to sleep in the guest room, and next morning rose refreshed and had one of the clearest meditations that I have had for many years. I seemed to go step by step, higher and higher, as it were, as if I was ascending a beautiful staircase made of silver and gold and adorned with precious gems. Perhaps it had something to do with the very beautiful new shrine room decorated by Chintamani with a Western-style Buddha-image and backdrop of cerulean blue with a magnificent peacock on either side. Perhaps it had something to with the proximity of Bhante and his spiritual influence pervading the place. Perhaps it also had something to do with the fact that I had been living the Dharma life rather more intensively and regularly in recent years, and was now beginning to experience the fruit of all that.

I have no time here to recount all my subsequent experiences in detail, and will have to pass briefly over those I do mention. There was a meeting with Dharmachari Kulamitra, with whom I drank a cup of coffee in a snack-bar in Roman Road. I was glad to see him looking so fresh and happy after a retreat at "Guhyaloka", and apparently completely recovered from his disappointments in trying to set up an FWBO Centre in Africa. There was a brief meeting with the ex-Mike McGhee, now Dharmachari Vipassi, his cutting edge as bright as one might have expected, and hardly more than a "Hello" to Dharmachari Jayamati, looking exceptionally well-washed and urbane. The day after my arrival, the Indian Order Members Vimalakirti, Chandrabodhi and Chandrasil arrived in the U.K. and were ceremonially welcomed at a public meeting in the large Shrine Room of the LBC, and there was a large and enthusiastic gathering of Order Members and Friends and mitras to welcome them. It was very heartening to see so many familiar and well-loved faces appearing the shrine room, and especially good now to see Indian Order Members there too. It really did seem as if an element that had been missing in the U.K. was now present, and each of the speakers, including the Indian Order Members themselves, gave expression to the significance of the occasion. Lokamitra was one of the speakers, but hardly had he begun his talk when he was assailed by nausea and unfortunately had to sit down and listen to the remainder of the talks from outside the shrine room door.

Whilst at 'Sukhavati', I telephoned my ex-wife and son Ben. Ben was now nineteen years old, and I had hardly exchanged a word with him since he was a small child. I spoke to his mother Vicky first. She sounded a bit distraught, and was rather more open about her feelings than she had been when I saw her four years ago. She was friendly enough, however, though she soon passed me over to Ben. Ben was much more forthcoming, and I soon discovered that he was uncertain about his future, but was interested in film making. He sounded lively and fairly positive, and I was very pleased indeed to discover it. Feeling that I would very much like to meet him, I suggested that we meet later in the day, when I was in any case coming up to North London to visit my Bank, which was very near where he lived. To my chagrin he declined, saying he was "not together", and suggested that I phoned him after the Convention. And with that I had to be satisfied.

I visited my bank, and proceeded on up to Hampstead Heath, visiting the Freud Museum on the way. The weather was very hot indeed for England, and had been like that, I gathered, for three months or more. But to me it was pleasantly warm, indeed rather pleasanter than Colombo, which is extremely humid. The exceptionally fine weather, in fact, appeared to be bringing out the best in people, who looked more relaxed, happy, and even colourful, than I ever remember seeing them in Britain.

Walking into the Freud Museum, which is the house the Father of Psychiatry moved into after leaving Vienna as the Nazi Terror approached, and now enshrined as a place of pilgrimage, I entered what used to be the Consulting Room. The collection of books in the large room, the muted half-tones of its decoration and fabrics, the collection of curios and pictures, lent it an air of mysterious calm, and I could almost overhear Freud's soft, slightly guttural voice welcoming a patient and inviting him (or her) to lie back and relax on the famous couch. There it was, in all its splendour, in one corner of the room. There was a large photo of the Grand Old Man himself on one of the walls. It was taken in his old age, when he must already have been suffering from cancer, for pain was written clearly on his face. His eyes, however, were exceptionally clear and penetrating, their brightness increased perhaps by the pain or by some drug he was taking. It was however an impressive picture, a picture of a man who refused to be cowed, refused to be afraid even as he was looking in the face of death; refused, even more pertinently, to be overawed by all the accumulated weight of the patriarchal authority of the Jewish race. Here was a man who was prepared to be stubborn to the nth degree, if necessary. I wonder what he would have made of Buddhism, or what Buddhism would have made of him.

I left the museum, not wishing to pay the £2 fee to watch the video about Freud, and made my way up through the back streets of Hampstead towards the Heath, which opened its sultry green and secret pathways to me as a welcome refuge from the chartered pavements of the Village. The Hampstead Village streets seemed lined with more and more expensive-looking shops and trodden by more and more expensive-looking people than ever. I took my shirt off and set off in the direction of Kenwood House, which I reached about lunch time feeling quite famished. I had a very pleasant vegetarian meal in the restaurant, and returning to the sales counter for a cup of tea, noticed a man of about seventy sitting by himself at a table. There was little to remark about him except that as I caught his eye, he gave a whimsical little smile, so when I had purchased my tea, I returned not to my original table, but sat down opposite him, having first asked if he minded, which he did not. We proceeded to have a very pleasant conversation, during which he remarked that I appeared to be rather interested in Psychology, to which I replied that in a way I was, but in a way I was not. I was much more interested in people, I said, not in mentally dissecting them, and was only interested in psychology insofar as it helped me to defend myself from neurotic people and to cultivate the friendship of healthy ones. "You're very shrewd", he said, and grew noticeably warmer. By the time we parted company, we were friends, and wished each other farewell.

I went to look at the interior of Kenwood House afterwards - particularly the Art Collection, and even more particularly, at the self-portrait of Rembrandt as an old man, supposed to have been made some four years before his death, bereaved and a pauper. It was an impressive picture, impressive for its simplicity and dignity, and the Gallery attendant was also impressive for the account he gave me of the picture. He was clearly deeply moved by it, and also, thankfully enough, pretty good at communicating. He was also proud of his English heritage and of the fact that none of the pictures in Kenwood House could be disposed of by greedy Art barons, he said. After passing quickly through the rest of the gallery, pausing only in front of a large portrait by Sir Joshua Reynolds, I made my way out, stopping on my way for a few minutes to sit in the Summer House in which, legend has it, Dr. Johnson used to sit with Mrs. Thrale. This was not the original site of the Summer House, of course; it had been saved for posterity from the rubbish-heap and brought from Streatham, where the Thrales had lived in Johnson's day.

Having taken my fill of cultural Hampstead (I had visited Keats' House some years earlier) I now made my way to the house of Mrs Fernando, a Sri Lankan whom I had met when I presided at the interment of the ashes of her late husband in Sri Lanka. Perhaps because I was in 'civvies', she hesitated a moment at her door before recognizing me, but after looking me up and down, she invited me in with a warm smile, and was glad to offer me a meal even though it was after mid-day. She said that she did not mind my not being in robes, and that both she and her daughter were very glad to have someone able to explain to them in easily-understandable terms what Buddhism really was. Being 'born Buddhists', they did not, she explained, have very much idea what Buddhism really was.

As time was getting on, and I did not have a key to the front door of Sukhavati, I took my leave and descended to the Underground at Chalk Farm Station. The scene that met my eyes as I travelled to Bethnal Green was almost incredible, accustomed as I had been for the last seven years to Eastern ideas of decorum in dress and behaviour. The Tube seemed to be full of people who had either just been to, or were about to attend, a fancy dress ball. Some men had hair cut and dyed to look like a sort of cockscomb, whilst the women looked like nothing so much as tarts on the rampage - tarts however still young and healthy. They were not, however, looking for custom, as they were either already paired up with a man, or with another or several of their own sex. The effect would have been provocative if it were not ludicrous. A young woman in a micro-skirt and bulging gluteals sat next to me and started clucking to a girl with a platinum-bleach hairdo and even shorter skirt and even longer legs who sat opposite her, and it was all I could do to prevent myself from bursting out laughing. I got back to Sukhavati before the last person had gone to bed, feeling that my day would have been even more enjoyable if I had been able to share it with a friend, but there had been no-one around to go with me at the time of my departure that morning.

Next morning I was in the Community Shrine Room before anyone else (as I was on every morning but the first), and I began to wonder whether spiritual vitality was not somehow lacking - after all, I was not the youngest person there, by any means. Perhaps everyone was working very hard at Right Livelihood projects. During breakfast, Bhante's companion Dharmachari Paramartha came to tell me, in answer to a request I had made, that Bhante was willing to see me at 4.30 that afternoon. I was ready at the appointed time. The tremors that had assailed me in the past before meeting Bhante were less in evidence this time for some reason, and I spent a pleasant twenty minutes or so in his company after handing over a couple of gifts from Sri Lanka. Though Bhante looked well enough, I thought he seemed a bit tired, and in fact at the end of our talk he said that now he wanted a rest. The feeling was actually mutual; for my part it was because of the strain of moving into the new Centre in Colombo, and during the last three weeks there being subjected mercilessly to continuous loud and crude chanting throughout the day and night from the nearby Temple. I had not had a good night's sleep during all that time, and the tiredness was now surfacing. Nevertheless, I was very happy indeed to be able to spend a little time with Bhante, and to be reassured that he himself, though now having to take medication to lower his blood pressure, seemed basically alright. It seemed odd, Bhante said, that he did not know what it was he was taking, and that it did not have any perceptible effect - that was the danger with blood pressure, apparently - that you did not know you were suffering from it in the absence of occasional tests, until you were under stress and then suffered an attack. There were apparently no side effects of the drug either, so it was not onerous taking it. But if Bhante was tired at the end, he certainly was not tired during our talk, and apart from pauses to allow me to answer occasional queries of his, or to pay attention to a particularly deep silence that might have come from his own mind or from some external source, he spoke with a sustained vigour that precluded any 'breaking in', and I felt refreshed and uplifted at the end of it, as if his words had been wish-fulfilling gems being carefully tucked away somewhere on my person.

After my talk with Bhante I arranged to visit my parents, and phoned my mother. She was very pleased to hear me, and suggested I contact my sister Susan in Dorking, about twenty miles South of London, in case she was willing and able to bring me by car to mid-Wales. Accordingly, I phoned Susan, who was also pleased to hear me, and who suggested I came and stayed with her husband Mike in Dorking before she took me to visit mother and father. So this I did, travelling by the excellent British Rail, in a new, clean, bright, quiet and fast train which left on time and arrived on time at my destination, and where I was met by Susan and Mike in one of their cars (he is an actuary in a Life Insurance firm, which accounts for the plurality of cars). Both of them were very glad to see me, and I was very glad to see them. Apart from differences of religion, which both of us seem able to set aside, my sister (actually my half-sister, with the same mother, but a different father) and we have got on very well since childhood. We have always been glad to see each other, and managed to keep to some extent in contact, although Susan is not keen on corresponding. Her response to me on this occasion was particularly warm, and I was very happy to see her. She was in a much better state of health than before her hysterectomy last year. There was another family member there - Susannah, the eighteen- or nineteen-year-old offspring of Susan's first marriage to Eli, a young man of Israeli-Arab extraction. Susannah was therefore my niece, and the adoptive or step-daughter of Michael, whom Susan had married after obtaining a divorce from Eli. Susannah had recently obtained an Upper Second degree in American Studies, and was relaxing after her success, in the company of her boyfriend, who, I could not help noticing, drank beer can after beer can. As I stayed two nights with the 'members of the marriage', I had a chance to get to know them a little.

Susan, my sister, having now gone beyond the possibility of child rearing, was evidently in a somewhat better frame of mind than I had previously experienced her, and had taken up voluntary teaching of English as a second language. She was clearly enjoying the experience, being quite proficient in languages herself, and I suggested to her that she might use the Jataka stories as material for study and comprehension. She did not know what they were, so I promised to send her a copy. Michael's chief interest seemed to be not the actuarial profession, but politics and management, and to some extent, religion. So I was able to spend the best part of two hours with him having a lively and intelligent bit of communication on these topics. Susan attempted to join in with us but on questions of religion she began to get out of her depth and to her credit, recognized her limitations and left to prepare lunch. With Michael I continued to explore the notions of truth, of charismatic leadership, of power, of democracy and several other related matters, and we ended up before lunch on really good terms. I felt that if one had a brother-in-law, I could hardly have a better one.

I had little chance to speak with Susannah because she was preoccupied with her boyfriend, but was able to observe them both at the dinner table. My sister had prepared a really excellent vegetarian lunch, with which wine was also served, but which I declined in favour of unfermented fruit juice. Michael partook liberally of the wine and so did Susannah's boyfriend. My sister and niece were more cautious. The boyfriend did much of the talking at first, out of nervousness, I suspected. And sure enough, when I asked him a few simple questions, he seemed unable to reply, at which Susannah laughed. Perhaps his drinking had incapacitated him to some extent, or perhaps he was just very shy. I wondered, though, whether this young man had bitten off more than he could chew in entering into a relationship with the much more urbane and confident Susannah.

During the afternoon, I took the opportunity to listen to some recordings of Chopin's piano music played by the great pianist Rubinstein. I do not now recall the names of the individual pieces, all I remember is the beautiful sound of tinkling and rushing notes, sometimes growing ponderous, sometimes joyous, and leaving a feeling of yearning and wonder in the heart. The periodic silences from the kitchen suggested that Susan was listening, and Susannah's boyfriend came and stood at the sitting room door and tried to say something but managed only a confused mumble. It seemed such a pity that an apparently healthy and normal young man should already be fuddling his mind with drink.

How the evening passed I do not now recall either, but next morning Susan was ready to take me to mid-Wales to visit our parents. I felt very confident with her driving as we picked up speed on the motorway, and not for a moment during the 200-mile motorway drive did she make a false or hasty move. There was a huge volume of traffic on the motorways; quite tangibly, technology was in process of stretching out into fertile nature and taking her over. The road ascended gradually, then began to descend a steep escarpment with a magnificent view over the surrounding countryside. I think it was the Cotswolds we had just traversed, and we stopped to eat the lunch which Susan had prepared, and to enjoy the view. Some distance further on, approaching the Welsh border, we passed a red brick church, and the sign-board bore an unusual but familiar name: it was the name of a friend who I had known in my primary school days, and who I had come across again during my year at Cambridge University. His friendship and influence had taken me on a brief excursion into Anglo-Catholicism, which I had quickly abandoned in favour of a sort of animism as soon I had left University. And now, there was his name up on the sign-board. I felt tempted to stop to see if he was there, and to find out whether age had mellowed him, but Susan was not keen to stop, so on we went. In a few minutes we were in Wales, and at this juncture both of us began to remark on the beauty of the evening. Indeed, it was of a quite exceptional, almost archetypal beauty, with little fluffy white clouds lining up in rows, in a sky of velvety blue, and the hills, woods and hedgerows glowing with every variety of green, from the palest emerald to the deepest and most mysterious verdigris. I felt at this moment that Britain was 'fairest of Isles, all Isles excelling', and wondered for a moment what fate it was that had led me to leave my native land. Susan and I were so absorbed in the beauty of the landscape that it seemed no time at all before we were in sight of our parents' home - now visible some way up on the opposite side of a narrow valley, bright in the warm evening sun. The valley was in fact something of a sun-trap, and evidently, so hot had the summer sun been here that the Southward-facing slope behind the row of four cottages, of which my parents occupied the last, looked more like one of the brown Bhaja hillsides in the hot season than the moist green grassy slope that memory conjured up. A few more minutes and we were ascending the steep, narrow road to 'Bronhaul', which is the Welsh name given to the four cottages, and meaning Sunny Prominence or Breast. We negotiated the hairpin bend just beyond which lay 'Bronhaul', and pulled up a few yards after the terrace on a sort of ledge dug out of the rocky hillside, and under a tree in which I used to sit as a child. I remembered I used to read the "Hotspur" there, seated on a branch, wondering what life would be like with one's companion a man made of iron like the one in the comic's main story, and at one's beck and call. Mother emerged from the nearest end of the terrace, the one dug deepest into the hillside, and came to greet us. I thought she looked a bit care-worn, but her face lit up as she came closer, and she was evidently as happy to see me as I was to see her. I already knew the reason for her cares, concerning which she had written to me in Sri Lanka. She was weighed down with the burden not only of looking after my step-father after his heart operation, (which she did not mind too much), but also that of looking after two ageing and ailing older sisters, both of whom had become very cantankerous, for the last couple of years, which she did mind. Auntie Ceinwen, had moved in with Essie, mother's eldest sister, who lived in the house at the other end of the little terrace, in the belief that she could look after Essie. But Ceinwen had herself become increasingly crippled, unfortunately, with Alzheimer's disease, with the result that my mother found herself in the position of looking after both of them. Eventually the situation had become impossibly demanding and strenuous for her, and arrangements had been made to move the two elderly sisters into separate homes - Essie, the oldest, but actually the most mentally alert, into an old people's home run by a young and enterprizing Irish couple, and Ceinwen into a geriatric hospital. So now Mother was recovering, or trying to, from the backlog of stress and worry, and even, I thought, irrational guilt, that had built up during the past few years. She had told me in one of her letters that her practice of reciting her TM mantra was of great benefit to her during her troubles, and that she didn't know what she would have done without it.

Father followed Mother out to the car, which my sister and I were now unloading. He was bare-chested in the warm evening sun, and a huge vertical scar was clearly visible, running from the base of his throat to his navel. He had had an ailing, almost defunct, bicuspid valve - a hereditary defect - replaced. He had suffered violent fibrillations during post-operative recovery, and his heart had stopped, but luckily the nurses attending him were quick off the mark, and had revived him. But now he looked far better than when I saw him last. He looked robust and healthy, and in good spirits. In fact he had put on quite a bit of weight. Physically at least, he looked a new man. I had been very distressed when I last said goodbye to him, thinking that I might not see him again, knowing as I did that he had decided to have the operation in the not far distant future. But now it looked as if the decision had paid off, and that he had probably not only got a longer lease of life, but good health into the bargain. He had written to me shortly after his recovery saying that "one thing a serious operation teaches one is that all that really matters in life is good health and loving personal relationships."

My parents support of my work in India and Sri Lanka had drawn us very close together, and though neither of them had developed any clarity concerning Going for Refuge, their attitude to life, both individually and 'collectively', was, I thought, very wholesome. It seemed to go quite a bit further than the attitude which they might have been directed towards an unconventional son: "Why aren't you contributing towards our material welfare?" So my happiness and feelings of gratitude towards them were great, too great, in fact, to find much outward expression, on this occasion. That evening, my parents and sister and I viewed some of the slides which I had taken on my travels during the past six and a half years. They looked particularly interested in the pictures of Sangharakshita that I had taken at Wardha during his talk, more interested, even, than they were in the pictures of me. I did not discover, unfortunately, whether that was in fact the case, and if so, why.

The next morning, the four of us went to visit Auntie Essie in the old people's home just outside Llanidloes. We found her sitting in a chair in a room with three other old people, and with the Television switched on, though she didn't appear to be paying it any particular attention. In fact, she seemed quite abstracted, as if she wasn't completely 'there', or not completely there all the time. However, she seemed to recognize me and to be pleased to see me, for she smiled every time I looked at her, which was actually a bit disturbing, because it was almost impossible to communicate under these circumstances. I remembered the times when she used to quote poetry - particularly the poetry of Robert Browning, for my benefit, and felt sad that all that seemed to have gone. The woman looking after the 'home' was I thought, perfectly suited for the job: healthy, young, intelligent and happy, and I was perfectly sure that my mother had no rational reason to feel guilty concerning the arrangements she had made for her eldest sister's welfare. My parents showed no inclination to take me to see Ceinwen in the geriatric hospital, and I did not press them. I suspected it was too distressing for them. "She probably wouldn't recognize you", Father said. "Last time I went to see her, she thought I was the Doctor."

I left Bronhaul the following day, taking a coach to Norwich and Padmaloka, in order to attend the Chairmen's meeting. British road transport seemed even more comfortable than I remembered it, especially when compared with its Eastern counterpart, and I arrived in Norwich after a twelve hour journey, not very much the worse for wear. I stayed the night in Vajrakula, sleeping in the lounge, since the available beds were already taken by the Indian Orders members Vimalakirti, Chandrabodhi and Chandrasil. The following morning after meditation and breakfast, I went into town with Dipankara. We went into a well-known multiple store, and I decided not to buy a pair of shorts, which would have cost the equivalent of two weeks rent for Tushitaloka, and settled for a pair of underpants, which didn't seem to have been subject to quite the same rate of inflation as the shorts. I noticed that the woman in front of me, who had selected a small heap of colourful summer clothing, had run up a bill of nearly two hundred pounds, at which she exclaimed to the cashier "I can't afford to clothe myself". She paid, nevertheless. Dipankara did not buy anything, and we left. We went for a cup of coffee to the Crypt Cafe, and brought each other up to date. Our communication was for some reason or other quite energising, and I began to feel very happy indeed in Dipankara's company. I then remembered that I had been on the retreat led by Bhante on Great Cumbrae (a little island in the middle of the Firth of Clyde) at which he had been ordained, together with Sangharatna, Danavira and Hridaya, and it certainly seemed that the event had created quite a special sympathy between us. After coffee, we went our separate ways, and I returned to 'the Kula'. After lunch I read one of Saddhaloka's pamphlets concerning the dumping of nuclear waste in Britain. When I had been studying Physics at University, I remember I had become very depressed at the thought of the likelihood of irreversible damage to the environment caused by nuclear wastes, and so convinced was I of the impossibility of avoiding accidents in the long run, that I came to the conclusion that nuclear waste-dumping was indefensible. That being the case, production of power by nuclear fission was indefensible also. That nuclear power stations had continued to be built and their waste piled up in the soil on which I was nurtured was a terrible thought, and the pamphlet produced by the agencies responsible for the management of the nuclear industry was incapable of offering any reassurance on the matter. To assert that man-made containers not only could, but actually would store those deadly toxic wastes for half a million years (the time calculated for the material to become harmless) was yet another example of scientific credulousness and lack of imagination. It could only be the result of wishful thinking - of rationalisation of the shallowest and most irresponsible kind. I earnestly hoped that everyone in a position to change things (i.e. the electorate), would come to their senses and re-think the whole question of energy production before the destruction of the human race as we know it by radioactive radiation became inevitable.

Trying to turn my mind in a positive direction, I played a disc of Monteverdi's Four Seasons - it was one of these new compact discs - a beautiful, rainbow-hued, mirror-like object that I had first met in a science-fiction story thirty years ago or more, when I thought that such things would be available only hundreds of years in the future. But now here it was, in my hands, ready to deliver to me, like an open window, the pure, undistorted sound of a concert orchestra. I soon worked out how to operate the machine, and sat back to listen. Sure enough, the sound seemed to be as pure as pure could be. Yet, something was missing. It is so easy nowadays to think, or expect that the medium is the reality; but for all its verisimilitude, it was not the sound of living music I was listening to, pure though it was in a technical or scientific sense. No technology can 'reproduce' the concert hall. Even the thorn-needled phonograph of my boyhood had brought more wonder and more magic, which is not to say that I regard the latter as better than the former. My solitary reflections were interrupted by someone coming into the sitting-room: the bus was ready to take us to Padmaloka. With a sense of relief, I packed my bags and was soon ready to go, and I began to look forward keenly to meeting so many old friends.

I will not attempt to give a connected account of the Chairmen's Meeting. I will simply say that it was characterized by a very high degree of harmony which seemed to come about for the most part perfectly naturally. There were a few rough edges here and there but these were resolved, I think, with little difficulty. I had the temerity to poke Ratnapriya in the middle of the night, but he promptly quit snoring and smiled at me seraphically for the rest of our time at Padmaloka. I even contrived to have a go at poor Kamalashila. Perhaps I am more competitive than I imagine myself to be - or is it that I am simply 'challenging'? The food on the Chairmen's Meeting was truly excellent, and my admiration for Vimalabandhu rose with every meal. The environment of Padmaloka - the Fens in early morning, for instance, was magical:

> Corn stubble, mist,
> Shrouded oak trees.
> A twig snaps underfoot;
> Wild geese take flight,
> Whirring and honking
> Into the veiled sun.

The feet turn shrinewards,
Why? the heart asks, aloof
Like the pale gold disc
Over the stubble fields;
The harvest's reaped,
The season's work done.

The path beckons,
Murmurs the heart.

I had felt my way very cautiously indeed into the Chairmen's Meeting, and did not feel very communicative at first. I had the impression that quite a few of the participants hardly knew me from Adam. So I probably appeared as a bit mouse-like to start with. But by the end of the Meeting, I was feeling in communication with everyone, and as if I never wanted to leave their company. I look forward very much indeed to the next one, and perhaps to a deeper exploration of certain themes, which began to appear from beneath the surface of much enjoyable, useful, but mostly inconclusive talk. There was a 'cultural event', with several brilliant performances. It was gratifying also to catch glimpses of Bhante from time to time, relaxing, for instance, after a lunch in the open air with the little Secretariat community, near the magnolia tree just outside the kitchen. In such a way time passed all too quickly, and soon it was time to proceed to the Order Convention, which was over all too soon, from at least one point of view, and to make my way back to Sri Lanka.

* * * * *

38   Back in Sri Lanka at last

I arrive at "Tushitaloka" by car, and having settled in, am obliged to listen to horror stories from the unfortunate Jinasena.

I ARRIVED IN SRI LANKA YESTERDAY after quite a comfortable flight on the Russian airline via Moscow and Karachi. My only complaints concerning Aeroflot were that I did not get the tour around Moscow that had been advertized, and the food after Karachi (courtesy of Air Pakistan), was not very good. However, I did arrive safely, together with my luggage. I had been taken to Heathrow (London) Airport by Arthadarshin and accompanied by Gunapala, who was on his way to Boston. Gunapala and I had been set down at Terminal 3 by Arthadarshin, but as he waved goodbye, I wondered whether I was in the right place. As I was wondering, Gunapala went on in ahead of me with a cheery wave and a "See you in there", but on inspecting my ticket, discovered that I should after all be in Terminal 2. I looked around to say goodbye to Gunapala but he had vanished. I thought it best to proceed forthwith to where I was supposed to be, knowing that things sometimes take longer than one expects in Airports, and although I was theoretically in plenty of time, I should not count on it. My last comment to Gunapala (and Arthadarshin) had been that I had not written my will - not that I had anything of great material value to leave, but that I had not stipulated what sort of funeral I would wish to have, 'just in case.' Gunapala had laconically remarked that in case of accident, there probably would not be a body to dispose of. He may have been right, but I added that I wanted a Buddhist funeral, and, in answer to Arthdarshin's comment "It's mainly for others, isn't it?" replied that such a funeral would give the best chance for the Dharma to emerge.

I had remarked earlier, as I had been leaving Sukhavati, on the morning of Padmasambhava Day, that I felt very much as if I was leaving for the Land of the Rakshasas, so what with the chance (though probably remote), of death in the air in the near future, and death at the hands of the Rakshasas (though not if I could help it), in the slightly more distant future, I felt in quite a sombre mood. In fact, whilst I had been packing the more important of my temporary belongings and leaving the less important, I had been almost overcome by an unaccustomed wave of nostalgia. I had spent two extraordinarily inspiring months in the U.K., seeing Bhante, seeing my Dharma Brothers and Sisters, seeing some of my family, and now I was leaving it all for two years or more. As my experience of life accumulates, I wonder more and more whether, when I say goodbye to people, I will ever see them again. I experience my attachment to things and people if anything more keenly than before, but try to take less notice of it. As I put the shirts lovingly pressed by mother to one side, even though I had told her that I would not be wearing them, tears came to my eyes, and I even considered for a ridiculous moment trying to take the shirts with me, adding even more to an already overloaded travelling bag.

The first thing I did on passing through Customs etc. at Colombo Airport, was to look for mitra Sumanapala, whom I had telephoned from London to tell him my arrival time. I soon spotted him waiting outside, and went to meet him. Jinasena together with Sumanapala's elder brother and his car were also there, so as well as being glad to see them, I was also thankful that I would not be obliged to use the Sri Lankan public transport, which is not of a very good standard. Thus I was able to reach 'Tushitaloka' in comfort, and after a cup of tea, got down to deciding, with the two mitras, on action to be taken to advertise my forthcoming public talk in celebration of Anagarika Dharmapala's birth Anniversary. Having decided that, I then had a talk with Jinasena concerning his future, bearing in mind what had been happening in the country since my departure two months ago.

Jinasena told me how he had decided one day to go on a visit to Galle with Michael, a New Zealand mitra who happened to be staying at Tushitaloka for a few days. As the bus they had taken was passing through a particular coastal town, a number of human bodies could be seen burning on the beach. The stench, Jinasena said, was almost unbearable, and all but made him panic with terror and jump off the bus. The point is that Jinasena's home town is Kandy, and recently the police have apparently discovered that young men from Kandy have been joining up with JVP people in Galle, and vice versa. He would therefore automatically be under suspicion, without any 'official' business to demonstrate as the reason for his travel - though they might believe his actual pretext - that of showing Michael around. On the other hand they might not. Imagine his feelings therefore when a bit further on from the burning bodies, there was a police roadblock stopping vehicles and examining the travellers inside. But for some reason or other - it seemed like a miracle, Jinasena said, the police waved on the bus he was in, and he arrived in Galle without mishap. Hundreds of young men, it is reported, have been taken away by the police and army. Some of them return to their families later. Some do not. It is horrifying. Everyone is in a state of terror, especially the young men, who, if they don't belong either to the Army or the Government, on the one hand, or to the JVP on the other, they are likely at any time to be abducted and dragooned, or else tortured by the opposing group.

* * * * *

39   Reflections on Bhante, the Order, and on the breakdown of Law in Sri Lanka

*Getting back to work in Sri Lanka, I discover a copy of **Shabda,** the Order newsletter, and despite my having only recently said farewell to quite a large number of Order Members, I read it avidly. I also discover that one friend is in police custody and that another is in danger from terrorists.*

YESTERDAY, TWO WEEKS AFTER arriving back in Sri Lanka after the 1989 Order Conventions in the West, I discovered the July edition of the Order newsletter under a pile of papers. It was unopened; the mitras here respect its confidentiality. I read it at the first opportunity, which was some 24 hours later, since there was a pressing matter to attend to, and have just finished reading it from beginning to end. There is much that I could comment upon, but my overwhelming desire is to rejoice in the Order: how truly wonderful it is, and how glad I am to be in communication directly with at least some of you and indirectly with all of you.

Sangharakshita's letter, if there is one, I always read first. Tears often come to my eyes when I think of Bhante. I cannot say how much I appreciate him. Words are not entirely useless, however, and sometimes whilst performing the Sevenfold Puja, something of what I feel for Bhante - and through him, for all the other great spiritual teachers, their teachings and communities - is given not entirely inadequate expression. As a direct result of meeting Bhante, my life has been radically changed. I am now living the sort of life which I feel is a reflection, however faint it may be, of Bhante's example. At a crucial period of my life, Bhante's presence and friendliness enabled me to take charge of myself and begin to direct my own life - a task which without his help I might never have been able to do. Bhante, since my effective Going for Refuge, has always been, as it were, poised above my head, except when I am in meditation, when it seems that he descends and gently touches it. I owe my life to Bhante.

Now I must turn to more sombre matters. Towards the end of my last letter I mentioned the torturings and killings which were brought to my attention by various people, notably Jinasena, but also by others, on my return to Sri Lanka. It is not my intention to harp on the violence on the island, but so widespread and horrible are the reports that it would I think be tantamount to psychological indifference not to say something about it. Ordinary people are intensely disturbed by the goings-on of Government, army, and the JVP, and often ask me what is the reason for it all - why it is that Sri Lanka has changed so much for the worse? I have been asking myself the same question, but have not been able to arrive at any cut and dried answer. Some people have traced the violence back to the unprincipled rule of Mrs. Bandaranayake, who they hold responsible for the mass slaughter of hundreds of students, thereby sowing the seeds for the JVP. Others attribute it chiefly to Tamil territorial ambition. But it would appear that these factors, though terrible enough in themselves if true - could have been contributory causes only to the general malaise. The bhikkhus, traditionally the upholders not only of culture but also of morality on the island, have much to answer for, I am ashamed to say. It is commonly held that ninety percent of the bhikkhu sangha involve themselves in practical politics, and of these, twenty to thirty percent are actually supporters of the JVP, the anti-Government terrorist organization. This, of course, is indicative of the degeneration and collapse of the moral backbone of the country and its falling away from what was, at least in principle, a Buddhist democracy (arguably the best possible kind of democracy). The general degeneration has given rise to political factionalism of the very worst kind, aided and abetted by foreign money and foreign arms traders, and traffic in drugs. This is of course true of practically every upsurge of violence in the world today, but one might least have expected it in an ostensibly Buddhist country. Not only that, it does seem that South East Asia quickly becomes a particularly inhuman and bloodthirsty place once the principles of citizenship break down.

It is conveniently forgotten - if, indeed, it was ever recollected - that morality has to be a conscious, active force in men and women, and that where it is not actively maintained, it degenerates and eventually disappears, so that we are left with nothing to deter people from the most inhuman behaviour imaginable. I have not heard of tortures anywhere in the world such as are said to have been inflicted on victims of the Sri Lankan conflict, and would not recount them in these pages. It is clear that the most dangerous creature ever to walk the earth on two legs is not the tyrannosaurus, but man himself.

So in the midst of all this, what am I doing, what indeed can I do? First; in case any of you should be unduly alarmed, I appear to be in a reasonably safe area, in this comfortable suburban bungalow just outside the city limits of Colombo - the one relatively safe city in the country, by all accounts. However, only a few days after my arrival, six young men were gunned down within earshot of here. Murder is therefore 'in the air' - the psychic stench of it is everywhere. So it is an opportunity for me to practice equanimity when, for instance, I see bands of soldiers standing at street corners, their modern automatic weapons freshly greased, or read or hear of this or that atrocity having just been committed somewhere. Sometimes the terror moves distressingly close to home, as when a young woman who had been attending our meditation retreats and been a good friend of the Movement, was denounced, it is believed, by a jealous villager and taken into police custody on Army orders. Everything that I know about Chula suggests that she is an exemplary woman, unfailingly kind and devoted to the welfare of her School for Street Children and Night Shelter for mothers. Yet this innocent and gentle woman, useful to society, has been kept in a jail for three weeks. I have added my tuppence worth to secure her release, dreading what might happen if army methods prevail.

I hear also that judges and legal officers unwilling to toe Government lines and wanting the Law to prevail, are sacked. What has been happening here is therefore tantamount to civil war, which I have been reluctant to admit to myself or anyone else, thinking as I did a couple of years ago that to make such a statement in public was irresponsible. However, there is no escaping the fact that there has been a drastic breakdown in the Law. Presumably there has been a breakdown in the Law because there has been a breakdown in morality, and on the heels of that, there follows the breakdown of democracy. Democracy should encourage morality, but when those who have been elected as the guardians of democracy abuse their powers, then people lose faith not only in democracy, not only in the Law, but in morality itself. Such terrible things are happening in Sri Lanka today.

Jinasena, quite understandably, is fearful for his prospects in Sri Lanka in the immediate future. But the likelihood of a future for him in India does not seem good either; having made application on two occasions to the Indian High Commission in Colombo, he has met with suspicion and rejection. The Indian who interviewed him was not impressed by the fact that Jinasena had spent six months in India with only forty Dollars in his pocket. Jinasena's disingenuous statement that he had Indian friends who looked after him only increased the suspicion that he was an armaments or drug smuggler. So I am open to the idea of Jinasena trying to go to the U.K., and would very much appreciate it if any Order Members that he approaches give him whatever assistance they can. He is a very enthusiastic worker, a very good cook, and would I think be an asset to any community of the FWBO.

* * * * *

40 Tannoys

This was to have been another 'ordinary' letter from 'Tushitaloka', and though I did indeed write it there, things moved very fast indeed immediately afterwards and I am writing this preface to that letter in India. Just prior to writing it, I visit the Ministry of the Buddha Sasana in Colombo to request a letter of recommendation so as to be able to renew my residence visa from the Immigration Department. However, I am rudely told by the officer in charge, who keeps me waiting in his 'surgery' for two hours, and without any offer of water, that a number of bhikkhus have sent letters of complaint about me to the Ministry of the Buddha Sasana. On asking whether I can see these charges in order to answer them, the officer says loudly and angrily, his eye flashing: "Certainly not. Go!" I immediately realise what this means. I will have to leave Sri Lanka unless the situation can be turned around with the help of a few influential friends. However, only a day or two later, I receive a curt note from the Police saying that in view of the non-renewal of my residence visa, I am required to leave the country within two weeks, and that if I do not do so, 'measures will have to be taken against me.' This all happens so quickly that I suspect it has been planned, and though I am not entirely unprepared, it comes as quite a shock. I reflect that if the Movement is to continue in Sri Lanka, it will now have to do so under the direction of the Sri Lankan mitras, some of whom might one day become Order Members. But they are far from ready to take on such responsibility.

There is no time to waste. However, by a stroke of good fortune, I am already making arrangements to leave Sri Lanka again, though for what I had thought would be a short period this time - to do another Indian tour. There is therefore no insuperable problem about leaving the country in the two weeks allowed me by the Police. I already have an outward flight booked. The unfortunate thing is that, contrary to my intentions and wishes, I will not now be allowed to return. I have therefore to pack the few possessions that I consider essential and leave the rest, including the beautiful old bungalow that I have named 'Tushitaloka', upon which so much time, effort and money has been expended, its library consisting of several hundred books and pamphlets, my growing network of friends and helpers, and the Centre bank account (the money deposited in which is non-transferable), and just go. It is very painful indeed to have to do this, but no alternative presents itself. In the remaining time I have made representations to the President, and tried to enlist the help of several influential friends to secure my continued residence in the country, but all to no avail.

In early January 1990, trailed by a CID Officer, who is spotted by Jinasena who comes along with me to carry my bag and say farewell, I catch a bus to Colombo International airport. Three hours later I am once again in India from where I am writing the preface to this letter . Hoping until the last that matters can be satisfactorily resolved, this last letter I write in 'Tushitaloka' gives hardly a hint of the consternation I am feeling. The only indication of impending disaster is my declared suspicion that the Temple bhikkhus want to "drive me away". I learn only later that the complaints to the Ministry of the Buddha Sasana had indeed come largely, though not wholly, from the bhikkhus in the temple adjacent to 'Tushitaloka'. I also hear, several years later, that the chief bhikkhu of that temple has disrobed.

I HAVE NOT BEEN DOING MUCH outside 'Tushitaloka' in recent months. I have been taking advantage of what was at first a more peaceful place of residence by doing quite a lot of reading and dharma study. I have read the whole of the *Digha Nikaya* and the *Samyutta Nikaya*, Thoreau's *On Civil Disobedience* and *Where I lived and What I lived For*, Plato's *Apology* (of Socrates), the *Crito* and the *Phaedo*, Thackeray's *Vanity Fair*, and *The Life of Marpa the Translator*, translated by a team led by Chogyam Trungpa Rimpoche. I have enjoyed all of them, and particularly, in the light of Sri Lanka's present plight, *On Civil Disobedience*. It has been particularly difficult to see in what sense one can be a good Sri Lankan citizen in the present circumstances, so I found Thoreau's trenchant protest against high-handed, exploitative and violent government heart-warming.

However, things on my doorstep have been far from peaceful of late. The bhikkhus in the adjoining temple - it is only fifty yards away - have been doing their utmost to disturb my peace of mind. Not only have I been informed that they have sent letters complaining about me to the Ministry of the Buddha Sasana, which is serious enough and of course, problematic to deal with, they have been continuously broadcasting chanting of the crudest kind on their outrageously intrusive tannoy system and thus disturbing not only me but the whole neighbourhood. They say they are performing 'Bodhi Puja', but it is very coarse, crude stuff indeed, rendered even cruder and more painful by their array of tannoys relaying what is in fact a recording endlessly looped. This recording has been replayed without respite all day and all night for the past five days, and I'm told that the 'Puja' is to continue for another sixteen days. Apart from being driven to the verge of collapse due to lack of sleep, and sickened by the crudity of what is being done in the name of Buddhism, I have begun to wonder why they are doing it. I am told by local friends that before our arrival here the Temple bhikkhus hardly ever did any chanting. I am beginning to suspect that they want to drive me away by their sheer noise. I would in fact have gone away, had there not, to my utter dismay, been a general transport strike, which makes travel impossible. So things being as they are, I am obliged to put up with the situation with the help of ear plugs and headache pills. My situation is reminiscent of Orwell's *Nineteen-Eighty Four* and the voice of Big Brother. There is nothing remotely spiritual about the 'Bodhi Puja'. It is a gross and insensitive imposition not only on me but on the people of the neighbourhood, many of whom are not Buddhists. In any case, none of the local Buddhists I have spoken to approve of what the temple bhikkhus are doing. I am very much hoping that the Transport strike will end so that I can go and stay with friends elsewhere until the Temple bhikkhus' paroxysm is over.

* * * * *

Postscript: a backward - and forward - glance

Despite the difficulties and setbacks I frequently experienced trying to spread genuine, practical, no-nonsense Buddhist teachings in Sri Lanka, I never lost faith in the Buddha. My own experience of daily meditation practice and participation in Puja was constant, living proof of the immediacy and effectiveness of the Buddha's message. I was also convinced that the necessary spirit for a re-birth of genuine, no-nonsense, real and practical Buddhism was and is present in the people of Sri Lanka today. I hope not only the Sinhalese, but all the inhabitants of and visitors to that beautiful Island will avail themselves both of the letter and the spirit of those great and ancient Buddhist Suttas which the bhikkhus who lived there more than two millennia ago played such an important part in transmitting.

Looking back now, some 24 years after my leaving Sri Lanka, I could speculate on what might have happened if only I had done, on such-and-such an occasion, something different. However, I will not. I will also refrain from offering advice, for which I was often asked by well-intentioned individuals on the Island. I know that advice is rarely if ever deemed appropriate or acceptable.

Of course, being a Buddhist, it goes without saying that I am as convinced as ever that the answers not only to Sri Lanka's ills but also to the world's, are to be found by as many people as possible actually putting into practice, from moment to moment, sincerely and deeply, the compassionate teachings of the human historical Buddha Shakyamuni.

Would I have left Sri Lanka, if I had not been removed by *force majeure*? I feel reasonably sure that sooner or later I would have done, if not permanently, then for considerable periods of time. It is a small Island and the whole world needs the Dharma.

My perceptions of Sri Lankan, or perhaps I should say modern Sinhala Buddhism, as witnessed on Island Hermitage and reinforced by visits to temples and forest hermitages, and by meetings with bhikkhus and ordinary Sri Lankans under all sorts of circumstances, remain, unfortunately, largely unchanged. Faith was there, yes, especially in the hearts and minds of ordinary people, but as a vital force for good in society, Buddhism with all its enlivening spiritual riches had, it seemed to me, all but vanished, swallowed up by dry-as-dust rationalist exposition and by religio-nationalism. What remained was, to all intents and purposes, a vestigial, merely ethnic Buddhism, which is at best a preparatory and therefore an incomplete Buddhism.

The intervening years have witnessed carnage in the north of the Island, with the Sinhalese army victorious over the LTTE forces at terrible cost to the civilian population; so much so that the Government and the Bhikkhus have been accused by numerous agencies and individuals both within and outside Sri Lanka of activities tantamount to ethnic cleansing[91]. Whether this is true or not, and whatever the verdict of historians may be, if there is to be any progress in the direction of a truly democratic and civil society, what to speak of higher human development, a radical re-evaluation of religion of all kinds as practised there is more than ever necessary.

Amongst the crucial questions to be asked not only by Sri Lankans but by men and women throughout the world is: 'What, from a human, though not from a merely *humanist* perspective, *is* religion? Is it possible for those professing different faiths to live together in harmony? Under what conditions might that be possible?' From the answers to these questions may come the answer to another question: 'What place should religion have, if any, in the world's affairs, today and tomorrow?' If the answers to these questions are sought urgently, earnestly and persistently, both inwardly and outwardly, not only by bhikkhus and by priests of all kinds but also by every thinking, self-aware, man and woman, there is hope. The answers to these questions must of course be sought with confidence in and aspiration towards the realisation of the universal brotherhood of Man. Motivation by any narrow, sectarian or fundamentalist agenda would immediately put up an impenetrable smoke-screen between those experiencing in its acutest forms the current human predicament and those having faith in and wishing to realise the transcendental goal. Much is said nowadays concerning the notions of multiculturalism, integration, and assimilation, with little reference to exactly what is being assimilated or integrated, as if it does not matter what people do, what people practice, or what people think, it can all go into the melting pot to produce a merry hotchpotch of fellow-travellers. This kind of approach to global integration is clearly failing, and must give way to a more earnest, more through-going, more practical and more realistic set of dialogues leading to actual commitment to a goal that can be shared world-wide by all men and by all women.

All men and women have mothers. All can inter-breed. The human race, with all its diversity, together with the whole of the natural world, is a unitary phenomenon of mutual dependence, of conditioned co-production. We are sailing through the heavens on one small planet. We have a simple choice before us: evolve spiritually so that we can live together sustainably, which means harmoniously, or perish.

There is however a much more positive motive than mere survival: "Opened for those who hear are the doors of the Deathless, Brahma", said the Buddha, "let them give forth their faith"[92]. He is represented in this passage as speaking to Brahma, 'The Lord of a Thousand Worlds', speaking as it were to the very highest level of the conditioned mind. He is saying, in effect: "The path to the Deathless has been opened, Brahma; let those who hear (with their hearts, with understanding) respond with faith". The Buddha here is seeing what faith really is: the response of what is highest in every human being to that Principle that is highest in the Universe. That principle is symbolised by a golden Dharma Chakra wheel, which is both Path and Goal.

It's as if the Buddha was saying "The Way to Nirvana, to the Deathless, has been shown, has been demonstrated. So, Brahma, it's no longer possible to confine the faith of individuals with spiritual insight within the old narrow religious boundaries. Let such individuals, seeing the Deathless, respond with renewed faith, with ever-deepening faith, in the Path to the Highest".

This profound utterance of the Buddha's was an expression of his confident realisation that, as a result of his own experience of the transcendental path, men who henceforth practiced in accordance with his teachings would be released from any fixed and narrow view or mere formulaic expression of faith. Nirvana would be clear before them. He had shown the way altogether beyond the old orthodoxies to the transcendental goal. He saw that so long as men's hearts were open to the possibility of an ever-deepening understanding of his teachings, then they would grow in compassion and wisdom; they would attain to the Deathless; they would experience inexhaustible realms of beauty and truth; they would begin to share in the transcendental realization that he himself had first attained under the wide-spreading Bodhi Tree beside the Nairanjara river one full-moon night in the Indian month of Vaisakha some 2557 or 2578 years ago (traditions differ slightly).

* * * * *

NOTES

91   See, e.g. *The Guardian*, 7 June 2007, *The Telegraph*, 26th May 2009
92   *Ariyapariyesana Sutta*, tr. I. B. Horner

INDEX

* * * * *